might suggest—and after all, they were in some cases the same people—the ideology behind it was based on the authority of writing over playing.

And while the world of HIP has loosened up significantly since those early days, there is another area in which the old ideologies maintain much of their grip: that part of the North American music-theoretical establishment that is concerned with performance. As expressed by Wallace Berry in his 1989 book *Musical Structure and Performance*, the aim is to explain 'how … a structural relation exposed in analysis can be illuminated in the inflections of edifying performance' (Berry 1989: 2). Put admittedly crudely, the idea is that the theorist knows how the music works, based on analysis of the score, and accordingly tells the performer how it should go. In essence it's a one-way street, from analysis to performance, from page to stage. In today's parlance, it is knowledge transfer rather than knowledge exchange.

In this way, established music-theoretical approaches to performance treat it as in essence an epiphenomenon of structure as specified by the score. Except within strict limits, performance oriented towards the projection of structure isn't seen as an option, a performer's choice, but rather as the paradigm of what performance is or should be. References to Murray Perahia's 'very natural and spontaneous musicianship',[1] for example, reflect a characteristic quality of articulacy in his playing that conveys the compositional structure, but with delicacy rather than insistence. You can hear this in the careful shaping of the phrases when he plays Schubert's G♭ major Impromptu Op. 90 No. 3 (Example 1 at https://www.britac.ac.uk/journal/2/cook-n.cfm):[2] he rounds off each phrase by playing more slowly and softly, articulating the phrases in such a way that they form a clearly perceptible framework within which slight but telling nuances of timing and dynamics highlight expressive junctures. It's the simplest possible illustration of Berry's principle that edifying performance involves identifying the structure and then finding ways to bring it out in performance.

Perahia is the most famous present-day musician to have acknowledged the strong influence of Heinrich Schenker, the turn-of-the-20th-century Viennese pianist, writer, and teacher whose methodical approach to the analysis of music from Bach to Brahms became the basis of the most theoretically informed of present-day performance pedagogies, particularly as regards the piano. Early in his career Schenker planned, partially drafted, and frequently talked about a book on performance, but he never completed it. And when they developed the analytical method of Schenker's later

---

[1] Stanley Sadie reviewing Perahia's recording of Mozart's Piano Concertos Nos 17, K453 and 18, K456 (Sony Classical 88691 91411-2), Gramophone, October 1981
(http://www.exacteditions.com/read/gramophone/murray-perahia-special-33385/13/2/, accessed 2 August 2013).
[2] Recorded in 1982 and reissued on Murray Parahia, Schubert Impromptus, Sony BMG Masterworks Classic Library 94732 (2005).

years into a theory and pedagogy of performance, post-war Schenkerians such as Charles Burkhardt and Carl Schachter saw themselves as bringing to fruition the project that Schenker had initiated. But there's a problem here, a quite fundamental issue of how theorists approach historical documents, whether musical scores or verbal texts.

Peter Johnson (2007) has shown how, when they wrote about Beethoven's Quartet Op. 135, mid-20th-century English musicologists and critics were actually writing about specific characteristics of the Busch Quartet's famous recording from 1933: they thought they were simply talking about what Beethoven wrote, but you can't make sense of notes—you can't imagine or even *read* them—without making assumptions of how they should be played. And the problem is that those assumptions have often been both unconscious and anachronistic. That's what happened with Schenker. When theorists from the second half of the 20th century read his analytical graphs and theoretical writings, they imagined the music he was talking about according to what had by then become mainstream performance style—a way of playing that was much less expressively inflected than had been the norm a generation or two earlier, and much more oriented towards the projection of structure.

We don't know how Schenker himself played, except through the thoroughly unsatisfactory medium of verbal description, but we do know how a pianist he greatly admired played the G♭ major Impromptu on a piano roll dating from 1905, and this pianist, Eugen d'Albert, took a quite different approach (Example 2 at https://www.britac.ac.uk/journal/2/cook-n.cfm).[3] As I said, Perahia structures his performance around the regular four-bar phrasing that Schubert composed into the music through the rhythm and contour of the melody, and through its harmonic and cadential patterning. D'Albert starts in the same way as Perahia, marking the end of the first phrase at bar 9 (about 16 seconds into the recording), but from then on he lets the phrase structure look after itself—which it can do very well, since the melodic and harmonic organisation specifies it so clearly. Instead d'Albert's basic strategy is to slow down over a series of beats in order to target and bring out some particularly expressive moment that may be located anywhere within the phrase. He plays through the phrase breaks, and it is only at bar 32—at the very end of Example 2—that his playing comes back into phase with the composed structure. Even then he does little more to underline the sense of closure than a brief expressive lingering on the note that initiates the final cadential motion (second beat of bar 30), nor does he need to: Schubert has taken care of it.

---

[3] Transferred on The Great Pianists Vol. 6, Dal Segno DSPRCD022 (1992). D'Albert is playing the music in Liszt's edition, which—like most of its time—transposed the music to G major and notated it in 2/2 rather than 4/2. Bar numbers in the text of this article and in Example 3 reflect this (to convert them into the bar numbers in modern editions subtract 1, divide by 2, and add 1).

Rather than translating structure as an analyst might see it into sound, then, d'Albert for the most part shapes his performance around what he sees as particularly expressive moments—or to be more precise, moments that embody a potential for expression that is realised through his intervention. In other words he doesn't think of performance as an epiphenomen of compositional structure. And no more, it seems, did Schenker. Twenty years after d'Albert made his piano roll, Schenker published an analytical article on the G♭ major Impromptu—arguably the first article in which what we think of as Schenkerian theory appears in a fully worked out form. And as in most of Schenker's analytical articles, there is a two-page section in which he gives a bar-by-bar commentary on how the music should be played (2005: 141–2). Modern Schenkerians hardly ever talk about these commentaries, because they can't make sense of them. The reason is that Schenker is talking about a style of performance quite different from that with which modern Schenkerians are familiar.

Even allowing for the fact that words can only communicate so much of the quality of performance, it is quite clear that what Schenker describes, or prescribes, has far more in common with d'Albert's playing of the G♭ major Imprompu than with Perahia's. Modern listeners and critics frequently complain about d'Albert's unsteady timing, but that is precisely the kind of playing Schenker is talking about: I count twelve specific invocations of hesitating, delaying, lingering, and pausing on the one hand, and of resuming motion, hurrying forward, pushing forward, and accelerating on the other. Schenker (2005: 141) might have been thinking of Example 2 when he wrote, 'One should not simply announce one note after the other: rather, one should lead toward and retreat from significant notes.' It's obvious that, when he wrote about the music, Schenker imagined it going quite differently from how modern Schenkerians imagine it going when they read what he wrote.

That doesn't of course mean that the structure-oriented style of performance that modern Schenkerians have read into Schenker's descriptions is wrong, in the sense of being misguided or meaningless. But it means it's just that, a *style* of performance, a performance option, and moreover one that is characteristic of the period from around 1950 on—and not a paradigm of performance in general, as theorists, teachers, and philosophers of music have represented it.

MUSIC AS PERFORMANCE

Even more than the HIP idealogues, then, analysis-to-performance theorists sought to discipline the act of performance: they located the meaning of music in the authored text, and so created a hierarchical relationship between, on the one hand, authors and their representatives—including musicologists and theorists—and on the other hand performers. It's hardly an exaggeration to say that to do that is to think of music as something other than a performing art. It's an extreme case of the bias towards written language and against the performative that Carolyn Abbate (2004) has identified in musicology, and James Winn (1998) in the humanities in general. And as such it stands at the furthest possible remove from performance studies, the amalgam of theatre studies and anthropology that has been one of the disciplinary success stories of recent decades. The basic principle of performance studies is that meaning is generated in the act of performance. To think of music as performance is therefore to focus on how meaning is created in real time—in the act of performing it, and equally in the act of hearing it, whether live or on a recording. It's to focus on the different meanings that result from the different ways that music is performed, or has been performed at different times and places, and on the relationships this involves or creates between performers, listeners, and the musical work as a tradition regulated—in the case of Western 'art' music—by documentation.

Theatre studies can be seen as a secession from traditional literary studies, a reaction against the latter's exclusive focus on the text: the history of Shakespeare studies makes the point. If theatre studies has a weakness, it is that in the act of secession it threw out the baby with the bathwater. Theatre studies, and even more the broader discipline of performance studies into which it fed, tend to swerve away from close engagement with the specifics of texts and the ways they condition the meanings that arise in the act of performance. W.B. Worthen (2003: 12) writes that 'Dramatic performance is not determined by the text of the play: it strikes a much more interactive, *performative* relation between writing and the spaces, places, and behaviors that give it meaning, *force*, as theatrical action.' That is a fair and balanced statement, but in asserting its disciplinary autonomy, its independence from traditional, text-based studies, performance studies has tended to create the impression that the meaning generated in the act of performance is the only meaning that matters. Another way of seeing it is that textual and performative meaning have been separated out through being assigned to different disciplines.

Given the extent to which musicology has traditionally been oriented towards the text, it's not surprising that there are calls for the establishment of a new discipline of music performance studies, focusing on the generation of meaning in the act of performance in the same way that performance studies does. But we don't have to follow the model of theatre studies, which by seceding from literary studies left the latter as an unreconstructed discipline and divided text from act. The problem with such a divison is that, while—as Worthen said—texts do not *determine* performances or the meanings they embody, they create a potential for the generation of certain meanings or kinds of meaning. These meanings emerge in the act of performance, and crucially, it is through performance that we come to know what meanings a given dramatic text or musical score may afford. (The Busch Quartet's recording of Beethoven's Op. 135 illustrates that.) There is in this way a reciprocality of text and act—of the written and the aural—that makes it essential to understand each in terms of the other, at least in the case of musical traditions as strongly conditioned by writing as Western 'art' music. And this means we can take advantage of the fact that musicology has taken so long to embrace the idea of music as performance: we can choose a different route from theatre and performance studies. Rather than creating a new discipline with its own societies and journals, we can create a broader musicology in which writing and playing are both understood as integral dimensions of music's existence and meaning.

With this proviso, performance studies forms a good model for the furthering of a performative perspective within musicology, and if musicology has borrowed approaches from performance studies, I'd like to think that in return it might offer the insights from close reading and close listening that, as an unreconstructed discipline, musicology has retained. Many of the areas in which musicological approaches to performance are developing reflect work in performance studies: issues of embodiment, ranging from the visual and kinesthetic dimensions of performance to the embodied dimension of listening (more on that shortly); the social dimensions of performance, for example how ensemble performance involves the negotiation of relationships that are at the same time social and musical; the relationship between explicit or declarative knowledge on the one hand, and tacit or procedural knowledge on the other. These are areas in which one of the most important research methods is participant observation, and a major ongoing transformation in musicology is an upsurge of ethnographical approaches applied to Western musics. Another way to put it is that musicology and ethnomusicology are converging around the study of performance.

In this article, however, I shall focus on a further approach to performance analysis, one that doesn't figure on the agenda of performance studies. Musicologists have customarily used research methods that are appropriate to data poor fields like medieval polyphony, where all the world's extant original sources could quite possibly be piled on a single, very large dining table. But they have also done the same in areas where far more data are available, resulting in a self-reinforcing focus on that tiny sample of the repertory that we call the canon. (Franco Moretti (2000: 57) has made the same complaint about literary studies.) Admittedly there are some signs of change. As digital libraries based on widely disseminated music representation languages develop, we are beginning to see more notation-based corpus studies, though they certainly aren't part of the musicological mainstream. Performance, however, offers much greater scope for data-rich approaches, partly because of the existence of over a century's worth of commercial recordings, with major repertory items in literally hundreds of different versions, and partly because of the extent to which salient aspects of performance can be captured in very concise codes (MIDI is an obvious example, at least in relation to keyboard music). That in turn means that key data extracted from performance—in particular data concerning tempo, dynamics, or articulation—are highly amenable to quantitative analysis. In fact it's hard to think of another creative practice that is so deeply cultural, evoking strong emotions and deeply held values, and yet so amenable to quantitative investigation.

There has been a certain amount of work along these lines in the areas of performance analysis I just mentioned. There has been a flowering of empirical investigation of gesture and other aspects of embodied performance, based on motion capture technologies, as well as research focusing on microtiming and other negotiated dimensions of ensemble performance. Again, however, such work has not permeated the musicological mainstream. But over the last two decades one quantitative approach to performance has made some headway in musicology and more specifically theory: this typically involves extracting tempo—that is, the pattern of beat durations over the course of a performance—and either representing it graphically or subjecting it to simple statistical analysis. And in repertory like 19th-century piano music, where rubato is a major source of musical meaning, this results in readily interpretable data.

Figure 1 graphs the central part of d'Albert's playing from Example 2, starting about 16 seconds in. The line graph represents durations: higher means longer, in other words, slower tempo. (The silhouette-like shapes at the top represent dynamics, but I will not discuss them.) There are divisions between composed phrases at bars 9 and 25—at left and right borders of Figure 1—and also at bar 17, which I have marked by a heavy line. But you can see that d'Albert doesn't shape his playing around them. Instead he slows down as he approaches bar 14; he is targeting the crotchet melody notes in that bar (first circle). You might imagine him trudging uphill. Then at bar 15 he reaches the crest and walks more freely, gathering speed and rushing through the phrase break at bars 16–17 in a way that it is hard to imagine a modern pianist doing (second circle). Only in bar 18 does he begin to slow down again: now he is targeting the appoggiatura and resolution in bar 19, easing up in bar 20 (third circle). From bar 21 he starts yet again to slow down, now targeting bar 25. While in terms of composed phrasing this is the beginning of a new eight-bar phrase, the effect of d'Albert's deceleration and prolongation of the first beat of bar 25 is to blur the boundary, creating a momentary effect that time is standing still.

The same kind of data can also be used in simple statistical analysis. As an example, a scattergram from Eric Grunin's 'Eroica' website[4] (Fig. 2) shows the degree of tempo flexibility in recordings of Beethoven's 'Eroica' Symphony from the 1920s

---

[4] http://www.grunin.com/eroica/ (temporarily unavailable at the time of writing).

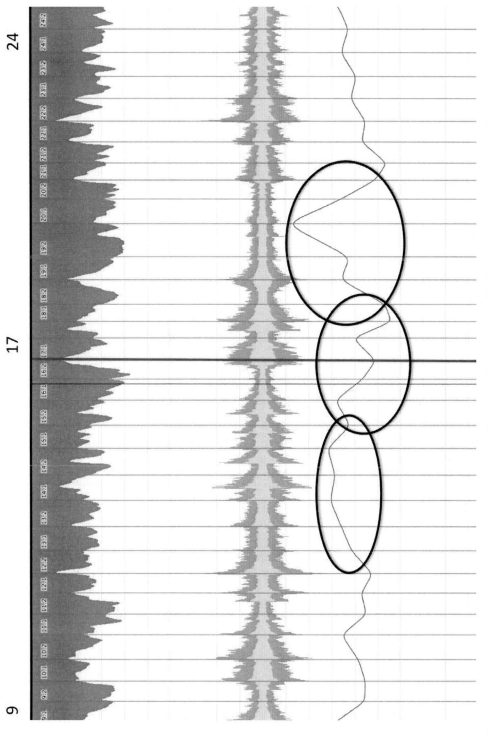

Figure 1. Beat duration graph for d'Albert's performance of Schubert's *Impromptu* Op. 90 No. 3, bars 9–24, created using Sonic Visualiser. Duration values are aligned with the end of the beat to which they refer.

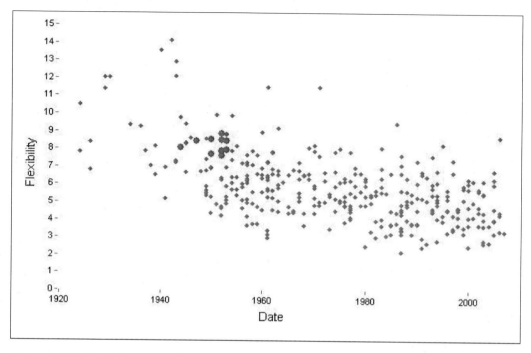

Figure 2. Eric Grunin's comparative measure of flexibility in recordings of Beethoven, Symphony no. 3 (first movement exposition), plotted against date of recording, with Furtwängler's recordings highlighted. Used by permission of Eric Grunin.

to the present day, where flexibility is defined by dividing the music into sections and comparing the average tempo of each section to that of the whole: each diamond represents a different recording, with Wilhelm Furtwängler's being highlighted, and you can see they are characterised by rather flexible tempos compared to most other conductors'. At the same time, it is important to recognise that approaches like this are highly reductive. For instance, the same average tempo in the 'Eroica' might mean that the conductor plods along at exactly the same speed throughout, or that wildly frenetic tempos alternate with monumental caesurae. (Furtwängler is closer to the second than the first.) In other words, there is no guarantee that such approaches relate meaningfully to the qualities of the performance as experienced.

But that doesn't necessarily mean you can't make musically significant deductions from them. I can illustrate this in terms of a project carried out at the AHRC Research Centre for the History and Analysis of Recorded Music (CHARM), where much of the research described in this article was based. One of the CHARM researchers, Craig Sapp, used a correlation technique based on tempo data to group recordings of Chopin mazurkas, discovering patterns that corresponded to a lesser or greater degree with chronology, nationality, or teacher–pupil relationships. That is what he expected to find. What he didn't expect was the fact that, in the course of this work, he kept finding implausibly high correlations between Joyce Hatto's recordings and those of another pianist, Eugen Indjic. But anybody who saw Victoria Wood's film 'Loving Miss Hatto', which the BBC screened on prime time television over Christmas 2012, will know what was going on.

In 1993 a recording of Chopin's mazurkas was issued under Hatto's name by Concert Artists, a label owned by Hatto's husband, William Barrington-Coupe; initially released on cassette, a slightly tweaked version of the recording appeared as a CD box set in 2006.[5] It was in fact a reissue of a recording by Indjic dating from around 1988— except that Barrington-Coupe had changed the order of the tracks, slightly altered some tempi and the recording acoustic, and helpfully corrected one track where Indjic had misinterpreted the notated pattern of repeats. Sapp's implausible correlations were in fact the first proof of the Hatto hoax. Most people think the hoax came to light when someone put a Hatto recording onto his iPod and the Gracenotes software identified the recording it had been taken from, but that's because our university was still worrying about the legal implications of going public when the story broke.

Even though CHARM missed the boat (we went public the following day), we found ourselves caught up in a media storm, and judging by the classical music chat lists, a lot of people got the impression that CHARM had been set up—at not inconsiderable cost to the taxpayer—in order to detect illicit recordings. Of course it hadn't, and that kind of forensic musicology has little to do with musicology as I understand it, the point of which is to understand music in its cultural context and to gain a better understanding of that cultural context through the study of music. The confusion arises because researchers come to empirical performance analysis from different disciplines, and carry it out for different purposes and on the basis of different assumptions.

For example, music psychologists are drawn to performance analysis because of the combination of cultural depth and ease of quantitative investigation to which I referred: they are primarily interested in general principles rather than the specific qualities of individual cases. That also applies to researchers in music information retrieval (MIR), whose approach is, however, more pragmatic: they are interested, for example, in developing algorithms to model listeners' tastes, with the aim of optimising the music preference systems that enable consumers to find what they want as the availability of digital music on the web explodes (and the music business is becoming more and more about selling services like this, rather than selling the music itself). MIR is in effect an applied area of computer science, and a number of more mainstream computer scientists have worked on recorded performances in order to develop and assess approaches such as data mining and artificial intelligence.

---

[5] Joyce Hatto, Chopin: The Mazurkas, Concert Artist CACD 20012 (2006).

Now, situations where different researchers work in the same area, and perhaps use the same techniques, but with quite different aims and on the basis of quite different epistemological assumptions, are generally fraught with misunderstanding. The study of performance is no exception, though interactions between empirical musicologists, music psychologists, and computer scientists have often been remarkably productive. The difficulties have rather arisen in relation to more traditional musicologists, who object to the use of empirical approaches in performance analysis or in music analysis more generally, on the grounds that quantitative methods cannot possibly tell you anything about culturally constructed and negotiated meanings. John Deathridge, for example, writes in his dust jacket endorsement of Adorno's *Towards a Theory of Musical Reproduction* (2006) that 'In his refreshing antidote to the mere collection and measurement of data that too often passes for research into the practice of music, Adorno effectively declares war on the impoverishment of musical performance in the modern era and the shallow empirical investigations that unwittingly reflect it.' And Richard Taruskin (1995: 24) complains of analysis in general that 'Turning ideas into objects, and putting objects in place of people, is the essential modernist fallacy—the fallacy of reification, as it is called. It fosters the further fallacy of forgetting that performances, even canned performances, are not things but acts.'

Actually the same kinds of objections are found across the range of digital humanities, particularly in relation to the use of empirical and statistical approaches for purposes of critical understanding. Stephen Ramsay (2011: 167) writes that 'The inability of computing humanists to break into the mainstream of literary critical scholarship may be attributed to the prevalence of scientific methodologies and metaphors in humanities computing research—methodologies and metaphors that are wholly foreign not only to the language of literary criticism, but to its entire purpose.' An example is when computational analysis is claimed to 'verify' critical hypotheses: Ramsay points out that critical insight is a matter of 'deepened subjectivity', not objectively verifiable data. Linked to this is an unhelpful tendency for digital humanities scholars to see their approaches as superior rather than complementary to traditional ones, as when Moretti gives the impression that traditional close reading has been rendered obsolete by what he calls 'distant reading': by this he means extracting statistical patterns from large textual corpora, a more sophisticated development of Grunin's approach to the 'Eroica'.

In contrast to this, Ramsay presents his own 'algorithmic criticism' as a ludic approach that is designed to provoke new critical responses through principled deformation or defamiliarisation of texts, in this way complementing traditional close reading. In this way, he says, quoting Jerome McGann, 'we are brought to a critical position in which we can imagine things about the text that we didn't and perhaps couldn't otherwise know' (Ramsay 2011: 172). That in turn resonates with Willard McCarty's claim that the value of computational models lies in their ability to facilitate processes of critical reading: as he says, 'what matters in this process is not the model but its perfective iteration at the hands of the modeller. What matters is not the model but the modelling' (McCarty 2007: 10). This is a perhaps even more relevant approach when one is dealing not with texts but with performances, or in the case of recordings with representations of performances.[6]

I can make the point in relation to musicologists' use of timing graphs such as Figure 1. Graphs of this kind appeared with some frequency in music-theoretical articles during the 1990s, but they suffered from a fundamental problem: it's easy enough to get the graph out of the music, but it's very hard to put it back. In other words, it's hard to relate the graph to the aural experience of the music in anything except the most broad-brush level (and at that level the graph probably serves little useful purpose anyhow). This problem encouraged a kind of deciphering approach in which people searched visually for possibly significant patterns or trends, often without really knowing what they were looking for. It resembled nothing so much as the way investment analysts try to make sense of financial data. For example, in December 2012 Dominic Frisby (2012), of *MoneyWeek*, published a graph of the price of gold between 2008 to 2012, and explained that he had added a red trend line below which one should not expect the price to fall; then, he said, he had added a 144-day moving average in green, which modelled the price beautifully between 2009–11, but for some reason ceased to do so thereafter. Finally he added wide blue and amber lines that show how since early 2011 the price has repeatedly tested, but failed to break through, a lower limit of $1,520 and an upper limit of $1,800. The bottom line was that he was holding his gold.

Given the socially constructed nature of the price of gold, not to mention the unpredictable swings that result from computer-based trading, there may not be any real alternative to this kind of approach. (Perhaps that is why most financial analysts have such a poor record of success; four months later, on 15 April 2013, the price of gold dropped by 8.7%, the largest drop in a single day since 1983.) But tempo graphs are different. As Wolff-Michael Roth and Michael Bowen (2001: 162) say, 'to interpret graphs means to build rich situational descriptions from reductionist and transformed mathematical representations', so that the same graph can have completely different meanings depending on the domain to which it refers. Unlike a graph of gold prices, Figure 1 is the representation from a particular perspective of a concrete phenomenological reality, and the way to make sense of it is to relate what you see directly back

---

[6] The nature of phonographic representation is a complex issue with major implications for performance research, on which I will not touch here; it is discussed in Cook 2013: chapter 11.

to the sonic experience. Patterns in the graph make sense to the extent that they orientate your listening, help you to hear the music in a particular way.

Technology has provided a solution to the problems analysts had with tempo graphs in the 1990s. Programs like Sonic Visualiser[7] can be used to generate such graphs, but more important, they synchronise them with playback of the music: this is illustrated by Example 3 (https://www.britac.ac.uk/journal/2/cook-n.cfm), which in effect puts together Example 2 and Figure 1.[8] Heard as well as seen, the graph brings to life the metaphor I previously invoked of wearily trudging up a slope, getting slower and slower, and then relaxing as you get to the top and walk more easily; perhaps thinking of the landscape of his native country, the Swiss theorist and pedagogue Matthis Lussy used just this image when describing performance in 1874.[9] The graph helps you hear more clearly, or more consciously, just how d'Albert shapes his playing to squeeze the maximum emotion out of the music—which is how I described his playing earlier on, and of course, my analysis was based on this kind of computer assisted listening. The graph means little if anything considered as a product, the outcome of an analytical process: its meaning lies rather in the process, in the analytical hearing that it facilitates. As McCarty said, what matters is not the model but the modelling. Or to put it another way, these graphs, like other music-analytical representations, signify not as things but in terms of the acts of listening they prompt—and that's my reply to Taruskin. As for Deathridge, I hope that by the end of this article you'll agree that empirical investigations of performance don't necessarily have to be shallow.

Used this way, technology serves as a means of training skills of close analytical listening, so that after a time you become able to hear far more, even without the graph. But that's not the only point of using an integrated visualisation and playback environment like Sonic Visualiser. It also makes it easy to do with recordings all the things that you take for granted in working with scores but can't do with a CD player: go straight to bar 36; jump between different points in the music to make comparisons; or compare the same point in different recordings (Sonic Visualiser can align different recordings of the same piece so that you hop from one to another as they play). One might draw an analogy between this kind of computer-assisted listening and the technologies of augmented reality that superimpose information on the scene in front of you when you view it on your mobile. This is a more powerful and flexible version of the close listening that lies at the heart of traditional musicology.

---

[7] http://www.sonicvisualiser.org/. Developed at the Centre for Digital Music at Queen Mary, University of London, Sonic Visualiser was partially funded by the AHRC through CHARM.

[8] Note that Sonic Visualiser shows a spurious value for the first note (the line graph should properly begin at 1.2, i.e. where the first beat ends and consequently acquires a duration value).

[9] Quoted from Lussy's *Traité de l'expression musicale* in Christiani 1885: 276.

PERFORMANCE AS CULTURE

Disciplinary change happens not when it becomes technically possible to do something, but when it becomes sufficiently easy that people can do it on an everyday basis. So I think the relatively modest uses of technology I've been describing, building on traditional skills and creating everyday ways of working with materials that have been largely disregarded by musicology, will have more impact on the discipline than the more ambitious applications of quantitative approaches that primarily engage the interest of specialist researchers in digital humanities. But I'd still argue that more ambitious quantitative approaches to performance have something to offer cultural musicologists, and in the rest of this article I'll make the point through two different analyses, both of which involve recordings of Chopin's mazurkas. The first revolves around a recording of Op. 33 No. 2 that Ignaz Friedman made in 1925 (Example 4 at https://www.britac.ac.uk/journal/2/cook-n.cfm).[10]

Friedman's playing of mazurkas lies at the core of his reputation, and this is frequently linked to his claim, if we are to trust his pupil Bruce Hungerford, that in his early years he had danced mazurkas in the Polish villages (Evans 2009: 7). There is a whole branch of scholarship, mainly Polish, that tries to relate Chopin's scores to different aspects of the various folk dances that fed into the umbrella category of the mazurka. But because of its role in the construction of Polish identity, not to mention the Polish tourist industry, the mazurka is a highly mythologised genre, the history of which is hard to reconstruct with any certainty. Besides, Chopin's mazurkas are not music to dance to, but rather representations of dance. And a major element in this representation is the extraordinarily strong sense of embodiment that you experience when you hear them, almost as if you were dancing yourself rather than sitting in a concert hall or living room. It is this phenomenon of the mazurka in live or recorded performance, rather than its largely irrecoverable origins in the 19th century or earlier, on which I shall focus.

In his 1925 recording of Op. 33 No. 2, Friedman creates the effect of embodiment through rubato, dynamics, and articulation. Actually to say that is to say very little, since those are the three measurable parameters of expressive pianism, but through measurement and close listening I developed a model of Friedman mazurka performance that is based on the idea of anacrusis.[11] By clipping notes or playing them up front—that is, before the beat—he generates dynamic momentum that may be discharged on a downbeat or climax, or alternatively rolled over, rather like the jackpot in a lottery. The effect of this rolling over is a kind of supercharging that can't be

---

[10] Reissued on Friedman: Complete Recordings, Volume 1, Naxos ADD 8.110684 (2003).
[11] For detailed explanation see Cook 2013: chapter 5.

obtained by purely compositional means or by those of standard performance practice: you can hear an example of it near the end of Example 4, just before the return of the opening section at 0'32". And when I say you can 'hear' it, this is hearing with the whole body. It's as if the surplus energy spills over from aural experience and is mapped onto your torso, arms, and legs. You may be sitting still, but you are dancing all the same. And rather than all this taking place against the backdrop of a steadily flowing, chronometric time, it's as if time is drawn into the body, shaped by the body.

That's just one example: other pianists have quite different ways of playing this mazurka. But what they all have in common is the creation through some kind of more or less continuous rubato of surplus anacrustic energy, resulting in an unusually vivid sense of embodiment. And that, in the context of the discrete historical repertory that is Chopin's mazurkas, is sufficient to trigger the range of social and cultural connotations that have accrued to them in the first 180 years of their existence. It would hardly be an exaggeration to say that mazurka performance has been seen as a kind of blood test of Polishness, and indispensably for such mythologisation, this can be traced back to Chopin, or at least to what Chopin is supposed to have said: that 'the French did not understand his Mazurkas, and that one had to be Polish to feel the subtleties of the national rhythm, and to render the proper local colour' (Eigeldinger 1986: 122, quoting Marie Roubaud).

Musicologists see the political signification of Chopin's music, and above all his mazurkas, as a 19th-century phenomenon. But thinking of music as performance changes your perspective on music history: playing (and listening to) 18th- and 19th-century compositions constituted a major dimension of classical music in the 20th century, but has barely figured in most so-called histories of 20th-century music (actually chronologies of innovation in 20th-century composition). And just as 'pictures of [Chopin] decorate classrooms in every Polish school, alongside those of Polish Nobel Prize winners, writers and scientists' (Mach 1994: 65), so Polish identity continues to be performed through the changing but unbroken pianistic tradition that is monumentalised in such publications as Stanisław Dybowski's *Słownik Pianistów Polskich* (2003), with its biographies, photographs, chronological tables, and genealogies.

But the central authority in this musical, cultural, and political performance of Poland is the International Fryderyk Chopin Piano Competition, which was set up in 1927 and in the postwar decades played a role in national consciousness that we might more readily associate with the Olympics. As Krystian Zimerman—who himself won the competition in 1975—recalls,

> if you took a train during the Chopin Competition hours, you'd find that every passenger would be discussing the contest. Everyone would be constantly checking their watches and say, 'It's ten o'clock now; that means the Russian pianist is playing

soon'. . . In that era, the Chopin Competition was not just a music competition, it was the life of the Polish people.[12]

And within such context a chart like Figure 3, based on the same correlational technique that led Sapp to identify the Hatto hoax, becomes something more than simply an exercise in empirical performance analysis. Based on their playing, pianists aggregate into clusters that are as much geographical or political as musical. Performance itself becomes a form of auditory cartography, giving rise to a map of the world based on a musical projection that places Warsaw at its centre.

The remarkable thing is that a correlational approach like Sapp's makes any sense at all, given that it reduces a performance to a single series of values representing the time between one beat and the next. But it is also possible to base the same kind of corpus approach on more perceptually salient dimensions of performance, and this takes me to my second example of a quantitative approach offering something to cultural musicologists. It's based on phrase arching, the tendency to play faster and louder as you enter a musical phrase, and slower and softer as you come out of it. (Phrase arching is one of the means by which Perahia brings out the structure of the Schubert Impromptu.) Music psychologists such as Neil Todd have seen this as a core attribute of expressive—or as people say, 'musical'—performance: Todd developed a computer model that takes the score as its input, together with an analysis of the phrase structure on multiple levels (2 bars, 4 bars, 8 bars, and so on), and outputs a tempo map in which each phrase is expressed through a combined timing and dynamic curve.

Schubert's Op. 90 No. 3 was one of Todd's examples, and when his model is used to control playback of a deadpan MIDI file of the piece, the result is Example 5 (https://www.britac.ac.uk/journal/2/cook-n.cfm). It's a quite impressive improvement over plain MIDI, though reassuringly characterless. You might even say it is more 'musical' than MIDI—and that is exactly Todd's claim. But psychologists have a habit of leaving history out of the equation when they investigate things like musicality. Indeed Todd (1992: 3549) suggests that phrase arching draws upon the general cognitive mechanisms that underlie the sense of self-motion: that, he says, is why phrase arching sounds so 'natural' (the same word Sadie applied to Perahia). The implication is that musicality is biologically determined rather than historically constructed.

Such a notion must incense any red-blooded musicologist, and so Sapp and I set out to establish—on the basis of several dozen recordings of Chopin's Mazurka Op. 63 No. 3—how far it was consistent with the evidence. Our approach was to extract tempo and dynamic information from this corpus of recordings dating from 1923 to the present day, and analyse it for evidence of phrase arching. This involved developing

[12] Chiao 2007, II: 6 (in Chinese translation).

Nicholas Cook

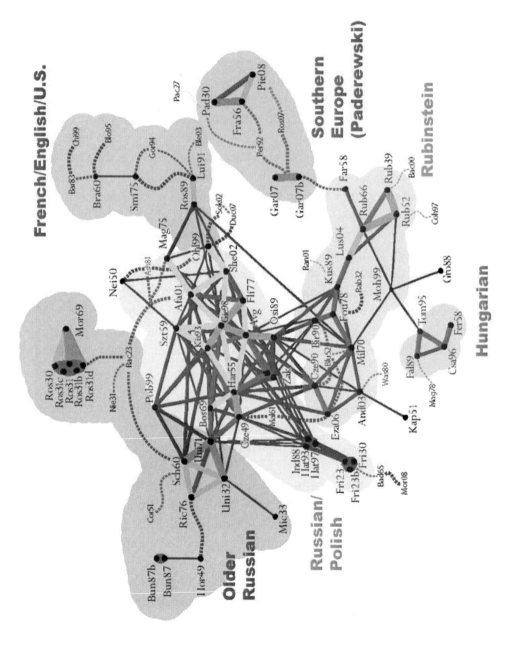

Figure 3. Tempo correlations in recordings of Chopin's Mazurka Op. 63 No. 3 (Sapp 2011: 37). Used by permission of Craig Sapp.

an algorithm that stepped through the data, matching them to rising or falling arch shapes, together with a range of visualisations that brought out different aspects of the data. Cutting to the chase, we used this as the basis of a formula that yielded an overall estimate of strength of phrase arching, which we could then plot against the date of recording. The resulting scattergram (Figure 4) looks much like Grunin's chart of flexibility in recordings of the 'Eroica' (Figure 2), but represents a much more salient dimension of listening experience.[13] As in Grunin's chart, each data point represents a different recording, but this time the vertical axis represents the strength of phrase arching: the higher in the scattergram a recording appears, the more phrase arching there is.

So what might this tell us? Many well known pianists today employ a high degree of phrase arching (I have marked Grigory Sokolov as a representative example). But it is obvious that the kind of phrase arching Todd describes is by no means universal: though there are elements of phrase arching in interwar recordings, it is only after the Second World War that tempo, dynamics, and composed phrasing became firmly locked together. In this way phrase arching is a historical style, and also to some extent a geographical one, disproportionately associated with Russian or Russian-trained pianists (marked by the squares in Figure 4): 68% of the Russians fall into the top half of the scattergram, as against 44% of the Poles and 37% of the others. In short, phrase arching is a cultural construction, and as such can be interpreted in light of broader cultural developments. Because today's dominant styles of performance are relatively uninflected, we tend to think of expressive practices such as phrase arching as survivals from the past. It makes more sense, however, to see the phrase arching style that was adumbrated between the wars and came to fruition after 1945 as exactly the opposite: a modernist reaction to the now obsolete style of pianists such as d'Albert and Friedman.

Pianists whose style was formed before the First World War aimed to draw the greatest possible emotion out of particular points in the music, resulting in a very detailed, even intricate style of performance that, from the mid-century perspective, must have seemed hopelessly cluttered in the same way as the antimacassars and knick-knacks of the Edwardian interior. The aesthetic embodied in phrase arching, by contrast, was one of simplification, along the lines of the functionalist aesthetic that developed between the wars and was given a boost by post-war austerity. Whether in interior decor, architecture, or fashion design, the modernism that swept across Europe in two waves, before and after the Second World War, revolved around a set of buzzwords that included structure, clarity, and simplicity.

---

[13] A later stage of this research, based on a larger data set and resulting in a rather more complex picture, is reported in Cook 2013: chapter 6.

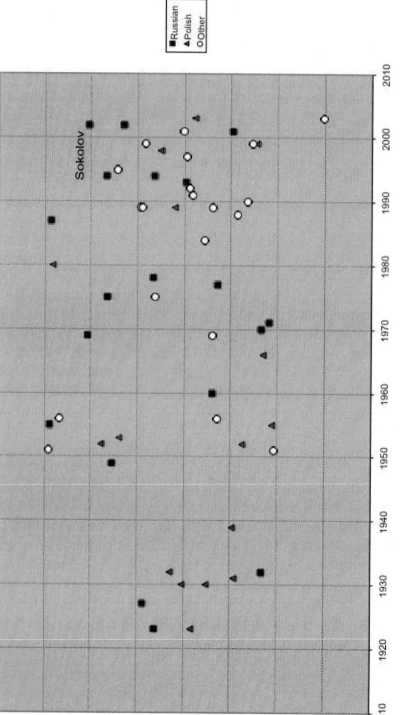

Figure 4. Phrase arching in recordings of Chopin's Mazurka Op. 63 No. 3, arranged by date of recording.

An article from *Vogue* in 1924 said of Coco Chanel's fashion designs that 'Simplicity . . . was the first thing. . . . [T]he simpler it was, the better'.[14] And if Coco Chanel's little black dress was an emblem of such values, then another prominent member of the chic Parisian set—and possible lover of Chanel—expressed them in musical terms. It was in 1942 that Stravinsky called for a new ideology of performance in his *Poetics of Music in the Form of Six Lessons*: he condemned the romantic idea of interpretation, describing it as lying 'at the root of all the errors, all the sins, all the misunderstandings that interpose themselves between the musical work and the listener and prevent a faithful transmission of its message' (Stravinsky 2003: 122). Instead he demanded execution, that is to say, a self-effacingly literal style of performance dedicated to the accurate reproduction of the composer's score. This is *Werktreue* in its most literal form.

It's notorious that Stravinsky didn't conform to his own injunctions, and the problem is something that has been obvious ever since the invention of MIDI: literal performance, where every *mezzo piano* is equally loud and every crotchet is twice as long as every quaver, is as unbearable for the listener as it is unachievable by the performer. That is why musical notation has always depended on, and made sense in terms of, aurally transmitted traditions of performance. And that is where the phrase arching style that came to fruition after the war comes in. It squared the circle. It drew on existing codes of expressive performance, but restructured and rationalised them. It eliminated what were now seen as the excessively subjective, personal, and arbitrary qualities of pre-war performance that emphasised the musician rather than the music, buttonholing the listener and so intruding upon private aesthetic experience. Through phrase arching, expressivity was relocated from the moment-to-moment progression of the performance to the more abstract and impersonal level of musical structure. It became the expressivity of the music itself, an embodiment of the qualities of self-effacement, faithfulness to the composer or work, and transparency that had now become installed as the permanent values of classical performance culture. In this way musical performance was not simply an expression of modernist culture. It was an aspect of modernism itself, one of the arenas in which modernism was constructed and contested.

I quoted Ramsay on the error of seeing computer-assisted research in the humanities as more 'scientific' or 'objective' than traditional approaches, and the study I have just described demonstrates his point: my attempt to interpret the data in light of broad cultural trends is typical of humanities scholarship, aiming at persuasion rather than proof. Yet the empirical, data-rich approach is fundamental to it because, in performance as in other aspects of culture, trends emerge not from individual cases but

---

[14] 'Before and after taking Paris', *Vogue* (New York), 1 Nov. 1924, p. 100, quoted in Davis 2006: 166.

at the statistical level. It's the same point Moretti (2003: 76, 90) is making about the history of the novel when he says that 'what we must explain is the pattern as a whole, not just one of its phases . . . individual episodes tend, if anything, to conceal it, and only the abstract pattern brings out the historical trend'.

Such approaches also help to counter some of the confounds of traditional humanistic approaches to the history of performance, such as the malleability of the ear. Like Bryce Morrison, who gave a recording of Rachmaninoff's Piano Concerto a far more glowing review when he reviewed it as Hatto's work than as Yefim Bronfman's,[15] we hear what we expect or even want to hear. And the resulting circularity combines with the cherry-picking inherent in using a handful of supposedly representative examples to advance your interpretation. It would be easy to narrate the development of phrase arching in terms of just those examples that illustrate the developing elements of the new style. What such a narrative would omit is the most important thing to come out of Figure 4: that playing with little or no phrase arching has persisted to the present day. It's not that there was a transformation of performance style as a whole, if indeed the idea of 'performance style as a whole' makes sense. It was rather the creation of a new option in performance.

And that bears directly on Taruskin's argument about turning ideas into objects and putting them in place of people. The implication is that music, and its history, can be understood only in terms of the choices of situated agents, rather than the impersonal forces to which historians in the Hegelian mould so readily resorted. But for all its apparent self-evidence and moral rightness, such a claim is far too sweeping. There are such things as style characteristics and trends that everyone takes for granted, that are seen as just the way things are: that's why archaeologists can date sites from the shaping of a pot handle. The same applies to the stylistic assumptions that many musicians internalise by their late teens, and then retain throughout their careers. Consequently, as Leech-Wilkinson (2009: 250) has argued, stylistic change in musical performance is generally best understood in terms of when performers were born.

But this doesn't apply to phrase arching. Among the cluster of recordings exhibiting strong phrase arching that appeared in the years after the war is one by Halina Czerny-Stefanska, who was just thirty when she made it, and still in her twenties when she won both the First Prize and the Polish Radio Mazurka Prize at the Fourth International Frederick Chopin Piano Competition in 1949, the first to be held after the war. So one might think of her as representing the new generation of post-war performers. But another recording in the same cluster—actually the most extreme example of phrase arching in any recording of Op. 63 No. 3 that I know—is by Heinrich Neuhaus, an immensely influential pianist and teacher at the Moscow

---

[15] The reviews in question appeared in the September 1992 and February 2007 issues of *Gramophone*.

Conservatory, and he was in his mid-sixties when he made it. And if you reformat Figure 4 according to date of birth rather than date of recording, no intelligible pattern emerges. What this tells us is that phrase arching was in essence a fashion, something that performers could choose to put on or not, like Chanel's little black dress. Rather than reifying style change, then, the data-driven approach makes it clear that we are dealing with individual acts of agency.

* * *

In this article I have tried to show two things. First, broadly scientific methods can open up otherwise inaccessible areas of culture for analysis: in doing this, they do not substitute for but rather add value to traditional humanities approaches. Secondly, fundamental dimensions of what music means, and particularly of what it means to the general public rather than just to specialists, lie in its performance. The music we hear sounds the way it does because performers play it that way: performers' choices constitute an essential dimension of the creativity of musical culture. Yet performance has always been the elephant in the musicological room. It has been written out of the books that represent music as a written tradition rather than a performing art. Even performers think of it this way: 'The psychological advantages of being able to justify their choices by attributing them to the composer', Leech-Wilkinson (2012: paragraph 1.2) observes, 'seem far to outweigh the uncertain likelihood of critical praise that might or might not accrue to them were there no higher authority to whom they could look for support'. Here, at the heart of classical musical culture, we see the continuing grip of the bias towards writing that Winn identifies across the humanities. Yet a case might be made that, contrary to the composer-based historiographies (or hagiographies) that still dominate both within and beyond the academy, it is performers who function as the primary motors of musical culture. Composers, after all, just write the notes.

Acknowledgements: This research would not have been possible without the financial support of the Arts and Humanities Research Council, who funded the AHRC Research Centre for the History and Analysis of Recorded Music (CHARM), and the programming expertise of Dr Craig Sapp, from 2005 to 2009 a Research Fellow at CHARM.

REFERENCES

Abbate, Carolyn (2004), 'Music—drastic or gnostic?', *Critical Inquiry*, 30: 505–36. http://dx.doi.org/10.1086/421160

Adorno, Theodor (2006), *Towards a Theory of Musical Reproduction: Notes, a Draft and Two Schemata*, ed. Henri Lonitz, trans. Wieland Hoban (Cambridge, Polity Press).

Barrett, Sam (2008), 'Reflections on music writing: coming to terms with gain and loss in early medieval Latin song', in Andreas Haug and Andreas Dorschel (eds), *Vom Preis des Fortschritts: Gewinn und Verlust in der Musikgeschichte* (Vienna, Universal Edition), 89–109.

Berry, Wallace (1989), *Musical Structure and Performance* (New Haven, Yale University Press).

Chiao YuanPu (2007), *The Colors Between Black and White*, 2 vols (Taipei, LinKing Books).

Christiani, Adolph (1885), *The Principles of Expression in Pianoforte Playing* (New York, Harper & Brothers).

Cook, Nicholas (2013), *Beyond the Score: Music as Performance* (New York, Oxford University Press).

Davis, Mary (2006), *Classic Chic: Music, Fashion, and Modernism* (Berkeley, California University Press).

Dybowski, Stanisław (2003), *Słownik Pianistów Polskich* (Warszawa, Selene).

Eigeldinger, Jean-Jacques (1986), *Chopin: Pianist and Teacher as Seen by his Pupils*, ed. Roy Howat, trans. Naomi Shohet with Krysia Osostowicz and Roy Howat (Cambridge, Cambridge University Press).

Evans, Allan (2009), *Ignaz Friedman: Romantic Master Pianist* (Bloomington, Indiana University Press).

Frisby, Dominic (2012), 'Gold's woes won't last—we're heading back to $1,800', posted on the *MoneyWeek* website, 20 December 2012, http://www.moneyweek.com/investments/precious-metals-and-gems/gold/gold-woes-wont-last-we-re-heading-back-to-1800-61920.

Johnson, Peter (2007), 'The influence of recordings on critical readings of musical works', paper presented at the *CHARM/RMA Musicology and Recordings Conference* (Egham, Surrey, 13–15 September 2007).

Leech-Wilkinson, Daniel (2009), 'Recordings and histories of performance style', in Nicholas Cook *et al.* (eds), *The Cambridge Companion to Recorded Music* (Cambridge, Cambridge University Press), 246–66. http://dx.doi.org/10.1017/CCOL9780521865821.028

Leech-Wilkinson, Daniel (2012), 'Compositions, scores, performances, meanings', *Music Theory Online*, 18/1.

Mach, Zdzislaw (1994), 'National anthems: The case of Chopin as a national composer', in Martin Stokes (ed.), *Ethnicity, Identity and Music: The Musical Construction of Place* (Oxford, Berg), 61–70.

McCarty, Willard (2007), 'Beyond retrieval? Computer science and the humanities' http://www.mccarty.org.uk/essays/McCarty,%20Beyond%20retrieval.pdf.

Moretti, Franco (2000), 'Conjectures on world literature', *New Left Review*, 1: 54–68.

Moretti, Franco (2003), 'Graphs, maps, trees: abstract models for literary history—1', *New Left Review*, 24: 67–93.

Ramsay, Stephen (2011), *Reading Machines: Toward an Algorithmic Criticism* (Champaign, IL, University of Illinois Press).

Roth, Wolff-Michael and Michael Bowen (2001), 'Professionals read graphs: A semiotic analysis', *Journal for Research in Mathematics Education*, 32(2): 159–94. http://dx.doi.org/10.2307/749672

Sapp, Craig (2011), *Computational Methods for the Analysis of Musical Structure*, Ph.D. thesis, Stanford University (http://purl.stanford.edu/br237mp4161).

Schenker, Heinrich (2005), *Der Tonwille: Pamphlets/Quarterly Publication in Witness of the Immutable Laws of Music, Offered to a New Generation of Youth, Volume II: Issues 6–10 (1923–1924)*, ed. William Drabkin, trans. Ian Bent *et al.* (New York, Oxford University Press).

Stravinsky, Igor (2003), *Poetics of Music in the Form of Six Lessons* (Cambridge, MA, Harvard University Press).

Taruskin, Richard (1995), *Text and Act: Essays on Music and Performance* (New York, Oxford University Press).

Todd, Neil (1992), 'The dynamics of dynamics: a model of musical expression', *Journal of the Acoustical Society of America*, 91: 3540–50. http://dx.doi.org/10.2307/749672

Winn, James (1998), *The Pale of Words: Reflections on the Humanities and Performance* (New Haven, Yale University Press).

Worthen, William (2003), *Shakespeare and the Force of Modern Performance* (Cambridge, Cambridge University Press). http://dx.doi.org/10.1017/CBO9780511484087

The author: Nicholas Cook is 1684 Professor of Music at the University of Cambridge. Author of *Music: A Very Short Introduction*, which has been translated into fifteen languages, his book *The Schenker Project: Culture, Race, and Music Theory in Fin-de-siècle Vienna* won the Society for Music Theory's 2010 Wallace Berry Award. His latest book, *Beyond the Score: Music as Performance*, was published in December 2013. In January 2014 he will take up a British Academy Wolfson Research Professorship, working on relational and intercultural musicology.

Contact: njc69@cam.ac.uk

This article was first published in 2014 in *Journal of the British Academy* (ISSN 2052–7217).

To cite the article: Nicholas Cook (2014) 'Between Art and Science: Music as performance', *Journal of the British Academy*, 2: 1–25. DOI 10.5871/jba/002.001

Journal of the British Academy, **2**, 27–41. DOI 10.5871/jba/002.027
Posted 17 March 2014. © The British Academy 2014

The appeal of Islamic fundamentalism

British Academy Lecture
read 26 February 2013 by

MICHAEL COOK
Fellow of the Academy

Abstract: In terms of its political appeal the Islamic revival of the last few decades is in some ways a unique phenomenon. We can plausibly understand this appeal to arise from the relevance of certain elements of the Islamic heritage to the predicament of Muslim populations living in Third-World conditions. At the same time we can argue that other religious heritages have less to offer their contemporary adherents in this context. Here the idea of fundamentalism can be helpful: on one simple definition it serves to highlight a feature of the Islamic revival that is particularly adaptive under contemporary conditions. Finally, it is worth noting that despite its exceptional features, the basic elements of the Islamic revival are familiar in contexts closer to home.

Keywords: Islamic revival, Islamic fundamentalism, Islamic heritage, religion and politics, Third World.

No one is in any doubt that one of the major changes in world politics over the last half century has been the Islamic revival—or, as it is often described and with some reason, the rise of Islamic fundamentalism.[1] This is not a development that people socialised into the secular values of a modern Western society find immediately comprehensible: it is thoroughly religious, and it is often marked by a determination to bring about the integration of religion and politics. But as with most human activities outside one's own culture, some relevant information combined with a bit of imaginative effort can help to make its aspirations intelligible to those who do not share its premises.

The first obstacle we face here is simply that terms like 'Islamic revival' cover too wide a range of phenomena for analytical convenience. So we should start by breaking down this revival into more manageable components.[2]

---

[1] Towards the end of this article I will take up the question just what it is about the Islamic revival that we might want to call fundamentalist.

[2] Most of the analysis that follows is drawn from parts of my forthcoming book, where a fuller discussion and documentation may be found (Cook 2014).

WHAT ARE THE COMPONENTS OF THE ISLAMIC REVIVAL?

The first and most widespread component is the process by which large numbers of people in the Muslim world have been 'getting religion', as the American idiom has it, in other words becoming more pious and observant. This may happen outside any institutional framework, but one movement that has contributed to this aspect of the revival, on a large scale and across the Muslim world, is the expressly apolitical Tablighi Jama'at. Its headquarters are located in the town of Raiwind in the Pakistani Punjab, and it holds an annual gathering there that is said to attract a larger crowd than any other event in the Muslim calendar bar the pilgrimage to Mecca. Since this component of the Islamic revival is apolitical, it will not be at the centre of our attention; it nevertheless underlies the other components.

The second component, to be found in most if not all Muslim countries, is political Islam, or as it is often referred to, Islamism. Here we are concerned with people who, like the Muslim Brothers and many others, are at pains to construe their politics out of their Islamic heritage. But since politics is at the centre of our concern, we need to break down this category into subcategories.

The first such subcategory is the politics of Muslim identity, a form of politics based on the axiom that Islam is the only political identity worthy of a Muslim. The phenomenon is widespread, but by far the most conspicuous instance of it is the ideology that led to the partition of India and the formation of Pakistan under the leadership of Mohammad Ali Jinnah and the Muslim League. A significant point about this kind of political Islam is that it does not have to be associated with any degree of Muslim piety. Jinnah himself was perhaps too good a politician to make this point explicitly, but it was aptly expressed by Kasim Razvi, an admirer of Jinnah's who led an ill-fated Muslim militia in Hyderabad at the time of the partition: in emphasising his pan-Islamic sentiments during an interview, he remarked that 'even if Muslim interests are affected in hell, our heart will go out in sympathy'.[3]

The second subcategory of political Islam is the politics of Muslim values. Here pietists with no commitment to Muslim interests in hell rally to impose Muslim norms on their fellow-believers, be it by getting women to wrap themselves up when appearing in public or by preventing men from drinking. Such activities may take the form of direct action by concerned believers, but they may also be a function of the state apparatus, as with the efforts of the vice police of the Islamic Republic to rein in the display of naked hair by young women on the streets of Tehran.

The third subcategory is the politics of the Islamic state. In this conception it is not enough for a state, perhaps a pre-existing state under new management, to represent a

[3] Guha (2007: 69).

Muslim identity or impose Islamic norms. Instead, the state must be an intrinsically Islamic one, constructed according to Islamic political doctrine from the ground upwards; for Sunnis this is likely to mean the restoration of the Caliphate.[4] By no means all Islamists seek such a restoration, but many do; an example is the Indian—later Pakistani—Islamist Abu'l-A'la Mawdudi (d.1979).

The final component of the Islamic revival is, of course, Jihadism. Typically Jihad is violence, but not just any old violence practised by the adherents of a religious faith. What is distinctive about Jihad is that it is violence mounted in fulfilment of a formal religious duty.

These, then, are the components of the Islamic revival that we need to keep in mind. In summary we can list them as follows:

1 'Getting religion'
2 Political Islam
    2a The politics of Muslim identity
    2b The politics of Islamic values
    2c The politics of the Islamic state
3 Jihadism

Equipped with this rough and ready breakdown, we can now go on to tackle a series of questions. The first of these is whether the Islamic revival is something unique in the world today. Or should we think of it as more or less typical of the times we live in?

IS THE ISLAMIC REVIVAL UNIQUE?

To answer this question, let us try a comparative exercise. Taking each of the components of the Islamic revival one by one, can we find a significant contemporary parallel outside Islam?

We start with 'getting religion'. Finding a non-Islamic parallel to this is no problem. Recent decades have seen a remarkable rise of Pentecostalism in Latin America and sub-Saharan Africa; in some Latin American countries today, over a fifth of the population is affiliated to Pentecostal and related churches. It is, moreover, a significant fact in this context that Latin America and sub-Saharan Africa are the regions of the Third World in which the religious market is most free. There is thus reason to

---

[4] For the main body of Shi'ites there can be no such restoration without the return of the twelfth Imam; in the meantime Khomeini's conception of 'the guardianship of the jurist' underpins the Islamic Republic of Iran, but is not universally accepted by the religious scholars of the community. The Shi'ite case thus bears comparison to the Jewish case, where it is unclear what would constitute an intrinsically Jewish state short of the advent of the Messiah.

think that religious liberalisation in other regions of the Third World would mean a rapid growth of Pentecostalism there too. There are, of course, differences, such as the much more prominent role of women in the Pentecostal context; but the basic phenomenon—a widespread increase in piety and observance—is the same.

We come now to Muslim identity politics, and again we have no problem finding a non-Muslim parallel. By far the largest phenomenon of this kind outside the Muslim world is the rise of Hindu nationalism in India, with its partially successful attempt to make being Hindu a political identity. Just as with Muslim identity politics, piety and observance are not of the essence: many members of the movement that stands guard over the ideological purity of the Hindu nationalist movement, the Rashtriya Swayamsevak Sangh (RSS), are not religious.[5]

Next comes the politics of Muslim values. Here too we have no problem finding a parallel that plays a prominent role in the affairs of a major country: the Christian Right in the United States. At its core, this movement is about using the ballot box to enlist the state in imposing Christian values on those who would not otherwise conform to them. It differs from what we saw in the Islamic Republic of Iran in that the control of the state apparatus by the Christian Right is rather limited; and as anyone who has seen a photograph of Michele Bachmann will know, it has no hang-up about naked hair—abortion rather than naked hair is the signature issue of the Christian Right. But the basic concern with imposing religious values on the population at large is the same.[6]

So far we have had no problem finding our parallels in large-scale phenomena. But from this point on the going gets harder. Thus in the case of the politics of the Islamic state we can again find a parallel in the United States, but not in the mainstream of the Christian Right. Instead we have to go to the outer fringes of the movement, to an obscure group known as the Christian Reconstructionists. I regularly ask audiences of fifty or sixty students at my university how many of them have heard of this group; to date only one student has raised a hand in response. But without question we have here a politics of the Christian state: not satisfied with the idea of commandeering the existing American state for Christian purposes, this movement would replace it with an intrinsically Christian state, one based on the Israelite polity as it was before the institution of the monarchy.[7] Yet even a group as small as the Christian

---

[5] Secular Zionists provide a further parallel, though a less satisfactory one to the extent that Jews are not just adherents of a religion but also members of an ethnic group.

[6] Again the Israeli scene provides parallels in the political activities of religious parties and the violence of vigilante groups.

[7] This points to a profound difference between the real-world implications of the Islamist and Christian Reconstructionist aspirations. The Islamist conception resonates with the strong modern state that Third-World nationalists would like to see, the Christian Reconstructionist conception with the weak state favoured by American libertarians.

Reconstructionists does not speak with one voice, and it is worth noting an internal disagreement regarding the current Constitution of the United States. Rousas John Rushdoony (d.2001), the founding father of the group, saw the Constitution in the manner of the mainstream Christian Right, namely as 'designed to *perpetuate* a Christian order'.[8] By contrast, his estranged son-in-law Gary North described it as a 'demonic plan', 'an apostate covenant', 'idol worship', 'covenanting with a new god, the sovereign People'.[9] Such rhetoric provides a stirring parallel to hard-line Islamist denunciations of democracy, but within the American context it is utterly marginal.

As to Jihadism, we can find violence all over the place, including violence performed by adherents of a variety of religions to further religious ends. But warfare as the performance of an express religious duty is not so common in the modern world. Perhaps the best example is the militancy of the Sikhs in India, originally directed against Muslims but more recently against Hindus. A couple of quotations from the 18th-century Sikh rulebooks will give the flavour of the Sikh duty. One states that 'The Sikh who ventures out unarmed shall be doomed to continued transmigration';[10] the other declares that 'The command of the Gurus is "Fight the barbarians, destroy them all!"'[11] But we are dealing here with the religion of a relatively small population—perhaps less than thirty million. That is vastly more than the number of Christian Reconstuctionists, but still numerically insignificant in a country the size of India.

So is the Islamic revival unique? In one obvious way it is not: as we have just seen, we can find a parallel for each of its components somewhere else. But in another way it is indeed unique. Nowhere else do we find a parallel to the entire complex; instead we had to be distinctly energetic, not to say eclectic, in trotting around the globe to find parallels, and some of them verged on the recherché. Moreover, there is a rather telling point to be made about two of the parallels we identified: they come from India, and in historical terms both can plausibly be seen as cases of non-Muslims emulating Muslims—their solidarity in the Hindu nationalist case, their militance in the Sikh case. So all in all, it seems that in seeking to understand the Islamic revival we are indeed trying to make sense of something exceptional.

Why then is it exceptional? There are two obvious places to look for an answer: one is the conditions under which contemporary Muslims live, and the other is the values entrenched in their heritage. This brings me to my second question.

---

[8] Rushdoony (1978: 2).
[9] North (1989: 696, 691, 655, 702, 654–5 respectively).
[10] McLeod (1990: 77).
[11] McLeod (1987: 150). The 'barbarians' are the Muslims.

HOW DOES THE ISLAMIC REVIVAL RELATE
TO THE THIRD-WORLD PREDICAMENT?

Muslim populations and the political movements that seek to mobilise them may be concerned with any number of issues, and it is in the nature of this short article that it makes no attempt to cover them. But apart from Islam, the single most obvious thing that all substantial Muslim populations have in common is that they belong to the Third World. This means that in terms of the global rat race they are not doing well in comparison with the populations of the First World, where wealth, power, and prestige are overwhelmingly concentrated. This is not a reassuring predicament to be in, and if you have the misfortune to be in it, it pulls you in more than one direction. Take international politics. On the one hand you want to respond to your inferior status by being defiant; but on the other hand you need to be cooperative because you desperately need the rich and powerful to be your friends and do you favours. In terms of cultural politics, you face a similar dilemma. On the one hand you want to save your heritage from being inundated by the tides of Westernisation; but on the other hand you want to adopt Western ways because they work better or are too prestigious to resist. One way or another these are major issues for a Third-World population, and we should certainly see the Islamic revival as responding to them. To put it counterfactually, if Muslim populations belonged overwhelmingly to the First World, I doubt if the British Academy would have organised a lecture on Islamic fundamentalism.

But against all this we have to come to terms with the fact is that there is nothing distinctive about the Third-World predicament as it affects Muslims, nothing about it that would explain why the *Muslim* response should stand apart from those of other Third-World populations. After all, the Third World contains many more non-Muslims than Muslims, and broadly they live in the same relatively disadvantaged situation as the bulk of the world's Muslims do. So it seems unlikely that we would find here an explanation of what is exceptional about the Islamic revival.

If we now bring the religious heritage of Muslims into the picture, and look at the way in which it can relate to the Third-World predicament, we may begin to do better. It is not hard to show that Islam makes available to its adherents a number of ideas that are powerfully relevant to this context. For simplicity, let us present these ideas in terms of extremes—a rejectionist extreme that maximises defiance and preservation of the native heritage, and an accommodationist extreme that maximises having rich and powerful friends and adopting beneficial aspects of Western culture. Of course in practice real people tend to be somewhere in between, and just where they stand is affected by many factors beyond the purview of this article; but this does not detract from the analytical convenience of looking at the extremes.

At the rejectionist end of the spectrum, we have no trouble identifying values available in the Islamic heritage that can be invoked to articulate and inspire a profound and violent alienation from the modern world. If anyone opts to believe that Islam is the only political identity worthy of a Muslim, that a Caliphate ruling over all Muslims is the only legitimate political order, that Muslims must wage war on non-Muslims, that Muslims must not imitate non-Muslims, and so forth, they will have no trouble finding immediate support for all this in the heritage. With regard to the imitation of non-Muslims, for example, such support is available in a well-known tradition that the Prophet Muhammad said: 'He who imitates a people is one of them.'[12] All this can readily be invoked to articulate Third-World rage, the sense of being involved in a struggle to the death against the prevailing world order, as no other ideology has done since the demise of revolutionary Marxism.[13] Moreover it does it by appealing to the heritage of a religion that a large fraction of humanity actually believes in.

Meanwhile at the accommodationist end of the spectrum there are various clever ways in which the heritage can be invoked to neutralise the rejectionist elements. But one does not always have to be clever. There are also—and this is what I want to elaborate on—features of the heritage to which one can make direct and positive appeal in such contexts. For example, if one wants to neutralise at least some of the force of the tradition about not imitating non-Muslims, one can cite the Battle of the Trench, a battle that Muhammad fought and won in 627. His problem in preparing for the battle was to secure the northern perimeter of the oasis of Medina against enemy cavalry. One of his followers, who happened to be of Persian origin, recommended digging a trench, observing that this tactic was used in his home country. Far from denouncing such imitation of a pagan practice, Muhammad immediately adopted it, and to good effect.[14] Here, then, we have Prophetic precedent for adopting beneficial aspects of non-Muslim cultures.

An accommodationist stance is also greatly assisted by what might be called the proto-republican values of the early Islamic polity. For example, when Muhammad Mursi gave his victory speech after being elected President of Egypt in June of 2012, this is what he told his fellow-countrymen: 'I have been given authority over you, but I am not the best of you . . . Help me as long as I act justly and righteously among you . . .; when I do not do so, you have no duty to obey me.'[15] In other words, he recognised that his subjects had the standing to judge the rectitude of his conduct and act accordingly. He was not being original: this was just what Abu Bakr is reputed to

[12] Abu Dawud (n.d.: 4: 44).
[13] Compare Che Guevara and Bin Laden as T-shirt icons.
[14] Waqidi (1966: 445).
[15] Anon. (2012).

have told the assembled Muslims in his accession speech of 632 when he was installed as the first Caliph following the death of Muhammad.[16] What we have here is a typical articulation of the values of the early Muslim polity.[17] It is not a democracy, nor is it a constitutional government, but it is very definitely a non-despotic form of rule. It is also anti-patrimonial, as another anecdote about the beginning of Abu Bakr's Caliphate shows. A day after he became Caliph, Abu Bakr was making his way to market with a pile of clothes that he planned to sell. He was, after all, a merchant, and he needed to feed his family. He was accosted by one of his supporters, who suggested to him that he could discharge his public duties more effectively if he applied to the treasurer for an allowance. He did so, and the treasurer proceeded to allocate one to him—not the highest allowance, but not the lowest either. The treasurer also equipped him with two suits of clothes, one for winter and the other for summer. 'If you wear something out', he concluded, 'you bring it back and you get another instead.'[18] This is not, of course, how things were done at the time in such imperial capitals as Constantinople and Ctesiphon. Alongside this aversion to despotism and patrimonialism we also find a rough and ready egalitarianism. 'People are equals like the teeth of a comb', as Muhammad is reputed to have said.[19] 'We Arabs are equals', as an Arab envoy to the Persians is reported to have told them within a few years of Muhammad's death.[20]

All this resonates powerfully with modern political values, and it means that these values can be seen as an authentic part of the native heritage, rather than as something adopted from the West in grudging recognition of its cultural superiority. Of course these values do not add up to democracy, the single most prestigious political value in the world today. Indeed, a real problem arises if one wants to see democracy as Islamic: how is popular sovereignty to be reconciled with divine sovereignty? Thus Ayman al-Zawahiri roundly denounces democracy as 'a new religion that deifies the masses',[21] in the same vein as Gary North condemns the American Constitution as 'covenanting with a new god, the sovereign People'. To find a way around this, one probably has to be clever—as Mawdudi was. He came up with the original—or perhaps Lockean—notion that God confers the Caliphate on each and every believer, and each of them in turn delegates his or her Caliphate to a single ruler whom the believers thereby appoint to rule over them.[22] Divine sovereignty thus engenders popular

[16] Cook (2013: 292). Different transmissions have different wordings, but the message is the same.
[17] The question how far what we read in our sources is later back-projection is a fair one, but it does not affect the argument.
[18] Cook (2013: 292).
[19] Cook (2013: 292).
[20] Cook (2013: 289–90), and see Kennedy (2007: 111–15).
[21] Cook (2013: 307).
[22] Cook (2013: 302). Mawdudi is not known as a feminist, but in this instance his inclusion of women is unequivocal.

sovereignty, thereby creating a space for democracy. We see here ways to share some very attractive Western values without the indignity of borrowing them from the West.

What I have just laid out are, so to speak, ideal types, but it is not hard to find phenomena reasonably close to them in the real world. Towards the rejectionist end of the spectrum we have the violence of Boko Haram against polio vaccination and modern education in northern Nigeria, and the violence of the Taliban against polio vaccination and education for girls in Pakistan. Towards the accommodationist end we have the Muslim Brotherhood in its various local incarnations; even Hamas, which tends to be thought of as rather extremist, believes in Islamic art in a manner that would be anathema to the Taliban. As the Hamas Charter has it, 'Man is a strange and miraculous being, . . . a handful of clay and a breath of soul. Islamic art addresses man on this basis.'[23]

Obviously religious traditions do not speak with one voice, and indeed in the Islamic case the polyphony is currently a deafening cacophony. My point is that there is a lot in the Islamic tradition that lends itself both to relatively rejectionist attitudes and to relatively accommodationist ones. Either way it is relevant, providing rich resources for thinking, feeling, and talking. And all this is entrenched in a heritage that is part and parcel of a religion that is accepted by entire societies from top to bottom. But is there anything exceptional about Islam in this respect? Could not similar things be said of the religious heritages of other Third-World societies? That brings me to my third question.

DOES ISLAM HAVE POLITICAL RESOURCES THAT OTHER THIRD-WORLD RELIGIONS DO NOT?

I believe that Islam does have such resources, and that a series of contrasts with other religious heritages would establish this. But for reasons of space, I shall do no more here than touch on one example, the Hindu heritage. It is a convenient one for our purposes thanks to the existence of a major political movement that mixes Hinduism and politics, namely Hindu nationalism. Let us adapt the analysis of the components of the Islamic revival set out near the beginning of this article, and seek Hindu counterparts of each component. In other words, we are looking for the following:

1　'Getting religion' in a Hindu context
2　Political Hinduism
　　2a　The politics of Hindu identity
　　2b　The politics of Hindu values

[23] See Article 19 in Mishal & Sela (2000: 188).

2c The politics of the Hindu state
3 A Hindu counterpart of Jihadism

With regard to 'getting religion', the literature on Hinduism over the last half century does not suggest that there has been a massive increase in piety and observance among Hindus. Though this is not central to the argument, it is well worth noting.

Turning to political Hinduism, the only form in which we find such a thing is the politics of Hindu identity. This is well developed in contemporary India; it is what Hindu nationalism is about, and it is accompanied by a strong antipathy towards the conversion of Hindus to Islam or Christianity. But it is not matched by anything we could call the politics of Hindu values, still less by the politics of the Hindu state. It is no doubt because of this almost exclusive focus on identity that we usually speak of the movement in question as Hindu *nationalism*—not Hindu revivalism or fundamentalism.[24] And even then, the movement is up against deep-rooted structural factors that make large parts of Hindu society unlikely to identify for political purposes as Hindu. In other words, they are up against caste.

As to violence directed at non-Hindus, there has been no shortage of this in recent decades. It is violence in support of a religious affiliation, but it is not normally violence as the performance of a religious duty.

If this is what we see in India today, how does it relate to the contents of the Hindu heritage?

Let us consider first one of the most pronounced features of the Hindu tradition: its resolute commitment to social inequality. Here are some typical pronouncements reflecting this tradition; they relate to Brahmins, who are at the top of the social order, and Shudras, who are at the bottom. First, choosing a name for a newborn child: 'For a Brahmin, the name should connote auspiciousness . . . and for a Shudra, disdain.' Second, the economic implications of the distinction: 'Even a capable Shudra must not accumulate wealth; for when a Shudra becomes wealthy, he harasses Brahmins.' Third, some everyday implications: 'They should give him leftover food, old clothes, grain that has been cast aside, and the old household items.' Finally, a general view of the role of Shudras in relation to Brahmins: 'For the Shudra . . . the highest Law leading to bliss is simply to render obedient service to distinguished Brahmin householders.'[25] This commitment to social inequality affects the prospects of any politics that is based squarely on the Hindu tradition, and it does so with regard to more than one of

---

[24] Likewise in the Israeli context we are comfortable describing as nationalist both secular Zionism and the religious Zionism of the National Religious Party. Islamism is of course similar to nationalism in significant respects, but it is also categorically opposed to it in the sense that it rejects any attempt to accredit ethnic difference within the Muslim community as a basis for loyalty or statehood.

[25] Olivelle (2005: 96 (2:31), 214 (10:129, 10:125), 207 (9:334) respectively, transcription modified).

the components that we are concerned with. Thus with regard to identity politics, it means that the tradition articulates social divisions inimical to the requisite sense of community, a serious liability in a democratic environment where one cannot be successful if one systematically gives offence to the majority of the population. The same problem arises with regard to the politics of Hindu values.

There is more. Consider the political values enshrined in the Hindu heritage: in addition to its commitment to inequality, its political vision is exclusively monarchist, and has no overlaps with modern Western values.[26] There is accordingly no viable basis for the politics of the Hindu state. The tradition likewise provides no counterpart to Jihadism: it is marked by a law of war that talks at length and without any discomfort about wars between rival Hindu rulers, yet has almost nothing to say about war against non-Hindus. And as to imitating non-Hindus, this is a heritage that does not even allow a Hindu to learn their languages[27]—a prescription that would undermine one of the most adaptive resources of Hindu society in the world today, the widespread knowledge of English among the elite.

In short, as a site for the construction of a modern political ideology, the Hindu heritage just does not have as much to offer as the Islamic heritage. So it is not surprising that the Hindu nationalists, who have done their best to articulate a Hindu identity with which they can hope to win elections, do not spend their time deriving their politics from the foundational texts of Hinduism.

This is not to say that the Hindu heritage has nothing to offer politicians active in the modern world. For example, it provides a rather precise territorial definition of India—something that religions with universal pretensions do not normally give their adherents. It makes available symbolic resources for mass mobilisation against Muslims—the Hindu nationalist enemy of choice—thanks to the sanctity of the cow (given that Muslims eat it) and the wide dissemination of the Ram cult (given the presence of a mosque on the site of Ram's birth). It supports the literal demonisation of the Muslim enemy thanks to the prominent role of demons in the *Ramayana*. Last but not least, its ritual practices, as modified by the Hindu nationalists with creative abandon, have a potential for political theatre unmatched by Sunni Islam.[28] All this lends itself to a politics of Hindu identity—but not to one of imposing Hindu values or creating a Hindu state.

---

[26] Gandhi took the traditional Hindu concept of non-violence (*ahimsa*) and gave it a new role as a political value, but the Hindu nationalists have not shown much enthusiasm for this notion.

[27] For the view that 'one should not study the language of the mlecchas' see Kane (1930–62: 2: 383).

[28] The creative abandon of the Hindu nationalists points to a deeper contrast with the Islamists. Virtually all modern adherents of ancient religious traditions tend to reshape their traditions in response to modern conditions, but the rules of the game will generally be found to be considerably more restrictive in the Islamist case.

If instead of Hinduism we were to turn to Buddhism or Christianity, the particulars would be very different but the upshot would be the same: neither provides its adherents with resources for modern Third-World politics comparable to those offered by the Islamic heritage.

WHAT PART DOES FUNDAMENTALISM PLAY IN ALL THIS?

Up to this point I have made little use of the term 'fundamentalism', and I have paid no attention to the question what exactly it might mean. As is well known, we owe the term to an American Protestant, Curtis Lee Laws (d.1946). Writing in 1920 about Protestants who shared his resolute opposition to what he saw as the corruption of religion by modernism, he launched the term in the following sentence: 'We suggest that those who still cling to the great fundamentals and who mean to do battle royal for the fundamentals shall be called "Fundamentalists".'[29] Laws had no intention of coining a term that would apply to non-Christian religions, but there is nothing in his definition that precludes that. So Muslim fundamentalists would be people who mean to do battle royal for the fundamentals of Islam, and the term is now in wide use in Muslim contexts. The difficulty, of course, is that it is not immediately obvious what we should count as the fundamentals of Islam. Laws had a clear idea what the fundamentals of Christianity were because he was a believing Christian with decided views; but a Catholic would hardly have agreed with him. The same indeterminacy affects the identification of the fundamentals in the Islamic case, and unsurprisingly those who use the term here do not display any unanimity about what they mean by it. So let me simply say what I propose to mean by it myself, without denying the right of others to mean something else. If your aim is to go back to the original source of your religion, by-passing what you think is its later corrupted form, and if you accordingly locate religious authority exclusively in the original source, and if you take this source seriously in a substantive way and not just as a symbol, then by my definition you count as a fundamentalist.

If this is what we choose to mean by the term, then the Islamic revival is not in general characterised by a doctrinaire fundamentalism, but it does display a marked fundamentalist tendency. Take the case of Mawdudi. As two of his disciples put it, Mawdudi was 'emphatic that the normative and immutable part of the Muslim heritage consists of the principles of the Qur'ān and the *Sunnah*, and nothing else';[30] the sources referred to here can readily be identified with the foundational texts of the

---

[29] Laws (1920: 834).
[30] Ahmad & Ansari (1979: 16).

religion. In other words, Mawdudi was indeed a fundamentalist in the sense that he wanted to go back to the original source of his religion, though in fact he was by no means doctrinaire or consistent about it. He himself catches the fundamentalist tendency of the Islamic revival very well in his remark that Muslims 'are still enamoured of Islam in its pristine purity, as it was preached and practised by the Prophet, his first four Caliphs and his Companions'.[31]

What is interesting to us about this tendency is that fundamentalising Islam works to enhance, as opposed to diminish, the force of the various elements I have been discussing. By going back to the beginnings one goes back to a time in the 7th century at which Muslim political identity was not yet weakened by ethnic divisions between Arabs and non-Arabs, at which all Muslims were still ruled by a single state, at which Muslims still spent their time making war on non-Muslims without as yet fighting each other, let alone allying with non-Muslims against other Muslims. The effect is likewise to sideline the despotic and patrimonial style of government that came to prevail in the Muslim world down the centuries, and to by-pass the acceptance of steep social hierarchy that soon came to mark Muslim societies. In other words, fundamentalism in this sense is not just a form of theological obstinacy: it pays real ideological dividends that in some ways can make one more comfortable with the modern world. A Hindu fundamentalism would not deliver any of this[32]—which is why, despite a 19th-century effort that went nowhere, Hindu fundamentalism in the sense in which I am using the term barely exists.[33] The same, I think, would hold true in different ways of other non-Muslim religions. Here again, Islam is different.

THE UNITY OF THE HUMAN RACE

In this article I have been concerned with showing how and why what we see in the contemporary Islamic world is exceptional. If we are to make sense of the political salience of Islam today, we need to understand this. But we also need to avoid over-emphasising the degree to which the Islamic case is exceptional. At the most basic level, there is nothing very arcane or mysterious about the ways of thinking we have encountered or the motivations behind them. Defiance, for example, is no monopoly of the Islamic world, or even of the Third World; anyone whose memory of British politics goes back to 1982 will recollect the message that the *Sun* reporter Tony Snow

---

[31] Mawdudi (1989: 19–20).

[32] It would also undermine the elements of the heritage I picked out above as politically serviceable.

[33] I should make it clear that I do not share the view that the nature of the Hindu tradition precludes the emergence of a Hindu fundamentalism; rather, it is a contingent historical fact, and a significant one, that the phenomenon was still-born. For more on this see Cook (2014), chapter 9.

inscribed on a missile about to be fired in the course of the Falklands War: 'Up yours Galtieri!'[34] At the same time Britain provides us with a much more recent and decorous example of the kind of thinking through which fundamentalists are sometimes able to appropriate alien ideas by finding them in their own heritages. At the annual conference of the Conservative Party in Manchester on October 5, 2011, the British Prime Minister David Cameron admonished those who had pointed to India, China and Brazil as economic models for Britain: 'We need to become more like us. The real us. Hardworking, pioneering, independent, creative, adaptable, optimistic, can-do.'[35] How truly fortunate that the *real* us turn out to have all the virtues of those enterprising Indians, Chinese, and Brazilians without the stigma of being foreign, just as the *real* Muslims already possess all those virtues that others have been telling them to acquire from the West. At a certain level, people don't seem to vary very much across the globe: when push comes to shove, they can all be heard talking the same kind of nonsense.

REFERENCES

Abu Dawud (n.d.), *Sunan*, ed. M.M. 'Abd al-Hamid (n.p., Dar al-Fikr).

Ahmad, K., & Ansari, Z.I. (1979), *Mawlana Mawdudi: An Introduction to his Life and Thought* (Leicester, The Islamic Foundation).

Anon. (2012), 'Mursi fi khitab al-fawz: sa-akunu ra'isan li-kull al-Misriyyin' (http://hespress.com/international/57009.html, June 24).

Burns, J.F. (2011), 'British leader pushes for "can-do optimism" and faith in austerity path', *New York Times*, 6 October.

Cook, M. (2013), 'Is Political Freedom an Islamic Value?', in *Freedom and the Construction of Europe*, ed. Q. Skinner and M. van Gelderen, vol. 2: *Free Persons and Free States*, 283–310. (Cambridge: Cambridge University Press).

Cook, M. (2014), *Ancient Religions, Modern Politics: The Islamic Case in Comparative Perspective* (Princeton, Princeton University Press).

Guha, R. (2007), *India after Gandhi: The History of the World's Largest Democracy* (New York, HarperCollins).

Kane, P.V. (1930–62), *History of Dharmaśāstra* (Poona, Bhandarkar Oriental Research Institute).

Kennedy, H. (2007), *The Great Arab Conquests: How the Spread of Islam Changed the World We Live in* (London, Weidenfeld & Nicolson).

Laws, C.L. (1920), 'Convention side lights', *Watchman-Examiner*, 8, no. 27, 1 July.

Mawdudi, A.A. (1989), *Islam Today* (Delhi, Crescent Publishing).

McLeod, W.H. (1987), *The Chaupa Singh Rahit-nama* (Dunedin, University of Otago Press).

McLeod, W.H. (1990), *Textual Sources for the Study of Sikhism* (Chicago, University of Chicago Press).

Mishal, S., & Sela, A. (2000), *The Palestinian Hamas: Vision, Violence, and Coexistence* (New York, Columbia University Press).

[34] We would nevertheless have to admit that Bin Laden never descended to this level of vulgarity.
[35] Burns (2011).

North, G. (1989), *Political Polytheism: The Myth of Pluralism* (Tyler, Texas, Institute for Christian Economics).

Olivelle, P. (2005), *Manu's Code of Law: A Critical Edition and Translation of the Manava-Dharmaśastra* (Oxford, Oxford University Press).

Rushdoony, R.J. (1978), *The Nature of the American System* (Fairfax, Virginia, Thoburn Press).

Waqidi (1966), *Maghazi*, ed. M. Jones (London, Oxford University Press).

Note on the author: Michael Cook is Professor of Near Eastern Studies at Princeton University. He studied at the University of Cambridge and SOAS, University of London, and went on to teach at SOAS until he moved to Princeton in 1986. His published work is mainly concerned with the formation and development of Islamic civilisation, including the role played by religious values in that process. He has also studied in detail a particular Islamic value across history: the duty of every Muslim to reprimand people for violating God's law. His publications include *The Koran* (in the OUP 'Very Short Introductions' series, 2000), *Forbidding Wrong in Islam: An Introduction* (Cambridge, 2003), and *Ancient Religions, Modern Politics: The Islamic Case in Comparative Perspective* (Princeton, 2014).
Contact: mcook@princeton.edu

This article was first published in 2014 in *Journal of the British Academy* (ISSN 2052–7217).

To cite the article: Michael Cook (2014), 'The appeal of Islamic fundamentalism ', *Journal of the British Academy*, 2: 27–41. DOI 10.5871/jba/002.027

Journal of the British Academy, **2**, 43–58. DOI 10.5871/jba/002.043
Posted 23 June 2014. © The British Academy 2014

Dyslexia: A language learning impairment

*Joint British Academy/British Psychological Society Lecture
read 24 September 2013 by*

MARGARET J. SNOWLING

Fellow of the Academy

Abstract: Without the ability to read fluently with comprehension there is a downward spiral of poor educational achievement and career prospects. Dyslexia is therefore a major problem for society and a key question is whether it is possible to intervene early to ameliorate its impact. Studies following the development of children at family-risk of dyslexia reveal that it is associated with language delays and speech difficulties in the pre-school years before reading instruction begins. Literacy outcomes for children depend not only on the risk factors that predispose to reading difficulties but also on protective factors which mitigate the risk. Together current evidence places dyslexia on a continuum with other language learning impairments.

Keywords: Dyslexia, SLI, language learning impairment, reading difficulties, risk studies.

Dyslexia is a life-time persistent disorder which affects the ability to read and spell. According to the new diagnostic manual of the American Psychiatric Association, DSM-5 (American Psychiatric Association, 2013), dyslexia is one of several learning difficulties classified together under the umbrella term 'Specific Learning Disorder'. It might seem reasonable at the outset to ask, 'Why a difficulty that primarily affects the ability to decode print should be classed as a form of mental disorder?' The question is apposite. But, if people with dyslexia are not properly supported, they can face a downward spiral of poor literacy, poor education and limited career prospects, with a negative impact on their adult well-being. Dyslexia is therefore not only a problem for the individual but also for society as a whole.

The first description of dyslexia in Britain was by a general practitioner, Dr Pringle-Morgan in 1896. After this, the causes of the condition, then referred to as 'congenital word blindness', remained the domain of medical specialists for some seventy years. An important study conducted by Rutter & Yule in 1973 was a turning point in terms of our understanding of this 'hidden' disorder. Rutter & Yule (1973) used a survey of the entire 9-year-old population of the Isle of Wight to differentiate two kinds of reading problem: children who had reading problems which were out of line with expectation given their age but in line with their Mental Age (they called these children 'children with general reading backwardness'); and children whose reading was out of line with expectation based on IQ (calling these, children with 'specific reading retardation'). Two points from this classic study resonate with current knowledge of children's reading difficulties. First, there was no evidence for a discrete condition of 'dyslexia', though the prevalence of specific reading retardation was greater than might be anticipated given just the normal distribution of reading skill. Second, and critically, children with both types of reading difficulty experienced delays and difficulties in language development, these being more circumscribed in the group with specific reading retardation.

At around the same time, researchers in the field of cognitive psychology were beginning to become interested in the process of learning to read and in reading difficulties. In 1979, Vellutino published a landmark text, *Dyslexia: Research and Theory*, in which he reviewed the large body of research suggesting that dyslexia is due to a perceptual difficulty. Instead, he argued that dyslexia was a verbal coding problem, an idea subsequently recast as the 'phonological deficit hypothesis' (Vellutino *et al.*, 2004). In short, learning to read, regardless of the script, requires the establishment of mappings between the spoken and written language domains. In an alphabetic system like English, these fine-grained mappings are between the letters of printed words, or graphemes, and the sounds of spoken words, the phonemes, and involve access to the phonemes of spoken language. This is no mean feat as many others have stated. Indeed, one might go so far as to say that cracking the alphabetic code is one of the major accomplishments of cognitive development. Furthermore, according to the phonological deficit hypothesis, the proximal cause of dyslexia is a difficulty at the level of speech sounds (phonemes), creating a problem in establishing the mappings—that is, a problem of phonological processing leading to a learning disorder. A growing body of evidence now shows that the phonological deficit in dyslexia may be universal, not only across alphabetic languages (Caravolas *et al.*, 2012), but also in Chinese (McBride-Chang *et al.*, 2011) and in the alphasyllabaries of southern India (Nag & Snowling, 2011).

It is perhaps useful to note at this point that dyslexia is the name given to a set of reading behaviours rather than a distinct category. These behaviours are the outcome of multiple factors, genetic and environmental which, through interaction, lead to a continuous distribution of outcomes with no clear cut-off (Pennington, 2006). Moreover, contrary to the view that dyslexia occurs in people of good cognitive ability, it is now agreed that 'dyslexia' occurs across the range of abilities and that the term can be equally applied to those of lower IQ (Snowling & Hulme, 2012 for review). It follows that 'diagnosing dyslexia' on the basis of a discrepancy between IQ and reading skill is no longer accepted practice.

It is argued in this paper that, regardless of the consensus that phonological skills are the prime determinants of learning to read, there is an 'elephant in the room'. The elephant is language. Learning to read builds on a foundation in spoken language skills and children who come to school with poor oral language skills are at high risk of reading difficulties (Bishop & Snowling, 2004 for a review; Catts *et al.*, 2002). Thus, although the theory that phonological deficits are the proximal cause of dyslexia is robust, an over-emphasis on these deficits does a disservice to those with language-learning impairments whose phonological skills are not well developed at school entry. The paper begins with a review of what is known about the precursors of dyslexia in the pre-school years, pointing to quite widespread delays and difficulties in speech and language development. It continues with a discussion of the relationship between dyslexia and specific language impairment, before outlining a new causal model of dyslexia and its implications for intervention. Taken together the findings reinforce the importance of language as a vital prerequisite for becoming literate.

PRECURSORS OF DYSLEXIA IN THE LANGUAGE DOMAIN

For many years, the study of dyslexia proceeded in laboratory-based studies of highly selected clinical groups. Such studies are subject to referral bias and often children with significant difficulties are excluded because of co-occurring issues. Quite a different approach is offered by longitudinal studies which follow the development of children at high risk of dyslexia from the pre-school years, and proceed to examine the characteristics of those who go on to be dyslexic compared to those who are deemed to be 'normal' readers.

The first of these studies was reported by Scarborough (1990). In this study she highlighted the crucial importance of language to literacy development, an issue which had been neglected for some years, arguably because of the dominance of both the 'discrepancy definition' of dyslexia and the phonological deficit theory (e.g. Stanovich 1994). Scarborough found that, in the pre-school years, children with dyslexia exhibited a changing profile of language strengths and difficulties. At 2–3 years old, although they used as many words as children in a control group without a family history of dyslexia, they were less intelligible and also had grammatical difficulties and from 3–5 years old they had difficulties in naming objects. These spoken language impairments presaged difficulties with phonological awareness and in the development of early reading skills. The study suggested that oral language difficulties were a distal cause of reading problems, in line with the earlier findings of the Isle of Wight study.

Since 1990, several studies of children at family risk of dyslexia have been completed and others are ongoing. The 'standard' paradigm has become to follow children with a first-degree relative who is dyslexic (normally a parent but sometimes an older sibling) alongside peers of the same age from families with no history of reading difficulties. The typical time frame is from pre-school to around Year 3, when the children are assessed and classified into three groups. The first group consists of children at family risk of dyslexia who are 'identified' as dyslexic (FR–dyslexia), the second group is of children at family risk of dyslexia who are deemed to be normal readers (family risk–normal reader; FR–NR) and the third group consists of typically developing (TD) children who, by definition, are at low risk of dyslexia and who do not have reading difficulties (TD–NR). In some but not all studies, a small group of the controls succumb to reading problems, as would be expected (about 10 per cent) and these children are excluded from further attention.

Having classified the children in Year 3, the next step is to conduct a retrospective analysis of group and sub-group differences at early developmental stages to reveal the precursors of reading difficulties (Snowling & Melby-Lervag, submitted, for a review). Together these studies confirm a heightened prevalence of dyslexia, some 44 per cent, in children at family risk compared to controls. Of course such data carry with them the assumption that dyslexia is a discrete category; as already discussed, this cannot be assumed. Indeed, examining literacy outcomes at the age of around eight, children at family risk who are not defined as dyslexic typically do less well on tests of reading and spelling than their peers. In short, although they do not qualify for the label of dyslexia, they still show some symptoms of reading and spelling disorder.

More importantly for our present argument, we can ask the question 'Do children who go on to be dyslexic experience phonological difficulties in the pre-school years and, if so, are they specific or part and parcel of a broader language delay?' With one or two exceptions, the emerging picture suggests that children who go on to be dyslexic do show significant difficulties with phonological skills; these difficulties include problems repeating novel words (non-word repetition), recalling verbal items in short term memory (which draws on phonological codes) and difficulties with phonological awareness (taking away the sound in a word, for example 'black → back') but they also experience broader difficulties with aspects of language comprehension, particularly receptive vocabulary.

Arguably, what is more surprising is that the FR–NR group also show the same broad range of linguistic problems in pre-school, though to a lesser extent. In fact, it is not until school age that the developmental trajectory indicative of slow language development in the two family-risk groups appears to diverge. According to the meta-analysis at school age, those with dyslexia continue to experience difficulties in language comprehension and in phonological awareness. In contrast, the FR–NR group appear to resolve their language problems though their phonological awareness remains weak. The finding that both family-risk groups, regardless of whether or not they go on to have significant reading problems, have problems with phonological awareness is important. Contrary to the classic view, it suggests that a phonological deficit alone is not sufficient to cause dyslexia; the likelihood of 'diagnosis' is increased when dyslexia occurs in the context of broader oral language difficulties, or possibly where there are additional co-occurring impairments, for example in attentional processes (Pennington, 2006; Snowling, 2008).

Following on from this, a slightly different way of conceptualising the phonological deficit in dyslexia is in terms of a risk factor, arguably the proximal cognitive cause. But like all risk factors it is probabilistic and can be moderated by additional risk and protective factors. Within a broader biological view in which dyslexia has a hereditary basis (Paracchini *et al.*, 2007), the phonological deficit can be considered as an intermediary between the genes associated with dyslexia and the behavioural disorder. Such an intermediate phenotype is sometimes referred to as a cognitive 'endophenotype' (Moll *et al.*, 2013). Endophenotypes are defined as processes associated with the disorder in the population but expressed at a higher rate in the unaffected relatives of probands than in the general population (Bearden & Freimer, 2006). Together the family-risk studies suggest that the key issue is how this endophenotype combines with other endophenotypes, as well as protective factors which are present at school entry to determine the course of literacy development.

THE RELATIONSHIP BETWEEN DYSLEXIA AND SPECIFIC LANGUAGE IMPAIRMENT

If the critical difference between children at family risk of dyslexia who go on to have reading problems and those who do not is the status of the language system at school entry, then this begs the question: what is the relationship between dyslexia and the language disorder known as 'specific language impairment' (SLI) (Bishop, 1997)? Interestingly, a longitudinal study following the outcomes of children with pre-school SLI came to similar conclusions: children whose language difficulties had resolved by 5½ years, went on to have normal literacy skills at 8½ (Bishop & Adams, 1990) and subsequently at school-leaving age (Stothard *et al.*, 1998). However, it is noteworthy that, at the later date, they were found to have some underlying weaknesses in phonological skills; these included poor performance on a test of Spoonerisms, a challenging task tapping phoneme awareness in which initial sounds of two words have to be exchanged (for example 'Phil Collins → Kill Follins') and poor non-word repetition relative to age and ability-matched controls.

Building on these findings, Bishop & Snowling (2004) reviewed the extant literature on the relationship between dyslexia and SLI, which is large and somewhat inconsistent in its findings. They proposed this inconsistency arises because the relationship between the two disorders is not a simple one, and two different dimensions need to be taken into account to specify it. The first dimension comprises the phonological skills that underpin the development of decoding (and the alphabetic principle), the second, the grammatical, syntactic and semantic skills that are critical for reading comprehension. Within this framework, dyslexia and SLI share deficits in phonological skills but differ with regard to broader oral language skills. There are continuities between the disorders since each of the 'dimensions' varies from impaired to superior. Broadly speaking, a similar view has emerged from two subsequent studies. On the basis of a large population study, Catts *et al.* (2005) concluded that dyslexia and SLI can be viewed as co-occurring conditions, the co-morbidity accounted for by shared phonological deficits (though bearing in mind that some children with SLI do not experience phonological difficulties, Nation *et al.*, 2004, and form a different subgroup). Similarly, Ramus *et al.* (2013) argued that SLI and dyslexia share deficits in phonological skills but also proposed that the profile of the two disorders is different. While SLI is associated with deficits at the level of phonological representations as well as in phonological skills, they proposed that dyslexia is primarily a deficit in the skills that operate on phonological representations and not the representations themselves.

More recently, we have been following the development from pre-school through to the age of eight, of children with a family risk of dyslexia, children with pre-school specific language impairment and controls. The research question driving this project is the developmental continuities between the two disorders and the shared risk factors. A key hypothesis is that phonological deficits represent a shared endophenotype between dyslexia and SLI; however, a further prediction is that the two disorders will differ in terms of co-morbidities, increasing the probability of diagnosis.

Recruitment to our study was a three-stage process. Following a call for volunteers of parents with pre-school children either at family risk of dyslexia, language impaired or typically developing, the parents (regardless of parental self-report) underwent objective assessment to determine their literacy status (Snowling *et al.*, 2012). This process led to classification of the families and their children into two groups: at family risk or not at risk. Next, following a language assessment, the children were grouped as to whether they fulfilled research criteria for language impairment. We defined language impairment as falling more than one standard deviation below the mean on two out of four measures of receptive and expressive language skills.

Our recruitment procedure yielded four groups of children: the first group were typically developing, the second, a group of children who had language impairment, third a group of children who were at family risk of dyslexia but without language impairment, and finally a group at family risk of dyslexia and who also had language impairment. A novel finding was that, amongst children at family risk of dyslexia, about a third appear to have language difficulties which are sufficient at 3½ years for them to be considered as having a pre-school language impairment (Nash *et al.*, 2013).

Our first question then was: are there differences between children who are language impaired and also at family risk of dyslexia and children with language impairments without family risk? The answer was 'No'—both groups showed broad deficits in oral language skills including poor phonology in pre-school and there was no significant difference between them; hence for present purposes, we can regard these two group as similar.

Turning now to children at family risk of dyslexia without SLI (FR-only), these children were found to have difficulties on phonological tasks that tapped speech production, namely articulation, word and non-word repetition. They were also impaired in the production of grammatical inflections, that is, with the endings of verbs (past tense -*ed*; third person singular -*s*) and in repeating sentences, particularly the function words within them. All of these tasks require access to phonological codes. The FR-only group also showed emerging difficulties with phonological awareness in an alliteration matching task.

Together, this pattern of deficit highlights the fact that poor phonological language is a risk factor for dyslexia, prevalent among children at family risk. The pattern was consistent across the first two phases of the study, though some of the grammatical impairments were beginning to resolve by the time children were 4½ years old (Nash *et al.*, 2013 for further details). Moreover, 44 per cent of the family risk sample had a significant non-word repetition deficit, commonly considered as a behavioural marker of SLI. This finding underlines the continuity between dyslexia and SLI. More generally our data are consistent with the hypothesis of a phonological endophenotype associated with dyslexia, with the differences between dyslexia and SLI hinging on additional co-occurring risk factors. For example, Gooch *et al.* (2014) showed that the children in the SLI groups are far more likely to have difficulties with executive attention and motor development than children at family risk without language impairment.

ENVIRONMENTAL INFLUENCES ON DYSLEXIA

Can these sorts of data be used to move toward a causal model of dyslexia? So far, rather little has been said about the etiology of dyslexia and the distal risk factors. Dyslexia is usually considered to be best characterised as a neurodevelopmental disorder, meaning that it is evident from early in development and has biological origins; furthermore, as is typical of most such disorders, there is a preponderance in males (Thapar & Rutter, in press). The ultimate cause of dyslexia is thought to be genetic and some candidate genes have been identified (Paracchini *et al.*, 2007). However, environmental variables also play a critical role.

Thus, it seems appropriate to choose a framework which could be applied to a range of neurodevelopmental disorders, including, for example, ADHD and autism; in all of these conditions, several risk factors act together through the environment to produce the behavioural phenotype of the disorder. The more risk factors that are present, the greater the likelihood of the disorder being diagnosed. It follows that clinical samples tend to be impure in the sense that there is more likely to be a referral leading to a diagnosis in children with multiple risk factors.

In relation to dyslexia it is likely that at least three aspects of the environment are important: the language of instruction, the home literacy environment and the teaching the child has received.

First, not all written languages are equally easy to learn to read. Alphabetic languages differ in the regularity or *consistency* with which the letters and sounds in them are related, as well as in their syllabic complexity. Both of these factors determine the rate of reading acquisition in a given language (Caravolas *et al.*, 2013; Seymour, 2005). For example, a child learning to read in the highly consistent Finnish language will on average do so much more quickly than a child learning in English. Nevertheless, a striking finding is that the predictors of individual differences in reading attainment across these languages are similar and include letter knowledge, phoneme awareness and performance on a test requiring the rapid naming of symbols or objects (rapid automatised naming, RAN) (Caravolas *et al.*, 2012). What this means is, if you have the genes which confer risk for dyslexia, you will have difficulties learning to read in any language, although the actual rate and extent of the difficulty might vary (Frith *et al.*, 1998).

Turning to the environment in the home, research on typical development suggests that in terms of home literacy, parenting styles differ and these differences affect reading development. Some parents provide fairly direct instruction about print concepts, letters and sounds when reading with their pre-school child and this practice appears to be a good predictor of early decoding skill. In contrast, some parents place an emphasis on oral language during shared-book reading, talking about the pictures, the characters and the story. This kind of language experience approach is more strongly predictive of individual differences in reading comprehension at a later stage in development than of decoding (Sénéchal & Lefevre, 2002). Turning to dyslexia, relatively few studies of home literacy environment have specifically focused on children at family risk. However, there is no strong evidence to date that children at family risk of dyslexia experience any different kind of literacy environment from controls of similar socio-economic status, though print motivation may be lower in older children who have actually developed dyslexia (Snowling *et al.*, 2007). In our own work we have shown that among children at family risk of dyslexia as for controls, shared reading mediates the impact of the mother's educational level on language and reading development (Hamilton, 2013). We have also looked at the predictors of pre-school letter knowledge in these groups because this is a measure which is thought to be highly dependent on environmental input; an interesting finding is that parental teaching of letters and sounds accounts for more variability in the family-risk group than in the low risk typically developing group. This finding is important—it suggests that typically developing children can learn the sounds of letters quite naturally from their environment, whereas children at family risk of dyslexia need more explicit teaching in order to do so.

WHAT WORKS FOR DYSLEXIA?

The starting point for an intervention should be a causal model. Based on the evidence discussed here and elsewhere, both from studies of typical reading development and of dyslexia, we can state confidently that learning to read requires phonological awareness and a primary risk factor for dyslexia is a phonological deficit. Moreover, we have seen that phonological deficits in dyslexia are prevalent in children at family risk of the condition even before reading instruction begins. But we also know from the study of Nash *et al.* (2013) that in about a third of cases these children have a language impairment. It follows that interventions for dyslexia need to remediate not only the phonological difficulties at the core of the disorder but also in some cases, residual or co-occurring language difficulties.

The main ingredients of a teaching approach to remediate the decoding deficit in dyslexia combine training in phoneme awareness with training in letter-sound knowledge and in which these two skills are reinforced in the context of reading. Hatcher *et al.* (1994) were the first group of researchers in the UK to assess the efficacy of such an approach using a controlled design. Children participating in this study were identified through a county-wide screening of all 7½-year-old children. The children were then provided with one of three types of intervention, and a fourth control group received the usual diet of remediation used at the time in the local education authority.

The three interventions that were evaluated consisted of: Reading alone (R) in which children read from texts which were selected to be at the appropriate level and teachers reinforced effective reading strategies to hone the children's skills; Phonology alone (P) which consisted of exercises training the development of oral phonological awareness at syllable, rhyme and phoneme levels; and Reading with Phonology (R+P) which combined the reading and phonology approaches and children were encouraged to practice their emergent skills through reading and writing activities. At the end of the 20 weeks of intervention, the children who received the combined programme (R+P) were significantly ahead of the other three groups in reading accuracy, spelling and reading comprehension and the gains in reading were maintained five months after the intervention ceased. Following on from this work, the programme was adapted for delivery by trained teaching assistants to children in Year 1 with dyslexic-like difficulties (Hatcher *et al.*, 2006). The programme yielded significant gains in reading accuracy scores on a standardised test of over 7 standard score points during the 20 weeks of the intervention. This rate of improvement can be regarded as educationally significant and an important first step for a child having difficulties with the acquisition of basic reading skills (Brooks, 2013).

But why wait for failure? As we have seen, a great deal is known about what places a child at risk of reading difficulties and therefore there would seem to be no good reason to wait until the child has failed before implementing intervention. With this in mind, Bowyer-Crane *et al.* (2008) evaluated a 20-week intervention programme using the principles of the R+P intervention for children who entered school at risk of reading failure. The programme was a modification of that used by Hatcher *et al.* (2006), suitable for younger children. It comprised three main components: letter-sound work, segmenting and blending, reading together and reading independently, and alternated between group and individual sessions on a daily basis. Four children worked together in a group on letter-sound knowledge, segmenting and blending, and in the individual sessions the work focused on reading, incorporating time to reinforce work on letters and sounds.

To evaluate the efficacy of this phonologically based programme, the gains of the children on tests of reading and reading-related skills were compared to those of a treated control group who received oral language work. The children who had received the intervention were significantly ahead of the controls in phoneme awareness, prose-reading accuracy, non-word reading and spelling. Moreover, comparison of the outcomes of these children in relation to a large sample of 700 classroom peers five months after the intervention was pleasing, with more than 50 per cent now performing within the average range for early word reading skills (and 7 per cent had standard reading scores above 115).

In summary, phonologically based reading intervention delivered by trained teaching assistants can be used to boost the foundations of decoding skill and to bring about improvements in reading in children with dyslexia. But there is a problem: if one of the important risk factors for dyslexia is language, then it is perhaps important to think about first of all intervening at the level of oral language as a foundation for phonological awareness. Second, the ultimate goal for literacy is to read fluently with understanding; unless we address the oral language weaknesses of children at risk of reading problems we will only ever find the imperfect solution to the remediation of dyslexia.

LANGUAGE INTERVENTION

To test the idea that oral language work can provide a strong foundation for learning to read, Fricke *et al.* (2013) conducted a study in which pre-school children with poorly developed language skills at 4 years old were randomly assigned either to receive a 30-week oral language programme or to a waiting control group who received 'business as usual'. The 30-week programme comprised three main components which ran throughout the sessions: work on oral narrative, vocabulary and listening skills. In nursery school, the activities were delivered to groups of two to four children, three times a week. In Reception class, the components of the programme remained the same but the intensity was increased to three 30-minute sessions a week and two 15-minute individual sessions in which narrative skills were honed; in addition, in the final ten weeks, the sessions were supplemented with work on letter-sound knowledge and phonological awareness. The interventions were delivered by trained and supported teaching assistants in early years' settings.

At the end of the intervention, the group who had received the intervention showed improvements in a broad range of oral language skills including vocabulary, narrative and listening comprehension as well as in expressive (but not receptive) grammar. There was also an impact on their emergent literacy skills namely letter knowledge, alliteration matching and phonetic spelling ability. Although there was no significant impact on reading *per se*, it needs to be borne in mind that the control group at that time had been receiving instruction in systematic phonics in the mainstream classroom. Some six months later the children who had received the invention were still ahead of their peers in the waiting control group in oral language, narrative skills and phonological awareness. But more importantly, at this stage they were also ahead of them in reading comprehension, an effect entirely attributable to their gains in spoken language skills (and not mediated by word-level decoding abilities).

TOWARDS A CAUSAL MODEL OF DYSLEXIA

Together, the large body of empirical research on dyslexia (Vellutino *et al.*, 2004) and more recent findings flowing from longitudinal studies of children at family risk of dyslexia, make a compelling case for viewing dyslexia as a language-learning impairment. A strong hypothesis is that it is a 'sub-type' of specific language impairment (SLI). To draw together the main issues, it seems likely that there are (at least) two separable causes of reading problems in children with language learning impairments: poor phonology and poor language. However, the shared liability between the circumscribed reading problems in 'dyslexia' and the broader spoken and written language problems associated with SLI is attributable to common risk factors in the domain of phonological skills. It can be hypothesised from the evidence reviewed that the trajectories of dyslexia and SLI diverge because the phonological deficit combines with other risk factors to lead to a more pervasive impairment in the SLI. Using evidence from twin studies, Bishop (2006) suggested that a problem with grammar (indexed by difficulties in morpheme generation) needs to be present alongside phonological problems (indexed by poor non-word repetition) for SLI to be diagnosed; interestingly, in the same study, poor non-word repetition was found to be a heritable marker of resolved language delay. There are synergies here with the current evidence from longitudinal studies in which children at family risk of dyslexia who do not succumb to reading problems appear to resolve their spoken language difficulties around the time of school entry. Similarly, we have shown that children with SLI often experience co-morbid difficulties in motor skills and executive attention (Gooch *et al.*, 2014).

The present evidence highlights the fact that phonological difficulties are circumscribed in children at family risk of dyslexia unless they have a concomitant language impairment that is persistent. Together then we can put forward a strong hypothesis. First, as others have proposed (e.g. Chiat, 2001; Baddeley *et al.*, 1998), the phonological deficit is the cause of language-learning difficulties. However, if the mechanisms involved in language learning are unimpaired (as we can infer they are in children whose early language delays resolve), then the phonological deficit will only affect written language skills. In essence, this hypothesis resonates with that of Scarborough & Dobrich (1990) who proposed the concept of 'illusory recovery' to describe children with language delay whose language difficulties apparently resolved, but who then went on to have reading problems. An alternative hypothesis is, not that the differences between dyslexia and SLI turn on the presence of additional risk and protective factors but rather, as proposed by Ramus *et al.* (2013), children with SLI have difficulties at the level of phonological representations which cause pervasive language problems, while children with dyslexia have difficulty in accessing these representations. Such access is critical to the formation of mappings between phonology and orthography that characterises learning to read.

CONCLUSIONS

Whilst the theoretical issues surrounding dyslexia and related language-learning impairments will continue to be debated, there is unequivocal evidence that a phonological deficit is the primary risk factor for dyslexia and that co-occurring language difficulties increase the probability of reading difficulties. Moreover, if we define dyslexia as a problem with the development of basic reading and writing fluency, then it is best regarded as the outcome of multiple risk factors and more likely to be identified when more than one deficit is present. This is not to say 'specific' dyslexia cannot occur and the fact that it does so in people of high ability with no other apparent behavioural difficulties is a testament to this.

The message is clear: poor oral language is a major risk factor for poor literacy. Risk factors accumulate towards the threshold for identification of dyslexia and the status of the language system at school entry is a good prognostic indicator. And, as far as we know, phonological aspects of language appear to be universally affected in dyslexia, but diagnosis remains difficult and the cut-off depends on agreed external criteria. On a positive note, we know from intervention research that the impact of phonological risk factors can be ameliorated, thereby preventing a downward spiral of poor educational achievement, disengagement and limited career prospects. To conclude, there needs to be a greater awareness of language as a barrier to learning (Bishop *et al.*, 2012) and the policy agenda needs to shift from a preoccupation with literacy standards towards a greater emphasis on oracy in the early years of education. Written language has its foundations in oral language: ensuring that all children are fluent users of the language of reading instruction is a vital ingredient of successful education.

Acknowledgements: The work described in this article was funded by grants from the Wellcome Trust and the Nuffield Foundation.

REFERENCES

American Psychiatric Association (2013), *Diagnostic and statistical manual of mental disorders* (5th edn) (Arlington, VA, American Psychiatric Association).
Baddeley, A., Gathercole, S. & Papagno, C. (1998), 'The phonological loop as a language learning device', *Psychological Review*, 105: 158–73. doi: 10.1037/0033-295X.105.1.158

Bearden, C.E. & Freimer, N.B. (2006), 'Endophenotypes for psychiatric disorders: ready for primetime?', *Trends in Genetics*, 22: 306–13. doi: 10.1016/j.tig.2006.04.004

Bishop, D.V.M. (1997), *Uncommon Understanding* (Hove, Psychology Press).

Bishop, D.V.M. (2006), 'Developmental cognitive genetics: How psychology can inform genetics and vice versa', *Quarterly Journal of Experimental Psychology*, 59(7): 1153–68. doi: 10.1080/ 17470210500489372

Bishop, D.V.M. & Adams, C. (1990), 'A prospective study of the relationship between specific language impairment, phonological disorders and reading retardation', *Journal of Child Psychology and Psychiatry*, 31: 1027–50. doi: 0.1111/j.1469-7610.1990.tb00844.x

Bishop, D.V.M. & Snowling, M.J. (2004), 'Developmental dyslexia and specific language impairment: Same or different?', *Psychological Bulletin*, 130: 858–88. doi 10.1037/0033-2909.130.6.858

Bishop, D.V.M., Clark, B., Conti-Ramsden, G., Norbury, C.F. & Snowling, M.J. (2012), 'RALLI: An internet campaign for raising awareness of language learning impairments', *Child Language, Teaching & Therapy*, 28: 259–62 doi: 10.1177/0265659012459467

Bowyer-Crane, C., Snowling, M.J., Duff, F., Carroll, J., Fieldsend, E., Miles, J., *et al.* (2008), 'Improving early language and literacy skills: differential effects of an oral language versus a phonology with reading intervention', *Journal of Child Psychology and Psychiatry and Allied Disciplines*, 49: 422–32. doi: 10.1111/j.1469-7610.2007.01849.x

Brooks, G. (2013), 'What works for children and young people with literacy difficulties: the effectiveness of intervention schemes', retrieved from http://www.interventionsforliteracy.org.uk/ (November 2013).

Caravolas, M., Lervåg, A., Defior, S., Seidlová Málková, G. & Hulme, C. (2013), 'Different patterns, but equivalent predictors, of growth in reading in consistent and inconsistent orthographies', *Psychological Science*, 24(8): 1398–1407. doi: 10.1177/0956797612473122

Caravolas, M., Lervåg, A., Mousikou, P., Efrim, C., Litavsky, M., Onochie-Quintanilla, E., *et al.* (2012), 'Common patterns of prediction of literacy development in different alphabetic orthographies', *Psychological Science*, 23(6): 678–86. doi: 10.1177/0956797611434536

Catts, H.W., Adlof, S.M., Hogan, T.P. & Ellis Weismer, S. (2005), 'Are specific language impairment and dyslexia distinct disorders?', *Journal of Speech, Hearing and Language Research*, 48: 1378–96. doi:10.1044/1092-4388(2005/096)

Catts, H.W., Fey, M.E., Tomblin, J.B. & Zhang, X. (2002), 'A longitudinal investigation of reading outcomes in children with language impairments', *Journal of Speech, Hearing & Language Research*, 45: 1142–57. doi: 10.1044/1092-4388(2002/093)

Chiat, S. (2001), 'Mapping theories of developmental language impairment: premises, predictions and evidence', *Language and Cognitive Processes*, 16: 113–42. doi: 10.1080/01690960042000012

Fricke, S., Bowyer-Crane, C., Haley, A.J., Hulme, C. & Snowling, M.J. (2013), 'Efficacy of language intervention in the early years', *Journal of Child Psychology and Psychiatry*, 54(3): 280–90. doi: 10.1111/jcpp.12010

Frith, U., Wimmer, H. & Landerl, K. (1998), 'Differences in phonological recoding in German and English speaking children', *Scientific Studies of Reading*, 2(1): 31–54. doi: 10.1207/s1532799xssr0201_2

Gooch, D., Nash, H., Hulme, C. & Snowling, M. (2014), 'Comorbidities in preschool children at family risk of dyslexia', *Journal of Child Psychology and Psychiatry*, 55(3): 237–46. doi: 10.1111/jcpp.12139

Hamilton, L. (2013), *The role of the Home Literacy Environment in the early literacy development of children at family-risk of dyslexia*, Ph.D. thesis, University of York.

Hatcher, P., Hulme, C. & Ellis, A.W. (1994), 'Ameliorating early reading failure by integrating the teaching of reading and phonological skills: The phonological linkage hypothesis', *Child Development*, 65: 41–57. doi 10.2307/1131364

Hatcher, P.J., Hulme, C., Miles, J.N.V., Carroll, J.M., Hatcher, J., Gibbs, S., Smith, G., Bowyer-Crane, C. & Snowling, M.J. (2006), 'Efficacy of small group reading intervention for beginning readers with reading-delay: a randomised controlled trial', *Journal of Child Psychology and Psychiatry*, 47(8): 820–27. doi: 10.1111/j.1469-7610.2005.01559.x

Moll, K., Loff, A. & Snowling, M. (2013), 'Cognitive endophenotypes of dyslexia', *Scientific Studies of Reading*, 2013: 1–13. doi: 10.1080/10888438.2012.736439

McBride-Chang, C., Lam, F., Lam, C., Chan, B., Fong, C.Y.C., Wong, T.T.Y., *et al.* (2011), 'Early predictors of dyslexia in Chinese children: familial history of dyslexia, language delay, and cognitive profiles', *Journal of Child Psychology and Psychiatry*, 52(2): 204–11. doi: 10.1111/j.1469-7610.2010.02299.x

Nag, S. & Snowling, M.J. (2011), 'Cognitive profiles of poor readers of Kannada', *Reading and Writing: An Interdisciplinary Journal*, 24(6): 657–76. doi: 10.1007/s11145-010-9258-7

Nash, H., Gooch, D., Hulme, C. & Snowling, M. (2013), 'Preschool Language Profiles of Children at Family Risk of Dyslexia: Continuities with SLI', *Journal of Child Psychology and Psychiatry and Allied Disciplines*, 54(9): 958–68. doi: 10.1111/jcpp.12091

Nation, K., Clarke, P., Marshall, C. & Durand, M. (2004), 'Hidden language impairments in children: parallels between poor reading comprehension and specific language impairment?', *Journal of Speech, Language & Hearing Research*, 47: 199–211. doi: 10.1044/1092-4388(2004/017)

Paracchini, S., Scerri, T. & Monaco, A.P. (2007), 'The genetic lexicon of dyslexia', *Annual Review of Genomics & Human Genetics*, 8: 57–79. doi: 10.1146/annurev.genom.8.080706.092312

Pennington, B.F. (2006), 'From single to multiple deficit models of developmental disorders', *Cognition*, 101: 385–413. doi: 10.1016/j.cognition.2006.04.008

Ramus, F., Marshall, C.R., Rosen, S. & van der Lely, H.K.J. (2013), 'Phonological deficits in specific language impairment and developmental dyslexia: towards a multidimensional model', *Brain*, 136(2): 630–45. doi: 10.1093/brain/aws356

Rutter, M. & Yule, W. (1973), 'Specific reading retardation', in L. Mann & D. Sabatino (eds.), *The First Review of Special Education* (Philadelphia, Buttonwood Farms), 49–62.

Scarborough, H.S. (1990), 'Very early language deficits in dyslexic children', *Child Development*, 61: 1728–43. doi: 10.1111/j.1467-8624.1990.tb03562.x

Scarborough, H.S. & Dobrich, W. (1990), 'Development of children with early language delays', *Journal of Speech and Hearing Research*, 33: 70–83. doi: 10.1044/jshr.3301.70

Sénéchal, M. & LeFevre, J. (2002), 'Parental involvement in the development of children's reading skill: a five-year longitudinal study', *Child Development*, 73(2), 445–60. doi: 10.1111/1467-8624.00417

Seymour, P.H.K. (2005), 'Early reading development in European orthographies', in M.J. Snowling & C. Hulme (eds.), *The Science of reading: A Handbook* (Oxford, Blackwell), 296–315.

Snowling, M.J. (2008), 'Specific disorders and broader phenotypes: the case of dyslexia', *Quarterly Journal of Experimental Psychology*, 61, 142–56. doi: 10.1080/17470210701508830

Snowling, M.J. & Hulme, C. (2012), 'Interventions for children's language and literacy difficulties', *International Journal Language & Communication Disorders*, 47(1): 27–34. doi: 10.1111/ j.1460-6984.2011.00081.x

Snowling, M.J. & Melby-Lervag, M. (submitted), 'Children at family risk of dyslexia: a review and meta-analysis'.

Snowling, M.J., Muter, V. & Carroll, J.M. (2007), 'Children at family risk of dyslexia: a follow-up in adolescence', *Journal of Child Psychology & Psychiatry*, 48: 609–18. doi: 10.1111/j.1469–7610.2006.01725.x

Snowling, M. J., Dawes, P., Nash, H. & Hulme, C. (2012), 'Validity of a Protocol for Adult Self-Report of Dyslexia and Related Difficulties', *Dyslexia*, 18: 1–15. doi: 10.1002/dys.1432

Stanovich, K.E. (1994), 'Does dyslexia exist?', *Journal of Child Psychology and Psychiatry*, 35(4): 579–95. doi: 10.1111/j.1469–7610.1994.tb01208.x

Stothard, S.E., Snowling, M.J., Bishop, D.V.M., Chipchase, B. & Kaplan, C. (1998), 'Language impaired pre-schoolers: A follow-up in adolescence', *Journal of Speech, Language and Hearing Research*, 41: 407–18.

Thapar, A. & Rutter, M. (in press), 'Neurodevelopment and Neurodevelopmental Disorders: Conceptual Issues', in A. Thapar, D. Pine, J. Leckman, S. Scott, M. Snowling & E. Taylor (eds.), *Rutter's Child and Adolescent Psychiatry*, 6th edn (London, Wiley), forthcoming.

Vellutino, F.R. (1979), *Dyslexia: Research and Theory* (Cambridge, MA, MIT Press).

Vellutino, F.R., Fletcher, J.M., Snowling, M.J. & Scanlon, D.M. (2004), 'Specific reading disability (dyslexia): what have we learned in the past four decades?', *Journal of Child Psychology & Psychiatry*, 45(1): 2–40. doi: 10.1046/j.0021-9630.2003.00305.

Note on the author: Maggie Snowling, FBA, FMed Sci, is Professor in the Department of Experimental Psychology, University of Oxford and President of St John's College. Her research focuses on children's language and learning and she is specifically interested in the nature and causes of children's reading difficulties and how best to ameliorate them. She is also a qualified clinical psychologist. She served as a member of Sir Jim Rose's Expert Advisory Group on provision for Dyslexia in 2009 and as an expert member of the Education for All: Fast Track Initiative group in Washington DC in 2011. Recent publications include:

Clarke, P.J., Truelove, E., Hulme, C. & Snowling, M.J. (2013), *Developing Reading Comprehension* (Oxford, Wiley-Blackwell).

Fricke, S., Bowyer-Crane, C., Haley, A., Hulme, C. & Snowling, M.J. (2013), 'Building a secure foundation for literacy: An evaluation of a preschool language intervention', *Journal of Child Psychology & Psychiatry*, 54(3): 280–90. doi: 10.1111/jcpp.12010

Nash, H.M, Hulme, C., Gooch, D. & Snowling, M.J. (2013), 'Preschool Language Profiles of Children at Family Risk of Dyslexia: Continuities with SLI', *Journal of Child Psychology & Psychiatry*, 54(9): 958–68. doi: 10.1111/jcpp.12091

Henderson, L., Clarke, P. & Snowling, M.J. (2011), 'Accessing and selecting word meaning in autism spectrum disorder', *Journal of Child Psychology & Psychiatry*, 52(9): 964–73 DOI: 10.1111/j.1469-7610.2011.02393.x

Contact: maggie.snowling@sjc.ox.ac.uk

This article was first published in 2014 in *Journal of the British Academy* (ISSN 2052–7217).

To cite the article: Margaret J. Snowling (2014), 'Dyslexia: A language learning impairment ', *Journal of the British Academy*, 2: 43–58. DOI 10.5871/jba/002.043

Journal of the British Academy, **2**, 59–99. DOI 10.5871/jba/002.059
Posted 26 August 2014. © The British Academy 2014

A heavenly aura:
Confucian modes of relic veneration

Elsley Zeitlyn Lecture on Chinese Archaeology and Culture
read 22 October 2013 by

JULIA K. MURRAY

Abstract: Although concepts and practices related to the veneration of relics are usually identified with Buddhism in China, this article will suggest that they are also relevant to Confucius (551–479 BC) and 'Confucianism'. Ideas about the special efficacy of great persons and things associated with them predate Buddhism, which spread from India to China in the 1st century AD. The display of personal items that had once belonged to Confucius and places that figured in his biography powerfully evoked the ancient sage to scholarly pilgrims who visited his home area and temple in Qufu, Shandong. Drawing on Buddhist scholarship for working definitions and typologies, I investigate the material forms of relic-related practices in the Confucian milieu, particularly at Qufu. I also analyse a now-destroyed shrine, near modern Shanghai, in which multiple media were employed to replicate relics of Confucius and bring his beneficent presence to a place he never visited.

Keywords: Confucius, relics, Qufu, Kongzhai, shrine, Confucian Religion Association, Kong lineage

INTRODUCTION

In this article, I examine ideas and practices related to the veneration of relics in China, focusing specifically on the forms that can be associated with Confucius and 'Confucianism' (*rujiao* or *ruxue*).[1] Known in Chinese as Kongzi ('Master Kong'), Confucius lived from 551–479 BC and has long been recognised as China's great

---

[1] The convenient though problematic terms 'Confucian' and 'Confucianism' will be used here to refer to Confucius's teachings and their later interpretations, as well as to certain aspects of ideology, institutions, and rituals of governance in dynastic times. For a fuller discussion of terms, see Csikszentmihalyi (2001: 243–4 and 292–7); for general introduction to Confucianism, see Goldin (2011), Richey (2013), and X. Yao (2000).

teacher.[2] His teachings, which were developed and modified by his disciples and later interpreters, are generally understood to be resolutely humanistic. Thus they would seem to be incompatible with the religious practice of relic veneration. However, the modern conception of Confucianism as a form of secular humanism has obscured important aspects of traditional Confucian ideology and practices that only now are beginning to be studied.[3] But even the scholars who are working to broaden our understanding of Confucianism have largely overlooked the place of relics in its traditions. By contrast, studies of Buddhism now routinely acknowledge the importance of relics to Buddhist doctrine, ritual, and devotional practices, as well as to the religion's spread across Asia.[4] Drawing on this scholarship for working definitions and typologies, the present article investigates relic-related practices and their material forms in the Confucian milieu. After considering early evidence, I survey the most significant elements that enabled Confucius's homeland of Qufu, Shandong, to become the premier destination of scholarly pilgrims seeking to pay homage to the relics of Confucius and be inspired by their auspicious aura. I then analyse a now-destroyed Confucian shrine at Kongzhai, near modern Shanghai, in which multiple media were employed to replicate relics of Confucius and provide a focus for scholar-pilgrims to experience his beneficent presence. Significantly, the locale had no direct connection to the ancient master, but purported to be a microcosm of his home, temple and tomb in Qufu. By imitating the defining features of Qufu's primordial sites, Kongzhai's patrons sought to maximise the efficacy of their shrine, despite its distance from Qufu.

DEFINING 'RELICS'

Recent scholarship on a variety of world religions and cults suggests that the term 'relic', from the Latin *reliquare*, 'left behind', covers a variety of media through which a devotee can gain connection to a special figure.[5] These include various forms of bodily remains, personal articles, sites of important events, music, and teachings. In

---

[2] For recent scholarship and references on the life of Confucius, see Nylan & Wilson (2010) and Csikszentmihalyi (2001).

[3] For recent studies of various aspects of the cult of Confucius as they relate to Confucian ideology, see essays in Wilson (2002*c*); also Sommer (2003), Tillman (2004), and Wilson (1996 & 2002*a*).

[4] I have gained many insights from the profusion of recent scholarship on Buddhist relics, especially Birnbaum (2007), Faure (1992 & 1995), Germano & Trainor (2004), Kieschnick (2003), Lee (2010), Ritzinger & Bingenheimer (2006), Ruppert (2000), Schopen (1998), Sharf (1999), Shen (2000), Strong (2004*a* & *b*), and Trainor (2004).

[5] Besides references on Buddhist relics cited in the preceding note, I have found scholarship on Christian and other Western relics useful; e.g. Bagnoli *et al.* (2010), Brown (1981), Head (1999), Smith (2012), and Vikan (2012).

many religions, relics are conceptualised as direct conduits to spiritual forces and often serve as objects of devotion. The Roman Catholic church recognised three categories of relic: the bodily remains of saints, objects belonging to or used by saints, and items that came into contact with either of the other two types.[6] Through their earthly relics, deceased saints in heaven could aid the living, such as through miracles of healing, or by interceding on the worshipper's behalf to attain eternal salvation. Sites where relics were present became destinations for pilgrims seeking to benefit from divine power. Physical relics are frequently preserved in magnificent containers, or reliquaries, and many mediaeval Christian examples survive in European and American museum collections.[7]

In China, and East Asia more generally, relics are most closely identified with Buddhism, a religion that originated in India with Shakyamuni, the historical Buddha, who lived from approximately 563 to 483 BC. According to the *Mahāparinibbāna-sutta*, an early scripture in the Pāli canon, he gave explicit instructions near the end of his life for his disciples to deal with his body after cremation.[8] They were to divide his corporeal remains into eight portions and enshrine them inside reliquary mounds, called *stupas*, so that worshippers could make offerings to them and receive blessings, even salvation. Not limited to the cremation remains, relics could also be created through monastic ritual, prayer, and meditation, thus continually increasing their quantity.[9] In addition, the deaths of particularly holy or charismatic monks of later times augmented the supply of relics, whether their bodies were cremated or miraculously preserved intact.[10]

Relics played an important role in the extension of Buddhism to other regions of Asia in the centuries before and after the start of the Common Era.[11] In the 3rd century BC, the Buddhist emperor Ashoka (304–232 BC) ordered 84,000 stupas built to distribute relics throughout South Asia and sponsored monks and monasteries to spread Buddhist teachings. Indian and Chinese monks brought Buddhist relics to China, and reliquaries attributed to Ashoka's distribution also were 'discovered' there, some allegedly appearing miraculously on their own.[12] John Kieschnick points out that before the introduction of Buddhism, China had no cult that focused on the physical remains of any great person, and he suggests that the numinous power attributed to Buddhist relics was a major factor in the religion's success.[13] John Strong observes that these relics 'served to link particular places and peoples to the life and

[6] Head (1999).

[7] e.g. see Bagnoli *et al.* (2010) for the catalogue of a major exhibition shown at several museums.

[8] Trainor (1997: 21); Trainor (2004: 9).

[9] Faure (1995: 214).

[10] e.g. see Kieschnick (2003: 34).

[11] Trainor (1997: 39–45); Huaiyu Chen (2007: 60–3).

[12] Huaiyu Chen (2007: 62–4); Faure (1995: 214).

[13] Kieschnick (2003: 30–2).

times of the Buddha', and they spread his teachings 'to places that the living Buddha never visited'.[14] More than merely signifying the Buddha or recalling his life events, relics constituted his presence and extended his biography, and in this sense, could 'have adventures of their own'.[15] Corporeal relics had charisma, they could perform miracles, and 'their possession brought prestige'.[16]

In addition to the corporeal remains that appear in cremation ash and related jewel-like particles, the Indian Buddhist discourse on relics also included two other major types, 'relics of use' and 'teaching (*dharma*) relics'.[17] Relics of use encompassed everyday objects that the Buddha had owned or handled, such as his clothing and begging bowl, which are often called 'contact relics' because he came into direct physical contact with them. Also classified as relics of use are places with which he was closely associated, such as the *bodhi* tree under which he achieved enlightenment and the park where he preached his First Sermon. As in Roman Catholic tradition, such objects and sites often inspired the construction of shrines and monasteries, which became destinations for pilgrimage by the devout. The emperor Ashoka made pious visits to thirty-two locations that were associated with events in the Buddha's life and built monuments at many of them.[18] The third category of Buddhist relics, teaching relics, includes everything that records the Buddha's message, from brief quotations to whole sutras. Shakyamuni himself told his closest disciples that his *dharma* would replace him after he died, implying that it was the most important of the three forms of relic.[19]

Strong notes that many modern scholars discuss visual images as a fourth kind of relic, belonging to the category of 'commemorative relics', which 'remind one of, or somehow point to, or represent the Buddha'.[20] However, as Strong points out, the doctrinal source that refers to images and their commemorative function is a sutra that enumerates different types of *shrines* and is not primarily concerned with relics as such. Commemorative relics are man-made and have no direct connection with the Buddha, unlike relics belonging to the other three major categories. Nonetheless, as Kieschnick suggests, the worship of images and attribution of special powers to them were important dimensions of Buddhism's impact on China, no less significant than

[14] Strong (2004*b*: 7).
[15] Ibid.
[16] Kieschnick (2003: 36–50).
[17] My discussion here draws particularly on Faure (1992), Ruppert (2000: Introduction), Sharf (1999), and Strong (2004*a*: Introduction).
[18] Dehejia (1997: 38).
[19] Strong (2004*b*: 8–9).
[20] Strong (2004*b*: 18–20).

the introduction of its cult of corporeal relics.[21] Relics and images were both capable of working miracles and causing supernormal events: 'In Chinese terms, the numinous (*ling*) evokes a miraculous response (*ganying*).'[22]

CONCEPTIONS OF CONFUCIUS AND CONFUCIANISM

Until recently, such overtly religious elements have not been part of our conception of the veneration of Confucius and the teachings associated with him. He and the important later figures who developed his ideas have generally been identified with purely secular and humanistic concerns, particularly those that address the roles and responsibilities of individuals within hierarchical social frameworks. Starting with the earliest account of his life, written around 100 BC, Confucius himself has been presented as an exemplary teacher, scholar, and authority on ancient rituals; and in recent years, as a political expert (*zhengzhi jia*).[23] For an individual, the primary concerns of Confucianism focus on learning, moral cultivation, and reciprocal obligations; for society at large, they centre on principles of rulership and social harmony. Its ancient texts offer a guide to self-cultivation and articulate lofty ideals of governance that remained influential for nearly 2,000 years of dynastic rule. These principles were premised on the belief that earthly concerns were integrally related to the cosmic order, and 'religious life and social organization were deeply intertwined'.[24] The ideal ruler aspired to bring harmony to the realm by carrying out appropriate and timely rituals and by exemplifying such virtues as benevolence (*ren*), filial piety (*xiao*), propriety (*li*), and righteousness (*yi*). Government officials mastered Confucian texts and were expected to perform local versions of appropriate rites and to promote social virtues within their jurisdictions. Ordinary people were taught to honour the obligations of the 'five bonds' (*wu gang*) that defined familial relationships.[25]

For virtually the entire dynastic period, Chinese emperors maintained a state cult for worshipping Confucius, his disciples, and later interpreters.[26] These figures received a succession of honorific posthumous titles over the centuries, and in 1530 Confucius was formally designated as the 'Ultimate Sage and First Teacher' (*Zhisheng xianshi*),

[21] Kieschnick (2003: 28–9).

[22] Ibid.

[23] Recent years have also seen a burgeoning of movements to apply versions of Confucianism to contemporary life, both in China and abroad; see Billioud & Thoraval (2007), Nylan & Wilson (2010: 262–5), and X. Yao (2000: chap. 5).

[24] Goossaert (2008: 211).

[25] On Confucian prescriptions for ordinary people, see Ebrey (1991).

[26] Wilson (2002*b*) provides a detailed introduction to the temple cult and further references.

the epithet referenced on a well-known 18th-century portrayal (Figure 1).[27] His ideas on moral self-cultivation, governance, and ritual were canonised in the 'Confucian Classics', which were fundamental to the education of scholars and government officials. Officials and other men who had passed the lowest-level civil-service examination performed sacrifices to the spirits of Confucius and the other canonised figures in government-funded temples at regular intervals. Following a prescribed liturgy and physical configuration, the celebrants offered wine, meat, vegetables, incense and silk, along with solemn prayers, ceremonial hymns, and ritual dance. However, as Lionel Jensen and others have demonstrated, these overtly religious aspects of Confucianism were deliberately obscured in recent centuries, first by Jesuit missionaries in China and Japan, and later by Chinese reformers and modernisers.[28]

Figure 1. Bust portrait of Confucius, entitled *Portrait of the Ultimate Sage and Foremost Teacher* (*Zhisheng xianshi xiang*). Rubbing of incised stone tablet erected by Prince Yinli, now in the Forest of Steles (Bei lin), Xian, China. Qing dynasty, 1734. After E. Chavannes (1909), *Mission Archéologique dans la Chine Septentrionale* (Paris, Leroux), 5: CCCXCIX no. 873. Photograph by author.

[27] On the succession of Confucius's honorific titles, see Wilson (2002*b*); for the 1530 ritual reforms, see Huang (2002) and Sommer (2002).
[28] For the role of European Jesuit missionaries in moulding a conception of Confucius to advance their own agendas, see Jensen (1997); also Demattè (2007). For the agenda of 20th-century Chinese modernisers, see Goossaert (2008); also Goldin (2011: 108–11).

During the 17th and 18th centuries, the Jesuits argued that Confucianism was an ethical philosophy, whose rituals merely expressed respect, and thus did not conflict with monotheistic requirements of Christianity. This characterisation of Confucianism allowed Chinese converts to continue to participate in sacrifices at the temples of Confucius and to express their filial piety in rites of familial ancestor worship. Although the papal authorities ultimately ruled that these observances were idolatrous and converts had to abandon them, the controversy helped to establish a European conception of Confucianism as primarily secular and humanistic. In the 20th century, some nationalistic reformers in China also promoted Confucius as the Chinese counterpart to the West's great rational philosophers, and this characterisation has reappeared under official auspices in contemporary post-Mao China.[29] By suppressing the elements of traditional Confucian beliefs and ritual practices that seemed idolatrous or superstitious, Confucius could be presented as a unifying national symbol and his legacy an important part of Chinese civilisation. As Herbert Fingarette has observed, modern Chinese and Western writers alike have often portrayed Confucianism 'either as an empirical, humanist, this-worldly teaching or as a parallel to Platonist-rationalist doctrines'.[30]

Other early 20th-century modernisers took a countervailing approach by attempting to establish Confucianism as China's national religion, on the model of Protestant Christianity in Western nations.[31] This movement was most prominently associated with Kang Youwei (1858–1927), an influential advocate of reform in the late Qing-early Republican period, and Chen Huanzhang (1881–1933), the founder of the Confucian Religion Association (*Kongjiao hui*). Organised in Shanghai in 1912, the Association brought together advocates for restoring Confucian texts to the educational curriculum and crusaders seeking official recognition for Confucianism as China's national religion, with Confucius as its founder and premier saint.[32] Members of the Association adopted a 'Confucian calendar' (*Kong li*) counted from the year of his birth, analogous to Jesus and the Christian calendar. After the Qing dynasty fell in 1911, they aspired to install Confucian ideology at the centre of republican governance, which replaced imperial rule, and they hoped to expand Confucian doctrines from an elite concern into a universal popular religion.[33] However, the Chinese Parliament voted in 1913 and again in 1916 not to accord official recognition to Confucianism as a 'religion' (*zongjiao*), and indeed rejected the idea of establishing

[29] Nylan & Wilson (2010: 194–5; Epilogue); also Goldin (2011: 111–13).
[30] Fingarette (1972: 1).
[31] For detailed treatments, see Hsi-yuan Chen (1999), Duara (2008: 49–51), Goossaert (2008: 220–1), and Nedostup (2009).
[32] Hsi-yuan Chen (1999).
[33] Goossaert (2008: 221).

any national religion for China. Instead, five religions were given official institutional status: Buddhism, Daoism, Catholicism, Protestantism, and Islam.

Confucian values versus Buddhist relic practices

Confucianism clearly differs from religions in which corporeal relics are important. One of its cardinal values is filial piety, whose fulfilment requires, among other things, that a person maintain the physical integrity of his body, which he had received from his parents. A body that was not intact at death could not be buried in the family cemetery, even if the deceased had been morally exemplary. Thus, there was no Confucian practice equivalent to the Buddhist worship of the bone fragments and crystalline particles left after the cremation of its holy persons. Indeed, a famous diatribe against the worship of body relics heralded the start of the fundamentalist revival known as Neo-Confucianism. In 819, Han Yu (768–824) wrote the 'Memorial Against Welcoming the Buddha Bone' (*Jian ying Fo gu biao*) to criticise the lavish reception of an alleged finger-bone of the Buddha, which was brought with great pomp to the palace for the emperor to worship.[34] Perhaps the most famous reliquary in China today is the set of nested boxes made of various precious materials to house it, which was discovered in the underground chamber of the Famen Temple pagoda in 1987.[35]

On the other hand, the Buddhist concepts of 'contact relics' and 'teaching relics' readily fit with Confucian predilections. The teaching relic was particularly congenial, as it aligned with longstanding Chinese tendencies to identify doctrines and texts with their authors.[36] The justification for official sacrifices to Confucius was that they honoured the Way of the ancient sages, which he had transmitted through his teachings and writings. The Confucian Classics were repeatedly monumentalised by carving the texts on large stone tablets, beginning with the Han dynasty's 'Xiping Stone Classics', erected in the capital at Luoyang between 175 and 183 AD.[37] As for 'contact relics' and other kinds of 'relics of use', devotees sometimes attributed spiritual power to objects and places that had an association with Confucius and other revered figures in his tradition. The term most often used for all these kinds of relics is *ji*, usually translated as 'traces' but also meaning 'footprints' or 'tracks', alternative translations that underscore their connection to human beings who had once walked the earth.[38] Confucian 'traces' were venerated in distinctive ways and for different reasons than Buddhist ones, and the origins of these practices predate the introduction of Buddhism

[34] Han Yu's memorial is translated in De Bary & Bloom (1999: 583–5).
[35] Wang (2005) provides a detailed description.
[36] Csikszentmihalyi & Nylan (2003: 59–60, 87–8, 91, 97–8).
[37] The latest set was carved between 1791 and 1794 and erected in the Qing dynasty capital at Beijing; see Nylan (2001: 48–9), von Spee (2013: 214), and Wilkinson (2000: 439–40).
[38] Wu (2012) discusses *ji* in the more general sense of 'ruins'.

to China. Perhaps the most important conceptual difference from Buddhist practice is that the purpose of Confucian veneration was to stimulate moral cultivation and benefit society, rather than to obtain blessings and gain merit toward salvation.

Ancient modes of venerating *ji*

The antiquity of ideas associating great figures of the past with their 'traces' is attested by poems in the *Book of Odes* (*Shijing*), also known as the *Classic of Poetry*, one of the books that Confucius is said to have compiled and edited from much older sources. A poem that is often quoted in commemorative inscriptions for shrines to worthy officials, who represented local exemplars of Confucian governance, is the short poem 'Sweet Pear' ('Gan tang'):[39]

> [This] umbrageous sweet pear-tree;
> Clip it not, hew it not down.
> Under it the chief of Shao lodged.

> [This] umbrageous sweet pear-tree;
> Clip it not, break not a twig of it.
> Under it the chief of Shao rested.

> [This] umbrageous sweet pear-tree;
> Clip it not, bend not a twig of it.
> Under it the chief of Shao halted.[40]

The poem calls for the protection of a tree identified with the Earl of Shao, a revered leader in the early Zhou dynasty, who had formerly stood under it. This association of man and tree inaugurated an enduring tendency to attribute human qualities or behaviour to trees, as will be further discussed below. A place where an admired figure had done something might become a site for venerating him in later times, marked by the installation of a commemorative stone stele, and perhaps an offering shrine. Literate visitors to the place would expect to be inspired to ponder the past while reflecting on the person's deeds and character. A classic example to which later writers often referred was a memorial stele on Mount Xian in Hubei, dedicated to the exemplary governor Yang Hu (221–78), which frequently (and perhaps conventionally) moved visiting scholars to tears.[41]

'Traces' were sometimes invisible or intangible. For Confucius himself, even music could function as a relic of the ancient sage-rulers, who became vividly present to him when he played or heard certain pieces. One piece induced him to visualise King Wen,

[39] Schneewind (2013: 348).
[40] Translation from Legge (1898: 26).
[41] Von Spee (2013: 223–4).

the founder of the Zhou dynasty, whom Confucius regarded as an ideal ruler.[42] And famously, during his sojourn in the neighbouring state of Qi, Confucius became oblivious to the taste of meat upon hearing the Shao music, which he associated with the even more ancient sage-emperor Shun.[43] To give material form to intangible traces, the most common strategy was to put up a commemorative stele, inscribed with a text that identified the object of veneration. Over the centuries, more than one stele was erected in Linzi, Shandong, to associate the locale with Confucius's experience of hearing the Shao music.[44] Another example is the installation of a stone inscribed 'Place Where Confucius Saw All-under-Heaven as Small (*Kongzi xiao tianxia chu*)' near the summit of Mount Tai, a plausible vantage point for honouring Confucius's observation that the world seemed small from the top of the mountain.[45]

Most important to Confucians of later ages, however, were the teachings of Confucius, which transmitted the principles of ancient sage rule without geographic limit: 'The Master's Way is broad, great, lofty, and bright; it is heaven and earth, sun and moon, pressing the borders of the universe.'[46] Educated men internalised his 'teaching relics' through memorisation and reflection, ideally to advance their own moral cultivation and create social harmony through proper governance.

RELICS AND THE TEMPLE OF CONFUCIUS IN QUFU, SHANDONG

Origins of the cult

The worship of Confucius originated in his homeland, the ancient feudal state of Lu (modern Qufu), centred at first on his grave. Qufu possessed the tomb of Confucius and thus his body relics. According to the Han Grand Historian Sima Qian (145–*c*.86 BC), who composed the first comprehensive biography of Confucius, rituals at the

---

[42] The event is noted in his earliest biography; see Sima (145–*c*.86 BC: 47.1925).

[43] Sima (145–*c*.86 BC: 1910).

[44] According to local records, early 19th-century residents unearthed an old stone inscribed with monumental characters reading 'Confucius Hears the Shao Music' (*Kongzi wen Shao yue*), but it disappeared amid late Qing social unrest, and a replacement was carved in 1911, just before the fall of the dynasty; see post at http://www.twwiki.com/wiki/%E9%BD%8A%E6%95%85%E5%9F%8E%E9%81%BA%E5%9D%80 (accessed 11.2.2014). A better image of the modern, refurbished stele is at http://www.panoramio.com/photo/83211904 (accessed 11.2.2014).

[45] A rubbing from a late Ming stele with this inscription, erected in 1637 by officials serving in the area, is reproduced in Baba (1940: 20). For the recently refurbished stone, *in situ* on top of Mount Tai, see http://upload.wikimedia.org/wikipedia/commons/a/a4/%E5%AD%94%E5%AD%90%E5%B0%8F%E5%A4%A9%E4%B8%8B%E5%A4%84.jpg (accessed 11.2.2014). The anecdote comes from Mencius (Mengzi), Confucius's major successor; see Legge (1933: 954 (VII.1.XXIV)).

[46] From a commemorative inscription by Zhang Jiude, dated 1610; transcribed in Sun (1716: 5.5 (339)).

tomb began shortly after his death in 479 BC.[47] Although Duke Ai of Lu had avoided employing Confucius in government, he performed a sacrifice *post mortem*, and subsequent rulers made offerings during annual festivals. Confucius's closest disciples remained at his grave to mourn him for three years, and one of them, Zi Gong, built a hut and stayed there for a further three. All of this was extraordinary because there was no blood relationship between Confucius and these men, and thus no ritual obligation to mourn him and make offerings to his spirit, as if for an ancestor.[48] Many disciples and others in the region moved their homes close to the grave, forming a settlement that came to be known as Kong Village (*Kongli*), from the surname of Confucius and his patrilineal descendants.[49] By the time of Sima Qian's visit, near the

Figure 2. Stump of the tree allegedly planted at the grave of Confucius by his disciple Zi Gong. Kong Cemetery (*Kong lin*), Qufu, Shandong. Photograph by author.

[47] Sima (145–*c*.86 BC: 47.1945–7). For detailed discussion of the evolution of the cult, see Wilson (2002*b*).
[48] For principles of ancestor worship, see Sommer (2003); also Ebrey (1991: chap. 2).
[49] Members of the Kong lineage have been recognised as the descendants of Confucius for over 2,000 years and have maintained genealogical records for much of that time. Now some eighty generations deep, their most recent genealogy, published in 2009, occupies eighty volumes.

Figure 3.   Stone pillars and figures on the 'Spirit Way' leading to the grave of Confucius. Kong Cemetery (*Kong lin*), Qufu, Shandong. Photograph by author.

end of the 2nd century BC, the cemetery had enlarged in area to over one *qing* (about 14 acres), implying that a considerable number of descendants and devotees had been buried *ad sanctos*. The disciples are said to have brought trees from their own native places, thus supposedly accounting for the great diversity of species growing in the cemetery. The remains of a Chinese pistache (*kai mu*) allegedly planted by the faithful Zi Gong is still to be seen near Confucius's grave (Figure 2). The grave itself was embellished or rebuilt numerous times over the centuries and up to the present. Although much refurbished, the basic elements that exist today were in place by the 12th century. A spirit way leads to an offering hall (Figure 3) in front of a tomb mound that was furnished with a stone stele, altar and incense burner (Figure 4).

The surrounding region boasted many other kinds of relics of the ancient sage. Sima Qian wrote that the former residence of Confucius had been turned into a temple, where his clothing, zither, carriage, and writings were preserved.[50] In 195 BC, the founding emperor of the Han dynasty offered a large-beast sacrifice (*tailao*) there.

---

[50] Sima (145–*c*.86 BC: 47.1945–6). The temple also replaced Confucius's tomb as the primary locus for sacrifice.

Figure 4.   Grave of Confucius. Kong Cemetery (*Kong lin*), Qufu, Shandong. Photograph by author.

As this imperial recognition marked a major milestone in the evolution of the cult of Confucius, the event is included in most versions of his hagiography (Figure 5). Sima's description makes it clear that Qufu had become a place for a special kind of pilgrimage in the Han dynasty, for he notes that lesser nobles and ministers often travelled there before taking up posts in the region. In the postscript to his biography of Confucius, Sima wrote of his own visit, in terms that suggest a deep emotional connection:

> The *Classic of Poetry* says, 'The great mountain, I look up to it! The great road, I travel it!' Although I cannot reach him, my heart goes out toward him. When I study Master Kong's works, I imagine that I see the man himself. Going to Lu, I visited his temple hall and contemplated his carriage, clothes and sacrificial vessels. Scholars regularly go to study ritual there, and I found it hard to tear myself away. The world has known innumerable princes and worthies who enjoyed fame and honour in their day but were forgotten after death, while Confucius, a commoner, has been looked up to by scholars for more than ten generations. From the emperor, princes and barons on down, all in the Central Kingdom who study the six arts take the Master as their final authority. Rightly is he called the Ultimate Sage.[51]

[51] Sima (145–*c*.86 BC: 47.1947); translation modified from H. Yang & G. Yang (1979: 27).

Figure 5. Han Emperor Gaozu sacrificing at the grave of Confucius, from *Shengji tu* [Pictures of the Traces of the Sage]. Page of a hand-coloured woodblock-printed album, published by Zhu Yinyi. Ming dynasty, 1548. Beijing University Library. Photograph by author.

Sima Qian's experience of visiting Qufu to pay homage to Confucius in turn became a model for educated men of later eras, who would have been well aware of it from studying his monumental history, *Records of the Grand Historian* (*Shi ji*). Moreover, his detailed chronology of Confucius's life helped to confer special significance on the places where particular events happened or teachings were expounded. It is no coincidence that the 15th-century compiler of the first pictorial hagiography of Confucius used Sima's text to order the scenes, and quoted excerpts from it to annotate them.[52]

Pilgrimage attractions in Confucius's homeland

Numerous sites in the Qufu region became stops on the scholarly pilgrim's itinerary and were described in later publications, including the private genealogies published by members of the Kong lineage under various titles, the official *Gazetteer of Qufu county* (*Qufu xianzhi*), and the numerous versions of the hybrid *Gazetteer of Queli* (*Queli zhi*), named for Confucius's home precinct.[53] In addition to recording places of significance to his life that could be visited, such works often included a convenient pictorial overview of the area, typically under the title 'Picture of the State of Lu' (*Lu guo tu*) (Figure 6).[54] Some also provide individual illustrations of the area's most significant places. For example, a short distance to the southeast of Qufu is Mount Ni (*Ni shan*), a particularly scenic location that figured importantly in accounts of the birth of Confucius. Sima Qian wrote that Confucius's mother made an offering to pray for a son at Ni 'hill' (*Ni qiu*); and when the baby was born with a slight depression in the top of his head, resembling the hill, he was given the personal name Qiu.[55] Illustrated separately in Kong-family publications since at least the 13th century, Mount Ni came to include geological features that the descendants linked to the nativity story. Adding apocryphal elements to embellish Sima Qian's terse account, they alleged that Confucius was born in a cave at the foot of the mountain, which is

---

[52] For detailed discussion of illustrated biographies and hagiographies, see Murray (1997).

[53] Agnew (2006: 158–82) provides detailed discussion of these different types of compilations and the sometimes competing interests that they represented. Of the genealogies compiled by various lineage members, the most relevant for my present purposes are Kong Chuan (1134) and Kong Yuancuo (1242). The administrative *Gazetteer of Qufu* was published in 1774, after the Kongs lost control over appointments to the local magistracy. Books titled *Gazetteer of Queli* (or close variants), first published in 1505 after a major reconstruction of the Qufu temple, recorded the long history, important people, and varied rituals associated with Confucius, his descendants, and his cult in Qufu. Although compiled at the instigation and under the supervision of high officials, it openly adopted material from Kong genealogies. Most later editions were published by Kong descendants and reflect their perspectives and interests.

[54] One updated edition of the *Gazetteer of Queli* gathers the diverse assortment of objects and places closely linked to Confucius into a separate chapter, under the title 'Treatise on Traces of the Ancient' ('*Guji zhi*'); see Kong Zhencong (1609: 8.1–4).

[55] Sima (145–c.86 BC: 47.1905).

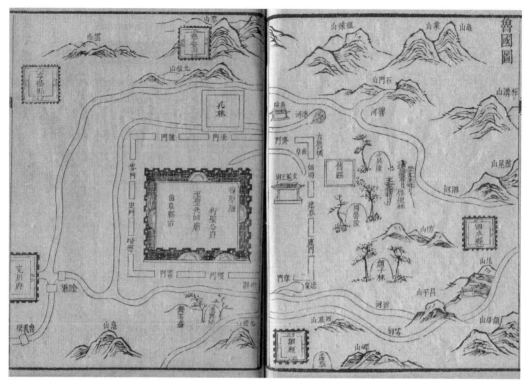

Figure 6. Picture of the State of Lu, from Song Ji & Song Qingchang (1673), *Queli guangzhi* [The Expanded Gazetteer of Queli], (repr. Qufu, n.p.,1870), 1: 6–7. Photograph by author.

marked 'Cave of Female Efficacy' (*Kunling dong*) on pictorial plans (Figure 7).[56] The name next to Mount Ni's highest section, Five Oldsters Peaks (*Wulao feng*), commemorates another family tale of five old men representing the essence (*jing*) of stars appearing in the sky on the night before Confucius's birth. Illustrations of Mount Ni also depict the shrine and academy established there in the mid-10th century, with separate buildings for sacrifices to Confucius and his father. The site even includes a hall for the spirit of the mountain, whom the Song emperor Renzong ennobled in 1050 with the title 'Marquis who Engendered the Sage' (*Yusheng hou*).

---

[56] The earliest depictions of Mount Ni appear in Kong Yuancuo (1242: tuben 4 & 9). A cave still exists in the location indicated on the pictures, but it is now called Cave of the Master (Fuzi dong); see photo at http://www.chinakongmiao.org/templates/T_common/index.aspx?nodeid=310&page=ContentPage&-contentid=1890 (accessed 15.3.2014). Sima Qian does not mention the physical circumstances of Confucius's birth, and hagiographical illustrations typically show his mother lying on a bed inside a comfortable house. According to the descendants' embellishment of the story, she abandoned the baby in the cave because he was so ugly, and he was cared for by wild animals until she relented and took him home; see Jing (1996: 30–2).

Figure 7. Picture of Mount Ni, from Song Ji & Song Qingchang (1673), *Queli guangzhi* [The Expanded Gazetteer of Queli], (repr. Qufu, n.p.,1870), 1: 10–11. Photograph by author.

The Qufu Temple of Confucius

Reverential visitors who came to experience something of the ancient master's aura in his home region invariably went to the great Temple of Confucius in Qufu itself, which evolved over the course of several dynasties into a magnificent complex comparable to the imperial palace (Figure 8).[57] After a devastating fire in 1724, the Yongzheng emperor provided generous funding for an expanded reconstruction of the temple and sent top craftsmen from Beijing to make replacements for the sculptural icons in the main sacrificial hall. His equally generous son, the Qianlong emperor, visited Qufu eight times and wrote many eulogistic inscriptions to carve on steles, in addition to bestowing material largesse. By the middle of the 18th century, the facilities had become particularly impressive, and many buildings had yellow-tiled double roofs in

[57] A thorough documentation of the evolution of the Qufu temple and all its components is provided in Nanjing Gongxueyuan jianzhuxi (1987). Miller (forthcoming) discusses its layout in relation to the ancient principles of palace and temple architecture that originated in the Zhou dynasty, which also influenced the design of Buddhist monasteries and Daoist temples.

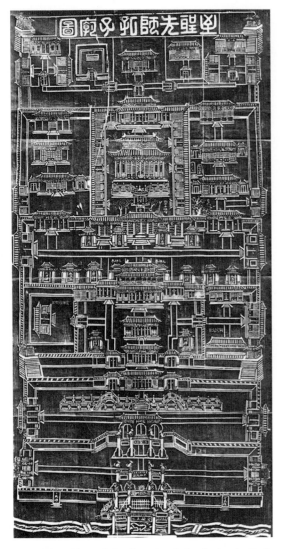

Figure 8. Plan of the Temple of Confucius in Qufu during the Qing dynasty. Rubbing of incised stone tablet. Qing dynasty, 18th c. After E. Chavannes (1909), *Mission Archéologique dans la Chine Septentrionale* (Paris, Leroux), 5: CCCXCVI no. 867. Photograph by author.

the imperial style. Although most of the structures required renovations from time to time, they never fell into serious dilapidation.

The visitor approaches the temple precincts from the south, as he would the imperial palace, passing through a series of ceremonial archways inscribed with appropriate phrases from Confucian texts. Written in monumental calligraphy by various emperors, they herald the entry into the temple precinct along its central axis. Further into the grounds stands the two-storey library, Pavilion of the Star of Literature (*Kuiwen ge*), and a large number of inscribed stone steles, some of them sheltered in pavilions and others set into walls or freestanding. The texts include celebratory inscriptions by emperors, officials, and private scholars; records of temple reconstructions, ritual equipment, and liturgies; and tributes to Confucius and the Way of the ancient sages. Other carved inscriptions identify mundane features attributed to the lifetime of Confucius and his early descendants, such as an old well at his residence and a wall where texts of the Classics had been hidden for safekeeping.

A more elaborate monument, the Apricot Platform (*Xing tan*), commemorates the place where Confucius had lectured to his disciples. First built in 1022, on the central axis of the courtyard in front of the sacrificial hall, the three-tiered stone pedestal appears disproportionately large in an early diagram of the temple (Figure 9).[58] A few decades later, under a new

[58] With the benefit of generous imperial patronage, a 45th generation descendant, Kong Daofu (986–1039), added the trilevel platform during his major reconstruction and enlargement of the temple; Kong Chuan (1134: *xia*.2b (106)).

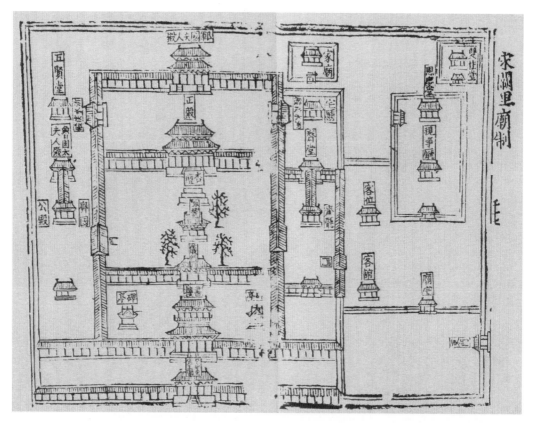

Figure 9. Plan of the Temple of Confucius in Qufu during the Song dynasty, from Kong Yuancuo (1242), *Kongshi zuting guangji* [An Expanded Record of the Kong Lineage]. After *Zhongguo zaizao shanben, Tang Song bian, Shi bu*, v. 82 (Beijing, Beijing tushuguan chubanshe, 2005), *tuben* 8. Photograph by author.

dynasty, a pavilion was added over the structure, along with a stele carved in the giant seal-script of a scholar-official who refers to himself as Confucius's latter-day pupil (*men sheng*). The pavilion became even grander in the Ming and Qing dynasties (Figure 10), and the Qianlong emperor added a stele inscribed with his own 'Eulogy on the Apricot Platform' (*Xingtan zan*).

The three trees schematically depicted near the Apricot Platform in the temple diagram were also significant relics, as they were believed to have been planted by Confucius himself. All Chinese cypresses (*kuai shu*, sometimes translated as juniper), the trees are rendered in more detail in a separate illustration, which gives them the hieratic appearance of an icon (Figure 11). Likened to the three legs of a tripod, an enduring symbol of legitimate rule, the cypress trees' flourishing, withering, and successive revivals allegedly responded to the moral condition of the polity, particularly as reflected in the status of Confucius's teachings and the welfare of his temple.[59]

---

[59] The tripod analogy comes from Kong Jifen (1762: 38.13) and is explained in Wang (2003: 212).

Figure 10. The Apricot Platform and the cypress tree planted by Confucius, from *Shengji tu* [Pictures of the Traces of the Sage]. Rubbing of recut version of incised stone tablet in the Hall of the Sage's Traces, Temple of Confucius, Qufu, Shandong. Ming dynasty, 1592 or possibly later. Marquand Library, Princeton University. Photograph by author.

According to an 8th-century writer, the trees had died in 309 when the heartland of China fell to northern invasion, but they revived in 601 after the resumption of native rule.[60] Because local people attributed curative powers to the bark, the trunks had to be coated with mud to protect them from being stripped.[61] Later authors note that the trees were again destroyed by fire in 1214, and only one cypress returned to life at the end of the century.[62] Revered as a direct link to Confucius, it was celebrated for its apparent ability to reflect heavenly principle, and scholar-officials composed panegyrics to it.[63] Although it periodically died, the tree repeatedly sprouted anew decades later, usually after a major reconstruction of the temple or demonstration of renewed imperial patronage. Besides being depicted at outsize scale on later temple plans, the cypress also appears in expanded versions of the pictorial hagiography of Confucius (see Figure 10), where it functions as a sign of his continuing presence.[64] During the turbulent decades of the mid-20th century, the tree again disappeared, but in recent years it is growing there once more.[65]

Just beyond the Apricot Platform stands the main sacrificial hall, the Hall of Great Accomplishment (*Dacheng dian*), the ceremonial heart of the temple. After the ritual reform of 1530, the Qufu temple was virtually unique in having fully three-dimensional and richly painted sculptural icons representing Confucius (Figure 12), the Four Correlates (his four major followers) and Twelve Savants (later Confucian scholars), in whose presence official sacrifices took place. In 1730, with the Yongzheng emperor's

---

[60] The 8th-century writer, Feng Yan, probably was referring to older local traditions; cited in Wang (2003: 211).

[61] Feng (8th c.: 8.4–5 (862/452)), implying that the trees' special qualities came from Confucius.

[62] Kong Jifen (1762: 2.12) chronicles the tree's successive deaths and revivals up to his own time; for a tabulation in English, see Wang (2003: 214).

[63] A stele that formerly stood beside the tree bore the great Song calligrapher Mi Fu's 1103-dated 'Encomium on the Cypress Planted by the Sage Confucius' (*Kong sheng shou zhi kuai zan*), incised in his distinctive cursive script; both the stone and a rubbing are reproduced online at http://qufubeike.com/html/ProductView.asp?ID=22&SortID=128 (accessed 12.3.2014). Perhaps because the stone later suffered damage, it was replaced by a 1600-dated late Ming stele in monumental regular script, which merely identifies the tree; a photograph of the recently refurbished stele beside the cypress is posted at http://img2.ph.126.net/l7jCsGKdXDkyf0IULgTQZw==/564075853346063303.jpg (accessed 15.3.2014).

[64] In addition to the tablet in the Hall of the Sage's Traces (i.e. Figure 10; the Hall is further discussed below) and later versions based on it, the tree has its own illustrated entry in the 18th-century expanded pictorial hagiography *Shengji quan tu* [Complete Pictures of the Sage's Traces]; the example in the Harvard-Yenching Library is reproduced online at http://nrs.harvard.edu/urn-3:FHCL :4913404?n=81 (accessed 18.2.2014). The anonymous author concludes that its pattern of flourishing and dying correlated with the rise and fall of dynasties. For a 17th-century temple plan that shows the cypress at exaggerated scale, see Song & Song (1673: 1.8b–9a).

[65] A Japanese sinologist who lived in Qufu in the 1920s and 1930s described the tree as a dried-out stump, and it is not even visible in his photograph of its enclosure; see Baba (1934: 155). Wang (2003: 211) says that only a dead stump remained in the 1950s. A tall tree stands there now, accompanied by the extensively restored late Ming stele (see above, n. 63).

Figure 11.   Cypress trees planted by Confucius, from Kong Yuancuo (1242), *Kongshi zuting guangji* [An Expanded Record of the Kong Lineage]. After *Zhongguo zaizao shanben, Tang Song bian, Shi bu*, v. 82 (Beijing, Beijing tushuguan chubanshe, 2005), *tuben* 11. Photograph by author.

generous patronage, palace craftsmen fashioned the over-lifesize statues and set them within elaborately decorated niches. Reflecting the successively higher posthumous titles and honours conferred on Confucius over the centuries, his effigy wears formal imperial garb and sits facing south in front of an ornately carved screen, like a ruler holding audience in his palace.[66] To the sides and overhead, panels in the gilded calligraphy of Ming and Qing emperors pay homage to him with eulogistic quotations from the Classics, and coiling dragons on the coffered ceiling complete the imperial ambiance.

At the north end of the temple's central axis stands a building whose explicit purpose was to collect the 'traces' of Confucius, as indicated by its name, Hall of the Sage's Traces (*Shengji dian*).[67] In keeping with Confucius's relatively modest status as

---

[66] After the ritual reform of 1530, which abolished Confucius's posthumous title as king and designated him Ultimate Sage and Foremost Teacher (see Sommer (2002)), this imperial regalia was anomalous. Perhaps the power of the Kong descendants enabled the Qufu temple to retain it.

[67] For detailed discussion of the Hall of the Sage's Traces and its pictorial hagiography, see Murray (1996).

Figure 12.   Sculptural icon and altar of Confucius in the main sacrificial hall (*Dacheng dian*) of the Temple of Confucius, Qufu, Shandong. 1984 replacement of destroyed Qing original. Photograph by author.

a teacher during his lifetime, it is a single-storey building with a green-tiled roof, in contrast to the grander structures that reflect his posthumous elevation to noble status. An expansive pictorial hagiography dominates the interior of the Hall, with 112 incised stones that portray the events of Confucius's life and milestones in the development of his posthumous cult (e.g. Figure 10). Eight more tablets bear celebratory inscriptions composed as the project neared completion in 1592–3 and identify its many participants and donors, who refer to themselves as the '60th generation of disciples'. One writer states his belief that the pictures will enable viewers to experience an 'audience' with Confucius, even if only by means of rubbings, which could circulate to people unable to come in person.[68] Three larger incised stones installed at the centre of the north wall reproduce the most venerated portraits of Confucius, transmitted through the generations by his descendants. Above is the Kangxi emperor's monumental inscription honouring Confucius as 'Teacher-Model for 10,000 Ages' (*Wan shi shi biao*), written in 1684 during the first of his six pilgrimages to Qufu, and subsequently carved on stone and disseminated empirewide through rubbings (Figure 13). The east wall displays several massive and ornate steles carved with additional inscriptions, records, and poems composed by the Kangxi and Qianlong emperors on their various visits to the temple. The west wall features additional stone tablets incised with images of Confucius, based on variations of the family heirloom pictures, and some are inscribed with eulogies composed by emperors or cultural luminaries (Figure 14).

'Living relics' of Confucius: the distinguishing presence of Kong descendants

Confucius became in effect the 'patron saint' of learning and governance with the adoption of the teachings of Confucius at the Han imperial court in the 1st century BC.[69] At the same time, his descendants, members of the Kong lineage, gained official recognition for their roles as caretakers of the cemetery and temple in Qufu, responsible for conducting periodic sacrifices on the emperor's behalf to benefit the entire realm. Men registered in Kong genealogies received noble titles of various levels, stipends, bequests of land, tax reductions, and exemptions from obligatory (corvée) labour service. From 1055 until 1935, the senior male of each generation was honoured with the title and perquisites of Duke for Perpetuating the Sage (*Yansheng gong*). Under the last two dynasties the duke was a powerful figure who lived and worked just east of the Qufu temple, in a grand mansion resplendent with imperial inscriptions and other

---

[68] Inscription by Zhang Yingdeng, dated 1592; transcribed in Baba (1940: 2).
[69] For detailed discussion of Confucius's posthumous honours and the rise of the Kongs, see Wilson (2002*b*: 45–57, 62).

Figure 13. 'Teacher-Model for 10,000 Ages' (*Wan shi shi biao*), calligraphy of the Kangxi Emperor, carved on stone tablets in the Hall of the Sage's Traces, Temple of Confucius, Qufu, Shandong. Qing dynasty, 1684. Photograph by author.

Figure 14. Portrait of Confucius and his disciple Yan Hui, with transcription of Yin Fuzhen's 'Encomium on the Small Portrait'. Rubbing of incised stone tablet erected by Kong Yu, now in the Hall of the Traces of the Sage, Temple of Confucius, Qufu, Shandong. Song dynasty, 1118. After E. Chavannes (1909), *Mission Archéologique dans la Chine Septentrionale* (Paris, Leroux), 5: CCCXCVIII no. 871. Photograph by author.

precious gifts.[70] The belief that lineage members shared the blood of the ancient sage, making them his 'living relics', contributed importantly to the successful perpetuation of their privileged status and to Qufu's distinction as the Confucian 'holy land'.

Soon after the fall of the Han dynasty in the early 3rd century, rulers also began offering sacrifices to Confucius at the imperial university in the capital, which was always located some distance from Qufu. In the 7th century, the Tang dynasty established a network of Confucian temples at government-sponsored schools in regional administrative centres, where students and officials were supposed to perform a major sacrifice twice a year.[71] As new administrative districts proliferated in later centuries, schools with temples continued to be added, generally following a standard architectural layout.[72] Kong descendants were rarely involved with these official temples, which did not include counterparts to the grave and residence of Confucius, nor did these temples claim to possess relics associated with his life. Instead they had libraries and sometimes stone tablets inscribed with the texts of the Confucian classics, his 'teaching relics'. Moreover, after the 1530 ritual reform, official temples were forbidden to display anthropomorphic icons, but instead had austere rectangular tablets simply inscribed with the names and honorific titles of Confucius, his disciples, and later interpreters and statesmen. If such a temple possessed an incised-stone replica of a lifelike portrait, as many did, it was not installed in the aniconic sacrificial hall, but elsewhere on the premises to inspire students and officials in daily life. Only the Qufu temple was allowed to keep representational images in the sacrificial hall, because of its dual role as both an official and family-ancestral temple.

The existence of numerous descendants of Confucius in the Qufu region and the requirements of their family-ancestral cult caused the Qufu temple to have a number of other features absent from Confucian temples elsewhere, marking it as special. Some of the buildings served as venues for the Kong lineage's ancestral rituals that were not part of the official cult.[73] West of the temple's main axis were separate buildings dedicated to Confucius's father and mother respectively, both of whom held posthumous titles of nobility. In the Family Temple (*Jia miao*) east of the central area, the Kongs worshipped distant ancestors of the entire lineage. Besides Confucius as progenitor, the honorees were his son, grandson, and 43rd-generation descendant Kong Renyu, the 'Restoration Ancestor', who had saved the family line from extinction in

---

[70] Agnew (2006 & 2009) and Lamberton (2002) provide detailed analyses of the Kongs' acquisition of power and privileges over the centuries. Often called the 'First Family of China', the Kongs were unique in maintaining hereditary aristocratic status throughout the dynastic era.

[71] For details of the ritual, which was also followed in later dynasties, see Wilson (1996: 577–8). Versions of it continue to be performed today; for video footage of a 1997 performance at the temple in Tainan, Taiwan, see http://academics.hamilton.edu/asian_studies/home/autumnalsacrifice/pages/videos.html (accessed 20.2.2014).

[72] For a comprehensive study of Confucian temples, see Kong Xianglin (2011).

[73] For details of the Kong family-ancestral cult and further references, see Nylan & Wilson (2010: chap. 6).

the 10th century.[74] The wives of these men also received offerings in the Family Temple, pointing up a major difference between family-ancestral rites and the official cult of Confucius. Confucius's wife additionally received sacrifices in the Resting Hall (*Qin dian*), the building immediately behind the Hall of Great Accomplishment on the temple's main axis.

Temples of Confucius elsewhere did not have special roles for Kong descendants or provide for observances of the Kong family-ancestral cult.[75] The ritual reform of 1530 did require official temples to add a building behind the sacrificial hall for the worship of Confucius's father and the fathers of the Four Correlates, in part because the Jiajing emperor wanted to provide his own father with higher ritual status.[76] Unlike the Qufu temple, where Confucius's mother and wife also received offerings, the new hall in the official temples did not include either woman. Its role was expanded in 1723 to accommodate the worship of five generations of Confucius's own ancestors, all given titles as king (*wang*). The name of the building was also changed from Shrine of the Progenitor of the Sage (*Qisheng ci*) to Shrine of Venerating the Sages (*Chongsheng ci*).[77] At the Qufu temple, however, Confucius's wife kept her place in the Resting Hall behind the main sacrificial hall, and the separate buildings for the worship of Confucius's father and mother were retained on the western axis. To comply with the order to establish a Shrine for Venerating the Sages, a new building was added on the eastern axis, in front of the Family Temple in which the Kongs worshipped important descendants of Confucius as lineage ancestors. While resulting in some duplication of offerings, these arrangements underscored the differences between the uniquely endowed Qufu temple and official temples everywhere else.

RELICS OF CONFUCIUS AT KONGZHAI

As described above, Confucius received regular sacrifices in the official temples attached to government schools and in the primordial Qufu temple for hundreds of

---

[74] Agnew (2009) demonstrates that the legend of Kong Renyu, a now-unchallenged tenet of Kong lineage history, emerged only in the 14th century in the context of legitimating a contender for the title of duke, and the emphasis of the story changed over time to meet new needs.

[75] The few exceptions were for temples at Kong-family outposts elsewhere. The most important of these is in Quzhou, Zhejiang, where the 48th-generation duke settled in the 12th century, when Song China was divided by invasion, and his heirs chose not to return to Qufu after the 13th-century Mongol reunification; for details, see Wilson (1996: 571–7).

[76] Nylan & Wilson (2010: 180). The new shrine also included the fathers of the Four Correlates of Confucius (Yan Hui, Zengzi, Zi Si and Mengzi) as attendants upon his father. Huang (2002: 268–70, 281) discusses the Jiajing emperor's motivations for mandating empirewide shrines to the father of Confucius.

[77] Zhao (1927: 84.2534).

years. In 1904, complementing the seasonal rites, the Qing dynasty also made the birthday of Confucius a national holiday.[78] His close identification with imperial rule became a liability when the 1911 Revolution toppled the Qing and ended the dynastic system. The new government of the Republic of China initially moved to abandon much of the classical heritage and school-based worship of Confucius in order to modernise the country.[79] However, President Yuan Shikai revived school sacrifices to Confucius in 1913, and the Confucian Religion Association marked the sage's birthday that year by organising a grand celebration and sacrifice in Qufu. Members from the Shanghai area who attended the fête intended to return the following year for another birthday observance, but an outbreak of fighting made travel to Qufu impractical. Instead, on 16 October 1914 (Min'guo 3/8/27), they performed a great sacrifice (*da si*) to Confucius at Kongzhai, a rural hamlet some 25 miles west of downtown Shanghai.[80]

The very name of the bucolic spot where the devotees gathered for their grand ceremony embodied a longstanding claim that the locality had direct connections with Confucius and his descendants.[81] The place-name Kongzhai, literally 'Kong Residence', was understood to refer to a 22nd-generation descendant who had sojourned there in the 2nd or 3rd century AD. Although situated a long distance from Qufu, the hamlet claimed possession of Confucius's robe and cap, intimate 'contact relics' that in a Buddhist context would signify the transmission of spiritual or doctrinal authority.[82] According to local traditions that were documented in the 12th century and much repeated in later sources, a 34th-generation descendant had buried these personal articles and a few jade ornaments in 606 AD. The relics themselves were never seen, but their presence was asserted by the so-called Tomb of the Robe and Cap (*Yiguan mu*), for which a stone-faced mound had been built in the 17th century

---

[78] Confucius's birthday initially was to be celebrated on the 28th day of the 8th lunar month, but the observance was changed to the 27th day of that month in 1910. The corresponding date in the Western calendar varies every year. In 1952 the birthday was fixed as 28 September, as currently observed in mainland China and Taiwan; however, birthday celebrations in Hong Kong still follow the lunar calendar. For further discussion, see Nylan (2001: 311), Hsi-yuan Chen (1999: 103–4), and Carroll (2006: 124).

[79] As several scholars have pointed out, earlier stages of this 'de-Confucianization' began in the last years of the Qing dynasty; see Goossaert (2006), Hsi-yuan Chen (1999), and Nedostup (2009).

[80] Yao Wendong (1915: preface). The circumstances are also described in a letter in English, dated 10 Aug. 1915, from one 'Chen Kuo chüan' to Sir James Haldane Stewart Lockhart, inserted into the Cambridge University Library's copy of the book. The rites for Confucius had been codified at the level of Middle Sacrifice (*zhong si*) from the 7th century until the early 20th (Wilson (2002*b*); it was raised in 1906 to a Great Sacrifice.

[81] The most comprehensive collection of documents pertaining to Kongzhai appears in the 18th-century edition of its gazetteer, *Kongzhai zhi*, whose compilation by Sun Hong was part of an effort (ultimately unsuccessful) to gain official certification and funding. I am currently writing a book about the site, provisionally titled 'Mysteries of Kongzhai: Relic, Representation, and Ritual at a Shrine to Confucius'.

[82] Faure (1995: 218–19).

Figure 15.   Plan of Kongzhai in the early 20th century, from Zhang Renjing & Yu Ding (eds) (1934), *Qingpu xian xuzhi* [The Continuation of the Gazetteer of Qingpu County], (Qingpu, n.p.), *juan shou: tu* 22. Photograph by author.

(Figure 15). Periodically refurbished, the 'tomb' and the sacrificial hall in front of it formed the nucleus of a shrine to Confucius that was not part of the official temple network. Its patrons repeatedly claimed that the clothing had brought Confucius's efficacious spirit (*ling*) to a place that he never even visited in his lifetime and caused auspicious or even miraculous events to occur in the vicinity.

In addition to the Tomb of the Robe and Cap, the Kongzhai shrine featured various kinds of representations that made Confucius visibly present. His sculptural effigy occupied the central position in the sacrificial hall, accompanied by statues of the Four Correlates. Copied from their counterparts in the Qufu temple, these anthropomorphic icons reinforced the claim of ancient connections between the two locales. To the west of the sacrificial hall, smaller buildings displayed stone tablets incised with portraits of Confucius, ultimately based on paintings handed down by his descendants in Qufu.[83] One of the stones had been brought to Kongzhai after being discovered in a nearby marsh in 1669, allegedly when mysterious lights flashing above it signalled its presence. Other incised stones depicted scenes from the life of Confucius and the beginnings of his cult, under the title 'Pictures of the Traces of the Sage, Confucius' (*Kongzi shengji zhi tu*). Appended inscriptions affirmed that the pictures brought ancient events to life and enabled viewers to feel that they had joined the company of disciples in the presence of Confucius.[84] Yet another set of incised stone tablets represented Confucius through teachings associated with him, in the form of a complete transcription of the *Classic of Filial Piety* (*Xiaojing*), purportedly based on a brush-written original by the great Ming calligrapher Dong Qichang (1555–1636).

Many important men from the Shanghai region took part in the 1914 ritual at Kongzhai, and hundreds of people attended the ceremony as spectators.[85] Joining with members of the local Kong lineage,[86] they presented various kinds of sacrificial offerings to the spirit of Confucius, including wine, three large animals, vegetables, grains, and silk; as well as prayers, prostrations, music, and dance. Afterwards, the celebrants established the Kongzhai chapter of the Jiangsu provincial branch of the Confucian Religion Association. To commemorate all these events, a founding member of the Association, the retired diplomat and Confucian scholar Yao Wendong (1852–1927), composed three poems, taking his rhyme and metre from an older verse that he found inscribed on a wall at Kongzhai. Yao subsequently circulated his poems nationwide and invited readers to send their own compositions matching the same rhymes. He received over 500 submissions from more than 300 individuals, which he published in three instalments in 1915.[87] These writings repeatedly affirm that the buried relics had endowed Kongzhai with the efficacious spirit of Confucius, creating an auspicious ambiance and conferring beneficial effects on the region. A couple of

[83] Members of the Kong lineage had first reproduced these pictures on incised stone tablets in the 11th and 12th centuries, and these were later installed in the Qufu temple's Hall of the Sage's Traces (discussed above). The images circulated through rubbings, facilitating replications and modifications of the original models elsewhere; discussed further in Murray (2011).

[84] The colophons that were carved on stones following the pictorial scenes are transcribed in Sun (1716: 5.2–6 (333–42)); I discuss them in detail in Murray (2014).

[85] Yao Wendong (1915) contains several accounts written by participants.

[86] Although the local Kongs were officially registered as descendants of Confucius, their more recent ancestors had moved to Kongzhai only in the 18th century. After the Duke for Perpetuating the Sage in Qufu recognised Kongzhai's claim to possess relics, he appointed Kong Yuxing to a hereditary position as Sacrificer at the Shrine and Tomb of the Robe and Cap (*Yiguan cimu fengsi sheng*); see Xiong & Chen (1879: 11.2).

[87] A fourth instalment was envisioned to accommodate submissions received after the Duanwu holiday (17 June 1915), and its publication was announced in the Shanghai newspaper *Shenbao* on 26 July 1915, but it may never have appeared; I have not been able to locate a copy.

the contributors prefaced their poems with accounts of their own pilgrimages to Kongzhai, in which they reverently described the shrine's architecture, images, and other significant features. Several mentioned the ceremonial archway at the boat landing, which was the main entrance to the shrine's precincts. Erected in the early 18th century, the arch bore an inscription in three large characters that read 'Little Queli' (*xiao Queli*), referring to Qufu. Thus the signboard identified Kongzhai as a microcosm of the premier destination for Confucian scholarly pilgrimage, which lay hundreds of miles to the north.

KONGZHAI AS 'LITTLE QUELI'

Kongzhai represents a rare case in which the presumed presence of contact relics and local lore concerning the sojourn of Kong descendants in antiquity combined to serve as a pretext for constructing a shrine to Confucius. Founded in the 17th century, outside the official temple network, its configuration was unique.[88] However, the epithet 'Little Queli' signalled that Kongzhai was meant to be a miniature facsimile of the grave, temple, and residence of Confucius and his descendants in Qufu. The alleged (and never verified) possession of clothing relics justified elements not shared by official temples but that imitated features distinctive to Qufu. Kongzhai's Tomb of the Robe and Cap, analogous to the tomb of Confucius, lay to the north of the main sacrificial hall, just as his actual grave was situated north of the Qufu temple. Inside Kongzhai's main hall, as in Qufu's, rituals were performed before sculptural representations, rather than aniconic inscribed tablets. At both sites, the building where five generations of Confucius's own ancestors received sacrifices was east of the main hall, rather than north of it as in official temples.[89] In another building, offerings were made to the two Kong descendants who were believed to have been active at Kongzhai in antiquity. Although no Kongs still lived in the area when the shrine was being built, lineage members moved there after it gained recognition, first from the Duke for Perpetuating the Sage and then from the Kangxi Emperor. The duke sent a lengthy commemorative inscription after verifying the claims made for Kongzhai, and in 1701

[88] The legends themselves were documented in the late 12th century but probably originated much earlier, and structures for venerating Confucius at the site existed for brief periods during the 13th and 14th centuries. The shrine where the 1914 sacrifice took place was established in the early 17th century and existed continuously up to the 20th century, although renovations introduced numerous changes during that period. For details of its history through the 1870s, see Xiong & Chen (1879: *juan* 11); an appendix to that history is Zhang & Yu (1934: 11.1–3).

[89] A separate shrine to Confucius's father also stood on the west side of Kongzhai's precincts until the mid-19th century; see Zhang & Yu (1934: 11.2). It was probably destroyed during the Taiping Rebellion (1851–64).

his text was carved onto a stone stele for prominent display in a pavilion.[90] The Kangxi Emperor bestowed eulogistic inscriptions, written by his own hand, while passing nearby during his 1705 inspection tour of the South. The large four-character epithet that he composed for Kongzhai, 'Lingering Emblems of the Sage's Traces' (*Shengji yihui*), echoed his 1684 monumental inscription 'Teacher-Model for 10,000 Ages' for the Hall of the Sage's Traces at the Qufu temple (see Figure 13). Kongzhai's patrons soon built a two-storey Tower of Imperial Calligraphy to house the emperor's brush-written originals and their reproductions on carved tablets, creating a counterpart to the imperial stele pavilions at the Qufu temple. Kongzhai's functional counterpart to the Hall of the Sage's Traces was the Hall of Being at Leisure (*Yanju tang*), where the stones incised with portraits and illustrations of the life of Confucius were installed. One of the accompanying inscriptions called them 'medicinal stones to awaken the heart-mind',[91] echoing the Qufu patrons' belief that pictures could stimulate the viewer to advance in moral self-cultivation.

As in Qufu, trees figured prominently in accounts of unusual occurrences at Kongzhai, which were interpreted as evidence of a numinous presence. A rhapsody composed by a 14th-century local literatus, Cai Tingxiu, celebrated five old sandal-wood trees that took turns flowering, such that only one bloomed each year.[92] His prose preface credited the nourishing beneficence of Confucius for this extraordinary manifestation, which suggests a natural-world counterpart to the Confucian virtue of gentlemanly deference (*rang*). Another story, recounted in the 1631 prefectural gazet-teer, claimed that a local man had begun bleeding from his nose and mouth when he tried to cut down one of the trees.[93] In the autumn of 1705, after the Kangxi emperor bestowed his imperial calligraphy in honour of the presence of 'traces' of Confucius at Kongzhai, a cassia tree produced four branches with auspicious red flowers among the usual yellow ones, a pattern of blooming that continued for a couple of years thereafter.[94] The occurrence became one of Kongzhai's 'Four Auspicious Phenomena' (*si rui*), which contemporary literati commemorated in suites of celebratory poems.[95] Several of the participants in the 1914 sacrifice at Kongzhai referred to the cassia's prodigious behaviour in the poems and prose notes published after the ceremony.[96] It

---

[90] For the text of the stele, see Sun (1716: 3.1–2 (261–4)). Another inscription sent by a later duke was carved on stone in 1849 for similar display; the text is transcribed in Xiong & Chen (1879: 11.3).

[91] The inscription, by the 17th-century literatus Ni Fuying, is transcribed in Sun (1716: 5:3–4 (335–7)).

[92] Transcribed in Sun (1716: 5.21–2 (371–3)).

[93] Fang & Chen (1631: 46.2 (1198)).

[94] Sun Hong recorded the phenomenon at the time and composed a panegyric to it; see Sun (1716: 5.20 (370) & 5.23–25 (375–9)).

[95] See examples in Sun (1716: 5.23–41 (375–412), passim).

[96] Yao Wendong (1915: passim).

seems somehow fitting that the only visible feature currently surviving at Kongzhai is a pair of 450-year-old gingko trees, which gained official protected status in 2002.[97]

Despite stories that attributed supernatural efficacy to Confucius's numinous presence, allegedly brought to Kongzhai by his buried clothing, the relics themselves did not become objects of worship. Nor did people come to Kongzhai seeking his aid or intervention, or hoping to accrue personal blessings by contributing to the shrine's upkeep. Devotees and patrons expected their offerings and material support to stimulate moral cultivation, not just for themselves but also for local residents and sojourners. Some writers expressed the belief that Kongzhai's very existence made its immediate environs superior to other localities within the Jiangnan region and raised the South more generally to a cultural level equalling or exceeding that of the North.[98] Even though Confucius himself had never come to the area in person, the arrival of his potent relic and lineal descendants had created favourable conditions for social and cultural progress. Later patrons assumed a responsibility for enhancing and perpetuating these spiritual benefits to the community by helping to build, restore, manage, or financially support Kongzhai. These men in turn were commemorated and posthumously received sacrifices in its Shrine for Reporting Merit (*Baogong ci*), east of the main hall.

CONCLUSION

The teachings of Confucius were unquestionably his most important 'relic', transmitted without geographic limit in the texts of the Confucian Classics. As one literatus associated with Kongzhai put it, 'Our Master's Way is manifested in the *Four Books* and *Six Classics*; it is like the sun in the centre of heaven'.[99] A major mode of veneration was through the proper performance of the sacrifice to Confucius and his canonised followers, which took place in Confucian temples throughout the realm at specified intervals. By fasting and other preliminary activities, the participant prepared himself to perceive the spirits coming down to receive the offerings. Ideally the

---

[97] See photograph titled 'Kongzhai—Qingpu de Kongzi houyi juzhu di' on the Qingpu Library blog, at http://bbs.qplib.sh.cn/forum.php?mod=viewthread&tid=652&highlight=%BF%D7%D5%AC, post no. 6 by shanghaipalm, dated 24.5.2009 (accessed 2.3.2014). Red Guards destroyed the rest of the shrine in 1966, during the Cultural Revolution (1966–76).

[98] For several such claims, see Zhang Baolian's mid-19th century commemorative inscription; transcribed in Zhang & Yu (1934: 11.2–3). South China was considered somewhat uncivilised until after the fall of the Han dynasty in the third century, which brought an influx of northerners, purportedly including the Kong descendants who figured in Kongzhai's history.

[99] Quoted by Ni Fuying in his inscription for incised stone tablets depicting the life of Confucius (see above, n. 91).

experience would stimulate him to renew his own commitment to the Way, which he had internalised by learning the Classics and cultivating his moral character. And Confucius himself was a role-model for self-cultivation, accessible through his biography and reported dialogues. The display and circulation of portraits and hagiographical pictures aided in this process, although critics sometimes argued that visual representations fostered only superficial understanding.[100] The ultimate ideal was to transmit and practice the Way.

Physical relics associated with Confucius played subsidiary roles in his veneration and, compared with his teachings, garnered far less attention from the scholars and officials who enacted his cult. Nonetheless, the material aspects of his identification with Qufu endowed his home region with special charisma. Qufu had the grave containing his body, various objects that he had used during his life, and many sites associated with his words and deeds. Furthermore, it harboured the senior line of his flesh-and-blood descendants, 'living relics' who shared his essence and represented an ostensibly continuous connection to him. Charged with maintaining the tomb and temple, the Kongs made themselves an integral part of the Qufu mystique, a phenomenon without obvious counterpart in other religions. For ordinary literati, steeped in Confucian learning, a visit to Qufu offered complete immersion in the master's aura and the potential for spiritual renewal. For emperors, although few made the pilgrimage and more bestowed patronage from afar, attention to Qufu also affirmed political legitimacy and publicly endorsed orthodox principles of governance.

By proclaiming Kongzhai to be a small-scale surrogate of Qufu, its patrons hoped to gain official credentials (*biaozhang*) and more reliable funding for the shrine. With its replication of Qufu's relics and representations of Confucius, validated by reports of supernormal occurrences, Kongzhai purported to offer the visitor a similar experience as he might have in Qufu. Official recognition of Kongzhai would bring the obscure locality renown and prestige, enhancing its vitality and importance. However, the effort achieved only limited success. Although the Kangxi emperor accepted Kongzhai's claims and bestowed his prestigious calligraphy during the 1705 inspection tour, this one-time interaction did not lead to formal recognition or financial support. His successors, the Yongzheng and Qianlong emperors, who were both very generous patrons of Qufu, either ignored Kongzhai or actively suppressed it.[101] On the other hand, the Duke for Perpetuating the Sage designated a nearby branch of

---

[100] This objection is raised even by an author of a commemorative inscription for the Hall of the Sage's Traces in Qufu; transcribed in Baba (1934: 171–3). Shao Yiren clearly worried that the Hall's hagiographical illustrations might lead a viewer astray, but reluctantly concluded that they could be inspirational.

[101] Qiao Zhizhong (2006) argues that Yongzheng and Qianlong both opposed unorthodox local shrines in order to assert tighter central control, and that the latter tried to destroy all copies of Kongzhai's gazetteer in order to conceal evidence of Kangxi's gullibility.

Kong descendants to tend the shrine and helped Kongzhai gain a hereditary Sacrificer position (*fengsi sheng*) from the Ministry of Rites in 1746 for the senior male.[102] The last incumbent, Kong Fanbang, officiated at the 1914 sacrifice and directed a planning office in the Jiangsu branch of the Confucian Religion Association. Over the intervening period, local activists occasionally donated land or made monetary contributions to Kongzhai, mounted campaigns to restore its facilities, performed sacrifices, held literary gatherings, and composed poems celebrating its distinctive features. Nonetheless, Kongzhai rarely aroused more than local interest, suggesting that unseen relics, assorted images, and obscure descendants could not create a fully persuasive aura to attract wider attention to a place where Confucius himself had never come.

Epilogue

Despite their numinous qualities as surrogates for Confucius's presence, his relics were not to be worshipped directly nor approached for aid with private concerns. As suggested above, appropriate ways to venerate them included erecting protective structures, heraldic archways, and commemorative steles; composing poems, panegyrics, and documentary records; writing calligraphy for monumental signboards and decorative couplets; copying hallowed images and circulating rubbings; and contributing to facility maintenance and renewal. Even more important and pervasive was the perpetuation of Confucius's teachings by disseminating the texts of the Classics, initially in sets of rubbings made from carved stone tablets and later in books produced with woodblock-printing technology.

Perhaps there was always a need to guard against attempts to treat Confucius like a boon-granting popular god, whose relics possessed special powers that supplicants could invoke for their own benefit. The 8th-century writer Feng Yan made this point with two colourful anecdotes about inappropriate behaviour at the Qufu temple. One was his account of how the tree planted by Confucius had to be plastered with mud, to keep people from stripping off the bark to use as medicine.[103] The other was a more lurid story describing how women would go into the main hall, remove their clothes and climb up on the dais, in hopes of conceiving a son who would grow up to become a high official. This egregious activity stopped only after an imperial edict of 472 barred women from entering the temple.[104] The underlying assumption is that only highly educated and disciplined males could approach the spirit of Confucius properly

---

[102] Wang Chang (1788: 17.1); however, unpublished documents in the Kong archives in Qufu indicate that negotiations for the position started as early as 1705.

[103] See above, n. 61.

[104] Feng (8th c.: 1.3 (862/422)).

and engage with the Way on an exalted level. For virtually the entire imperial era, access to Confucian temples was limited to men.

The dramatic unheavals of the 20th century displaced the cult of Confucius and Confucian learning from their central roles in Chinese governance, and Maoist persecution rendered Confucian temples completely defunct. After post-Mao changes of policy permitted temples to reopen in the 1980s, the long rupture enabled new practices to develop. The sacrificial ceremony has undergone numerous contemporary revivals, with some that deliberately modernise it for touristic purposes, as well as others that attempt to recreate the traditional liturgy. Most notably, monumental statues of Confucius and sometimes his disciples have been added at many of the restored temples in recent years, and visitors of both sexes make offerings, burn incense, hang votive placards, and pray for personal blessings.[105] Because Confucius historically was closely identified with learning, and arduous examinations dominated the traditional path to a prestigious career, it is not surprising that supplicants initially sought his aid in passing university entrance examinations. But Confucius and his disciples now receive appeals for the full array of traditional concerns, such as having sons, getting rich, advancing in a career, enjoying good health, and living to old age. These once exclusive figures have become almost interchangeable with the Buddhist, Daoist and popular gods who have also returned to the arena of public religious expression. The modes of venerating Confucius are continuing to evolve.

REFERENCES

Agnew, C.S. (2006), 'Culture and Power in the Making of the Descendents [*sic*] of Confucius, 1300–1800', Ph.D. dissertation, University of Washington.

Agnew, C.S. (2009), 'Memory and Power in Qufu: Inscribing the Past of Confucius's Descendants', *Journal of Family History*, 34: 327–43. http://dx.doi.org/10.1177/0363199009337393

Baba Haruyoshi (1934), *Kôshi seiseki shi* [Treatise on the Traces of the Sage Confucius] (Tokyo, Daitô Bunka Kyôkai).

Baba Haruyoshi (1940), *Kô Mô seiseki zukan* [Reflection in Pictures of the Traces of the Sages Confucius and Mencius] (Tokyo, Santô Bunka Kenkyûkai).

Bagnoli, M., Klein, H.K., Mann, C.G. & Robinson, J. (eds) (2010), *Treasures of Heaven: Saints, Relics, and Devotion in Medieval Europe* (Cleveland, Cleveland Museum of Art; Baltimore, Walters Art Museum & London, The British Museum).

Billioud, S. & Thoraval, J. (2007), '*Jiaohua*: The Confucian Revival in China as an Educative Project', trans. N. Jalladeau, *China Perspectives*, 4: 4–20. http://dx.doi.org/10.3406/perch.2007.3569

Birnbaum, R. (2007), 'The Deathbed Image of Master Hongyi', in B.J. Cuevas & J.I. Stone (eds), *The Buddhist Dead: Practices, Discourses, Representations* (Honolulu, University of Hawaii Press), 175–207.

---

[105] See Billioud & Thoraval (2007) and Wang-Riese (2012).

Brown, P. (1981), *The Cult of the Saints: Its Rise and Function in Latin Christianity* (Chicago, University of Chicago Press).

Carroll, P.J. (2006), *Between Heaven and Modernity: Reconstructing Suzhou, 1895–1937* (Stanford, Stanford University Press).

Chen, Hsi-yuan (1999), 'Confucianism Encounters Religion: The Formation of Religious Discourse and the Confucian Movement in Modern China', Ph.D. dissertation, Harvard University.

Chen, Huaiyu (2007), *The Revival of Buddhist Monasticism in Medieval China* (New York, Peter Lang).

Csikszentmihalyi, M. (2001), 'Confucius', in D. Freedman & M. McClymond (eds), *Rivers of Paradise* (Grand Rapids, Eerdmans), 223–93.

Csikszentmihalyi, M. & Nylan, M. (2003), 'Constructing Lineages and Inventing Traditions through Exemplary Figures in Early China', *T'oung Pao*, 89: 59–99. http://dx.doi.org/10.1163/156853203322691329

De Bary, W.T. & Bloom, I. (eds) (1999), *Sources of Chinese Tradition*, v. 1, 2nd edn (New York, Columbia University Press).

Dehejia, V. (1997), *Discourse in Early Buddhist Art: Visual Narratives of India* (New Delhi, Munshiram Manoharlal Publishers Pvt Ltd).

Demattè, P. (2007), 'Christ and Confucius: Accommodating Christian and Chinese Beliefs', in M. Reed & P. Demattè (eds), *China on Paper: European and Chinese Works from the Late Sixteenth to the Early Nineteenth Century* (Los Angeles, Getty Research Institute), 29–51.

Duara, P. (2008), 'Religion and Citizenship in China and the Diaspora', in M.M. Yang (2008), 43–64.

Ebrey, P.B. (1991), *Confucianism and Family Rituals in Imperial China* (Princeton, Princeton University Press).

Fang Yuegong & Chen Jiru (1631), *Songjiang fuzhi* [The Gazetteer of Songjiang Prefecture], repr. in *Riben cang Zhongguo hanjian difangzhi congkan* (Beijing, Shumu wenxian chubanshe, 1990).

Faure, B. (1992), 'Relics and Flesh Bodies: The Creation of Ch'an Pilgrimage Sites', in S. Naquin & C. Yü (eds), *Pilgrims and Sacred Sites in China* (Berkeley, University of California Press), 150–89.

Faure, B. (1995), 'Substitute Bodies in Chan/Zen Buddhism', in J.M. Law (ed.), *Religious Reflections on the Human Body* (Bloomington & Indianapolis, Indiana University Press), 211–29.

Feng Yan (8th c.), *Fengshi wenjian ji* [Mr Feng's Record of Things Heard and Seen], repr. in *Yingyin Wenyuange Siku quanshu* v. 862 (Taipei, Taiwan shangwu yinshuguan, 1983).

Fingarette, H. (1972), *Confucius: The Secular as Sacred* (New York, Harper and Row).

Germano, D. & Trainor, K. (eds) (2004), *Embodying the Dharma: Buddhist Relic Veneration in Asia* (Albany, SUNY Press).

Goldin, P.R. (2011), *Confucianism* (Berkeley, University of California Press).

Goossaert, V. (2006), '1898: The Beginning of the End for Chinese Religion?', *Journal of Asian Studies*, 65.2 (2006), 307–36. http://dx.doi.org/10.1017/S0021911806000672

Goossaert, V. (2008), 'Republican Church Engineering: The National Religious Associations in 1912 China', in M. M. Yang (2008), 209–32.

Head, T. (1999), 'The Cult of the Saints and Their Relics', posted on *The ORB: On-line Reference Book for Medieval Studies*, http://www.the-orb.net/encyclop/religion/hagiography/cult.htm (accessed 9.2.2014).

Huang, C. (2002), 'The Cultural Politics of Autocracy', trans. C.D. Smith & T.A. Wilson, in Wilson (2002c), 267–96.

Jensen, L.M. (1997), *Manufacturing Confucianism: Chinese Traditions and Universal Civilization* (Durham, North Carolina, Duke University Press).

Jing, J. (1996), *The Temple of Memories: History, Power, and Morality in a Chinese Village* (Stanford, Stanford University Press).

Kieschnick, J. (2003), *The Impact of Buddhism on Chinese Material Culture* (Princeton, Princeton University Press).

Kong Chuan (1134), *Dongjia zaji* [Miscellaneous Records of the Eastern House], repr. in *Kongzi wenhua daquan* (Ji'nan: Shandong youyi shushe, 1990), 1–200.

Kong Jifen (1762), *Queli wenxian kao* [Examination of the Documents of Queli] (repr. Taipei, Zhongguo wenxian chubanshe, 1966).

Kong Xianglin (2011), *Shijie Kongmiao yanjiu* [Research on Temples of Confucius Worldwide] (Beijing, Zhongyang bianyi chubanshe).

Kong Yuancuo (1242), *Kongshi zuting guangji* [An Expanded Record of the Kong Lineage] (Qufu, n.p.), facsimile reproduction in *Zhongguo zaizao shanben, Tang Song bian, Shi bu*, v. 82 (Beijing, Beijing tushuguan chubanshe, 2005).

Kong Zhencong (1609), *Queli zhi* [Gazetteer of Queli] (Qufu, n.p.).

Lamberton, A. (2002), 'The Kongs of Qufu: Power and Privilege in Late Imperial China', in Wilson (2002*c*), 297–332.

Lee, S.S. (2010), *Surviving Nirvana: Death of the Buddha in Chinese Visual Culture* (Hong Kong, Hong Kong University Press).

Legge, J. (1933), *The Four Books: Confucian Analects, The Great Learning, The Doctrine of the Mean, The Works of Mencius* (Shanghai, Chinese Book Company).

Legge, J. (1898), *The Chinese Classics* v. 4: *The She King or Book of Poetry* (Oxford, Oxford University Press).

Miller, T.G. (forthcoming), 'The Architecture of the Three Teachings', in J. Lagerwey (ed.), *Modern Chinese Religion I: Song-Liao-Jin-Yuan* (Leiden, EJ Brill).

Murray, J.K. (1996), 'The Temple of Confucius and Pictorial Biographies of the Sage', *Journal of Asian Studies*, 55.2: 269–300. http://dx.doi.org/10.2307/2943360

Murray, J.K. (1997), 'Illustrations of the Life of Confucius: Their Evolution, Functions, and Significance in Late Ming China', *Artibus Asiae*, 57.1–2: 73–134.

Murray, J.K. (2011), 'Heirloom and Exemplar: Family and School Portraits of Confucius in the Song and Yuan Periods', *Journal of Song-Yuan Studies*, 41: 227–66. http://dx.doi.org/10.1353/sys.2011.0021

Murray, J.K. (2014), 'Competing Lives of Confucius: The *Shengji tu* at Kongzhai', in S. McCausland & Y. Hwang (eds), *On Telling Images of China: Essays in Narrative Painting and Visual Culture* (Hong Kong, Hong Kong University Press), 31–60.

Nanjing Gongxueyuan jianzhuxi (1987), *Qufu Kongmiao jianzhu* [The Architecture of the Temple of Confucius in Qufu] (Beijing, Zhongguo jianzhu gongye chubanshe).

Nedostup, R. (2009), *Superstitious Regimes: Religion and the Politics of Chinese Modernity* (Cambridge, MA, Harvard University Asia Center).

Nylan, M. (2001), *The Five 'Confucian' Classics* (New Haven, Yale University Press).

Nylan, M. & Wilson, T.A. (2010), *Lives of Confucius: Civilization's Greatest Sage through the Ages* (New York, Doubleday).

Qiao Zhizhong (2006), 'Kongzhai zhi qi shu yi ji xiangguan lishi wenti: Riben xiancang guben Kongzhai zhi fafu' [Record of Kongzhai and Related Historical Problems: The Rediscovery of the Only Existing Version of Record of Kongzhai in Japan [*sic*]], *Qiushi xuekan*, 33.5: 132–8.

Richey, J. (2013), *Confucius in East Asia: Confucianism's History in China, Korea, Japan, and Viet Nam* (Ann Arbor, MI, Association for Asian Studies).

Ritzinger, J. & Bingenheimer, M. (2006), 'Whole-body Relics in Chinese Buddhism: Previous Research and Historical Overview', *Indian International Journal of Buddhist Studies*, 7: 37–94.

Ruppert, B. (2000), *Jewel in the Ashes: Buddha Relics and Power in Early Medieval Japan* (Cambridge, MA, Harvard University Asia Center).

Schneewind, S. (2013), 'Beyond Flattery: Legitimating Political Participation in a Ming Living Shrine', *Journal of Asian Studies*, 72.2: 345–66. http://dx.doi.org/10.1017/S0021911812002203

Schopen, G. (1998), 'Relic', in M. Taylor (ed.), *Critical Terms for Religious Studies* (Chicago, University of Chicago Press), 256–68.

Sharf, R. H. (1999), 'On the Allure of Buddhist Relics', *Representations*, 66: 75–99; repr. with minor revisions in Germano & Trainor (2004), 163–91.

Shen, H. (2000), 'Buddhist Relic Deposits from Tang (618–907) to Northern Song (960–1127) and Liao (907–1125)', D.Phil. thesis, Oxford University.

Sima Qian (145–*c.*86 BC), *Shi ji* [Records of the Grand Historian] (repr. Beijing, Zhonghua shuju, 1982).

Smith, J.M.H. (2012), 'Portable Christianity: Relics in the Medieval West (*c.*700–1200)', 2010 Raleigh Lecture on History, *Proceedings of the British Academy*, 181 (*2010–2011 Lectures*), 143–67. http://dx.doi.org/10.5871/bacad/9780197265277.003.0006

Sommer, D. (2002), 'Destroying Confucius: Iconoclasm in the Confucian Temple', in Wilson (2002*c*), 95–133.

Sommer, D. (2003), 'Ritual and Sacrifice in Early Confucianism: Contacts with the Spirit World', in W. Tu & M.E. Tucker (eds), *Confucian Spirituality*, v. 1 (World Spirituality; New York, Crossroad Publishing Company), 197–219.

Song Ji & Song Qingchang (1673), *Queli guangzhi* [The Expanded Gazetteer of Queli] (repr. Qufu, n.p., 1870).

Strong, J.S. (2004*a*), 'Buddhist Relics in Comparative Perspective', in Germano & Trainer (2004), 27–49.

Strong, J.S. (2004*b*), *Relics of the Buddha* (Princeton, Princeton University Press).

Sun Hong (ed.) (1716), *Kongzhai zhi* [The Gazetteer of Kongzhai], repr. in *Kongzi wenhua daquan* (Ji'nan, Shandong youyi shushe, 1990), 201–593.

Tillman, H.C. (2004), 'Zhu Xi's Prayers to the Spirit of Confucius and Claim to the Transmission of the Way', *Philosophy East and West*, 54.4: 489–513. http://dx.doi.org/10.1353/pew.2004.0036

Trainor, K. (1997), *Relics, Ritual, and Representation in Buddhism: Rematerializing the Sri Lanka Theravāda Tradition* (Cambridge, Cambridge University Press).

Trainor, K. (2004), 'Introduction: Beyond Superstition', in Germano & Trainer (2004), 1–26.

Vikan, G. (2012), *From the Holy Land to Graceland: Sacred People, Places and Things in our Lives* (Washington, American Alliance of Museums Press).

Von Spee, C. (2013), 'Visiting Steles: Variations of a Painting Theme', in S. McCausland & Y. Hwang, *On Telling Images of China* (Hong Kong, Hong Kong University Press), 213–36.

Wang Chang (ed.) (1788), *Qingpu xianzhi* [The Gazetteer of Qingpu County] (Qingpu, Zunjingge).

Wang, E.Y. (2003), 'The Rhetoric of Book Illustrations', in P. Hanan (ed.), *Treasures of the Yenching: 75th Anniversary of the Harvard-Yenching Library* (Cambridge, MA, Harvard-Yenching Library), 181–217.

Wang, E.Y. (2005), 'Of the True Body: The Famen Monastery Relics and Corporeal Transformation in Tang Imperial Culture', in H. Wu & K. Tsiang (eds), *Body and Face in Chinese Visual Culture* (Cambridge, MA, Harvard University Asia Center), 79–118.

Wang-Riese, X. (2012), 'Popular Religious Elements in the Modern Confucius Cult', in P. Clart (ed.), *Chinese and European Perspectives on the Study of Chinese Popular Religions* (Taipei, Boyang wenhua shiye youxian gongsi & Konfuzius-Institut Leipzig), 96–127.

Wilkinson, E. (2000), *Chinese History: A Manual*, rev. edn (Cambridge, MA, Harvard University Asia Center).

Wilson, T.A. (1996), 'The Ritual Formation of Confucian Orthodoxy and the Descendants of the Sage', *Journal of Asian Studies*, 55.3: 559–84. http://dx.doi.org/10.2307/2646446

Wilson, T.A. (2002*a*), 'Sacrifice and the Imperial Cult of Confucius', *History of Religions*, 41.3: 251–87. http://dx.doi.org/10.1086/463684

Wilson, T.A. (2002*b*), 'Ritualizing Kongzi/Confucius: The Family and State Cults of the Sage of Culture in Imperial China', in Wilson (2002*c*), 43–94.

Wilson, T.A. (ed.) (2002c), *On Sacred Grounds: Culture, Society, Politics, and the Formation of the Cult of Confucius* (Cambridge, MA, Harvard University Asia Center).

Wu, H. (2012). *A Story of Ruins: Presence and Absence in Chinese Art and Visual Culture* (London, Reaktion Books Ltd).

Xiong Qiying & Chen Qiyuan (eds) (1879), *Qingpu xianzhi* [The Gazetteer of Qingpu County] (Qingpu, Zunjingge).

Yang, H. & Yang, G. (1979), *Selections from Records of the Historian: Written by Szuma Chien* (Beijing, Foreign Languages Press).

Yang, M.M. (ed.) (2008), *Chinese Religiosities: Afflictions of Modernity and State Formation* (Berkeley, GAIA Books).

Yao Wendong (ed.) (1915), *Kongzhai shi* [Poetry of Kongzhai] (Shanghai, n.p.).

Yao, X. (2000), *An Introduction to Confucianism* (New York, Cambridge University Press). http://dx.doi.org/10.1017/CBO9780511800887

Zhang Renjing & Yu Ding (eds) (1934), *Qingpu xian xuzhi* [The Continuation of the Gazetteer of Qingpu] (Qingpu, n.p.).

Zhao Erxun (ed.) (1927), *Qing shi gao* [Draft History of the Qing] (Beijing, Qing shi guan).

Note on the author: Julia K. Murray is Professor Emerita of Art History, East Asian Studies, and Religious Studies at the University of Wisconsin, and Associate in Research at the Fairbank Center for China Studies at Harvard University. Her research focuses on the visual and material culture associated with the worship of Confucius, particularly pictorial portraits, sculptural images, and hagiographical illustrations. Among her publications are *Confucius: His Life and Legacy in Art*, co-authored with Wensheng Lu (China Institute in America, 2010)); '"Idols" in the Temple: Icons and the Cult of Confucius' in the *Journal of Asian Studies* (2009), and *Mirror of Morality: Chinese Narrative Illustration and Confucian Morality* (Cambridge, 2007).

jmurray@wisc.edu

This article was first published in 2014 in *Journal of the British Academy* (ISSN 2052–7217).

To cite the article: Julia K. Murray (2014), 'A heavenly aura: Confucian modes of relic veneration ', *Journal of the British Academy*, 2: 59–99. DOI 10.5871/jba/002.059

Journal of the British Academy, **2**, 101–123. DOI 10.5871/jba/002.101
Posted 14 August 2014. © The British Academy 2014

Education and opportunity:
Is the UK departing from a common tradition?

Sir John Cass's Foundation Lecture
read 18 March 2014

LINDSAY PATERSON
Fellow of the Academy

Abstract: There is an assumption in public debate that Scotland and England are drifting apart in social policy, whatever the outcome of the referendum in Scotland in September 2014 on whether Scotland should become an independent country. Three broad examples of policy divergence in education are discussed to examine the claim— in connection with student finance in higher education, with the structure of secondary education, and with the school curriculum. It is concluded that the apparent divergence owes more to rhetoric than to the reality of policy, of public attitudes or of social experience. Despite the origins of a shared educational philosophy in the post-war welfare state, and despite the partisan strife of current politics, a weakening of that state through greater Scottish autonomy does not in itself signal an end to the project of common welfare.

Keywords: Education, welfare state, universalism, Scotland, England, curriculum, student finance, school governance.

INTRODUCTION

It has become the common-sense view of public debate recently that devolution has made the UK less united even well in advance of the referendum on Scottish independence in September 2014. *The Economist*, in November 2013, said that 'even if Scotland votes to stay in the United Kingdom, the union is fraying'. Devolution had already disrupted the common social experience of the UK so profoundly that this process 'appears not just irreversible but unstoppable'. Steve Richards, in the *Guardian*, in August 2013, made a similar point, having spent a few days at the Edinburgh Festival:

> there may be no divorce [in the referendum], but devolution combined with a right-wing Westminster government is moving our nations in separate directions. . . . In its political culture and its powers to define what form that culture takes, Scotland is already so incomparably different from England that a form of separation is taking place in front of our eyes.   (Richards 2013)

Talking to a mixed audience of English and Scots, he said, was now like addressing a mixture of 'Americans and Swedes'.

The Scottish journalist Iain Macwhirter has summed up what he sees as the implications for the very nature of the state and society:

> England is dismantling the traditional welfare state through marketisation of the NHS, welfare caps and free schools, while Scotland retains faith in the monolithic health service, social security and universal comprehensive education.   (Macwhirter 2013)

If Scotland were to become independent, he went on, it would be likely to 'evolve into a relatively high-tax, high-spend oil-rich Nordic state within the European Union, emulating Denmark or Finland. England may seek its own form of independence, probably leaving the EU to become a finance-led market economy with low taxation and diminished social protections.'

Such perceptions that Scotland is already profoundly different contribute sharply to the debate about Scottish independence, although the political disputes in Scotland itself tend to be about what the most appropriate version of a left-wing response should be to such divergence, since the main partisan conflict is between two large left-of-centre parties, the Scottish National Party and the Labour Party (What Scotland Thinks website 2014). Reflections on a common British welfare state have underpinned the most sociologically well-informed of the contributions from both sides of that debate, politicians asking whether the shared project of a common welfare state is any longer viable. Opponents of independence, notably the former UK Labour prime minister Gordon Brown, regret this loss of common purpose. In a speech in summer 2012, Mr Brown celebrated what he called 'a community of values that cuts right across the United Kingdom', and said that this shared commitment would be lost if Scotland votes to 'break up the Union' (Brown 2012, developed more fully by Brown 2014). Supporters of independence, by contrast, argue that the only way to recover the old welfare-state ethic is to make Scotland diverge even further from England. For example, the deputy first minister of Scotland, the SNP politician Nicola Sturgeon, said, in 2012, that 'the creation of the welfare state played an overwhelming role in giving the union a new purpose,' replacing the empire that had created a union out of disparate nations: 'Britain lost the colony of India, but we all gained a new territory in the shape of free health care and social protection from cradle to grave. Alongside the BBC, these things began to define Britishness' (Sturgeon

2012). These shared institutions, she said, had now been so much undermined by what she referred to as 'the Westminster system of government' that Scotland could retain them only by becoming politically independent. Thus it was not Scotland that was breaking away from the old Britishness but rather governments in London.

There is some irony here, to which we shall return, since essentially what Ms Sturgeon and others are arguing is that to retain what might be characterised as British values of the past it is necessary for Scotland to break away from the Britain of the present. Indeed both Mr Brown and Ms Sturgeon argue that these values of the past—the shared values of common welfare—are also values for the future. They differ profoundly only on the constitutional framework that might translate these values into policy.

So the claim discussed in this paper is that the common project of the British welfare state is coming to an end, and that devolution and possible Scottish independence are part of this erosion. Constitutional disintegration is not the only way in which the old welfare-state settlement has been undermined. There are many other ways in which common welfare and common citizenship seem to be treated now with some scepticism by the UK state—targeted benefits, growing inequality, social polarisation, withdrawal of the state from responsibility to be replaced by private responsibility (Taylor-Gooby 2012). But the overarching guarantor of a common citizenship achieved through common welfare was a state possessed in common throughout Britain. Therefore if that weakens or ends, so—it is claimed—do the projects of common social citizenship. In particular for this paper, education and common educational opportunities were at the heart of this project of common welfare, in Britain as elsewhere. If educational practices depart too far from common principles, then education not only ceases to be a foundation of common social citizenship, but in fact becomes a source of differentiation. If young people in Scotland and in England are inducted into a different kind of society, then education itself becomes a further source of divergence.

The paper is in three parts. It starts by looking at some examples of educational policy in more detail. Then it considers how we might understand what is meant by saying that the welfare state rested on common traditions, and considers academic rather than journalistic evidence relating to the question of whether the common traditions are being eroded. It finishes by reconsidering the educational debates in the light of that evidence, and drawing some general conclusions about the relationship between political autonomy and social distinctiveness.

THREE EDUCATIONAL EXAMPLES

Three examples from education will illustrate the apparent divergence more clearly, in detail. They also show that, if there is divergence, it is largely not because of anything which Scotland (or Wales) has done but because of radical change in policy for England. In that sense, these examples would appear to confirm the Scottish nationalist claim that it is England or the UK state which has departed from the British values of the past. The three educational examples concern student finance in higher education, the structure of secondary schooling, and—perhaps most fundamentally of all—the school curriculum.

Student finance in higher education

The question of the ways in which the cost of taking a higher-education course is paid for is the best-known example of all the policy difference between Scotland and the rest of the UK. Crudely put, it is usually summed up as something like this: 'students from Scotland at Scottish universities don't pay fees while those from the rest of the UK do pay fees, wherever they go to university'. In more detail, but still glossing over many of the complications in order to concentrate on the essential political points, the background may be summarised quite straightforwardly (Barr 2012; Barr and Johnston 2010; Dearden, Goodman and Wyness 2012; Wakeling and Jefferies 2013). Following the Dearing review of higher education which reported in 1997, the Labour government introduced fees and ended grants. That was a radical departure from the policy which had been in place since the introduction of state grants for students in higher education in 1962. The new financial arrangement then became controversial during the first elections to the Scottish Parliament in 1999. Although Labour was the largest party there, the proportional electoral system led to there being a majority in the parliament against the new arrangements, and so Labour was forced to concede a further review of student finance as part of its negotiations with the Liberal Democrats to form a coalition government in Scotland.

The result in Scotland was in effect a graduate tax—a loan to cover fees that was repayable after graduation at a rate related to salary. This applied to students domiciled in Scotland at Scottish universities, and to rest-of-EU students because EU rules prevent Scottish universities' treating students from other member states differently from home students. But the new arrangements did not apply to students from the rest of the UK. It was thus Scottish Labour and the Scottish Liberal Democrats—not the nationalists—who inaugurated the different treatment of citizens of the same state. But the nationalists have not demurred.

The essential differences in student finance between Scotland and the rest of the UK have remained broadly the same ever since, through various further changes in England and Wales—the capping of fees for Welsh-domiciled students in Wales in 2007, the UK Labour government's increasing fees after 2006 in England, but their replacement by the same kind of postgraduate tax-like repayment as in Scotland, and the UK coalition government's removal of the cap on fees in England from 2012 along with their introduction of a new system of bursaries and of repayment methods that the Liberal Democrats forced on their Conservative partners and that made the English arrangements now more redistributive than Labour's regime before 2010, and more redistributive than the arrangements in Scotland (Chowdry *et al.* 2012). Whatever the complexities, the essence of the contrasts are not changed: Scottish students don't pay, Welsh students don't pay very much, and English students pay a lot.

One reason why this policy is the most visible of all the post-devolution divergence is cross-border flows of students, so that in university classes now in Scotland there are students paying nothing and students paying a great deal. Of course that has always been so, and is true also elsewhere in the UK, insofar as students from outside the European Union are charged very large fees, but the difference here is that the divergence is between citizens of the same state. The contrast is also symbolically exacerbated in Scotland by the fact that citizens from other EU states do not pay fees and so are now treated differently from citizens of the rest of the UK. That is another irony in the context of the referendum of 2014, since independence would force the same free treatment of students from the residual UK, which would then be a separate member state.

Whatever the complexities, this difference has now become so entrenched that the Scottish First Minister has famously said in a flight of Burnsian rhetoric in 2011 that the rocks would melt with the sun before he would preside over the introduction of fees for undergraduate higher education in Scotland (BBC 2011).

Structure of secondary schooling

The second example of educational divergence within the UK also stems from an innovation in English policy: the introduction of greater diversity in secondary schooling. This diversity is a departure in England from the system of common secondary schooling that was generally the outcome in all three British countries that stemmed from the 1960s moves to non-selective secondary schools in the public sector. This had never gone quite as far in England as in Wales or Scotland, insofar as some areas of England retained selective schools, and also insofar as the independent sector remained larger in England than in Scotland or Wales, and therefore offered more competition to public sector schools. But the deliberate creation of diversity in school provision in England that was started by the Conservative governments of Margaret Thatcher and John Major was given a strong impetus under the Blair government, and has become the most visible education policy of the present UK government, articulated energetically and eloquently by the former Education Secretary Michael Gove. The stark contrast is then with both Wales and Scotland, which have done absolutely none of this. Scotland and Wales have still essentially a common structure of comprehensive, non-selective secondary schools, not diversified in any way, with only small independent sectors alongside them.

The diversity of provision introduced by the Conservatives in the 1990s in England was limited essentially to the City Technology Colleges that were intended to strengthen technical education, in partnership with commercial finance, and these did not get very far because of a reluctance by both business and local government to develop them (Hatcher 2011; Machin & Vernoit 2011). The Conservatives responded by trying to develop specialist secondary schools which Labour embraced with enthusiasm. By the end of its first term in office, in 2001, around 20 per cent of English secondaries had become specialist, and in April of that year, during the general election campaign, Tony Blair said that there would be no limit on the number (Paterson 2003). Now almost all secondary schools in England have a specialism (West & Bailey 2013: 148).

The development of academy schools outside the local authority sector was an even stronger challenge to the previous uniformity of provision. They were described by the Department for Education and Employment in 2000 as 'part of a wider programme to extend diversity within the state sector' which were related to new forms of governance, 'allowing new schools to be established within the state sector, . . . allowing existing private schools to become part of the publicly-provided education system, . . . [and] allowing new promoters from the voluntary, religious or business sectors to take over weak schools or replace them with City Academies' (quoted by Hatcher 2011: 486). That policy already took the structure of secondary schooling in quite different directions from those in Scotland and Wales.

Michael Gove's policy of 'free schools' went even more radically in that same direction (Hatcher 2011). These are publicly funded schools that are not managed by the local authority and that are in principle almost as free from central control as independent schools: they are not required to follow the national curriculum, may decide (within limits) which pupils to admit, and are not bound by national standards of staffing. Mr Gove borrowed the ideas from Sweden, where somewhat similar schools were enabled during a brief period in the mid-1990s of a government led by conservative parties; that reform in Sweden was not rescinded by the social democrats when they came back to power (Lindbom 2001; Lidström 1999).

This whole programme of radical diversity of schools in England has been criticised by writers on the left as the end of the ideals of common educational provision that were the founding ideas of common schooling. For example, Beck described Mr Gove as holding 'a profoundly anti-statist ideology, that includes an attempt to complete Margaret Thatcher's work of radically marginalising any local government presence in education'. The programme, Beck argues, 'aims . . . to create a new "common sense" that uncritically accepts that neoliberal modes of governing are natural . . . or inevitable in the modern world' (Beck 2012: 9, 11).

So the apparently sharp divide between policy for the structure of secondary schooling in England on the one hand and policy in Scotland and Wales on the other seems, as with the question of university student fees, to bring the common principles of the original welfare state to an end.

School curriculum

Despite all the controversy surrounding secondary-school structures and higher education fees, perhaps the deepest changes are happening in connection with what is being taught in schools, and these certainly lead to the appearance of the sharpest philosophical disagreements between the direction of education policy in Scotland and that in England. On the whole, this is an area where the differences only really became significant when Michael Gove became Education Secretary.

Mr Gove was determined to distance himself from all recent curriculum policy in England, and was determined to restore what he sees as a traditional curriculum based on subjects and on rigour. He said in 2010, for example, that 'the great tradition of our literature—Dryden, Pope, Swift, Byron, Keats, Shelley, Austen, Dickens and Hardy—should be at the heart of school life'. In 2008, before becoming a minister, he described this approach as based on the emancipating power of knowledge:

> knowledge is the mother, father and midwife of understanding—totally indispensable. For those who grow up in homes rich in knowledge, where conversation is laced with learning and childhood curiosity is easily satisfied, future learning is made easier, deeper understanding comes more readily. . . . [W]ith the abandonment of subject disciplines, the poorer lose out again.   (Gove 2008: 24)

He described the pedagogical philosophy that he rejects as 'Progressivism, or Constructivism or Child-Centred Education,' 'championed [he adds] in different ways, with different emphases, at different times, by John Dewey, by Jean Piaget, by Lady Plowden and by successive Department of Education luminaries'. 'What has united the followers of this ideology,' he argued, was 'hostility towards traditional, academic, fact-rich, knowledge-centred, subject-based, teacher-led education' (Gove 2008: 20).

That signals a radical departure, but what makes Mr Gove's reforms particularly relevant to the debate here is that policy on the curriculum in Scotland is moving in quite the opposite direction from Mr Gove's favouring of a traditional curriculum. There is almost complete consensus on this in Scotland across the political spectrum, and embracing most shades of professional opinion and of opinion among academic commentators (Paterson 2014; Priestley & Humes 2010). The Scottish reforms are called the 'Curriculum for Excellence', and the general principles are described officially as entailing that 'the child or young person is at the centre of learning provision' (Scottish Government 2008: 22). The aim is not directly to instil knowledge: 'the purpose of the curriculum is to enable the child or young person to develop the "four capacities"', by which are meant becoming 'successful learners, confident individuals, responsible citizens, and effective contributors'. The curriculum framework 'sets out what a child or young person should be able to do and the experiences that contribute to their learning, rather than detailed definitions of content or prescribed hours of study' (Scottish Government 2008: 5).

Priestley & Humes (2010: 355) describe the Scottish approach as 'a process curriculum', characterised by aiming for 'individual growth and intrinsic purposes', as opposed to purposes set by, for example, the nature of knowledge or the needs of the economy. Michael Young—doyen of curriculum studies in England—draws the explicit comparison between this and what is happening in England. In the emerging Scottish approach, he says, 'the teacher becomes a facilitator of learning and the distinctiveness of the pedagogic relationship between teachers and pupils in providing students with access to specialist knowledge is played down'. This is, Young adds, 'what Gove and his colleagues see themselves as combating; hence his enthusiasm for returning to the past' (Young 2011: 268).

Not surprisingly, in the light of this, Mr Gove fell out spectacularly with the dominant academic opinion in England. Young, commenting further on the constructivist philosophy underlying Curriculum for Excellence, makes the point in explicitly political terms: 'with its emphasis on access and participation,' he says, 'and its confidence in claiming that no form of knowledge is necessarily more reliable than any other, it appears progressive and democratic and has been seen as attractive, in its less extreme forms, on the Left and among some researchers in educational studies' (Young 2011: 269). Implicitly following such a line in their criticism of Mr Gove, 100 education academics wrote a letter to *The Independent* newspaper in 2013 alleging that the new English 'curriculum consists of endless lists of spellings, facts and rules. This mountain of data will not develop children's ability to think, including problem-solving, critical understanding and creativity' (*The Independent* 20 March 2013). Mr Gove responded with his characteristic sarcasm, describing the signatories as criticising 'the [UK Government] Coalition for our indefensibly reactionary drive to get more children to spell properly, use a wider vocabulary and learn their times tables' (Gove 2013). The rudeness of that had previously been prefigured by an equally *ad hominem* attack from one of Mr Gove's many academic critics on the left, the philosopher John White: 'we know [that Mr Gove] adored the traditional fare he got at his Aberdeen grammar school, but only an education minister one tree short of an arboretum would impose a personal preference on a whole nation' (White 2011).

We shall return to this, since White gets his history of Scottish education wrong, but the serious point amidst the political bluster is the philosophical difference between (to put it too starkly) a knowledge-centred and a child-centred curriculum, between Matthew Arnold's view of liberal education as passing on the best that has been thought and said—a view praised by Mr Gove—and John Dewey's view that shifting the curriculum's centre of attention from the teacher to the child was as profound a change in its own way as that brought about by Copernicus (Dewey 1915: 35). If devolution has enabled such sharp differences to emerge between these two neighbouring systems of education, then surely—it might reasonably be supposed—it has destroyed the once common educational project of the welfare state.

WELFARE STATE AND COMMON TRADITIONS

That, then, is the evidence for disintegration of policy in education. How now might we understand the claim that devolution is threatening the very foundation of the welfare state? The premises here are that the British idea of social citizenship rested on common traditions of social thought, and that education was the heart of that. These premises are indeed plausible. There are two strands to this, both directly related to the nature of the education systems: the first aspect is a universal structure of opportunity; the second is a certain kind of universalism of learning.

The structure of opportunity

In a report published in 1947, the Scottish Advisory Council on Education commended what later came to be called comprehensive education but which in those days in Scotland was usually referred to as the omnibus school: 'the case for the omnibus school is that this is the natural way for a democracy to order the post-primary education of a given area' (Scottish Education Department 1947: 36). Among the civic advantages which the Council saw was the manner in which a school educating the whole community could contribute to 'inculcating the community virtues'.

A belief that providing a common set of opportunities would create a democratic culture was then one of the several reasons why a pattern of common secondary schooling came to be the preferred mode of secondary-school organisation throughout Britain by the 1960s. Anthony Crosland, for example, argued in 1956 in *The Future of Socialism* that 'if the state provides schools and hospitals, teachers and doctors, on a generous scale and of a really high quality . . . then the result will be, not indeed a greater equality of real incomes, but certainly a greater equality in manners and the texture of social life' (Crosland 1956: 85). In particular, he argued later, comprehensive schooling ought to be justified 'in terms of a sense of community, of social cohesion, of a nation composed of people who understand each other because they can communicate' (Crosland 1974: 204).

These are the local political expressions of a principle that has been described by Boli *et al.* (1985) as universalistic individualism. It was about individual opportunity, but was universal in that it sought to make a reality of the liberal claim that everyone is equal. There are three aspects of the way in which this rested on a shared British state. First, as in many other places, the state expanded education, and achieved new political legitimacy in the era of mass democracy by doing so. Second, educational growth strengthened nation building, again as elsewhere but with the complication in Britain that it involved three distinct nations nested within a larger one. Thus through sanctioning the democratisation of education systems that remained distinctive in the separate parts of Britain, the newly democratic British state found a new way of showing British identity to be complementary to the other national identities, not antagonistic to them. Then the third role for education underpinning universalistic individualism is an overarching liberalism. Mass education has been the link between politics and the individual in the very construction and definition of what Ramirez and Boli (1987: 10) call 'the European model of a national society'. The British state, then (to paraphrase these authors) was the guardian of all the nations that constitute Britain by being a guarantor of individual progress through education.

Individual opportunity, the argument goes, evoked a common British identity because it was believed that the opportunity depended on the welfare project of the British state, depended, that is, on the universalism which the very concept of 'Britain' seemed then—till about the 1960s—still to embody. So if the structure of opportunity is no longer essentially the same throughout Britain, then one of the pillars of the British welfare state is weakened.

Universalism of learning

These common opportunities were not only about structures, however. They were also about what is learnt, about the common culture which a common education system was supposed to bring about. That view was recurrent and strong among those people whose influence led throughout the first half of the 20th century to the fully developed welfare state of the post-war period—indeed was strong earlier than the belief in common structures of opportunity, which was not widely held on the political left until the 1950s with thinkers such as Crosland.

Harold Laski—socialist intellectual and professor at the London School of Economics—wrote in 1923, for example, that 'we have made the electorate commensurate with the majority of the adult population, but we have failed, in any creative sense, to fit that electorate to grasp either its responsibilities or its powers', which would require that the average person 'be trained to feel a moral responsibility for the results of the political process' (Laski 1923: 50). To that end, the most effective means was immersion in a tradition:

> for what, in the handling of material, it is essential for the student to encounter is the great mind which has formed the civilised tradition. He will rarely find it easy to wrestle with; but he will gain infinitely more from surmounting the difficulties of the supreme book than by digesting a second-hand summary of what the supreme book contains. (Laski 1930: 97)

Percy Nunn, the influential professor of education at the Institute of Education in London, noted in 1920 that 'the strongest opponents of vocational training are among those who speak for labour,' and explained this by their 'claim for the poor the heritage of culture from which they have so long been unjustly excluded' (Nunn 1920: 204). R.H. Tawney, admirer of Nunn and the person with greatest claim to have shaped Labour's education policy as it moved towards consolidating and extending the welfare state, argued that 'no one can be fully at home in the world' without acquaintance with the cultural traditions of society, in which he included 'literature and art, the history of society and the revelations of science' (Tawney 1964 [1953]: 88). James Chuter Ede, the Labour MP who spoke for the party on education in the 1930s, who was co-author (with the Conservative Minister of Education, R.A. Butler) of the wartime coalition's Education Act of 1944, and who was Home Secretary in the 1945 Labour Government, wrote in 1929 that

> if we are to have a democracy capable of shouldering th[e] great burden [of responsibility for decisions that used to be relegated to the few], I am quite sure that it can only be done through giving to the children of all classes of the community a greater opportunity of entering into those great heritages of literature, of art and of beauty that should enrich the lives of the community. (Quoted by Barker 1972: 139–40)

The culture which all these reforming political thinkers admired was not a particular culture, not a class culture or any other kind of sectional culture. There was no inkling of relativism among the social democratic and liberal reformers who created the welfare state, absolutely no sense that the best that has been thought and said was anything other than the basis of the first truly common culture to be created deliberately through education. The inherited intellectual culture, they believed, could provide all the ideas needed to reform capitalist society even in the most fundamental ways.

To sum up the delicate balance that was sought between tradition and change, consider A.D. Lindsay, founder (in 1949–51) of the innovatory University of Keele, philosopher, socialist, political activist, and in 1938 anti-appeasement parliamentary candidate in a by-election in Oxford (which he nearly won)—yet steeped in the past, in the traditions of Scottish religious thought, as Master of Balliol, and as Vice-Chancellor of the University of Oxford. Lindsay said that 'the problem [is] this conception of a standard which was corrigible and progressive, creative and authoritative' (Lindsay 1950: 145). So the socialist and philosopher—and Scot—Lindsay sought radical inspiration in the tradition of English poetry just as surely as Mr Gove does today:

> an understanding and appreciation of English poetry, of its history and its relations to the history of English culture, is a far more effective way of teaching a common outlook on the world, and a common understanding of our heritage, than a technical instruction in Philosophy.   (Scott 1971: 370)

These founders of the idea of the welfare state were all then of Matthew Arnold's view that people 'of culture are the true apostles of equality,' that 'the best that has been thought and said' would enable us—in the often forgotten second half of that sentence—'through this knowledge [to turn] a stream of fresh and free thought on our stock notions and habits' (Arnold 1960 [1869]: 6). So to undermine a common culture in whatever way—to define the common curriculum in such a radically different way as is now happening between Scotland and England—is to destroy a common heritage, a belief in which lay at the heart of the development of universal education in the middle of the 20th century.

THE COUNTER ARGUMENT

Yet there is a paradox in all this legacy of social democratic thinking. The common culture in which these old socialists believed is very similar to the common culture that the radical Tory Michael Gove wanted to introduce in England. Should that particular point about one of these policy differences not at least give us pause for thought? Might the differences of policy that we have noticed not be in fact really variations on common themes, the differences exaggerated by the rhetoric of politics, and mistaken for profound change (by too credulous journalistic and some academic commentators)? Might the difference be about means rather than ends, and indeed might these differences of means be not much greater now than they have often been in the pre-devolutionary past, when Scotland already had, through administrative autonomy, distinctive universities, and a pattern of secondary schooling that was somewhat more comprehensive than that in England?

One of the striking features of the whole constitutional debate about Scotland's place in Britain is how little public values differ between Scotland and the rest of Britain. Take for example what the British Social Attitudes Survey tells us about attitudes to the welfare state. In 2010, the proportions agreeing that the government should redistribute wealth were 41per cent in Scotland and 34 per cent in England:[1] a difference, true, but hardly great enough, one would have thought, to undermine the very structure of the state, and only a minority in favour of redistribution in each country.

The same is the case with other topics. The proportion hostile to the welfare state on the grounds that it weakens communities—in the sense of believing that the welfare state discourages people from helping each other—was 29 per cent in Scotland and 40 per cent in England, a difference again, certainly, but in both countries a minority.[2] The proportion not very sympathetic to the unemployed—in the sense of believing that they could find work if they tried—was around one half in each country: lower in Scotland (at 46 per cent) than in England (55 per cent) but again not qualitatively different.[3] The proportion nevertheless looking back with some pride on the welfare state, and agreeing that it was one of Britain's proudest achievements, was almost identical: 49 per cent in Scotland and 52 per cent in England.[4] These differences, though generally placing Scotland on average to the left of England, are not so huge as to signal a fundamental gulf of social values.

We can see this all the more clearly if we look at some measures of attitudes towards democracy and the state across Europe, as recorded by the European Social Survey.[5] In 2012, that Survey found that the proportion believing that democracy in their state worked well was 86 per cent in the UK, almost identical in England (where it was 87 per cent) and Scotland (where it was 84 per cent).[6] By contrast, the range across Europe was from the mid-90s in the Scandinavian states, and around 90 per cent in Germany and the Netherlands, through 70 per cent in Spain, to 54 per cent in Russia. Thus Scotland and England were both near the top end of this scale.

In the 2004 European Social Survey, the percentage believing that state benefits could create a more equal society was 45 per cent in Scotland and 41 per cent in England, but the range was far wider elsewhere: from around 66 per cent in Scandinavia, through about the same in Germany as in Britain, to 32 per cent in the Czech Republic and 14 per cent in Hungary.[7] We shall look at some other more specifically educational attitudes below, but the main point to make here is that, though there is some

---

[1] BSAS 2010 data set from UK Data Service, Study Number 6969. Variable REDISTRB. Percentages are weighted; unweighted sample sizes are 273 (Scotland) and 2,360 (England).
[2] See above, n. 1. Variable WELFHELP.
[3] See above, n. 1. Variable UNEMPJOB.
[4] See above, n. 1. Variable PROUDWLF.
[5] Data from European Social Survey web site, http://www.europeansocialsurvey.org/data/.
[6] Variable DMCNTOV, percentage scoring 5–10 on a 10-point scale. Percentages are weighted; unweighted sample sizes are 173 (Scotland) and 1,515 (England). Sample sizes in other countries were between about 1,800 and 2,200.
[7] See above, nn. 5 and 6. Variable SBEQSOC.

basis for the political claim that Scotland is to the left of England, the differences are not so great as to indicate a profound territorial rupture in social values.

More generally, we still live essentially in the world of the Enlightenment. Throughout Europe, what purport to be national values are actually just the local translation of what Joppke calls 'the universal creed of liberty and equality that marks all liberal societies . . . the universal, nationally anonymous creed of the liberal state' (Joppke 2004: 253–4). All that differs is language and accent: 'the various national labels are only different names for the same thing, the liberal creed of liberty and equality'. Thus in the European Social Survey we find general agreement on some basic principles of liberal society. For example, there is very clear majority agreement in 2012 with the propositions that 'people should be treated equally' and have 'equal opportunities in life'—between about 66 and 80 per cent agreeing in almost all countries.[8] Even stronger is the agreement that it is important 'to live in a country that is governed democratically'—almost all countries have agreement proportions between 90 and 95 per cent.[9] Both Scotland and England share in this common European liberalism.

If part of these common values is what is referred to as globalisation—the penetration of the free market everywhere—then that is not new either. Liberalism has always been both emancipatory and potentially oppressive because standardising, and education in the service of liberal universalism can seem to the particularist to be what the Irish nationalist Padraig Pearse called an imperial 'murder machine' (Lyons 1973: 652). Consider John Stuart Mill—great Victorian liberal, hero of the left ever since, admired everywhere still today for his pioneering concern with human rights, notably the rights of women. Consider how Mill expressed the claims of liberal modernity rather unashamedly, writing in 1861:

> nobody can suppose that it is not more beneficial to a Breton, or a Basque of French Navarre, to be brought into the current of the ideas and feelings of a highly civilized and cultivated people—to be a member of the French nationality, admitted on equal terms to all the privileges of French citizenship, sharing the advantages of French protection, and the dignity and prestige of French power—than to sulk on his own rocks, the half-savage relic of past times, revolving in his own little mental orbit, without participation or interest in the general movement of the world. The same remark applies to the Welshman or the Scottish Highlander as members of the British nation. (Mill 1861: chap. 16)

We might note, too, that statistical measurement and therefore educational research are themselves part of this standardisation, implying—in the words of Theodore

---

[8] See above, nn. 5 and 6. Variable IPEQOPT.
[9] See above, nn. 5 and 6. Variable LVDTC.

Porter—'the subordination of personal interests and prejudices to public standards' (Porter 1995: 74). Using statistics to create norms conflates the idea of normal as a criterion with normal as a description of a state of affairs: 'the normal', in a comment by Ian Hacking about Comte, 'as existing average [and] as figure of perfection to which we may progress' (Hacking 1990: 168). Originally—in the period of 19th-century development of statistics about which Porter and Hacking were writing—statistical standardisation was a national project, but it is now much more than that. As Grek has noted in connection with the OECD's Programme for International Student Assessment, 'evaluations of national education and training systems require international points of comparison,' which—as she points out—is a transfer to the international level of the standardisation which the very invention of statistics as an agency of the state originally brought about internally: 'statistics and numbers which elide the local are . . . important to the construction . . . of a commensurable education policy field' (Grek 2009: 25).

We might then ask whether the three examples that we looked at of education policy within the UK are in fact as straightforwardly to be interpreted as evidence of radical divergence as may have appeared plausible. On the question first of student finance, if we take the point of comparison to be opportunity rather than mechanisms of opportunity, the conclusion from careful research is that the differences in the regimes of fees and of student support have no effect on the outcomes, and thus no effect on the deeper matter of opportunities or denial of opportunities. Nicholas Barr, for example, has noted that 'a widespread and central argument was that variable fees would deter students from poorer backgrounds, making higher education even more the province of the rich'. But, he notes (from UCAS data), 'that has not happened'. There is no evidence that the much-noticed difference in student finance between Scotland and England has led to any differences in social-class inequality of access: thus between 2002 and 2008, as Barr points out, 'applications in England [from] the bottom three socioeconomic groups rose by 6.5 per cent [annually], compared with 0.5 per cent in Scotland, 3.1 per cent in Northern Ireland and 3.7 per cent in Wales (Barr 2010: 14, 17). Though the differences of student finance are greater than at any time since 1962, they were much larger in the interwar period, at a time when the Union was far more secure than it is today: grants from the Carnegie Trust enabled many able young Scots of limited means to attend university when their counterparts in England had only very restricted access to bursaries of any kind (Anderson 2006: 92 and 118).

Despite the changes brought about by the Scottish Parliament, there is little difference in public attitudes on this matter. The level of support for means-tested fees is similar in Scotland and in England: in the 2010 British Social Attitudes Survey, it was 63 per cent in Scotland and 70 per cent in England, and indeed Scotland became

slightly less favourable to the current Scottish policy in the decade following its introduction: in 2000, 57 per cent favoured means-tested fees (thus 6 points higher in
2010).[10] More directly relevant to the underlying principles of opportunity is the quite
close agreement between opinion in Scotland and opinion in England on whether
opportunities to enter higher education should be expanded: in 2010, 43 per cent in
Scotland, 35 per cent in England, each similar to 2004 and about five points less than
in 1999.[11] This difference between Scotland and England is again a difference of degree
rather than of fundamental social ethos.

On the structure of secondary schooling, the effect on opportunity is not in fact
the major factor that it was once thought to be. On the whole, the structure of a
school system—even the presence or absence of selection—seems to make little
difference to outcomes, whether these are achievement in examinations, social
mobility, or civic values (Boliver & Swift 2011; Kerckhoff *et al.* 1996; Paterson 2013).
Comprehensive education neither raises nor harms attainment when compared to
selective school systems; neither makes people more civic-minded nor diminishes their
engagement with society.

Again, research on school structures contributes to the common fundamental
principles, as with the international statistical comparison of nominally independent
countries. Even where radically different structures are being introduced, the criteria
used to evaluate them—for example the evaluation of academies in England by
Machin & Vernoit (2011)—are the same as for comprehensive schools, and the same
as they have been since, say, A.H. Halsey or J.W.B. Douglas and colleagues carried
out their research on the operation of the old selective school system in the 1950s (for
example, Douglas *et al.* 1966; Floud & Halsey 1957). Implicit in this common framework of analysis is a common epistemological framework, and therefore also a common ethical framework. Thus when the critics of English academies question whether
Machin & Vernoit have adequately controlled for selection bias, they are accepting in
principle that such schools are part of the same framework of understanding as any
other kind of school. To engage in this debate at all on statistical grounds is to accept
that the variation in policy—radical though it may be—is taking place on top of a
ground of agreement about the importance of opportunity, and about how to measure it. Political debate implicitly rests on that common ground too. When a politician
says that 'education [i]s the only reliable means of realising a young person's potential'
or 'education is the key to social mobility', or 'schools should be engines of social

[10] For 2010, see above, n. 1; variable HEDFEE. British Social Attitudes Survey 2000 has UK Data Service
Study Number 4486.
[11] For 2010, see above, n. 1; variable HEDOPP. British Social Attitudes Survey 2004 has UK Data Service
Study Number 5329, and 1999 has Study Number 4318.

mobility', there is no clue within the rhetoric as to which side of the debate that person is on, nor indeed as to whether they are speaking about Scotland or England.[12]

Any differences in public views about school structures go back to before the Scottish Parliament was created in 1999: if the stronger support for comprehensive education in Scotland than in England contributes to the fragility of the Union, then it is not to be attributed to devolution, but developed in the 1980s (for example, see Brown *et al.* (1999: 96–107), using the British Election Surveys of 1997, 1979 and 1974). Moreover, on most matters attitudes concerning school structures are little more favourable in England than in Scotland to private firms or charities running schools. In the 2007 British Social Attitudes Survey, the proportion in favour of private companies running schools was 17 per cent in Scotland and 20 per cent in England. For charities running schools, the proportion in favour was 30 per cent in Scotland and 37 per cent in England.[13] There is not much evidence here of fundamental divergence between Scotland and England so far as the ways in which schools relate to society politically are concerned.

Then on the curriculum we are back to the irony that we have already briefly seen, that Mr Gove is closer to the dominant tradition of liberal education than his critics, and thus closer also to his left-wing critics' predecessors half a century or more ago than they are. He does indeed—as we noted John White saying—conscientiously draw upon his own school experience in Aberdeen, but Mr Gove's critics on the political left rather neglect the social purpose to which that old Scottish academic curriculum was put. In the words of Guy Neave, writing around the time when Mr Gove was at school:

> in most Western countries the distinction between 'academic' and non academic courses is regarded as one of the major historic obstacles to a democratic system of education. In Scotland, the reverse is true. The concept of a curriculum dominated by a highly academic content has been justified in the name of creating a 'common course' for all.   (Neave 1976: 131)

In truth then, the apparent contrast in the cultural meaning of different approaches to the curriculum is less significant than that there are multiple interpretations of a common tradition. The Scottish tradition which Neave notes, and to which such a pre-eminently British academic leader as A.D. Lindsay was heir in the first half of the 20th century, was part of a common current of ideas about liberal education that, in both England and Scotland, owed its main debt to Matthew Arnold and, further

---

[12] The two social mobility quotations are respectively from Tristram Hunt (28 Oct 2013) and Michael Gove (Department for Education, 2010: 6); Hunt speaks for Labour on education in England. The one about realising potential is from Michael Russell (27 March 2013), Cabinet Secretary for Education in the Scottish Government.

[13] BSAS 2007 data set from UK Data Service, Study Number 6240. Variables SCHPRV and SCHVOL. Percentages are weighted; unweighted sample sizes are 189 (Scotland) and 1,741 (England).

back, to the classical tradition as renovated from the Renaissance onwards (Rothblatt, 2007). Variation in how that tradition was interpreted was about means, not ends, as it is still today. Being part of this liberal tradition, too, Mr Gove is not the reactionary traditionalist that his critics allege: as Michael Young has pointed out, 'Gove has claimed that his approach is based on the principle of equality. In the sense that he is proposing a common "curriculum for all" he is right' (Young 2011: 275). Young continues: 'to the extent that a subject-based curriculum is based on concepts, not facts alone, it is not only a reproducer of inequalities, but also potentially a carrier of universal knowledge—knowledge that is not dependent for its validity on its social origins or when or how it was produced' (Young 2011: 276). There would probably be nothing there with which Mr Gove would disagree, and undoubtedly he has repeatedly acknowledged the importance of concepts built on a secure foundation of knowledge about facts, and has never said that all he wants is facts. He wrote in 2008 on the relationship of knowledge to ideas that 'we learn by using existing knowledge to construct models, parallels, paradigms and analogies which enable us to grasp new concepts and insights' (Gove 2008: 24). But, as Young's comments here exemplify, some of Mr Gove's critics are not the unthinking ideologues that he alleges, and some of them remember the history of left-wing support for a liberal education as the welfare state was being established.

More to the point for our present discussion, the new Scottish curriculum is perhaps better thought of as a reform of pedagogical methods than necessarily an abandonment of knowledge or of the traditions of intellectual enquiry. Alongside the constructivist ideas which we noted as tending to break down inherited structures of knowledge, the Curriculum for Excellence principles also include judgements such as this commendation of disciplinary knowledge:

> subjects are an essential feature of the curriculum, particularly in secondary school. They provide an important and familiar structure for knowledge, offering a context for specialists to inspire, stretch and motivate.   (Scottish Government 2008: 20)

The old predilection for the academic curriculum in Scotland will not vanish by ministerial fiat, and what actually will happen in Scotland will thus depend on practice, on the 'specialists' cited but not explained in that quotation. Trusting the teachers, which Curriculum for Excellence does, must mean also trusting those who choose an approach to knowledge as traditional as Mr Gove's.

So the Scottish approach allows for Mr Gove's, just as it is a caricature to reduce his ideas to a mechanical philistinism. Both approaches are really elements of the always evolving tradition of liberal education. As Sheldon Rothblatt once noted (1976: 199):

> the phrase 'a liberal education' . . . enjoys an extraordinary continuity and has survived each of the revolutions that should have disposed of it. . . . The words continue to

exercise a hold on the imagination, and scarcely any educational change of significant proportions is undertaken without reference to some aspect of its history,

the common element being, in some form, the belief that 'liberal education [is] the pathway to civilisation' (Rothblatt 1976: 23).

CONCLUSIONS

Three points might be made in conclusion. The first is that there are far more continuities of culture, of opportunity, and of liberal ideas than the rhetoric of politics sometimes indicates (Raffe 2004). By this is meant continuities not only over space, though there are indeed greater similarities of social philosophy in the parts of Britain than is usually supposed, as we have seen. If Scotland secedes, it will not be directly because the country has a fundamentally different social philosophy from England. The continuities are also over time, and they help to consolidate the sense of a common culture. The values that led to the welfare state, and the values that underpinned a common system of education, continue to be strong. That is not because of anything specifically to do with Britishness, but rather because these values are part of the common culture of universalistic individualism that is found across the developed world.

The second point is about research. Research itself contributes to this process of standardisation, in that in order to compare social groups it has to create common categories in terms of which to compare. The only way in which we could prevent an impact from research on the maintenance of common criteria would be if we kept our results secret. So the inclination of academics to engage in public debate is itself a contribution to processes of standardisation.

The final point is that none of this really has much to say about the future of Britain as a constitutional entity. Scottish independence could happen without disturbing these commonalities, just as social values can be quite similar among Scandinavian countries, or indeed between them and other places, as we noted in passing earlier from the European Social Survey. The UK may be departing from common traditions so far as politics and specific policies are concerned—the means of social philosophy—but for the social traditions that really matter it would take much more than the ephemera of politics or even the accident of constitutional change to bring to an end the shared history of values, ideas, and principles.

Acknowledgements: I am grateful to Dr Fiona O'Hanlon (Edinburgh University) for comments on a draft of the paper, to Natalie Papanastasiou (Edinburgh University) for advice on specialist schools in England, and for comments from an anonymous referee and from audiences at the British Academy, and at the Policy and Governance research group in the School of Social and Political Science at Edinburgh University, where versions of the paper were given as lectures in March 2014.

REFERENCES

Anderson, R.D. (2006), *British Universities Past and Present* (London, Hambledon).

Arnold, M. (1960 [1869]), *Culture and Anarchy*, J. Dover Wilson (ed.) (Cambridge, Cambridge University Press).

Barker, R. (1972), *Education and Politics, 1900–1951* (Oxford, Oxford University Press).

Barr, N. (2010), *Paying for Higher Education: What Policies, in what Order?*, Submission to the Independent Review of Higher Education Funding and Student Finance, London School of Economics.

Barr, N. (2012), 'The Higher Education White Paper: the good, the bad, the unspeakable—and the next White Paper', *Social Policy and Administration*, 46: 483–508. http://dx.doi.org/10.1111/j.1467-9515.2012.00852.x

Barr, N. & Johnston, A. (2010), *Interest Subsidies on Student Loans: A Better Class of Drain* (London, Centre for the Economics of Education, London School of Economics).

BBC (2011), 'SNP Conference: Salmond in Free Education Pledge', 12 March, http://www.bbc.co.uk/news/uk-scotland-12711509, accessed 18 April 2014.

Beck, J. (2012), 'Reinstating knowledge: diagnoses and prescriptions for England's curriculum ills', *International Studies in Sociology of Education*, 22: 1–18. http://dx.doi.org/10.1080/09620214.2012.680322

Boli, J., Ramirez, F.O. & Meyer, J.W. (1985), 'Explaining the Origins and Expansion of Mass Education', *Comparative Education Review*, 29: 145–70. http://dx.doi.org/10.1086/446504

Boliver, V. & Swift, A. (2011), 'Do Comprehensive Schools Reduce Social Mobility?', *British Journal of Sociology*, 62: 89–110. http://dx.doi.org/10.1111/j.1468-4446.2010.01346.x

Brown, A., McCrone, D., Paterson, L. & Surridge, P. (1999), *The Scottish Electorate* (London, Macmillan). http://dx.doi.org/10.1057/9780230376823

Brown, G. (2012), speech at Edinburgh Book Festival, 13 August.

Brown, G. (2014), *My Scotland, Our Britain* (London, Simon & Schuster).

Chowdry, H., Dearden, L., Goodman, A. & Jin, W. (2012), 'The Distributional Impact of the 2012–13 Higher Education Funding Reforms in England', *Fiscal Studies*, 33: 211–36. http://dx.doi.org/10.1111/j.1475-5890.2012.00159.x

Crosland, A. (1956), *The Future of Socialism* (London, Jonathan Cape).

Crosland, A. (1974), *Socialism Now* (London, Jonathan Cape).

Dearden, L., Goodman, A. & Wyness, G. (2012), 'Higher Education Finance in the UK', *Fiscal Studies*, 33: 73–105. http://dx.doi.org/10.1111/j.1475-5890.2012.00153.x

Department for Education (2010), *The Importance of Teaching* (London, DfE).

Dewey, J. (1915), *School and Society* (Chicago, University of Chicago Press).

Douglas, J.W.B., Ross, J.M., Maxwell, S.M. M. & Walker, D.A. (1966), 'Differences in Test Score and in the Gaining of Selective Places for Scottish Children and those in England and Wales', *British Journal of Educational Psychology*, 36: 150–7. http://dx.doi.org/10.1111/j.2044-8279.1966.tb01863.x

The Economist (2013), 'Even if Scotland Votes to Stay in the United Kingdom, the Union is Fraying', 9 November.

Floud, J. & Halsey, A.H. (1957), 'Intelligence Tests, Social Class and Selection for Secondary Schools', *British Journal of Sociology*, 8: 33–39. http://dx.doi.org/10.2307/587403

Gove, M. (2008), 'Higher Standards, Freer Minds', Haberdashers' Aske's Education lecture, 18 November.

Gove, M. (2010), Speech to Conservative Party Conference, Birmingham, 5 October, http://centrallobby. politicshome.com/latestnews/article-detail/newsarticle/speech-in-full-michael-gove/, accessed 1 May 2014.

Gove, M. (2013), article in *Daily Mail*, 23 March.

Grek, S. (2009), 'Governing by Numbers: the PISA "Effect" in Europe', *Journal of Education Policy*, 24: 23–37. http://dx.doi.org/10.1080/02680930802412669

Hacking, I. (1990), *The Taming of Chance* (Cambridge, Cambridge University Press). http://dx.doi.org/10.1017/CBO9780511819766

Hatcher, R. (2011), 'The Conservative-Liberal-Democrat Coalition Government's "Free Schools" in England', *Educational Review*, 63: 485–503. http://dx.doi.org/10.1080/00131911.2011.616635

Hunt, T. (2013), 'Labour's New Education Chief Tristram Hunt Vows: I'm on a Crusade to Make Bad Schools History', *Daily Mirror*, 28 October, http://www.mirror.co.uk/news/uk-news/tristram-hunt-interview-im-crusade-2648047, accessed 14 February 2014.

The Independent (2013), 'Gove will Bury Pupils in Facts and Rules' (letter), 20 March.

Joppke, C. (2004), 'The Retreat of Multiculturalism in the Liberal State: Theory and Policy', *British Journal of Sociology*, 55: 237–57. http://dx.doi.org/10.1111/j.1468-4446.2004.00017.x

Kerckhoff, A.C., Fogelman, K., Crook, D. & Reeder, D. (1996), *Going Comprehensive in England and Wales* (London, Woburn Press).

Laski, H. (1923), 'Knowledge as a Civic Discipline', in H. Laski, *The Way Out: Essays on the Meaning and Purpose of Adult Education* (Oxford, Oxford University Press), 47–59.

Laski, H. (1930), *The Dangers of Obedience, and Other Essays* (New York, Harper and Brothers).

Lidström, A. (1999), 'Local School Choice Policies in Sweden', *Scandinavian Political Studies*, 22: 137–56. http://dx.doi.org/10.1111/1467-9477.00009

Lindbom, A. (2001), 'Dismantling the Social Democratic Welfare Model? Has the Swedish welfare state lost its defining characteristics?', *Scandinavian Political Studies*, 24:171–93. http://dx.doi.org/10.1111/1467-9477.00052

Lindsay, A.D. (1957 [1950]), 'Philosophy as a Criticism of Standards', paper read to The Scots Philosophical Club, September 1950, reprinted in A.D. Lindsay, *Selected Addresses* (privately published).

Lyons, F.S.L. (1973), *Ireland Since the Famine* (London: Fontana).

Machin, S. & Vernoit, J. (2011), *Changing School Autonomy: Academy Schools and their Introduction to England's Education* (London, Centre for the Economics of Education, London School of Economics).

Macwhirter, I. (2013), 'Scotland and England are Growing Apart. A No vote won't stop that', *Guardian*, 18 August.

Mill, J.S. (1861), *Considerations on Representative Government* (London, Parker, Son and Bourn).

Neave, G. (1976), 'The Development of Scottish Education, 1958–1972', *Comparative Education*, 12: 129–44. http://dx.doi.org/10.1080/0305006760120204

Nunn, T.P. (1920), *Education: Its Data and First Principles* (London, Edward Arnold).

Paterson, L. (2003), 'The Three Educational Ideologies of the British Labour Party', *Oxford Review of Education*, 29: 165–86. http://dx.doi.org/10.1080/0305498032000080666

Paterson, L. (2013), 'Comprehensive Education, Social Attitudes and Civic Engagement', *Longitudinal and Life Course Studies*, 4: 17–32.

Paterson, L. (2014), 'Competitive Opportunity and Liberal Culture: the significance of Scottish education in the twentieth century', *British Educational Research Journal*, 40: 397–416. http://dx.doi.org/10.1002/berj.3089

Porter, T. (1995), *Trust in Numbers* (Princeton, Princeton University Press).

Priestley, M. & Humes, W. (2010), 'The Development of Scotland's Curriculum for Excellence: Amnesia and déjà vu', *Oxford Review of Education*, 36: 345–61. http://dx.doi.org/10.1080/03054980903518951

Raffe, D. (2004), 'How Distinctive is Scottish Education? Five perspectives on distinctiveness', *Scottish Affairs*, 49: 50–72.

Ramirez, F.O. & Boli, J. (1987), 'The Political Construction of Mass Schooling: European origins and worldwide institutionalisation', *Sociology of Education*, 60: 2–17. http://dx.doi.org/10.2307/2112615

Richards, S. (2013), 'Scotland is Going it Alone—Regardless of the Referendum', *Guardian*, 23 August.

Rothblatt, S.R. (1976), *Tradition and Change in English Liberal Education* (London, Faber and Faber).

Rothblatt, S.R. (2007), *Education's Abiding Moral Dilemma* (Oxford, Symposium).

Russell, M. (2013), 'From Good to Great: building equity and success in Scottish education', speech at Glasgow University, 27 March. http://www.scotland.gov.uk/News/Speeches/school-attainment-27032013, accessed 14 February 2014.

Scott, D. (1971), *A.D. Lindsay* (Oxford, Blackwell).

Scottish Education Department (1947), *Secondary Education* (Edinburgh, HMSO).

Scottish Government (2008), *Curriculum for Excellence: Building the Curriculum 3* (Edinburgh, Scottish Government).

Sturgeon, N. (2012), 'Bringing the Powers Home to Build a Better Nation', speech at Strathclyde University, 3 December, http://www.scotland.gov.uk/News/Speeches/better-nation-031212, accessed 18 April 2014.

Tawney, R.H. (1964 [1953]), 'The Workers' Educational Association and Adult Education', in R.H. Tawney, *The Radical Tradition* (Harmondsworth, Penguin), 86–97.

Taylor-Gooby, P. (2012), 'Root and Branch Restructuring to Achieve Major Cuts: the Social Policy Programme of the 2010 UK Coalition Government', *Social Policy and Administration*, 46: 61–82. http://dx.doi.org/10.1111/j.1467-9515.2011.00797.x

Wakeling, P. & Jefferies, P. (2013), 'The Effect of Tuition Fees on Student Mobility: the UK and Ireland as a natural experiment', *British Educational Research Journal*, 39: 491–513.

West, A. & Bailey, E. (2013), 'The Development of the Academies Programme: "privatising" school-based education in England, 1986–2013', *British Journal of Educational Studies*, 61, 137–59. http://dx.doi.org/10.1080/00071005.2013.789480

What Scotland Thinks web site, http://whatscotlandthinks.org/questions/how-do-you-think-you-would-vote-in-the-european-election#line, accessed 17 April 2014.

White, J. (2011), 'Gove's on the Bac Foot with a White Paper Stuck in 1868', *Times Educational Supplement*, 21 January.

Young, M. (2011), 'The Return to Subjects: a sociological perspective on the UK Coalition government's approach to the 14–19 curriculum', *The Curriculum Journal*, 22: 265–78. http://dx.doi.org/10.1080/09585176.2011.574994

Note on the author: Lindsay Paterson is Professor of Educational Policy in the School of Social and Political Science, University of Edinburgh. He has written extensively on the expansion of higher education, on social mobility, on the relationship between education and civic values, and on Scottish politics. Among his recent relevant publications are:

Paterson, L. (2014), 'Education, social attitudes and social participation among adults in Britain', *Sociological Research Online*, 19 (1). http://dx.doi.org/10.5153/sro.3235

Paterson, L. (2009), 'Civic values and the subject matter of educational courses', *Oxford Review of Education*, 35: 81–98. http://dx.doi.org/10.1080/03054980802351801

Paterson, L. (2008), 'Political attitudes, social participation and social mobility: a longitudinal analysis', *British Journal of Sociology*, 59: 413–34. http://dx.doi.org/10.1111/j.1468-4446.2008.00201.x

lindsay.paterson@ed.ac.uk

This article was first published in 2014 in *Journal of the British Academy* (ISSN 2052-7217).

To cite the article: Lindsay Paterson (2014), 'Education and opportunity: Is the UK departing from a common tradition?', *Journal of the British Academy*, 2: 101–123. DOI 10.5871/jba/002.101

Journal of the British Academy, **2**, 125–152. DOI 10.5871/jba/002.125
Posted 3 December 2014. © The British Academy 2014

Charlemagne and Europe

Raleigh Lecture on History
read 12 November 2013

JINTY NELSON
Fellow of the Academy

Abstract: This paper, 'Charlemagne and Europe', is a revised and expanded form of the lecture I read on 12 November 2013. I begin by asking what Europe has meant to medieval historians in recent times, focusing on some answers given in the 1990s and around the year 2000, and reflecting on the different ways Charlemagne is being commemorated in different parts of Europe now, 1,200 years after his death. I then re-examine Charlemagne through evidence from his own time, as a ruler of a recognisably European empire, and, in the light of recent research and new approaches, I reconsider his record as a political figure. A brief survey of his posthumous reputation as man and myth in the middle ages, and after, leads into a closer look at the roles assigned to him in post-war rhetoric. Finally I ask whether Charlemagne has, or might have, anything to offer Europeans today.

Keywords: Charlemagne, Europe, empire, commemoration, myth

To be invited to give the Raleigh Lecture is, as it has been since it was endowed almost a century ago, a tremendous honour. It also presents a new challenge, for the British Academy is changing with the times, and today's Raleigh Lecturer is now invited to connect the Academy with a broad public. The occasion has become part of the Academy's opening-wide of its doors. Implicit in my chosen title, therefore, is an assignment to ask if or why Charlemagne and Europe should ever have mattered, and to whom, and to show why this pairing could still matter today to a broad public interested in history. Sir Walter Raleigh, whom the Lecture commemorates, and whose *History of the World in Five Books* was published in 1614, took seriously the wide dimensions of Europe 'with all the islands adjoining and compassing it about'. The Europe of my theme was and is one that included the isles.

Christopher Clark, author of a fine book on 1914, *The Sleepwalkers*, said recently: 'our [meaning British] culture is obsessed by anniversaries'.[1] In 2014, Britons are

---

[1] *The Guardian*, 16 Jan. 2014, 22.

commemorating, as are very many others, but perhaps with particular British determination, the anniversary of 1914. In 2014 too, many Europeans are commemorating
another anniversary, the 1,200th anniversary of the death of Charlemagne, on 28
January 814. The planned commemorations are very unevenly distributed, though. In
Germany, there are to be quite a number, including a large exhibition at Aachen and
several big academic events, and at least two conferences in France. Elsewhere in
Continental Europe there is not much to report, not even in Italy, or Catalonia, where
some public consciousness of Charlemagne's legacy might have been expected. In the
UK, there took place on 28 January 2014, the anniversary of Charlemagne's actual
death-day, an interdisciplinary commemoration in London (involving some 200
people including sixth-formers), and a small academic symposium in Edinburgh. And
that seems to be it: not a lot for a Europe of 28.

This concerns me as a historian of Europe. Myths apart—and there have been
plenty of those—Charlemagne has loomed large in the academic study of European
history and culture since recognisably modern university curricula came into being in
the 19th century, and especially in Germany. The critical editions of texts by the
Monumenta Germaniae Historica allowed Charlemagne's reign to be examined critically.[2] Political events in Germany and France generated huge interest in Charlemagne
and his legacy not just among university students but for a wide reading public that,
later in the 19th century when national governments made schooling compulsory,
came to include schoolchildren. German and French textbook writers produced
attractive books on Charlemagne, naturally with different spins on his significance for
the two different nations who competed for the role of Charlemagne's heir.[3] The divergent branches of the same thematic stock flourished into the 20th century; and in
Germany, divergent offshoots generated ideological conflict that was brief but fierce.[4]
There will be more to say presently about divergence. But here at the outset, I want to
raise the question of what has become of Charlemagne since the Second World War,
and in our times. One answer is that he has become an icon of Europe. Another is that
he has become an irrelevance to Europe. This lecture's object is to explain why both
answers are true, up to a point—but also to explore the possibility that the second is
truer than the first, then to see how that has come about, and finally to ask if the icon
can be remodelled, or re-imagined, so as to become helpful in connecting Europe past
with Europe present.

In 2001, I was invited to give a talk to a scholarly audience in Warsaw on
'Charlemagne—the father of Europe?'[5] I answered my own question with five reasons

---

[2] Knowles (1963: chap. 2).
[3] Morrissey (1997); Kapfhammer (1993); Kintzinger (2005).
[4] Lambert (2012: 97–125); Lambert (2013: 13–6).
[5] Nelson (2002: 3–20).

for saying yes: first his empire in territorial terms bore some resemblance to what was to come—admittedly long after—in the shape of the EEC, and less obviously the EU, which in 2001 did not include Poland though the Poles' application was already on the table; second, a conception of Europe as containing multiple laws and languages, combined with governmental decentralisation, and willingness, in practice, to coexist with neighbouring peoples, seemed to foreshadow such modern arrangements as subsidiarity; as did, third, the empire's mixed economy, in which public fiscal interests operated alongside 'private and non-fiscal ones', including market exchange, with a potential for the development of urbanism; fourth, a style of consensual government in which oaths of loyalty were sworn in return for royal acknowledgement of responsibilities; and fifth and finally, a government determined to realise justice, and demanding that all (women were included, even if seldom mentioned in official pronouncements) who lived in its territories should try to do the same at micro-level, prefigured in some ways the rights to justice that modern states and citizens are concerned to defend.

That was 2001. By then, I had been inspired by Jacques Le Goff's confident insistence, in the preface to each volume in the series he began to edit in 1994, celebrating the year of his seventieth birthday, *The Making of Europe*, that 'a Europe without history would be orphaned and unhappy', and that it was on the combined foundation of Europe's history and geography, 'rich and creative, united yet diverse—that Europe's future will be built'.[6] Invited to Budapest in 1994 to speak on 'Les peripheries de l'Occident médiévale', and asked about the different evolutionary speeds of 'the two or three Europes' proposed by the Hungarian historian Jenö Szücs, Le Goff protested that this perspective 'made little sense from his point of view . . . [a view in which] Europe extended from the *Ultima Thule* of Ireland to Jerusalem, from Santiago de Compostela to the lands of the ferocious Scythians. Europe was, and is, something to be made and remade, which cannot be done by enumerating the defections of internal and external peripheries, but rather by integrating them while learning from their differences.'[7]

Both past and future look different today; and I would put the points I made in 2001 differently today, partly because I didn't make enough allowance for Europe's changed realities, and meanings, over recent times, partly because I am no longer sure that it's plausible, even with a three-line *mutatis mutandis*, to make any very specific claims for Charlemagne paternity of today's Europe, and partly because it matters where as well as when you ask a question. Yet still ringing in my ears is Le Goff's clarion call for a perspective that integrates rather than divides. In Germany, no fewer than three books on Charlemagne, plus one on Einhard have appeared in 2013 or are

---

[6] The first volume came out in 1994, and more than twenty have followed.
[7] Klanizcay (1997: 223–37), at 236–7 (where 'defects' rather than 'defections' seems to have been meant).

imminent.[8] All these books have got, or will get, reviewed in national broadsheet newspapers. All, it must be said, are Germany-focused, and yet all devote some thought to the European dimension of their theme. If German minds have not lost long-term historical memory, and encompass 814 as well as 1914, they also have room for the space that is Europe.

Certainly there are historians writing in French, Italian and English today who would still assign Charlemagne a key role in Europe's making: that of inventor and promoter of a cultural renewal that historians have called and still call the Carolingian Renaissance. The term is a modern construct, but the renewal it denoted was real to the men and women who made it and absorbed it. Renovating, and 'baptizing', ancient knowledge was a task for an intellectual elite of professional clergy. Had it stayed in those hands, Jacques Le Goff would have been right to call this 'hoarding not sowing', and to deny it the name of 'renaissance'.[9] But it did more than sow, it harvested and nurtured and scattered again across Charlemagne's Europe. It evolved, already in Charlemagne's lifetime, and then over centuries, into something that resembled mass engagement, engaging lay people too, peasants as well as elites, women as well as men, in reforming religious structures and practices not only in large churches but small and local ones, not only in big houses and at courts, but in small houses and villages.[10] The teachings of the clergy reached the laity through sermons and admonitions and ritual ministrations, scholarly supply meeting lay demand. Vernaculars as well as Latin were the media. Not just a set of directives and duties and dues imposed from above, this renaissance included responses from below: as for example when a letter from Charlemagne himself reported that he had found prospective godparents failing to pass the test of knowing the Lord's Prayer and the Creed and sent them home again to learn, or when within months of Charlemagne's requiring a general oath of fidelity in the spring of 802 a Bavarian charter dated 14 August 802 records locals at a legal assembly actually having sworn the oath.

Mutual communication and exchange underlay the making of Charlemagne's Europe. Far beyond it, the same processes persisted and spread throughout what would later be called, understandably if somewhat misleadingly, Latin Europe: understandably because of the need to distinguish Latin-using west from Greek-using east, or Byzantium; misleadingly, because within the west, Latin was the language of the Church and of lay elites, but the vast majority spoke forms of a *lingua romana* (a Roman language) that increasingly diverged both from classical Latin and from each

---

[8] Weinfurter (2014); Patzold, (2013); Bredekamp (2014); Fried (2014). See also Hack (2011).

[9] Le Goff (1957: 11–14).

[10] For a small selection of many recent and forthcoming works but all with many suggestions for further reading, see Mayr-Harting (2002: 113–24); Nelson (2001: 76–88); Wood (2006); Ganz (2010: 18–32); Nelson (2014a); Diesenberger (2014, forthcoming).

other, and in the reigns of Charlemagne and his heirs, basic Christian texts like the Lord's Prayer and the Creed were being translated into and written down in Germanic vernaculars.

Rather as some powerful politicians in modern times have lured academics, including those learned in humanities, perhaps in history especially, to their court-equivalents, *mutatis mutandis*, Charlemagne lured scholars to his court. This renewal was never the preserve of the Franks: most of the scholars at, or connected with, the court of Charlemagne were not Franks, that is, they did not belong to the people to whom Charlemagne himself belonged, who lived in the lands now known as northern France, Belgium, the Netherlands and Luxembourg, and west Germany. The scholars came from other places where Roman Christian culture was deeply if differently rooted: Italy, Spain, and from the British Isles, Ireland and especially Anglo-Saxon England.[11] The most prolific and famous of them was Alcuin, lured from York *c.*786: a polymath, interested in astronomy and philosophy, theology and liturgy, rhetoric and history, a scholar who was not a monk but a sub-deacon, that is, a secular cleric, with a teaching vocation that necessarily involved him in using the media of his day.[12] His teaching at Charlemagne's court was diffused far beyond it by means of the script which was the forerunner of the one you are reading at this moment: Caroline minuscule. The language he spoke and taught in was a pure Latin, as taught at York, and he frowned on the romance languages he encountered on the Continent. He encouraged friends and former students at York to imitate the keeping of annals, as practised in Francia. He wrote a great many letters, to other scholars but also to kings and royals, and elite personages, in Charlemagne's realm and beyond it, in his homeland, Northumbria, and in other kingdoms in the isles of Britain.[13] Europe's geographical identity was real in Alcuin's mind.

* * *

Alcuin was heir to long scholarly traditions. Herodotus, the father of history, in the 5th century BC wondered 'why three names [Asia, Africa, Europa] had been laid on the earth [that were] all names of women'. Patrick Geary observed in 2006 that origin-myths typically begin with women.[14] Apropos Europa, St Augustine commented, talking about pagans and Christians in 426, that history and fable appealed to different audiences.[15] Isidore of Seville described the ways in which scriptural terms fitted onto parts of circle of the earth, Europe being the area occupied by the descendants

[11] Brown (1994: 1–51); Fried (1997: 25–43); see also Nelson (2015, forthcoming).
[12] Bullough (2004), posthumously published (the author had died in 2002); see further Ganz (2003: *passim*).
[13] Garrison (1997: 97–124); Story (2003).
[14] Geary (2006).
[15] Augustine ([426], 1955), XVIII, 12.

of Noah's third son Japhet.[16] The earliest example of Christian scholars' so-called 'T-O' map of Europe dates from the 9th century and shows Europe constituted by the lands west of the River Don (Tanis)—modern Ukraine, the Carpathian Basin and Balkans, and Greece.[17] But Europe had special meaning for what turns out to be a more specific group. Virtually every early medieval text that refers to *Europa* was written by someone who was Irish or Anglo-Saxon. Cathwulf, for instance, probably Anglo-Saxon, possibly Irish, wrote *c*.775 when Charlemagne had just taken over the Lombard kingdom in Italy urging him to 'thank God for raising you to the honour of the glory of the *regnum Europae*'.[18] Alcuin in 793, not long after returning to Francia after a 3-year stay in England, heard that the monastery of Lindisfarne had been attacked by pagan Northmen, and he wrote to the abbot offering some history as consolation: 'nearly all *Europa* was laid waste [in the 5th century] by . . . the Goths and Huns but now, thanks to God, Europe shines adorned with churches as the heavens shine with stars'.[19] A generation before Alcuin, a much wider audience had been evoked by the probably Irish author, *c*.700, of the *Life of St Gertrude*: 'Who living in *Europa* does not know the loftiness, the names and the localities of [Gertrude's] lineage?'—'as if', commented Karl Leyser, 'there were a European public to discuss such matters'.[20] That 'as if . . .' tempts the thought that such a public did exist, and that lay elites too were familiar with a concept of Europe that combined mythological and geographical meanings with a social reality of courts, halls, linked with family-endowed churches: places where 'birth, names and localities' mattered, milieux not wholly confined to elites. The very people portrayed by the Roman poet Virgil as in a land 'sundered far from the whole world', that is, people in and from the British Isles, where Charles never ruled, reached out to what would become his empire in their claims to belong within Europe.

* * *

The author of the epic 'Charles the Great and Pope Leo', one of a number of poets at

[16] Isidore of Seville, *Etymologiae* XIV, at points in the text that differ in different manuscripts, and *De natura rerum* following c. 48, 'de partibus terrae'. See below, n. 17.

[17] The 'T-O' Map (in French 'la carte OT') was so-called because within the O of the *orbis terrarum* (circle of lands) the cross-bar of a T formed schematically by the rivers Don and Nile marked off Asia in the upper half of the circle, while in the lower half of the circle the T's column formed schematically by the Mediterranean divided Europe to the onlooker's left and Africa to the right: see Gautier Dalché (1997), chap. VIII, 693–764, esp. 705–8, 709–33, and Plates I, II (9th-century), III, VIII (9th-century). Gautier Dalché has demolished the idea that Isidore's own text (or any now-lost early copy) was accompanied by a T-O Map, though he thinks that later readings of Isidore's text could have given rise to such a map.

[18] Cathwulf to Charles, Epistolae variorum Carlo magno regnante no. 7, in Dümmler, (1895: 501–5, at 503).

[19] Alcuin, *Ep*. 20, to Bishop Higbald of Lindisfarne, in Dümmler (1895: 56–8, at 57).

[20] Leyser (1992: 25–47, at 28–9).

or linked to Charles's court, was the only one to call his patron *pater Europae*, thereby situating the king's paternity firmly in the present, *c*.800, and in a world of patriarchal authority linked to the classical past.[21] The theme of the epic was Charles's reign up to July 799: his deeds in war and in peace, his learning and patronage, his building of Aachen. There was a vivid description of Charles's royal hunt preceded by a splendid court procession. The rest of the poem told how the king, while taking a nap during the hunt, had a terrible dream that Pope Leo III had been attacked in Rome (this was on 25 April 799, when an enemy faction blinded him and cut out his tongue but by a miracle he recovered) and had fled Rome to journey across the Alps, and how Charles received him at a great military assembly at Paderborn in Saxony. The details on the ritual staging of Leo's arrival and reception suggest a date of composition not far from the time of these events.

The poet began by imagining himself a sailor, his boat blown 'to where the light-house or beacon of Europe [*Europae pharus*] gleams with light from afar'. Later, the poet extolled 'King Charles . . . | the venerable apex of Europe [*Europae apex*], best father, hero, | Augustus, and also mighty in the city where a second Rome | flowering anew, arises with its mighty mass to great heights.' The king was described setting out for the hunt, as 'the venerable beacon of Europe'. The poem's climax was the meeting at Paderborn of 'the king, *pater Europae*, and Leo, the highest pastor in the world'. Charles makes a tremendous show of his military power; and when Pope Leo comes close, he's astonished to see 'the peoples of such diverse parts of the world, and how varied they are in looks, speech, clothes and weapons'.

The king as lighthouse belonged with the nautical metaphor of the poet's voyage towards his patron.[22] Charles in 811 ordered the rebuilding of the actual lighthouse at Boulogne 'put up in antiquity for the guiding of sailors'.[23] Imperial lighthouse-building at (probably) Boulogne is mentioned in the Roman historian Suetonius's *Life of Caligula*. Charles's courtier Einhard (d.840) drew heavily on Suetonius's *Lives of the Twelve Caesars* in his own *Life of Charles* written in (probably) 829.[24] What makes

---

[21] 'Karolus magnus et Leo papa' Dümmler (1881a: ll. 1–536, 366–79) (here attributed to Angilbert). The authorship of the poem is much debated: Schaller (1976: 136–68), greatly improves on an older case for Einhard as author; Godman (1985: 22–4, 196–207) (translating ll. 1–176 only), proposes '?Einhard' as author; and Godman (1986: 82–91), leaves the authorship uncertain; Stella (2001: 19–33) proposes Moduin as author; Hack (1999: iii: 19–33, at 22–4) sits on the fence; Scheck (2012: 13–38) feistily proposes a nun as author, but disregards the major themes of the poem. See below.

[22] See Curtius (1953: 128–30).

[23] *Annales regni Francorum* (*s.a.* 811), ed. F. Kurze (1895: 135). Sea-borne enemies were already active in 810 when a Danish fleet of '200 ships'(!) attacked the Frisian Islands, possibly en route for the mouths of the Loire and the Garonne: Astronomus, *Vita Hludowici imperatoris* c. 15, ed. Tremp (1995: 325 and n. 181).

[24] Tischler (2001: i: 151–235).

Einhard plausible as the author, perhaps 30 years before, of 'Charles the Great and Pope Leo' is that he is mentioned in a poem on the court written by Alcuin in 796 as a skilled designer and manager of great building works, hence his nickname 'Bezaleel', after the temple-builder in Exodus 31: 2–5, and also as 'expert in poems about Troy', that is, Virgil's *Aeneid*.[25] 'Apex of Europe' comes in the lengthy Virgil-inspired section on the construction of 'second Rome' at Aachen, including its splendid church, still to be seen today. Einhard, in charge of all this building, perhaps rebuilt the lighthouse too, and even saw to its being mentioned in the court-produced Royal Frankish Annals. Empire was being reinvented in practical as well as ideological dimensions. Einhard's poem (and I am going to assume it is Einhard's) conveys the built and written legacies of ancient Rome, and the geographical extent of Charles's realm as viewed from Aachen in 799.

If poetry were all there was to it, there would be room for scepticism. But by 799, there were signs in a range of prose genres that Charles's sights were fixed on empire in the Roman sense of an accumulation of provinces. In 790, a huge treatise correcting Greek (that is, Byzantine) errors on images and image-veneration was begun at Charles's behest. The preface gave Charles's title an imperial ring: king of the Franks, the Gauls, Germany, Italy, and the provinces neighbouring these.[26] At the Council of Frankfurt in July 794, the bishops of the various provinces sent letters in varied styles which could also be seen as representing multiple lands and peoples, as in the Roman Empire.[27]

Charlemagne's wars looked Roman too. They played a crucial part in his empire-building in the 790s: new momentum, vital for military success, was gained not so much by wars against the Saxons which continued, on and off, for 30 years, but the wars launched from Bavaria in 791–3. Using old Roman military roads and forts along the Danube river, as well as the river itself, Charlemagne's armies and boatmen took the eastern frontier (or at least zone of influence) to Rome's old frontier region, Pannonia, which resulted in the annexation of what would later become Austria and part of Hungary.[28] In 795–6, armies recruited from plural peoples led by generals appointed by Charles crushed the power of the Avars, a Eurasian people long settled in Central Europe. Vast quantities of Avar loot were brought back to Aachen: Einhard wrote in *The Life of Charles*, 'the Franks seemed to have been poor until then, so rich

[25] Alcuin, *Carmen* XXVI, in (Dümmler, 1881b: l. 21, 245): 'Beleel [i.e. Bezeleel] Hiliacis [i.e. Ilianis] doctus in odis'.

[26] *Opus Caroli regis contra Synodum* [i.e. against the Council of Nicaea of 787] (*Libri Carolini*), ed. Freeman & Meyvaert (1998: 97).

[27] Concilium Franconofurtense of 794, ed. Werminghoff (1908: 110–71, at 111–56). See Close (2011: 101–19, 146–53). See also Fried (1994: 25–34).

[28] Wolfram (1987: 253–60); Pohl (1988).

did they now become'.[29] Though Einhard characteristically highlighted the Franks, they were not the only beneficiaries. A contemporary Anglo-Saxon author writing annals at York, presumably informed by Alcuin from Aachen, wrote that transporting all the gold and silver and precious robes of silk from Avaria [central Hungary] to Aachen took 15 wagons, each pulled by 4 oxen.[30] The *Royal Frankish Annals* reported: 'God's steward [Charles] sent a large part of the treasure to Rome to the thresholds of the apostles, but the rest he distributed to his great men, clerical and lay, and to his other faithful men.'[31] Roman-style triumph was followed by imperial largesse. The contemporary Byzantine chronicler Theophanes (died 817/818), registered the new reach of Charlemagne. Theophanes' historical work went back to antiquity, and included information on the Avars from the 5th century down to the 8th. He clearly had in his mind a division of space that resembled Isidore's and gave rise to a T-O map of the world. Theophanes consistently locates the Avars in Europe, that is, west of the Don, Ukraine and the Balkans, and he distinguishes them from other enemies of the 'Romans' in Asia.[32]

As it happened, there was what might be retrospectively identified as a Europe-wide window of opportunity, opening onto eastern as well as western parts, in the years between 797 and 802. To appreciate the window, it's necessary to stand back, and look at the early years of Carolingian rule in the Frankish kingdom. Between the 720s and the 750s, two successive Byzantine emperors had commanded the destruction of icons, whose veneration had bonded for centuries the whole of Christendom, in east and west.[33] The first Carolingian king Pippin, Charles's father, stood firm in support of icon-veneration and a series of popes denounced Greek heresy. But this did not prevent growing contacts with the Greeks, sometimes Pippin taking the initiative, sometimes responding to theirs. There was an attempt to forge a dynastic marriage alliance in 767, when the Greek Emperor Constantine V urged Pippin to agree to the marriage of his daughter to the young Byzantine emperor Leo IV.[34] Pippin died in 768, and the princess became an abbess. In 774, Charlemagne took power in most of Italy, in a near-bloodless conquest.[35] This I think was the most important single

[29] Einhard (1911: 16).

[30] On these 'York Annals', the so-called *Annales Nordhumbrani*, preserved in Symeon of Durham's (12th-century) *Historia regum* (*s.a.* 795), see Story (2003: 101).

[31] *Annales regni Francorum* (*s.a.* 796: 98, 99).

[32] Mango & Scott (1997: 446–7).

[33] For this and an excellent account of what followed, see Noble (2009: 46–110, 140–5); see also McCormick (2004: 221–41).

[34] *Codex Carolinus*, ed. Gundlach (1892: no. 45: 562); see McCormick (1994: i: 130–1).

[35] Cathwulf to Charlemagne (see above, n. 18), 502, where this is the seventh of God's blessings on the king: 'Alpes intrasti, inimicis fugientibus, opulentissimam quoque civitatem etiam Papiam cum rege sine cruoris effusione et insuper cum omnibus thesauris eius adprehendisti.'

moment in Charlemagne's reign. It recreated what had been the transalpine axis of the western Roman Empire, linking Gaul with Italy under one ruler. Still more important, it brought the Franks into quite new relationships with a set of Mediterranean powers, including the papacy but also Byzantium. In 781, a year after Leo IV's death, envoys of his widow Irene, now the regent, came west to seek Charles's eldest daughter Hrotrude as a bride for the ten-year old Constantine VI.[36] What was envisaged was a traditional diplomatic alliance, where the bride was given by her parents and sent to live in her husband's land. During her betrothal, Hrotrude prepared herself by studying 'Greek language and literature and Roman imperial ways' with a scholar sent from Constantinople.[37] The decision of 'the most pious Eirene' and her son Constantine in 786 to restore icon veneration was intended to win support in the east and to restore harmonious relations with the papacy and the Franks. But Charles's response was at first hostile. He knew that the Greeks were intriguing against him on the southern border of his Italian kingdom, with the duke of Benevento, de facto a separate Lombard principality. In 788, Charles broke off Hrotrude's betrothal (let's hope she did not see all that learning of Greek as a waste of time), personally led a war against a Greek force that had landed in Benevento, and won a great battle: Alcuin wrote to an Irish friend, '4,000 Greeks were slain and 1,000 have been taken captive'.[38] News (and this news sounds reliable) travelled from one end of Europe to the other.

By the late 790s, the situation had changed dramatically. In a classic royal family scenario—as the anthropologist Jack Goody pointed out: 'the history of monarchy is stained with the blood of close kin'[39]—relations between Irene and her son had deteriorated. His lacklustre performance as emperor enabled her to stage a coup in August 797: she had him blinded in such a way that (unlike Pope Leo) he could make no come-back; her five-year stint as empress regnant astonished contemporaries. She sent embassies in 797 and 798, to seek 'peace and alliance' with Charles. He returned envoys of his own.[40] These were times of many travels. When the pope, miraculously healed, fled to Charles's protection in Francia in July 799, envoys from Constantinople were with him at Paderborn.[41]

Charlemagne may well have had personal experience of being stained with the blood of close kin. After his younger brother's death back in December 771, his widow had fled with her sons to Italy 'for no apparent reason, having spurned her husband's

[36] *Annales Mosellani* (*s.a.* 781), ed. Lappenberg (1859: 497).

[37] Theophanes, *Chronicle* [*s.a.* 781/782], ed. Mango & Scott (628).

[38] Alcuin, *Ep.* 7 [to Colcu], 32.

[39] Goody (1966: 142).

[40] *Annales regni Francorum* (*s.a.* 797, 798: 100–1, 104–5). For the evidence of the so-called 'Cologne Notice', see Nelson (2007a: chap. XII: 17).

[41] *Annales Guelferbytani* (*s.a.* 799), MGH SS I, 45: 'Et hic [ad Phaderprunnin] venit papa Leo ad eum et alii Romani consiliatores eius 203; et missi imperatissa [*sic*] ibi fuerunt.'

brother': thus Charlemagne's biographer Einhard writing disingenuously or deeply ironically in *c.*829.[42] In Italy, during the early months of 774 in which Charlemagne consolidated his power in northern Italy, he captured his nephews. They are never heard of again. In 806, in the projected division of the *regnum* after his death, Charlemagne forbade any of his sons to 'cause to be accused before him, to kill or mutilate or blind or tonsure against their will' any of their nephews, 'our grandsons'.[43] Bad memories lay behind those words. When it came to ruthlessness Irene and Charles were a match for one another. Observing this is not to condemn but to understand. Both were in positions of high office in hereditary succession systems which Goody's larger view enables European historians to see in their own histories as structurally requiring dynastic exclusion, shedding, demotion, or being 'quietly liquidated' in a wicked uncle scenario.[44]

Could this hard-bitten middle-aged pair (they were aged respectively 52 and perhaps 50) have contemplated marriage? According to Theophanes, they could— though he imputes the proposal to Charlemagne.[45] True, they lived 2,250 km apart. But chaste spiritual marriage of elderly couples was a venerable Christian tradition, and the role of women in peace-making was an even more general and not specifically Christian one. Their rule together could, as Theophanes put it, 'unite Eastern and Western parts', meaning parts of Europe. In the west, Alcuin's letters reverberated with biblically derived warnings: '*tempora periculosa sunt.* These are dangerous times . . .'[46] In Charlemagne's imperial coronation by the pope in Rome as emperor of the Romans on Christmas Day 800 were many meanings, but one was eschatological, that is, it pertained to measurings of time and prophesies about the end of time. Calculations based on the Book of Daniel's six ages reckoned the end of the sixth age would fall at the end of 800, or, to be precise, and since writers of annals frequently reckoned the new year from Christmas Day, it would fall on 24 December 800. Roman prophesies were reworked and amplified in the 7th-century work on the Apocalypse by a Syriac writer Pseudo-Methodius, translated into Latin early in the 8th century, to predict 'a Last Emperor of the Greeks, that is, the Romans, who would come out against the enemies of God, establish himself in Jerusalem, destroy the Son of Perdition, and

---

[42] Einhard, *Vita Karoli* c. 3, 6: '. . . defuncto Karlomanno, uxor et filii . . . Italiam fuga petiit et nullis existentibus causis, spreto mariti fratre, sub Desiderii regis Langobardorum patrocinium se cum liberis suis contulit'. Translators have handled this statement delicately.

[43] *Divisio regni*, ed. Boretius (1883: 130).

[44] Goody, 'Introduction' (1966: 24–39, esp. 29–34).

[45] Theophanes, *Chronicle*, ed. Mango & Scott (653).

[46] Brandes, (1997: i: 49–79, at 66–70) pointing out that the future tense in 2 Tim. 3, 1: 'in novissimis diebus instabunt tempora periculosa', frequently cited by Alcuin, was turned into a present tense in a number of the adaptations of this warning in his own letters: Epp. 116, 121, 122, 174, 193, 206, in MGH Epp. KA II: 171, 176, 179, 288, 320, 342.

ascend Golgotha to place his crown upon the Cross'.[47] In the late 790s (there's something about the '90s isn't there?), men interested in prophecies were to be found close to both Irene and Charlemagne.[48] Archbishop Hildebald of Cologne, Charlemagne's archchancellor, had a collection of calculations and synchronicities made which included: 'in 798 AD king Charles received one third of the people of Saxony as hostages, and envoys came from Greece to hand over *regnum et imperium* to him'.[49] Not everyone thought about or knew, let alone succumbed to, the terrors of the end-time. But eschatology was grist to the rumour-mills of courts in Aachen and Constantinople, and also Jerusalem whence the patriarch in 799 sent an envoy to Charlemagne with relics from the holy sepulchre. The king responded by sending back an envoy, whom the patriarch sent back along with two envoys of his own in 800, 'bearing the keys of the sepulchre and the keys of the city and mount Zion, with a banner'.[50] They arrived at Rome on 23 December 800. These people were capable of timing long-distance travel connections to a T. Shrewd diplomatic plans jostled with eschatological fantasies in the brains of Charles and Irene and their counsellors. Could the problem of the imperial title be solved at a stroke in this window of opportunity?

As things turned out, it couldn't—but not because the solution itself was unthinkable. The window closed when a former henchman of Irene's removed the empress from power on 31 October 802, and later that same day had himself crowned emperor in the Great Church, Haghia Sophia. From this moment, *femineum imperium* was a thing of the past (Irene died in exile a few months later). Normal service had been resumed as soon as possible. Intermittent hostilities and negotiations between east and west ended only when a two-emperor solution was agreed in 811/812 between the Emperor of the Romans (meaning Greeks) in the east and the emperor (without further definition) in the west. There followed a long-term stand-off. As for a united Europe: that had already been postponed indefinitely by the time Charlemagne died on 28 January 814. Soon springing to life were fictions and fantasies about him.

This is a good time to pause and take stock: to assess from the vantage-point of 814 how historians nowadays assess Charlemagne's achievement, making allowances for what he himself could not possibly have achieved, or even conceived. My focus in this section will be, as it were, on Charles before Charlemagne, without anachronism, and on his government's impact across much of what is now Europe. The effectiveness of that government is currently being reaffirmed, chiefly because the administrative

---

[47] Brandes (1997: 51–63); see now also Latowsky (2013).

[48] Theophanes, *Chronicle*, ed. Mango & Scott (638–9); Brandes (1997: 56–7).

[49] See Brandes (1997: 56). For a convincing reconstruction of how the York Annals, and specifically their account of 800, were compiled (cf. above, n. 30), see Story (2003: 112–26, esp. 115).

[50] *Annales regni Francorum* (*s.a.* 799, 800: 108–13).

records have been undergoing an overdue re-evaluation.[51] The surviving records are being recognised for what they are: chance survivals, tips of an iceberg. There were a lot of records about in Charles's realm, and in them his agents were encouraged to see themselves as office-holders, competent accountants, made literally accountable. I have chosen just one such record, both for its exemplary significance, and because though long known it has only very recently become possible to appreciate, thanks to the fine work of Michael McCormick.[52] This is a copy, perhaps made in the late 820s in the same routine administrative format as the original, that is, a roll, of a document made in 808. *Breve Commematorii*, 'Summary of a report' could not look more ordinary. In fact it is quite *extra*ordinary. It reports on the houses of God and monasteries in the Holy Land viewed, and their inmates enumerated, by Charles's *missi*, officers-cum-envoys, in 808. Its purpose was to allocate financial support, alms, from the west. Lines 22–3 have a little gem of information: *Monasteria puellarum xxvi, de imperio domni Karoli quae ad sepulchrum Domini serviunt Deo sacratas xvii*, 'a convent of 26 women, of whom 17 are nuns or consecrated widows from the Lord Charles's empire who serve at the Holy Sepulchre': a little outpost of Europe in Asia.[53]

Especially in Charles's imperial years, high functionaries were being summoned frequently to Aachen: so frequently, in fact, that some built and maintained houses there.[54] There they heard a peremptory voice urging greater efforts, castigating in anger but also in sorrow their corruption and carelessness, reminding them of the needs of the *pauperes*, the less powerful and unprotected—for the empire needed their services too.[55] Charles's empire was an empire of the mind—or minds: a collective enterprise. There were some large assemblies, usually at Aachen but sometimes at other important palaces; but there were far more local ones, attested chiefly in private charters.[56] The state was always a congeries of statelets, to which power devolved. Charles himself said he could not supervise everyone, but that each must strive to observe their own duties to God and emperor 'as far as understanding and strength

[51] Innes (2011: 155–203); Esders & Haubrichs (2015, forthcoming); Davis (2015, forthcoming), with comprehensive and up-to-date bibliography; and the AHRC-funded 'Making of Charlemagne's Europe' project, directed by Alice Rio, a searchable database of all charters, public and private, known from the reign of Charlemagne (in progress).

[52] McCormick (2011).

[53] McCormick (2011: 65) (with text and translation at 206–7) noting that 42.8 per cent of all monastic personnel in Jerusalem in 808 were women.

[54] See Innes (2011: 186–203), for the 802 assembly and its spin-offs; for 811, see Nelson (2001). For magnates' houses, see Nelson (2007b: chap. XIV: 7–8).

[55] Nelson (2010a: 383–401).

[56] Major assemblies documented in capitularies include those of Thionville & Nijmegen (805, 806), and Aachen (808, 809, 811), MGH Capit. I, nos. 43–6, and 8–53, 61–5, 72–3. Regional and local assemblies documented in charters include the Bavarian ones discussed by Fouracre (1995: ii: 771–803), and by Brown (2001: esp. 102–23), on the role of Archbishop Arn.

allow'.[57] Like many political utterances, this was trite, but true. Viewed spatially, elites regionally and locally held the stage, intimately involved in sharing and grasping power, intermittently in touch with the palace. Decentring was required then. Historians need to decentre now. Structurally, and in terms of lived experience, assembly politics at local and regnal levels were geared in to one another.[58] Charles, given such embedded forms of social power, and limited communications technology, could never have contemplated changing this situation. The workings-out of dynastic inheritance made division inevitable, and the parts increasingly separate, especially those that would become Germany and France, and Charles never planned otherwise. Italy was different, in that attempts to restore a working transalpine axis and imperial presence recurred. After the 10th century, however, this had little to do with Charlemagne, except as a form of myth-history.[59] The longer-run consequence was that decentred power in regional territories and in lordships survived the weakening of royal government.

Nevertheless, as long as Charlemagne ruled, and thereafter through the reigns of his sons and grandsons, assembly politics could never be separated from the needs of war. The keeping of the peace within the patria, and the defence of local people, were main tasks of counts and bishops, abbots and abbesses, and their deputies and sub-ordinates, whether the threats came from human predators, such as feuding nobles or troops marching towards the frontiers, or wild animals like wolves. Taking armed men beyond the frontiers was almost an annual event. All earlier medieval kings were expected to direct and often to lead campaigns. Charlemagne's youthful training was in war, and his reputation grew during and after his lifetime, thanks especially to his wars against the Saxons, which loom large in the narrative of the Royal Frankish Annals, and thence in Einhard's Life of Charles. Bloody battles in the civil wars that dogged the reign of Charlemagne's successor were described, exceptionally, by participants who were also laymen: Nithard, Charlemagne's grandson, and a noble, Angilbert. Nithard praised Charlemagne for having in his lifetime 'tamed the ferocious iron hearts of Franks and barbarians with controlled terror [*moderato terrore*]'.[60] The two rebellions of Franks in Charlemagne's reign were ruthlessly crushed but the very few documented exemplary executions of ringleaders were apparently enough to deter imitators.

Can Charlemagne, then, be regarded as a man of peace, a suitable icon for Europe post-1945? Or has he been thus represented by post-war Germans, to fit a German bill? The answers to both questions may be, yes: but that does not make them

[57] Capit. I, no. 33, c. 3: 92.
[58] Reuter, (2006: 193–216).
[59] Wickham (1994: 275–93); MacLean (2010: 394–416); Bullough (2003: 389–97, esp. 393–7).
[60] Nithard (2012: 4).

historically wrong. In the early Hitler years, many north Germans refused to stomach Charles the Saxon-slayer, perpetrator of a 'bloodbath' at Verden in Saxony, where, according to both versions of the Royal Frankish Annals (but no other sources), 4,500 Saxons were beheaded on a single day at Charles's behest.[61] These were legal proceedings, justified on the grounds that *fides*, fidelity, had been sworn by those Saxons on oaths, and the oaths then flagrantly broken. The men who handed over those Saxons to death were other Saxons who had kept their oaths. The exemplary punishments apparently had the desired effect. By 785, further large numbers of Saxons had accepted Christianity and sworn faith to Charlemagne. Later, when still-resisting Saxons were deported en masse with their families into Frankish territory, there is no mention in any source of slaughtering the men and enslaving the women and children. The aim, rather, was to assimilate the deportees into Christendom, just as the high-born sons of the Saxon nobility were held as hostages in the households or on the properties of Charlemagne's regional elites. Similarly, the defeats of the Avars in 795 and 796 were immediately followed by a drive for conversion, and strong warnings from Alcuin that to repeat the harshness shown to some of the Saxons would be counter-productive. The limited evidence suggests Avar elite conversion accompanied by intermarriage with Slav populations, and slow christianisation in the course of the 9th and 10th centuries.

Something similar had occurred in the religious practice of those in the Franks' own territories, and in conquered areas that had long been nominally Christian from Brittany to Bavaria, and from Frisia to central Italy. The Carolingian Renaissance helped generalise processes of internal and expansionary christianisation. Promoting these was the work of elites and functionaries and patrons, ecclesiastical and lay. Charles drove their efforts forward, and funded them up to a point; but they mostly operated in regions far away from the court, and it was in the regions that these efforts persisted after 814, and increasingly from the 830s.[62] Decentring is, again, the right word for a realistic approach. Alms-giving, and relic-veneration may stand as emblematic.[63] In both, huge collective investment was involved, before and after Charles's reign, in material terms. Yet Charles's reign was critical in setting a standard for practice and extending it, however patchily, across Europe. It might be said that he won wars, and also won a series of truces, which in time became peaces entrenched under his successors, and repeated in regions such as Carinthia and Normandy. Neither in Saxony nor Avaria did Charlemagne make a wilderness and call it peace.

Geography focused Charles's mind, and constrained what he could do. Economic change, even growth, had already begun before Charles's reign began, but there is

---

[61] *Annales regni Francorum* (*s.a.* 782: 62, 65); see now Nelson (2013: 1–29, at 23–9); cf. above, n. 4.
[62] Wood (2006), Part II.
[63] Mordek, (2005: 1–52); Smith (2012: 143–67).

considerably more evidence during and after it than before. Charles's coinage, and interventions in market prices during times of famine (and here I would stick with what I said in 2001) show a new combination of public and private interests. In the countryside, markets proliferated, and peasant producers could participate because credit was available. [64] A cluster of small monasteries datable to the late 8th century with a quality of artwork signalling powerful patronage were remote from population centres, but they served as, and protected through the relics they housed, commercial thoroughfares between Italy and southwest Germany.[65] The Rhine was an artery of trade that very effectively linked south-central Germany with Frisia. Two of Charles's three greatest projects, the building of a bridge across the Rhine at Mainz, and the making of a canal linking the Main (and via that the Rhine) and the Danube which flowed across Europe to its eastern frontier, were inspired not just by military and ideological (though certainly those), but also commercial concerns. The third project, the creation of a capital at Aachen, was strongly ideological. All three were in some sense short-lived, yet the trends that were already shaping the European economy unfolded long-term. The canal of 793, abandoned because of difficult climatic and geological conditions (a contemporary recognised these as occurring *naturaliter*), would have needed to be less than 4 km long. Both Napoleon and King Ludwig of Bavaria in the 19th century, and Hitler's engineers in the twentieth, made fresh attempts using different routes, but were unsuccessful. In 1991 the canal, taking still another route, was finally finished at 171 km long: its economic impact has been great. Some 2 km of Charles's canal survive at a place called Graben, 'ditch', conspicuous in the landscape, and recent excavations have revealed how Charles's men attempted to prop up the sides of their digging with oak timbers dendrochronologically dated to 793.[66]

* * *

How was Charles made to connect with Europe after him? How did an empire of the mind became an empire of memory? Through an inexorable process of forgetting, neither the Carolingian Renaissance nor the administrative developments were to be greatly celebrated by medieval posterity. The memory of the Saxon Wars was smoothed into peaceful acculturation, the memory of Avaria obliterated. Two memories that endured were transmitted by Einhard. One, in chapter 9 of the *Life of Charles* dealing with events in 778, I shall deal with presently. The other, in chapter 16, was the

[64] The case was formidably made by Hendy (1988: 29–78). See further Bruand (2002: 155–84); Bougard (2010: 439–78).

[65] Nelson (2010b: 116–48, at 120–3).

[66] Ettel, Daim, Berg-Hobohm *et al.* (eds) (2014). My warm thanks go to Falko Daim of the Römisch-Germanisches Zentralmuseum at Mainz for keeping me abreast of his research and sharing the excitement of the team's findings.

description in the years *after* the imperial coronation of the arrivals at Charles's court of embassies from the king of the Persians, also known as the Caliph Har'un al-Rashid, in 801–2 and 807, bearing fabulous eastern gifts. Einhard deployed an old classical topos in which eastern gifts signalled submission to a universal empire. Rhetorically, the 'king of the Persians' displaced the emperor of the Greeks as the submissive ruler.[67] In 886, Notker of St-Gall, drawing on Einhard but viewing the Greeks in an 'orientalising mirror' (Chris Wickham's felicitous phrase), affirmed universality by contrasting the Greek king to the imperator in the west.[68] 'When Charles's chief envoy told the king at Constantinople that all was at peace in Charles's realm except for the trouble caused by the Saxons, that man [!] who was sluggish in idleness and useless for war replied, "O dear, why does my son [Charles] struggle against enemies who are very few and totally lack reputation or manly courage? You can have that people [the Saxons] with all that belongs to them!" When the envoy returned and reported this to the most warlike Charles, he laughed and said, "That king would have done you a lot more of a good turn if he'd granted you [a pair of] linen pants for your long journey back."' No matter whether the all mouth and no trousers joke was actually Charles's, or Notker's (the words Notker uses for linen pants are those used in 9th-century church legislation on monks' apparel): either way, to dismiss the joke as 'coarse and vulgar' is to miss an entrée to 9th-century meanings and double-entendres which disparage both Saxons and Greeks as weak and unmanly, while asserting the manliness of Franks whether laymen or monks.[69]

Yet throughout the Middle Ages, prophecies and dreams connecting Charlemagne with some kind of united Europe became part of the European imaginary.[70] Among the earliest of such texts was one written for the West Frankish queen who was also the sister of the East Frankish king by an author hedging bets in the mid-10th century. Charlemagne's transferring of empire to the Franks paved the way for, in some unspecified future, a Frankish emperor to come to Jerusalem and hang his crown on the Mount of Olives. A more elaborate Italian version depicted King Harun assigning Charlemagne his power over the Holy Sepulchre: a unifying vision. The *Description of the Lord's Key and Crown*, produced in France at the royal court or at St-Denis,

---

[67] See Latowsky (2005: 25–57), and also Latowsky (2013) (see above, n. 47).

[68] Haefele (1959: 53); and see Wickham (1998: 245–56, at 55). (The translation below improves slightly on the one I offered in, 'Did Charlemagne have a private life?', in Bates, Crick & Hamilton (eds)) Nelson (2006: 15–26, at 26).

[69] Barbero (2000: 142): 'la grossolanità e diciamo pure la volgarità'; cf. Latowsky (2013: 38–57). For the manliness of monks, see Coon (2010: 69–97).

[70] For what follows, see Morrissey (1997: 71–160); Gabriele (2011: 13–70, 107–28); Latowsky (2013: 58–96, and chaps 4 & 5, *passim*). For Germany, see Folz (1950); and for competing French and German appropriations, see Folz (1953), English trans. (1969), and especially Ehlers (2001), and Kintzinger (2005: 49–74 and *passim*). For Charlemagne in Spain, see Herbers (2003: 15–28).

presented a French Charlemagne who reached Jerusalem with a vast army, making the pagans flee without a battle. Charlemagne received relics of the Passion from the Greek emperor, and returning west via Constantinople ordered a magnificent church to be built at Aachen: a pacific imperial vision. In 1165, the emperor Frederick Barbarossa had Charlemagne canonised by the bishop of Liège, the diocese in which Aachen lay, and to whom the anti-pope Paschal III had delegated his authority in this particular case.[71] A huge candelabra in the Aachen church still documents the occasion. By now, the appeal of Charlemagne's journey to the East had been registered by a mass constituency. Prophecy had absorbed history, and with dynastic and military alliances between the Comnenan emperors in Byzantium and the Staufer in the West, a European project became, briefly, a reality. It dissolved in new rivalries between Germany and France.

Students of literature have contributed much to explaining how and why the legendary Charlemagne was a disputed legacy. But to my mind the best and certainly the briefest discussion remains the interdisciplinary one of James Fentress and Chris Wickham, where the disciplines in question are history and anthropology:[72] this may account for the relative neglect of their book by literary specialists. The emphasis here is on memory's transmission and contextualisation through time. Though Charlemagne was 'ever-present' in historical writings in almost every area historically connected with him, in the central medieval period, it was in France and Germany that he was remembered, but differently. In France (to simplify), oral traditions transmitted notably through the vernacular epic *The Song of Roland* constructed Charlemagne as protagonist of Christian victory not against the Basques of history in 778, but against the Saracens of timeless legend; the historic Roland, already attested in one segment of the manuscript tradition of Einhard's *Life of Charles*, is the heroic noble, faithful unto death. His last act was to blow his horn to summon Charlemagne—too late. 'The memory of the story . . . is as strong and stable as the memory of the actual events at Roncesvaux is fragile.' In Germany, Charlemagne was largely an ecclesiastical construct, a saint. In the 12th century, the two traditions merged with the production of a Latin version of the Roland legend, the *Historia Karoli Magni et Rothlandi*, purportedly by archbishop Turpin of Reims; and this was incorporated into the texts authorising the cult of Santiago de Compostella as well as into the *Grandes Chroniques* of France. Charlemagne, uniquely, was 'a generalized symbol of legitimacy that anyone could claim an association with'. 'The socially irrelevant gets forgotten'; that, and genre itself, explain why neither the Carolingian Renaissance nor administration were remembered in vernacular epic. Unexpected new forms of relevance account for

---

[71] Görich (2011: 268–82).
[72] Fentress & Wickham (1992: esp. 154–62, 171). The quotations below come from 155, 59, 161, 162 & 108.

the memory of the emperor in post-Risorgimento southern Italy as a dealer of justice: 'brigands put on the mantle of Charlemagne, and invested him with local meaning, local attributes and even a local geography'.

At the level of the state, Charlemagne's legend, came to reflect and augment not unity but division in Europe. The Holy Roman Emperor Charles IV developed Aachen in the 14th century as a cult-site for Karl der Grosse; and there was no French look-in. At Cologne in 1521, the first printed edition of Einhard's *Life of Charles* was dedicated to Charles V, seen by some contemporaries as a future Last Emperor.[73] At Paris in 1623, the first ever map of Charlemagne's empire was made for the French king Louis XIII who saw in it a blueprint for France's eastward expansion.[74] Napoleon briefly created a single Europe over the name of Charlemagne. He looked back to the role of the Rhineland, or *Francia media*, in Charles's empire, the historic heartland between Meuse and Rhine, from the mid-9th century called Lotharingia: Lothar's-land. This region proved to be 'the natural heart of Napoleon's empire'.[75] The geography that underpinned 'the social, economic and cultural elements at the core of the Napoleonic state system', what had already been 'the hub of European cultural and economic dynamism in the early modern period', was now 'central'. Here Michael Broers invokes two theories: the first is acculturation, signifying the elimination of indigenous traditions in an empire of conquest but in which the conquering power acknowledged underlying geopolitical forces, in this case the predisposition of compliant elites and already well-policed and assimilable urban populations willing to accept the new regime's laws and tax demands in return for security and prosperity; the second theory is the blue banana.[76] Here are Lotharingia/the Rhineland viewed *c.*1990 from a satellite, and looking palely blue because of the light emanating from concentrated homes and factories and nodes of power—the heart of Europe. And here's the blue banana itself—invented by French geographers who were not innocent academics: their map was meant to inspire politicians to move French industry eastwards—into the imagined banana. Economic geography isn't the sole arbiter of boundaries.

What it offered were European possibilities, perceived with particular sharpness by Jean Monnet. I have read his *Memoirs*: Charlemagne is mentioned only once and not by Monnet. In March 1950, Monnet wrote that Adenauer was for pooling German and French sovereignty, but that Schuman thought this not yet feasible. 'To me [Monnet] it mattered little whether these attitudes were sincere or not . . . Like the

---

[73] Tischler (2001: II: 1667–8).

[74] Goffart (1997: 53–60, at 54 with n. 6).

[75] Broers (2001: 135–54, esp. 138–4).

[76] A Google-search reveals the tendentious view of the geographer, Michel Brunet, who 'revealed' the Blue Banana.

chorus of some Greek tragedy, General de Gaulle added his eloquent commentary: "If one were not constrained to look at matters coolly, one would be dazzled by the prospect of what could be achieved by a combination of German and French strength . . . it would mean giving modern economic, social, strategic and cultural shape to the work of the Emperor Charlemagne." But if in fact we had to look at matters coolly and to reject the dream of a Carolingian Europe totally and immediately integrated, was this any reason for making no effort at all? . . . [T]he time had come to act . . .'[77] What drove Monnet was not the memory of Charlemagne, but the thought of coal and steel as the basis of a Franco-German-Benelux economic community. De Gaulle, like most of the founding Fathers of Europe had a strong sense that Christianity still provided distinctively European ideals and values, not necessarily linked with Charlemagne. What drove all these men inexorably was the need for peace, and for Europe's reconstruction. Winston Churchill shared these views passionately and consistently, from the 1930s through to the 1950s, without ever remembering—or anyway ever mentioning—Charlemagne at all.[78]

Monnet's contemporary the German medievalist Ernst Curtius pointed to another way of saving Europe post-war. *Europäische Literatur und lateinisches Mittelalter* appeared in Switzerland in 1948: 'When the German catastrophe came, I decided to serve the idea of a medievalistic humanism . . . [My book] grew out of a concern for the preservation of Western culture. It seeks to serve an understanding of the Western cultural tradition . . .'[79] Norman Cantor wrote in 1991, 'It is through the study of literature, art and philosophy of the Middle Ages that further code-breaking entry into the medieval mentality will primarily occur well into the 21st century.'[80] That is where we are now! You may well agree that Cantor, in pressing the claims of medieval studies in the USA, had a point, though to my mind, further code-breaking will depend on the social sciences as well, and on comparing western with other cultural traditions.[81] A humanist education that has space for the Middle Ages has added value. Only so, will the connection between Charlemagne and Europe remain an intellectual freeway.

In 2000, Max Kerner of the University of Aachen asked, 'Hat Karl der Grosse eine Zukunft?'—has Charlemagne a future?[82] In Germany, interest in Charlemagne still generates large amounts of cutting-edge research, some of it reaching a wide public. The Paderborn Exhibition was visited by 311,000 people between July and

---

[77] Monnet (1976), cited from the English trans. by Mayne (1978: 221–2).

[78] I am very grateful to Roland Quinault for letting me read his unpublished paper, 'Churchill and Europe'.

[79] Curtius (see above, n. 22) (1953: Foreword, viii).

[80] Cantor (1991: 161).

[81] See for instance Goody (2010).

[82] Kerner (2000: 272–7).

Figure 1. Once the Eastern Emperor at Constantinople had agreed to recognise Charlemagne's imperial title in 812, Charlemagne ordered a small number of mints to produce an imperial coinage. Only about 40 coins are extant, reflecting the very short period of issue, possibly as late as September 813–January 814; but at least 11 mints produced them, suggesting relatively high productivity. This one bears on the obverse Charles's portrait in profile, with the inscription KAROLUS IMP[erator] AUG[ustus] and the mint-name M[ainz], and on the reverse XPICTIANA (for Christiana) RELIGIO and a temple, standing perhaps for the Christian Church. This may be considered the only strictly contemporary 'portrait' of Charlemagne, depicted Roman-style, in profile, with imperial laurel-wreath, but also barbarian-style (imitating Theoderic?), with a moustache, and in a military cloak held at the right shoulder with an understated brooch.

Courtesy BnF.

October 1999.[83] The 1,200th anniversary of Charlemagne's imperial coronation in 2000 was widely celebrated, not just by scholars but by the public. Interest was intensified by the launch of the euro in various European countries. Kerner insisted that it remained 'important and essential to commit oneself to a European image of Charlemagne (*ein europäisches Karlsbild*)'. Charlemagne had a future in Europe, then?

But does today's Europe, the Europe of 28, want Charlemagne? Relatively few French or Italian historians have devoted themselves to Charlemagne recently. German or North American historians have turned instead to exposing myth-histories. In the United Kingdom Charlemagne is enthusiastically studied in select universities. Yet my media contacts say the Great Man lacks 'name-recognition' among the British public. Most English voters today express little interest in Europe. Many want out of Europe altogether. They are not the only ones to have lost faith in Europe. Mistrust is widespread now in countries most hard-hit by the banking crash of 2008 and its aftermath. A study in 1999 of German politicians' attitudes as expressed in speeches in the Reichstag, found that Charlemagne was 'cold coffee'.[84] Is the coffee any warmer in

[83] Nelson (2000: 295–9).
[84] Kerner (2000: 277).

Germany today? Or in any other EU member state, when so many European citizens feel powerless and voiceless, and perceive EU institutions as remote and unaccountable? Couldn't more be done with the Charlemagne Prize, awarded annually by the city fathers of Aachen for contributions to European unity?[85]

If Charlemagne can play a part in a re-imagined European future, it will be for new reasons.[86] It will be a matter not of falsifying history, but distinguishing it from myth, addressing it squarely and writing about it in terms meaningful to 21st-century Europeans. Here are some thoughts. First, in its multiple and often conflicted forms, Christianity has a part to play in unlocking Europe's medieval and modern pasts. Literacy and Latin learning in Charlemagne's world were modes of communication accessible to lay-people through signs and symbols, sermons and prayers, and coins, all with messages to be decoded. But for access to Europe's multi-religious or irreligious, and multicultural, present and future, other elements are needed as well. Charlemagne's contacts with the emperors in Constantinople and the caliph in Baghdad, his alliances with local powers in Muslim Spain, his gifts to monasteries in the Holy Land, suggest ways of understanding cultural interchange which exclude Charlemagne as proto-crusader. Second, the widespread sense of political belonging inherent in graduated levels of assembly politics, and collective interactions of people with Charlemagne's government, could freshen responses to a perceived deficit of legitimacy in the EU today. Third, Charlemagne enlisted relatively large numbers of local men in the delivery of justice and peace, in grassroots contexts where the boundaries between free and unfree were negotiable and where effective communication was a priority. If History teaches no lessons, it can signpost oracles and provoke questions from us who live in the EU.

Charlemagne and his contemporaries thought much about peace, but to explain *how* they thought, historians have to work like anthropologists, treating another culture on its own terms, thinking across cultures, comparatively and historically. The late Satish Sabarwal, an anthropologist of India who also read widely in European history, saw what was distinctive about Europe not in its science and technology but in its capacity 'progressively to reconstitute itself'.[87] Ideas certainly were reconstituted in Charlemagne's Europe, of conquering peace expressed in liturgy, of rights enshrined in diverse laws, of the responsibilities of office-holders to ruler, and the answerability of ruler to peoples. At Aachen, on 11 September 813, Charlemagne exacted from his son and successor what was in effect a coronation oath. Recently, a Swiss scholar took

[85] An inspection of the list of prize-winners via Google is instructively puzzling.
[86] What follows is an English version (without the endnotes) of the last paragraph of my '*Pater Europae*? Karl der Große und Europa', Nelson (2014b: 420–7).
[87] Sabarwal (1992: 145–61). See Pearson (2011: 504–6).

a pot shot at the Holy Roman Empire: 'No empire, but, for us Europeans, rather what must remain holy is what brings together and holds together peoples and human beings as different—and this entails a recognition of their differentness.'[88] Diverse we are. What makes Europe is a bundle of paradoxes, but these include historical inspirations for fresh attempts at 'innovating and retouching', 'progressively to reconstitute'. Therein could lie futures for Charlemagne and for Europe.

Acknowledgements

I am very grateful to John Gillingham for critical comment on, and suggested improvements to, the lecture as read.

REFERENCES

Alcuin (1895), '*Ep.* 20, to Bishop Higbald of Lindisfarne', in E. Dümmler (ed.), MGH Epistolae Karolini Aevi II (Berlin), 56–8.

Augustine ([426], 1955), *City of God*, ed. B. Dombart and A. Kalb, *Corpus Christianorum*, 47, 48, 2 vols (Turnhout, Brepols), XVIII, 12.

Barbero, A. (2000), *Carlo Magno un padre dell'Europa* (Rome, Laterza).

Boretius, A. (ed.) (1883), *Divisio regni*, Capit. no. 45 (806), c. 19, MGH Capitularia regum Francorum I (Hanover), 130.

Bougard, F. (2010), 'Le crédit dans l'Occident du haut Moyen Âge', in Jean-Pierre Devroey, Laurence Feller & Régine Le Jan (eds), *Les élites et la richesse*, Collection Haut Moyen Âge 10 (Turnhout, Brepols), 439–78.

Brandes, W. (1997), '"*Tempora periculosa sunt*". Eschatologisch im Vorfeld der Kaiserkrönung Karls des Großen', in Rainer Berndt (ed.), *Das Frankfurter Konzil von 794*, 2 vols (Mainz, Verlag der Gesellschaft für mittelrheinische Kirchengeschichte), i: 49–79.

Bredekamp, H. (2014), *Der schwimmende Souverän. Karl der Große und die Bildpolitik des Körpers* (Berlin, Klaus Wagenbach).

Broers, M. (2001), 'Napoleon, Charlemagne, and Lotharingia: acculturation and the boundaries of Napoleonic Europe', *The Historical Journal*, 44: 135–54. http://dx.doi.org/10.1017/S0018246X01001704

Brown, G. (1994), 'Introduction: the Carolingian Renaissance', in Rosamond McKitterick, ed., *Carolingian Culture: emulation and innovation* (Cambridge, Cambridge University Press), 1–51.

Brown, W. (2001), *Unjust Seizure. Conflict, Interest and Authority in an Early Medieval Society* (Ithaca, NY, Cornell University Press).

Bruand, O. (2002), *Voyageurs et marchandises aux temps carolingiens* (Brussels, De Boeck Universite).

Bullough, D.A. (2003), 'Recycling Charlemagne in the fifteenth century, north and south', *Early Medieval Europe*, 12: 389–97.

Bullough, D.A. (2004), *Alcuin. Reputation and Achievement* (Leiden, Brill).

Cantor, N. (1991), *Inventing the Middle Ages* (Cambridge, The Lutterworth Press).

Close, F. (2011), *Uniformiser la foi pour unifier l'Empire. Contribution à l'histoire de la pensée politico-théologique de Charlemagne* (Brussels, Académie royale de Belgique), 101–19, 146–53.

---

[88] Muschg (2004: 101–16, at 114).

Coon, L.L. (2010), *Dark Age Bodies. Gender and Monastic Practice in the Early Medieval West* (Philadelphia, PA, University of Pennsylvania Press), 69–97.

Curtius, E.R. ([1948], 1953), *European Literature and the Latin Middle Ages*, trans. Willard R. Trask ([Bern, Francke]; London, Routledge & Kegan Paul), 128–30.

Davis, J. (2015 forthcoming), *Charlemagne's Practice of Empire* (Cambridge, Cambridge University Press).

Diesenberger, M. (2014 forthcoming), *Predigt und Politik im Frühmittelalterlichen Bayern* (Vienna, Verlag der Österreichischen Akademie der Wissenschaften).

Dümmler, E. (ed.) (1881a), 'Karolus magnus et Leo papa', MGH Poetae latini I (Berlin), ll. 1–536, 366–79.

Dümmler, E. (ed.) (1881b), Alcuin, *Carmen XXVI*, in MGH Poetae latini I (Berlin).

Dümmler, E. (ed.) (1895), MGH Epistolae Karolini Aevi II (Berlin).

Ehlers, J. (2001), *Charlemagne: L'Européen entre la France et Allemagne* (Stuttgart, Thorbecke).

Einhard (1911), *Vita Karoli* c. 13, ed. Oswald Holder-Egger, MGH SSRG (Hanover), 16.

Esders, S. & Haubrichs, W. (2015 forthcoming), *Verwaltete Treue. Ein oberitalienisches Originalverzeichnis (breve) mit den Namen von 174 vereidigten Personen aus der Zeit Lothars I*, MGH Schriften.

Ettel, P., Daim, F., Berg-Hobohm, S., Werther, L. & Zielhofer, C. (eds) (2014), *Grossbaustelle 793. Das Kanalprojekt Karls des Großen zwischen Rhein und Donau* (Mainz, Verlag des Römisch-Germanischen Zentralmuseums).

Fentress, J. & Wickham, C. (1992), *Social Memory* (Oxford, Wiley-Blackwell).

Folz, R. (1950), *Le Souvenir et la légende de Charlemagne dans l'empire germanique médiéval* (Paris, Les Belles Lettres).

Folz, R. ([1953], 1969), *The Concept of Empire in Western Europe*, trans. Sheila A. Ogilvie ([Paris, Aubier]; London, Edward Arnold).

Fouracre, P. (1995), 'Carolingian justice: the rhetoric of reform and the contexts of abuse', *Settimane di Studi*, 2 vols (Spoleto, Centro italiano di studi sull'alto medioevo), 44, ii: 771–803.

Freeman, A. & Meyvaert, P. (eds) (1998), MGH Concilia, II, Supplementum I (Hanover).

Fried, J. (1994), 'Karl der Große in Frankfurt am Main. Ein König bei der Arbeit', in Fried & Lieselotte E. Saurma-Jeltsch (eds), *794. Karl der Große in Frankfurt am Main* (Sigmaringen, Thorbecke), 25–34.

Fried, J. (1997), 'Karl der Große, die *Artes liberales* und die karolingische Renaissance', in Paul Leo Butzer, Max Kerner & Walter Oberschelp (eds), *Karl der Große und sein Nachwirken. 1200 Jahre Kultur und Wissenschaft in Europa* (Turnhout, Brepols), 25–43.

Fried, J. (2014), *Karl der Grosse. Gewalt und Glaube* (Munich, C.H. Beck).

Gabriele, M. (2011), *An Empire of Memory. The Legend of Charlemagne, the Franks and Jerusalem* (Oxford, Oxford University Press).

Ganz, D. (2003), 'Donald A. Bullough. Unpublished lectures', *Early Medieval Europe*, 12, 4: *passim*.

Ganz, D. (2010), 'Giving to God in the Mass: the experience of the Offertory', in Wendy Davies & Paul Fouracre (eds), *The Languages of Gift in the Early Middle Ages* (Cambridge, Cambridge University Press), 18–32.

Garrison, M. (1997), 'English and Irish at the court of Charlemagne', in Paul Leo Butzer, Max Kerner & Walter Oberschelp (eds), *Karl der Große und sein Nachwirken. 1200 Jahre Kultur und Wissenschaft in Europa* (Turnhout, Brepols), 97–124.

Gautier Dalché, P. (1997), 'De la glose à la contemplation. Place et fonction de la carte dans les manuscrits du haut moyen âge', in his *Géographie et culture. La representation de l'espace du VIe au XIIe siècle* (Aldershot, Ashgate), 693–764.

Geary, P. (2006), *Women at the Beginning: Origin Myths from the Amazons to the Virgin Mary* (Princeton, NJ, Princeton University Press).

Godman, P. (1985), *Poetry of the Carolingian Renaissance* (London, Duckworth).

Godman, P. (1986), *Poets and Emperor* (Oxford, Clarendon Press).

Godman, P., Jarnut, J. & Johanek, P. (eds) (2002), *Am Vorabend der Kaiserkrönung. Das Epos* 'Karolus Magnus et Leo Papa' *und der Papstbesuch in Paderborn* (Berlin, Akademie Verlag). http://dx.doi.org/10.1524/9783050056272

Goffart, W. (1997), 'The first venture into "Medieval Geography"', in Jane Roberts, Janet L. Nelson & Malcolm Godden (eds), *Alfred the Wise. Studies in Honour of Janet Bately* (Cambridge, Brewer), 53–60.

Goody, J. (1966), 'Circulating succession among the Gonja', in Jack Goody (ed.), *Succession to High Office* (Cambridge, Cambridge University Press), 142–76.

Goody, J. (2010), *Renaissances. The One or the Many?* (Cambridge, Cambridge University Press).

Görich, K. (2011), *Friedrich Barbarossa. Eine Biographie* (Munich, Beck).

Gundlach, W. (ed.) (1892), Codex Carolinus, MGH Epp. KA I, 45 (Berlin), 562.

Hack, A. (1999), 'Das Zeremoniell des Papstempfangs 799 in Paderborn', in Christoph Stiegemann & Matthias Wemhoff (eds), *799. Kunst und Kultur der Karolingerzeit. Karl der Große und Papst Leo III in Paderborn*, 3 vols (Mainz, Philipp von Zabern), iii: 19–33.

Hack, A. (2011), *Abul Aziz. Zur Biographie eines Elefanten* (Badenweiler, Bachmann).

Haefele, H.F. (ed.) (1959), Notker, *Gesta Karoli Magni*, II, 5, MGH SSRG, ns 12 (Berlin), 53.

Hendy, M. (1988), 'From public to private: the western barbarian coinages', *Viator*, 19: 29–78.

Herbers, K. (2003), 'Carlomagno y Santiago. Dos Mitos Europeos', in Klaus Herbers (ed.), *El Pseudo-Turpin Lazo entre el Culto Jacobeo y el Culto de Carlomagno. Actas del VI Congreso Internacional de Estudios Jacobeos* (Santiago de Compostela, Xunta de Galicia), 15–28.

Innes, M. (2011), 'Charlemagne, Justice and Written Law', in A. Rio (ed.), Law, *Custom, and Justice in Late Antiquity and the Early Middle Ages* (London, Centre for Hellenic Studies, King's College London), 155–203.

Kapfhammer, G. (1993), *Sagenhafte Geschichte. Das Bild Karls des Großen durch die Jahrhunderte* (Munich, Bayerische Vereinsbank).

Kerner, M. (2000), 'Ausblick', in Max Kerner (ed.), *Karl der Grosse. Entschleierung eines Mythos* (Cologne, Weimar, Vienna, *Böhlau*), 272–7.

Kintzinger, M. (2005), *Die Erben Karls des Grossen. Frankreich und Deutschland im Mittelalter* (Ostfildern, Thorbecke).

Klanizcay, G. (1997), 'Le Goff, the *Annales* and Medieval Studies', in Miri Rubin (ed.), *The Work of Jacques Le Goff and the Challenges of Medieval History* (Woodbridge, Boydell & Brewer), 223–37.

Knowles, D. (1963), *Great Historical Enterprises* (London, Thomas Nelson).

Kurze, F. (ed.) (1895), *Annales regni Francorum, s.a.* 811, MGH Scriptores rerum Germanicarum in usum scholarum (Hanover).

Lambert, P. (2012), 'Duke Widukind and Charlemagne in Twentieth-Century Germany', in Catharina Raudvere, Krzysztof Stala & Trine Stauning Willert (eds), *Rethinking the Space for Religion* (Lund, Nordic Academic Press), 97–125.

Lambert, P. (2013), 'The Immediacy of a Remote Past: the afterlife of Widukind in the Third Reich', *British Academy Review*, 22: 13–6.

Lappenberg, J.M. (ed.) (1859), *Annales Mosellani, s.a.* 781, MGH SS XVI (Hanover), 497.

Latowsky, A. (2005), 'Foreign embassies and Roman universality in Einhard's Life of Charlemagne', *Florilegium*, 22: 25–57.

Latowsky, A. (2013), *Emperor of the World: Charlemagne and the Construction of Imperial Authority, 800–1229* (Ithaca, NY, & London, Cornell University Press).

Le Goff, J. (1957), *Les intellectuels au moyen âge* (Paris, Éditions du Seuil).

Leyser, K. (1992), 'Concepts of Europe in the Early and High Middle Ages', *Past & Present*, 137: 25–47. http://dx.doi.org/10.1093/past/137.1.25

McCormick, M. (1994), 'Textes, images et iconoclasm dans le cadre des relations entre Byzance et l'Occident carolingien', in *Testo e imagine nell'alto medioevo*, Settimane di Studi, 2 vols (Spoleto, Centro italiano di studi sull'alto medioevo), 41, i: 130–1.

McCormick, M. (2004), 'Pippin III, the Embassy of Caliph al-Mansur, and the Mediterranean World', in Matthias Becher & Jörg Jarnut (eds), *Der Dynastiewechsel von 751* (Münster, Scriptoria), 221–41.

McCormick, M. (2011), *Charlemagne's Survey of the Holy Land* (Washington DC, Dumbarton Oaks Research Library).

MacLean, S. (2010), 'Legislation and politics in late Carolingian Italy: the Ravenna constitutions', *Early Medieval Europe*, 18: 394–416. http://dx.doi.org/10.1111/j.1468-0254.2010.00304.x

Mango, C. & Scott, R. (trans.) (1997), *The Chronicle of Theophanes Confessor: Byzantine and Near Eastern History AD 284–813* (Oxford, Clarendon Press).

Mayr-Harting, H. (2002), 'Charlemagne's Religion', in Peter Godman, Jörg Jarnut & Peter Johanek (eds), *Am Vorabend der Kaiserkrönung. Das Epos 'Karolus Magnus et Leo Papa' und der Papstbesuch in Paderborn* (Berlin, Akademie Verlag), 113–24. http://dx.doi.org/10.1524/9783050056272.113

Monnet, J. (1976), *Mémoires*, cited from the English trans. by Richard Mayne (London, Collins).

Mordek, H. (2005), 'Karls des Großen zweites Kapitular von Herstal und die Hungersnot der Jahre 778/779', *Deutsches Archiv*, 61: 1–52.

Morrissey, R. (1997), *L'empereur à la barbe fleurie* (Paris, Gallimard).

Muschg, A. (2004), 'Karl der Große—Kleineuropa?', in *Karl der Große und Europa*, ed. the Swiss Embassy in the Federal Republic of Germany in collaboration with the German Historical Museum (Frankfurt-am-Main, Peter Lang), 101–16.

Nelson, J. (2000), 'Representing Medieval Pasts', *History Workshop Journal*, 50: 295–9. http://dx.doi.org/10.1093/hwj/2000.50.295

Nelson, J. (2001), 'The Voice of Charlemagne', in Richard Gameson & Henrietta Leyser (eds), *Belief and Culture in the Middle Ages. Studies presented to Henry Mayr-Harting* (Oxford, Oxford University Press), 76–88.

Nelson, J. (2002), 'Charlemagne: "father of Europe"?', *Quaestiones medii aevi novae*, 7: 3–20.

Nelson, J. (2006), 'Did Charlemagne have a private life?', in David Bates, Julia Crick & Sarah Hamilton (eds), *Writing Medieval Biography. Essays in Honour of Frank Barlow* (Woodbridge, Boydell & Brewer), 15–26.

Nelson, J. (2007a), 'Why are there so many different accounts of Charlemagne's coronation?', in J. Nelson, *Courts, Elites and Gendered Power* (Aldershot, Ashgate), chap. XII: 17.

Nelson, J. (2007b), 'Aachen as a place of power', in J. Nelson, *Courts, Elites and Gendered Power* (Aldershot, Ashgate), chap. XIV: 7–8.

Nelson, J. (2010a), '*Munera*', in Jean-Pierre Devroey, Laurent Feller & Régine Le Jan (eds), *Les élites et la richesse au haut Moyen Âge* (Turnhout, Brepols), 383–401.

Nelson, J. (2010b), 'The setting of the gift in the reign of Charlemagne', in Wendy Davies & Paul Fouracre (eds), *The Languages of Gift in the Early Middle Ages* (Cambridge, Cambridge University Press), 116–48.

Nelson, J. (2013), 'Religion and Politics in the Reign of Charlemagne', in Ludger Körntgen & Dominik Waßenhoven (eds), *Religion and Politics in the Middle Ages*, 29 (Berlin, Prince-Albert-Studien), 1–29. http://dx.doi.org/10.1515/9783110262049.17

Nelson, J. (2014a), 'Religion in the age of Charlemagne', in John A. Arnold (ed.), *The Oxford Handbook to Medieval Christianity* (Oxford, Oxford University Press), 490–514.

Nelson, J (2014b), '*Pater Europae*? Karl der Große und Europa', in F. Pohle (ed.), *Karl, Charlemagne, der Grosse. Orte der Macht, Essays*, im Auftrag der Stadt Aachen (Dresden, Sandstein Verlag), 420–7.

Nelson, J. (2015 forthcoming), 'The Carolingian Renaissance revisited', in Helmut Reimitz (ed.), *Religion, Politics and Society: from Constantine to Charlemagne. Essays in Honor of Peter Brown* (Princeton, Princeton University Press).

Nithard (2012), *Histoire des fils de Louis le Pieux*, ed. Philippe Lauer, revd Sophie Glansdorff (Paris, Les Belles Lettres), 4.

Noble, T.F.X. (2009), *Images, Iconoclasm, and the Carolingians* (Philadelphia, PA, University of Pennsylvania Press).

Patzold, S. (2013), *Ich und Karl der Große. Das Leben des Hoflings Einhard* (Stuttgart, Klett-Cotta).

Pearson, G. (2011), 'Obituary of Satish Saberwal', *South Asia: Journal of South Asian Studies*, 34: 504–6. http://dx.doi.org/10.1080/00856401.2011.620558

Pohl, W. (1988), *Die Awarenkriege Karls des Großen 788–803* (Vienna, Österreichischer Bundesverlag).

Reuter, T. (2006), 'Assembly politics', in his *Medieval Polities and Modern Mentalities*, ed. J.L. Nelson (Cambridge, Cambridge University Press), 193–216.

Sabarwal, S. (1992), 'On the Making of Europe: Reflections from Delhi', *History Workshop Journal*, 33: 145–61. http://dx.doi.org/10.1093/hwj/33.1.145

Schaller, D. (1976), 'Das Aachener Epos für Karl den Kaiser', *Frühmittelalterliche Studien*, 10: 136–68. http://dx.doi.org/10.1017/CBO9780511497216.013

Scheck, H. (2012), 'Nuns on parade: memorializing women in Karolus Magnus et Leo Papa', in Margaret Cotter-Lynch & Brad Herzog (eds), *Reading Memory and Identity in the Texts of Medieval European Holy Women* (Basingstoke, Palgrave Macmillan), 13–38.

Smith, J.M.H. (2012), 'Portable Christianity: relics in the medieval west (*c.*700–*c.*1200)', *Proceedings of the British Academy*, 181: 143–67.

Stella, F. (2001), 'Autore e attribuzioni del "Karolus Magnus et Leo Papa"', in Peter Godman, Jörg Jarnut, and Peter Johanek (eds.), *Am Vorabend der Kaiser Krönung: das Epos "Karolus Magnus et Leo papa" und der Papstbesuch in Paderborn 799* (Berlin, Akademie), 19–33.

Story, J. (2003), *Carolingian Connections: Anglo-Saxon England and Carolingian Francia* (Aldershot, Ashgate).

Tischler, M.M. (2001), *Einharts Vita Karoli. Studien zur Entestehung, Überlieferung und Rezeption*, 2 vols (Hanover, Hahnsche Buchhandlung).

Tremp, E. (ed.) (1995), Astronomus, *Vita Hludowici imperatoris* c. 15, MGH Scriptores rerum Germanicarum in usum scholarum 64 (Hanover).

Weinfurter, S. (2014), *Karl der Grosse: der heilige Barbar* (Munich, Piper).

Werminghoff, A. (ed.) (1908), Concilium Franconofurtense of 794, in MGH Concilia I, I (Hanover), 110–71.

Wickham, C. (1994), 'Lawyers' Time: History and Memory in Tenth- and Eleventh-Century Italy', in C. Wickham, *Land and Power: Studies in Italian and European Social History* (London, British School at Rome), 275–93.

Wickham, C. (1998), 'Ninth-century Byzantium through western eyes', in Leslie Brubaker (ed.), *Byzantium in the Ninth Century: Dead or Alive?* (Aldershot, Ashgate), 245–56.

Wolfram, H. (1987), *Die Geburt Mitteleuropas* (Vienna, Siedler Verlag), 253–60.

Wood, S. (2006), *The Proprietary Church in the Medieval West* (Oxford, Oxford University Press).

The author: Jinty Nelson is Emeritus Professor of Medieval History at King's College London. Her main research interests have focused on the earlier middle ages, especially on politics, political ideas and religion, and more recently on gender. She served as a Vice-President of the British Academy in 2000–1, and as President of the Royal Historical Society in 2000–4. She has published four volumes of papers, the most recent *Courts, Elites and Gendered Power in the early Middle Ages* (2007), and is planning a fifth. She is a member of an AHRC-funded database project based at King's College London, 'The Making of Charlemagne's Europe', which structures and makes searchable the rich and complex data derived from charters produced in Charlemagne's realm and reign. She is currently writing a biography of Charlemagne.

jinty.nelson23@gmail.com

This article was first published in 2014 in *Journal of the British Academy* (ISSN 2052-7217).

To cite the article: Jinty Nelson (2014), 'Charlemagne and Europe ', *Journal of the British Academy*, 2: 125–153. DOI 10.5871/jba/002.125

Journal of the British Academy, **2**, 153–211. DOI 10.5871/jba/002.153
Posted 2 December 2014. © The British Academy 2014

Getting a word in: Contact, etymology and English vocabulary in the twelfth century

Sir Israel Gollancz Memorial Lecture
read 26 November 2013

RICHARD DANCE

Abstract: English vocabulary owes an enormous debt to the other languages of medieval Britain. Arguably, nowhere is this debt more significant than in the 12th century —a complex and fascinating period of 'transition', when (amongst many other things) influence from both Norse and French is increasingly apparent in writing. This lecture explores the etymologies, semantics and textual contexts of some key words from this crucial time, as a way to think about the evidence for contact and change at the boundary of Old and Middle English, and to illustrate how rich, diverse, challenging and surprising its voices can be. It concludes with a case study of words meaning 'rich' and 'poor' in Old and early Middle English, concentrating on the vocabulary of the manuscript Oxford, Bodleian Library, Bodley 343.

Keywords: Old English, Middle English, language contact, etymology, semantics, 12th century

The Middle Ages are full of surprises. In a manuscript probably from Kent, from the very end of the 12th century, nestling in a series of otherwise French proverbs with Latin verse equivalents,[1] there are two small passages of English. One of these is a

---

[1] The manuscript is Oxford, Bodleian Library, Rawlinson C. 641. For descriptions see esp. Ker (1990: 426–7, no. 348) (summarised for *The Production and Use of English Manuscripts 1060 to 1220* (hereafter *EMSS*) by Swan & Roberson (2010)), Laing (1993: 140), *Early English Laws* (hereafter *EEL*) at http://www.earlyenglishlaws.ac.uk/laws/manuscripts/rl/; Ker dates the main part of the manuscript (containing legal texts) to *s.* xii², and the hand of the proverbs (ff. 13v–18r) to *s.* xii/xiii. Kentish origin is implied by the script of ff. 7v–10 and the fact that the English glosses on ff. 32r–40v are shared with the copy of *Instituta Cnuti* in the *Textus Roffensis* (Ker 1990: 427); see also Richards (1988: 47), Wormald (1999: 252), O'Brien (2003: 180 n. 17). It may be added that the dialect of the two English proverbs resembles very closely that of the so-called 'Kentish Sermons' in Oxford, Bodleian Library, Laud Misc. 471, on which see Bennett & Smithers (1968: 390–3). The manuscript contains two collections of vernacular proverbs, 364 in total, all except the two discussed here being in Anglo-French; 48 of the proverbs in the first set are accompanied by (one or more) translations into Latin hexameters. (Ker (1990: 427) states that the two proverbs containing English versions 'are trilingual', a claim repeated by some subsequent

reflection on the suddenness of change: 'On dai bri*n*gd þet al ier ne mai' ('one day brings what a whole year cannot').[2] For medievalists, there are indeed times when everything seems to happen at once, never more so than during the 12th century. This is a period so often characterised as a frantic cultural 'renaissance'—in literary modes, in the law, in religious thinking, in architecture—and also one which witnessed significant linguistic change.[3] This manuscript, with its English and French and Latin, exemplifies just one of a long series of multilingual interactions which had taken place in medieval England, including, if we trace them back through the Norman Conquest, relations between English speakers and those of Scandinavian and Celtic languages, amongst many others.[4] Sometimes the meetings of these languages are dramatised on the manuscript

---

commentators, e.g. Pulsiano (2000: 193), Swan & Roberson (2010); but these two proverbs in fact appear only in English and Latin versions in this manuscript.) All the proverbs in Rawlinson are edited by Stengel (1899), with the English material reprinted by Förster (1900). The proverbs with Latin equivalents are extant in several further manuscripts, the Latin texts being attributed to or associated with the 12th-century Anglo-Latin poet Serlo (or Serlon) of Wilton; for critical editions see Friend (1954) and Öberg (1965: 113–20, 144–57). The French material is furthermore associated with the corpus of proverbs known as *Li proverbe au vilain* (many of the proverbs in Rawlinson being versions of the concluding 'morals' which circulated with the longer stanzas of that tradition; the classic edition and account is Tobler (1895)).

[2] Rawlinson C. 641, f. 13v, col. 1 l. 16, with abbreviations expanded in italics; unless otherwise indicated, all translations in this lecture are my own. The Latin version (which follows at ll. 17–18) reads: 'Q*uo*d donare mora neq*ui*t a*n*nua dat br*e*vis hora. Anno cura dat*ur* t*ame*n una dies op*er*at*ur*' ('what the space of a year cannot give, a short hour gives; concern is given to a year, nonetheless one day performs it'). There are variants of the same English proverb in Dublin, Trinity College, B.3.5 ('Oft yift o dai yat alle yeir ne mai'), Oxford, Bodleian Library, Douce 52 ('Oft bryngeth on day þat all þe ȝere not may') and Manchester, John Rylands Library, Lat. 394 ('Ofte bryngeth o day þat after alle þe ȝere ne may'; see Pantin 1930: 95). None of the editions and handbooks I have consulted seems to know all these versions: see variously Friend (1954: 189, who records only the Rawlinson and Rylands variants), Öberg (1965: 115, Rawlinson and Dublin only), Whiting & Whiting (1968: 119, no. D56), Boffey & Edwards (2005: 174, no. 2668.5) and *DIMEV* (record 4244, http://www.dimev.net/record.php?recID=4244) (the last three record only Rawlinson, Douce and Rylands). For comparable sayings see further Smith (1970: 169).

[3] The classic accounts of the 12th-century as a 'renaissance' are Haskins (1927), Southern (1960), Brooke (1969), Benson & Constable (1982), and see also the important collection of essays in Thomson (1998). There is a convenient survey of intellectual and artistic developments in England in this period in Bartlett (2000: 506–34).

[4] As recent studies have compellingly demonstrated, the Norman Conquest only compounded the already rich and complex linguistic situation in early medieval England. The bibliography on this subject is very large, but for important recent accounts of language contact and multilingual textual culture in the period see notably O'Brien (2011: esp. 69–121), O'Donnell, Townend & Tyler (2013), and the essays in Trotter (2000), Kennedy & Meecham-Jones (2006), Tyler (2011), and Jefferson & Putter (2013); and for further discussion of some of the literary, documentary and historiographical contexts see *inter alia* Ashe (2007), Treharne (2011), Clanchy (2013), Harris (2013). In addition to these (and to the various studies of specific issues cited in what follows), for discussion and further references regarding Anglo-French (a.k.a. Anglo-Norman) and its contexts see e.g. Crane (1999), Short (2007), Wogan-Browne *et al.* (2009), Ingham (2010) and the introduction to the online *AND* (at http://www.anglo-norman.net/sitedocs/main-intro.shtml?session=SAB15757T1396452066); on Anglo-Scandinavian bilingualism see especially Townend (2000), Parsons (2001), Townend (2002); and on contact with the Celtic languages and some of its (possible) effects consult e.g. Higham (2007: esp. 165–244), Filppula & Klemola (2009).

page, occasionally in a very grand manner, as in the famous trilingual enterprise of the Eadwine Psalter (Cambridge, Trinity College, R.17.1).[5] But far more often the contacts happened off-stage; sometimes their circumstances can only be hypothesised, and sometimes their most visible consequences reside in their effects on the languages concerned. In this lecture I would like to examine just one aspect of these linguistic exchanges, that is how they affected the vocabulary of medieval English; and to look at some of the evidence for this in texts from the 12th century. This era is not, of course, the only one when English words show influence from other languages; but it is perhaps uniquely interesting as the period not only when French loanwords appear in quantity in English texts for the first time, but also when words of Old Norse origin start to become really widely attested.[6] And moreover these changes in vocabulary are happening in the context of one of the most notoriously difficult stages in the history of English, and one which we still do not understand as well as we might, the 'transition' from Old English to Middle English. Here, while I shall be interested to some extent in these 'big' changes, the grand historical narratives, I would like to concentrate instead on some of the little stories which underlie them, and which more often go untold. Drawing on some important research tools which have opened up early medieval text and language studies in the last few years, I shall focus on a small number of particular words, chasing their etymologies and their semantic contexts, and culminating in a case-study of expressions for one related group of concepts in writings from late Old to early Middle English. I hope to show that words like these, and the evidence for their usage, are significant not just for the part they play in the larger accounts of contact and transition, but that what they have to say is compelling and important in its own right.

TWELFTH-CENTURY ENGLISH: PIGGY IN THE MIDDLE?

Let us begin by thinking about the written evidence and some perspectives on it, and return to the manuscript we started with. Rawlinson C. 641 sits intriguingly at the

---

[5] On the Eadwine Psalter see especially Harsley (1889), Verfaillie-Markey (1989), Ker (1990: 135–6, no. 91), Gibson, Heslop & Pfaff (1992), Pulsiano (2000), Treharne (2010c), Treharne (2012: 167–87), Harris (2013: 50–61); digital images of the entire manuscript may be viewed at http://sites.trin.cam.ac.uk/james/show.php?index=1229. There are few other 12th-century manuscripts in which a single text is designed to display the same content in all three languages; for a notable example see the formulas for the visitation of the sick from Rufford Abbey, Nottinghamshire, preserved in London, British Library, Cotton Titus D. xxiv (Ker 1990: 263–4, Swan & Kato 2010; for facsimile and remarks see O'Brien 2011: 99). It is more common to find texts in one (or two) original languages annotated in one or more others; for some discussion see Da Rold & Swan (2011, esp. p. 260 n. 14, for a helpful list of relevant manuscripts), Swan (2012), and for an important case study of Anglo-French annotations in manuscripts of Ælfric's *Grammar* see Menzer (2004).

[6] For general accounts of lexical borrowing in English, see now esp. Miller (2012) and Durkin (2014).

cross-roads of Anglo-Saxon, Anglo-Scandinavian and Anglo-Norman textual cultures. By the time the proverbs were added in about 1200, its contents already included Latin translations of Old English law-codes including Cnut's, the recent Latin text known as the 'Laws of Edward the Confessor', and an extract from Guernes de Pont-Sainte-Maxence's Anglo-French *Life of Thomas Becket*.[7] (And as if all that wasn't emblematic enough a mixture, a few years later someone inserted a copy of Magna Carta.)[8] The English-language material in this manuscript is not quite so epoch-making. Apart from a few glosses,[9] it is limited to the 'on dai' proverb and one other saying, whose subject is nothing if not earthy: 'Si stille suge fret þere grunninde mete' ('The quiet sow devours the grunting one's food').[10] If it hadn't seemed ill-advised to begin a lecture with a proverb about the virtues of staying quiet, then I might equally well have used this one as an epigraph, since it too seems as though it could be appropriate. English has often been characterised as playing a marginal role in 12th-century textual culture in England, carefully keeping its voice down next to the more impressive outputs in French and Latin. But while that may certainly be true of this manuscript, a very important body of recent research, led by and often associated with the *Production and Use of English Manuscripts 1060 to 1220* project, has very productively

---

[7] These texts are respectively: the so-called *Instituta Cnuti*, printed by Liebermann (1903–16: I.612–17) as *Instituta Cnuti aliorumque regum Anglorum* (for an important discussion see O'Brien (2003), who is preparing a new edition for *EEL*); the second version of *Leges Edwardi Confessoris* (Liebermann (1903–16: I 627–70), O'Brien (1999), with a digital edition and introduction by O'Brien in *EEL* at http://www.earlyenglishlaws.ac.uk/laws/texts/ecf2/); Guerne's *Vie de saint Thomas le Martyr* (Walberg (1922), and see O'Donnell (2011) and the description at *EEL* at http://www.earlyenglishlaws.ac.uk/laws/texts/con-clar-fr/). For some recent discussion of 12th-century responses to Anglo-Saxon legal and administrative culture see further Gobbitt (2013), Harris (2013: 104–30).

[8] See Ker (1990: 427) ('The text of Magna Carta, ff. 21v–29, is an early addition.')

[9] Six interlinear glosses to the *Instituta Cnuti* on ff. 32r, 33r, 34v, 40v; see Ker (1990: 426), Laing (1993: 140).

[10] Rawlinson C. 641, f. 13v, col. 1 l. 13. The Latin version (ll. 14–15) reads 'Sus taciturna uorat dum garrula uoce laborat. Sus dape fraudatur clamosa. tacens saciatur.' ('the quiet sow eats greedily, while the noisy one labours with her voice; the loud sow is cheated of her feast, the silent one is sated'). There are close variants of Rawlinson's English proverb in the collections in Dublin, Trinity College, B.3.5 ('þe stille suwe het þene grunende mete') and Cambridge, Trinity College, O.II.45 (a.k.a. 1149) ('þe stille sohghe het þare gruniende mete'); the text in Oxford, Bodleian Library, Digby 53 ('þe stille sue æt gruniende hire mete') is also close, but has been recast to feature just the one sow. As with the 'one day' proverb above, none of the editions and handbooks records all English variants: see Förster (1900: 6; notes Rawlinson, Digby and Cambridge only), Friend (1954: 204–5; Rawlinson, Dublin, Digby), Öberg (1965: 150; Rawlinson, Dublin, Digby), Whiting & Whiting (1968: 536, no. S535; Rawlinson and Digby); Friend and the Whitings notice later similar proverbs, to boot. I follow *DOE* (s.v. *grunian* (1)) in parsing Rawlinson *þere grunninde* as def. art. plus pres. ptcp. (used substantivally) in the fem. gen. sg., i.e. 'the grunting one's' (*contra* Förster (1900: 19) who takes *þare* in the Cambridge text as a form of OE *þǣr* and punctuates so as to imply a meaning 'while grunting'; Förster has seemingly been misled by the reading in Digby 53, itself probably a misunderstanding of the original construction). (The proverb is on f. 16 in Digby 53, not f. 53 as claimed by Ker (1990: 427); Ker's error seems in turn to have misled Laing (1993: 128).)

challenged simplistic assumptions of this century as a 'gap' in English literary history.[11] What is more, despite the abiding impression that 12th-century evidence for developments in the English language is more equivocal and harder won than it is in the centuries on either side, there have nonetheless been massive advances in its study, particularly the period from about 1150, which is covered in glorious detail now by the *Linguistic Atlas of Early Middle English*.[12] All the same, the vocabulary of 12th-century English remains relatively underexplored. The main focus of research has tended, understandably, to fall on the most important 'new' compositions, especially those hailing from the East Midlands and which most clearly illustrate linguistic features identifiably en route to mainstream modern (standard English) usage—the additions to the *Peterborough Chronicle*, and the extraordinary *Orrmulum* (from Lincolnshire), have in particular long been textbook staples.[13] But there are many other surviving pieces of English from this period whose vocabulary, while it has been the subject of some pioneering and important research, has not yet been investigated in the detail it deserves.[14] This comparative dearth of attention has to do at least partly, I think, with the awkward relationship that 12th-century texts often seem to have with the major period divisions we apply to medieval English. To pose a question which I have avoided so far, is their language Old English, or Middle English, or neither?

The names we give to varieties of English from this century have, of course, long been subject to debate.[15] Since the end of the 19th century, we have been fairly clear

[11] For *EMSS* see the website at http://www.le.ac.uk/ee/em1060to1220.index/html. The most significant recent contributions to this discussion are otherwise Lerer (1999), Swan & Treharne (2000), Georgianna (2003), Traxel (2004), Kennedy & Meecham-Jones (2006), Treharne (2006), Conti (2007a), Faulkner (2008), Roberts (2009), Treharne (2012), Treharne, Da Rold & Swan (2012), Younge (2012), Faulkner (forthcoming); see further the helpful reviews of scholarship in Da Rold (2006), Faulkner (2012b). Some typically dismissive statements about 12th-century English material are collected by Treharne (2012: 93–6).

[12] For *LAEME* see the website at http://www.lel.ed.ac.uk/ihd/laeme1/laeme1.html, and see also the important associated *Corpus of Narrative Etymologies* project at http://www.lel.ac.uk/ihd/CoNE/CoNE.html. For the period 1000–1150, the fullest account of orthography and phonology is Schlemilch (1914). For some recent work on particular texts/manuscripts, in addition to the work on vocabulary cited below, see e.g. Liuzza (2000), Traxel (2004), Roberts (2009: esp. 27–42).

[13] The Peterborough text of the *Anglo-Saxon Chronicle* in Oxford, Bodleian Library, Laud Misc. 636 (MS E) is edited and its language discussed by Irvine (2004); on the manuscript and the language especially of the 12th-century interpolations and continuations see further Clark (1952–3), Clark (1970), Da Rold (2010) and the essays in Bergs & Skaffari (2007). *The Orrmulum* in Oxford, Bodleian Library, Junius 1 is edited by Holt (1878); on manuscript, date and language see *inter alia* Burchfield (1956), Parkes (1983), Laing (1993: 135–6), Laing (2008: 161–3), Faulkner (2010).

[14] Notable studies are Pelteret (1978), Stanley (1985), Fischer (1996; 1997), Nevanlinna (1997), Skaffari (2009), Faulkner (2012a), Pons-Sanz (2013: 469–502), beside the work specifically on Bodley 343 (see below, n. 87); see also the important investigation of the early 13th-century Worcester 'tremulous hand' in Franzen (1991), and further Dance (2011).

[15] On the history of this debate see notably Fisiak (1994), Kitson (1997: 221–2), Matthews (1999), Lass (2000), Curzan (2012), Momma (2013: 126–9), and further on some of the principles and problems Nicolaisen (1997), Lutz (2002), Cannon (2005), Skaffari (2009: 40–2).

about what we mean by 'Old English' and 'Middle English', at least as prototypical stages in the history of English grammar—Henry Sweet defined them as the periods with 'full' and 'levelled' inflections, respectively.[16] But drawing a definitive line somewhere in the continuum of developments in between these two stages (what Sweet called 'transition Old English') has always seemed a much more difficult proposition;[17] and those authorities which for practical purposes have needed to draw such a line have never completely agreed on which texts to count on which side. This issue has special consequences when it comes to the lexicon, divided as it is nowadays between separate period dictionaries of Old and Middle English. Our two Rawlinson proverbs are a good example of this contested territory, since they are claimed by both the *Dictionary of Old English* and the *Middle English Dictionary*.[18] So, are they Old English, or are they Middle English? At a fundamental level, one might think, it doesn't really matter what we call them—it won't alter their contents, their actual linguistic features. What's in a name? But in reality, these texts are a very good example of how the perspective we take, the period vantage point from which we view them, can have serious consequences for our contexts of interpretation, and hence for how we perceive their vocabulary.

Let us take one word from our 'quiet sow' proverb, the verb *grunnin*, and think about its linguistic relationships and historical connotations. From an etymological point of view, it is natural to begin with the Old English form *grunian* (whose suffixed counterpart *grunnettan* is the ancestor of modern *grunt*),[19] and to think our way backwards and outwards to its broader Germanic setting, and perhaps beyond. Most etymological authorities explain it as an 'echoic' (or ideophonic) formation, whose nearest parallels are to be found in High German verbs with closely related meanings (notably the early modern HG *grunnen*); elsewhere in the Indo-European family we meet forms like Latin *grunniō*, which may ultimately share an origin with our Old

---

[16] Sweet's fullest discussion is in Sweet (1873–4: 617–21). His later categorisation of periods for the medieval stages of English, as set out at Sweet (1892: §594), is: 'Early Old English', 700–900; 'Late Old English', 900–1100; 'Transition Old English', 1100–1200; 'Early Middle English', 1200–1300; 'Late Middle English', 1300–1400; 'Transition Middle English', 1400–1500.

[17] Sweet himself recognised this difficulty perfectly well; see for instance his remarks at Sweet (1873–4: 619) ('if we take the intermediate stages into consideration, we find it simply impossible to draw a definite line'). Before Sweet, when pre-Conquest English was distinguished as something nominally quite separate from what came later ('Anglo-Saxon') and 'English' was felt to be identifiable as such only from the 13th century, the transition between these two stages was sometimes labelled still more awkwardly as 'Semi-Saxon' (see Matthews (1999), Lass (2000: 14), Momma (2013: 128 n. 29)). Since Sweet, the most significant attempts to readdress the boundary between Old and Middle English on morpho(phono)logical grounds are Malone (1930) and Kitson (1997).

[18] *DOE* groups both proverbs under the heading '*Prov 4* (Förster)'; in *MED* they are '*On dai bringd* (Rwl C.641)' and '*Þi stille suge* (Rwl C.641)' (both mis-dated in the stencil as '*a*1300').

[19] See *DOE* s.vv. *grunian* (1), *grunnian* and *grunung, grunnung*; and *grunnettan*.

English verb or may be simply analogous.[20] If we focus on the Old English word itself, then inevitably we look backwards to its Anglo-Saxon literary contexts, vernacular and Latin. In the Old English corpus, *grunian* is only used of animals, especially (though not only) of pigs.[21] Sometimes it occurs as a direct translation equivalent of Latin *grunniō*, in fact, as in Ælfric's catalogue of animal noises in his *Grammar*:[22]

> *canis latrat* hund byrcð, *lupus ululat* wulf ðytt, *equus hinnit* hors hnægð, *bos mugit* oxa
> hlewð, *ouis balat* scep blæt, *sus grunnit* swin grunað *et similia*

Amongst other things, this frequent bilingual partnering of *grunian* with Latin *grunniō* opens up the possibility that Latinate writers in this period equated the two words, and perhaps even that the form of the Latin (with its double /n/) influenced some variants of the English one.[23] But if instead we come at this word in our Rawlinson proverb *c.*1200 from a Middle English perspective, we get quite a different impression. The relevant entry in *MED* is for its verb *groinen*. We seem now to be in a different (and possibly more barbarous) age, where our verb is used not only of pigs (sense (b), 'of a sow: to grunt') and other animals (sense (c), 'of a dog: to growl, snarl'; sense (d), 'of a bull: to bellow'), but also of people (sense (a), 'to murmur, mutter, grumble'). More importantly, the linguistic context now draws in early French comparanda. *MED* derives *groinen* jointly from 'OF *groignier, gro(u)gnier* & OE *grunnian, grunian*', making no attempt to separate words of Old English and early French (including Anglo-French) etymological heritage.[24] Indeed, it is often quite hard to do so: some

---

[20] See *OED* s.v. *grunt* (v.) ('an echoic formation parallel with Latin *grunnīre*'), Lloyd & Lühr (2009: s.v. *grunzen*), Pokorny (1959: I.406, s.v. *gru-*). Lat *grunniō* 'I grunt' descends from an earlier *grundiō*, with which cp. further Grk *grúdzō* 'I grunt' (see de Vaan (2008: s.v. *grundiō, -īre*), Beekes (2010: s.v. γρῦ)). Holthausen's (1934: s.v. *grun(n)ian*) attempt to connect OE *grunian* instead with the noun OE *gyrn* (*gryn*) 'sorrow, misfortune' and its OHG cognate *grun(nî)* 'undoing, misfortune, misery, wailing' seems to me implausible, and has not been followed in more recent work; compare notably Lloyd & Lühr (2009: s.v. *grun*, and (with respect to another of Holthausen's rather remote comparanda) s.v. *granôn*).

[21] *DOE* records four attestations of forms of the verb *per se*, and six of the verbal noun. Apart from the Rawlinson proverb cited above, and the instance in Ælfric's *Grammar* given below, these are (with *DOE*'s title abbreviations): *AldV 1* 4219 <grunian> and *AldV 13.1* 4337 <grunnian>, glossing *grunnire*; *AldV 1* 4257 and *AldV 13.1* 4378 <grunnunge>, glossing *rugitus*; *AldV 1* 2344 <grununga>, <grunung> and *AldV 13.1* 2387 <grunnunga>, glossing *barritus*; *GD 3 (C)* 4.184.29 <grununge> (translating Gregory's *stridores*). Notice that, while the instances in Ælfric, *GD 3 (C)* and at *AldV 1* 4219 (*AldV 13.1* 4337) refer to the sounds made by pigs, the other Aldhelm glosses have to do with altogether more fearsome creatures: lions at *AldV 1* 4257 (*AldV 13.1* 4378) and elephants at *AldV 1* 2344 (*AldV 13.1* 2387).

[22] Zupitza (1966: 129 ll. 1–4), based on Oxford, St John's College 154.

[23] Old English spellings in <nn> occur only in the Aldhelm glosses, at *AldV 13.1* 4337, *AldV 1* 4257 and *AldV 13.1* 4378, and *AldV 13.1* 2387 (not all of which however gloss forms of Lat *grunniō*); see above, n. 21.

[24] *MED* s.v. *groinen* (v.). *OED* moreover gives only French derivation s.v. *groin* (v.1), and its *grunny* (v.) is described simply as a variant of this. The French verb is a descendant of Lat *grunniō*, via the VL variant **grŭniare*; see *DEAF* s.v. *groignier*, *FEW* s.v. *grŭndīre* (3. *grogner*).

spellings look more like Old English, and the vocalism of others (indicating /ɔi/) must show French input; but forms of both origin are used with the 'grumble' sense,[25] and it is possible this meaning developed first in French (where it is found from the late 12th century onwards).[26] So how far we think of this verb's etymological inputs as Germanic or English, and how far as French (and even Latin) is a moot point, and depends to some extent on the perspective we take.

Now, you might well be thinking that we can expect this sort of problem with words like this one, which at some level imitate or represent noises; that is that they are always liable to end up sounding similar in different languages. And to a certain extent that is true. But words for animal noises are actually a famous example of the conventionality of linguistic signs, since they can be startlingly different in different languages. (English dogs go *bow-wow* or *woof*, but in French they say *ouah ouah*, and in Greek *ghav ghav*.)[27] All this is not to say that medieval authors could not and did not think about the noises animals actually made, and could not represent and perhaps even pun on them. I suspect I am not the only person, for instance, ever to wonder whether it is deliberate that the first word spoken by the Owl in the Middle English poem *The Owl and the Nightingale* is 'Hu' (i.e. /huː/, in '*Hu* þincþe nu bi mine songe?', '*How* does my song seem to you now?').[28] But conventional, lexical items describing animal noises do not really have less 'proper' or 'normal' a history in English than do any other words. One only has to look at the set of animal noise verbs in Ælfric's list (cited above) to see how instantly recognisable (apart from that for the wolf) these words still are. Far from being spontaneously generated or regenerated, they are a very good indication of the continuity that there *can* be, not just across the murky Old and Middle English divide, but right up to the present; and morever that change to vocabulary (to form, to sense, or whatever), as to any received linguistic feature, is not just random or capricious, it is a process that we can at least try to explain—in the context both of what *has* changed, and what has *not*.

[25] Compare for instance (following *MED*'s title stencils) (1340) *Ayenb.*(Arun 57) 67/8 <grunny> (on the *Ayenbite*'s -*y* infinitive ending see Gradon (1979: 99–101)) with (a1382) *WBible(1)* (Dc 369(1)) Is29.4 <groyne>, both under sense (a).

[26] See *AND* s.v. *groigner*, where the second sense ('(of people) to grunt, grumble') is attested in Guerne's *Life of Thomas Becket*; and see further *AFW* s.v. *groignier*, *DEAF* s.v. *groignier*, *DMF* s.v. *grogner*.

[27] For discussion see Durkin (2009: 126).

[28] Cartlidge (2001), l. 46 from London, British Library, Cotton Caligula A. ix. I have been unable to find anyone who is willing to own up in print to wondering this; but for evidence of a homophone denoting an owl-call in Middle English see *MED* s.v. *hou* (interj.2) sense (c) 'used to represent the hooting of an owl' (one attestation from a1475 *Holy berith beris* (Hrl 5396) p. 94).

LOANS AND THEIR STORIES

There are many interesting words which occur in 12th-century texts, and which one could choose to explore further. By way of a few highlights from amongst those first attested in English in the 12th century, I present in Table 1 sixty or so which are usually recognised as borrowings from other languages and which are still in common use today.[29] Taken together, these words are an arresting bunch. At least impressionistically, they give a powerful sense of how much the development of vocabulary in this period, especially its expansion from 'foreign' sources, contributed to the evolution of the English language—lending us our modern words for everything from the noblest of accoutrements (*grace, justice, mercy, skill*) to the most quotidian (*custom, fruit, root, seat*), not to mention some key small 'grammatical' items (*both, though, they/their/them*), and the word we use to describe this whole category of imported vocabulary, *loan* itself. In etymological terms, all these words have been argued to come either from French (and/or Latin; it isn't always easy to tell the difference)[30] or from Old Norse.[31] Even if

---

[29] I include amongst 12th-century attestations words occurring in the *Lambeth* and *Trinity Homilies*, on which see below, n. 71.

[30] Clearly derived from a variety of early French (including Anglo-French, a.k.a. Anglo-Norman) are: *accord* (early Fr *acorder*; see *OED* s.v. *accord* v., *MED* s.v. *accōrden* v.), *clerk* (early Fr *clerc*; *OED* s.v. *clerk* n., *MED* s.v. *clerk* n.), *council* (early Fr *cuncile*; *OED* s.v. *council* n., *MED* s.v. *cŏunseil* n.), *court* (early Fr *curt*; *OED* s.v. *court* n.1, *MED* s.v. *cŏurt* n.1), *custom* (early Fr *custume*; *OED* s.v. *custom* n., *MED* s.v. *custūm(e* n.), *easy* (early Fr *aisié*; *OED* s.v. *easy* adj., adv. and n., *MED* s.v. *ēsē* adj.), *ermine* (early Fr *(h)ermine*; *OED* s.v. *ermine* n., *MED* s.v. *ermīn* n.), *feeble* (early Fr *feble*; *OED* s.v. *feeble* adj. and n., *MED* s.v. *fēble* adj.), *fruit* (early Fr *fruit*; *OED* s.v. *fruit* n., *MED* s.v. *fruit* n.), *grace* (early Fr *grace*; *OED* s.v. *grace* n., *MED* s.v. *grāce* n.), *honour* (early Fr *(h)onur*; *OED* s.v. *honour, honor* n., *MED* s.v. *honŏur* n.), *justice* (early Fr *justis*; *OED* s.v. *justice* n., *MED* s.v. *justīce* n.), *large* (early Fr *large* (fem.); *OED* s.v. *large* adj., adv. and n., *MED* s.v. *lārǧe* adj.), *lecher* (early Fr *lecheur*; *OED* s.v. *lecher* n.1, *MED* s.v. *lechŏur* n.), *marble* (early Fr *marbre*; *OED* s.v. *marble* n. and adj., *MED* s.v. *marble* n.), *mercy* (early Fr *merci*; *OED* s.v. *mercy* n. and int., *MED* s.v. *mercī* n.1), *miracle* (early Fr *miracle*; *OED* s.v. *miracle* n., *MED* s.v. *mīrācle* n.), *peace* (early Fr *pes, pais*; *OED* s.v. *peace* n., *MED* s.v. *pēs* n.), *poor* (early Fr *pover, pore*; *OED* s.v. *poor* adj. and n.1, *MED* s.v. *povre* adj.), *rhyme* (early Fr *rime*; *OED* s.v. *rhyme* n., *MED* s.v. *rīm(e* n.3), *robber* (early Fr *rob(b)er(e)*; *OED* s.v. *robber* n., *MED* s.v. *robber(e* n.), *scorn* (early Fr *escarnir*; *OED* s.v. *scorn* v., *MED* s.v. *scōrnen* v.), *spouse* (early Fr *spus(e)*; *OED* s.v. *spouse* n., *MED* s.v. *spŏus(e* n.), *treasure* (early Fr *tresor*; *OED* s.v. *treasure* n., *MED* s.v. *trēsŏur* n.), *war* (early (northern) Fr *werre*; *OED* s.v. *war* n.1, *MED* s.v. *wer(re* n.). Of possible French or Latin origin (or both, with the one reinforcing the other) are: *advent* (early Fr *advent* or Lat *adventus*; *OED* s.v. *advent* n., *MED* s.v. *advent* n.), *bar* (early Fr *barre* or late Lat *barra*; *OED* s.v. *bar* n.1, *MED* s.v. *barre* n.), *duke* (early Fr *duc* or Lat *duc-*; *OED* s.v. *duke* n., *MED* s.v. *dūk* n.), *feast* (early Fr *feste* or Lat *festum*; *OED* s.v. *feast* n., *MED* s.v. *fēste* n.), *rent* (early Fr *rent(e)* or medieval Lat *renta*; *OED* s.v. *rent* n.1, *MED* s.v. *rent(e* n.), *sermon* (early Fr *sermun* or Lat *sermŏun-*; *OED* s.v. *sermon* n., *MED* s.v. *sermŏun* n.), *serve* (early Fr *servir* or Lat *servīre*; *OED* s.v. *serve* v.1, *MED* s.v. *serven* v.1). For discussion of the French (and/or Latin) influence on the medieval English lexicon, and for further references, see most recently Skaffari (2009), Miller (2012: 148–91), Skaffari (2012) and Durkin (2014: 223–80).

[31] I use the term 'Old Norse' (ON) here in its traditional Anglophone philological sense to refer to any

Table 1.   Present-day English words first attested in the 12th century and usually recognised as borrowings.

accord (v.)	duke	lecher	scathe
advent	easy	low	scorn (v.)
bank	ermine	marble	seat
bar	feast	meek	seem
bond	feeble	mercy	sermon
boon	flit	miracle	serve
both	fruit	nay	skill
cast	get	peace	sly
clerk	grace	poor	spouse
club	honour	raise (v.)	they, their, them
council	ill	rent	though
court	justice	rhyme	treasure
crooked	kid	robber	want (v.)
custom	large	root	war
die (v.)	loan	same	wrong (adj.)

we go no further, this is extremely potent information: these words are living witnesses to medieval contact situations, actual cultural artefacts from the Normans or the Vikings (and how often can we say that about items we use on a daily basis in the 21st century?). Nevertheless, and inevitably, there are difficulties lurking in lists like this.

Scandinavian language variety down to about 1500 AD. The words in question are: *bank* (cp. ODan *banke*; see *OED* s.v. *bank* n.1, *MED* s.v. *bank(e* n.1), *bond* (cp. OIcel *band*; see *OED* s.v. *bond* n.1, *MED* s.v. *bōnd* n.), *boon* (cp. OIcel *bón*; see *OED* s.v. *boon* n.1, *MED* s.v. *bōn* n. 2), *both* (cp. OIcel *báðir*; see *OED* s.v. *both* adj. and adv., *MED* s.v. *bōthe* num. (as n., adj., and conj.)), *cast* (cp. OIcel *kasta*; see *OED* s.v. *cast* v., *MED* s.v. *casten* v.), *club* (cp. OIcel *klubba*; see *OED* s.v. *club* n., *MED* s.v. *club(be* n.), *crooked* (cp. OIcel *krókr* 'hook'; see *OED* s.v. *crooked* adj., *MED* s.v. *crōked* ppl.), *die* (cp. OIcel *deyja*; see *OED* s.v. *die* v.1, *MED* s.v. *dīen* v.), *flit* (cp. OIcel *flytja*; see *OED* s.v. *flit* v., *MED* s.v. *flitten* v.), *get* (cp. OIcel *geta*; see *OED* s.v. *get* v., *MED* s.v. *gēten* v.1), *ill* (cp. OIcel *illr*; see *OED* s.v. *ill* adj. and n., *MED* s.v. *il(le* adj.), *kid* (cp. OIcel *kið*, Sw, Dan *kid*; see *OED* s.v. *kid* n.1, *MED* s.v. *kide* n.), *loan* (cp. OIcel *lán*; see *OED* s.v. *loan* n.1, *MED* s.v. *lōn(e* n.1), *low* (cp. OIcel *lágr*; see *OED* s.v. *low* adj. and n., *MED* s.v. *loue* adj.), *meek* (cp. OIcel *mjúkr*; see *OED* s.v. *meek* adj. and n., *MED* s.v. *mēk* adj.), *nay* (cp. OIcel *nei*; see *OED* s.v. *nay* adv.1 and n., *MED* s.v. *nai* interj.), *raise* (cp. OIcel *reisa*; see *OED* s.v. *raise* v.1, *MED* s.v. *reisen* v.1), *root* (cp. OIcel *rót*; see *OED* s.v. *root* n.1, *MED* s.v. *rōte* n.4), *same* (cp. OIcel *samr*; see *OED* s.v. *same* adj. (pron., adv.), *MED* s.v. *sām(e* adj.), *scathe* (cp. OIcel *skaða*; see *OED* s.v. *scathe* v., *MED* s.v. *scāthen* v.), *seat* (cp. OIcel *sæti*; see *OED* s.v. *seat* n., *MED* s.v. *sēte* n.2), *seem* (cp. OIcel *sæma*; see *OED* s.v. *seem* v.2, *MED* s.v. *sēmen* v.2), *skill* (cp. OIcel *skil*; see *OED* s.v. *skill* n.1, *MED* s.v. *skil* n.), *sly* (cp. OIcel *slœgr*; see *OED* s.v. *sly* adj., adv. and n., *MED* s.v. *sleigh* adj.), *they, their, them* (cp. OIcel *þeir, þeira, þeim*; see *OED* s.vv. *they* pron., adj., adv. and n., *their* poss. pron., *them* pron., adj. and n., *MED* s.vv. *thei* pron., *their(e* pron., *theim* pron.), *though* (cp. OIcel *þó* (earlier **þóh*); see *OED* s.v. *though* adv., conj. and n., *MED* s.v. *though* conj.), *want* (cp. OIcel *vanta*; see *OED* s.v. *want* v., *MED* s.v. *wanten* v.), *wrong* (cp. OIcel *(v)rangr*; see *OED* s.v. *wrong* adj. and adv., *MED* s.v. *wrong* adj.). For studies of the Old Norse influence on English and Scots lexis see most notably Björkman (1900–2), Rynell (1948), Hofmann (1955), Townend (2002), Dance (2003a), Kries (2003), Skaffari (2009), Pons-Sanz (2013) and references there cited, and for recent survey accounts see esp. Miller (2012: 91–147), Dance (2012a), Durkin (2014: 171–221).

As we saw with *grunnin*, identifying the extent and type of foreign input in a word's history can be challenging, and this is true not only of words for noises. Lists of loan-words from Old Norse, in particular, always conceal a great deal of etymological complexity. Large-scale contact between speakers of Old English and the early Scandinavian languages goes back to the late 9th century, principally in the North and East of England, and the great majority of loans had probably already entered English by 1066, even though many only appear in writing in the 12th century and later. As we might expect, many of these newly recorded words surface first in texts from the old Danelaw, especially the *Peterborough Chronicle* continuations and *The Orrmulum*— but by no means all do so, something which is symptomatic of the amount of time they had already been circulating in spoken English before this.[32] By the major texts of the early 13th century a great many Norse loans are well established throughout England.[33] The 12th century, then, is likely to be a crucial period if we want to understand the diffusion of originally 'Viking words' into English at large; but to do so we first need to work out what is Viking about them. Old English and the Old Norse of the Viking Age were of course closely related and very similar languages.[34] Sometimes this can be a help in tracing the genealogy of words which are first attested in English

[32] Of the words in Table 1, *bond*, *both* and *though* are first attested in the 12th-century additions to the *Peterborough Chronicle* (the latest of which were made in 1155; on Norse-derived lexis in this text see in particular Clark (1970: lxiii, lxix), Kniezsa (1994), Skaffari (2009), Pons-Sanz (2013: Appendix IV)). Words for which *The Orrmulum* (dated *c*.1160–80 by Parkes (1983)) provides clear earliest witnesses are *bank*, *flit*, *get*, *ill*, *kid*, *low*, *meek*, *nay*, *raise*, *same*, *scathe*, *seat*, *seem*, *skill*, *sly*, *they*, *their*, *them*, and *want* (and see further esp. Brate (1885), Townend (2002: 208–10), Skaffari (2009), Dance (2012b: 166–8)). For *boon*, *die* and *root*, Orrm competes with the approximately contemporary main section of Oxford, Bodleian Library, Bodley 343 (on which see further below), which attests them in (using *DOE* short titles) *LS 18.1 (NatMaryAss 10N)* (Pons-Sanz 2013: 488), *LS 5 (InventCrossNap)* (see Dance (2000), Pons-Sanz (2013: 493–4)) and *HomU 4 (Belf 13)* and *LS 5 (InventCrossNap)* (see Pons-Sanz (2013: 485)) respectively. Uncontested in its first appearance in Bodley 343 is *loan* in *ÆHomM 7 (Irv 2)* (see Pons-Sanz (2013: 489), and further below). (Note that I include *low* as first clearly attested in Orrm; it also occurs in the short poetic fragment known as 'The Grave' in Bodley 343, but despite *MED*'s date stencil (c1175 *Body & S.(1)* (Bod 343)), this piece is in a later hand, dated by Ker (1990: 374) to *s.* xii/xiii.) Other first attestations of the Norse-derived words in the list are (with *MED* or *DOE* short titles): *cast* in the *Lambeth* and *Trinity Homilies* (a1225(?OE) *Lamb.Hom.*(Lamb 487); a1225(?a1200) *Trin.Hom.*(Trin-C B.14.52); on these manuscripts see below, n. 71); *club* as a surname in (1166) in *Pipe R.Soc.9*; *crooked* in *LS 9 (Giles)* (Pons-Sanz 2013: 109, 287, 386); *wrong* (adj.) in a place-name form in (a1153) *Coucher Bk.Kirkstall.*

[33] Of those in Table 1, occurring frequently in early 13th-century texts from the South-West Midlands and further south are *bond*, *boon*, *both*, *cast*, *die*, *flit*, *loan*, *low*, *meek*, *nay*, *root*, *seat*, *seem*, *skill*, *sly* and *want*. See the *MED* entries for each cited above, n. 31, and on the South-West Midland texts see esp. Dance (2003a).

[34] For discussion and references see notably Townend (2002), including a comparison of the linguistic systems of the two languages (pp. 19–41) and an important argument for their mutual intelligibility. On the etymological evidence for Norse influence on the English lexicon, the foundational work is Björkman (1900–2); for recent discussion of the issues see Dance (2011; 2012a), Pons-Sanz (2013), Durkin (2014: 190–213).

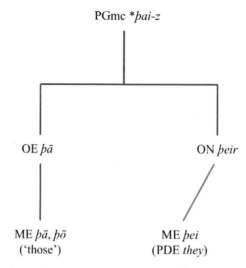

Figure 1.   The etymology of ME *þei* (PDE *they*).

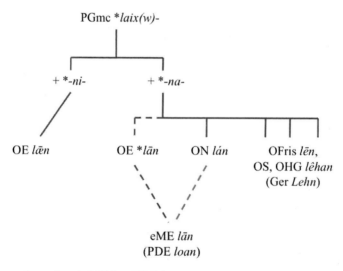

Figure 2.   The etymology of early ME *lān* (PDE *loan*).

during or after the period of contact. Take for instance ME *thei*, PDE (Present-Day English) *they* (earliest recorded in *The Orrmulum*), whose vocalism is an absolutely secure sign that it descends via the Old Norse branch of the Germanic tree, and that it cannot come from Old English (which gives ME *þā, þō* 'those' instead) (see Figure 1).[35] But, at least equally often, this genetic similarity is a source of uncertainty, since there are many proposed Norse loans whose form might have been the offspring of

---

[35] See *OED* s.v. *they* (pron., adj., adv. and n.), Holthausen (1934: s.v. *ðā*), de Vries (1977: s.v. *þeir*), Ásgeir Blöndal Magnússon (1989: s.v. *þeir*), Björkman (1900–2: 50), Dance (2003a: 456–7), Pons-Sanz (2013: 501).

either sibling. The word *loan* itself is one of these. On the face of it, OE *lǣn* and ON *lán* are again formally distinct reflexes of their Germanic parent form (a PGmc **laix-(w)-n-*). But closer investigation of their etymology (see Figure 2) shows that this case is not quite analogous to *they*. Here, it is not the evolution of the Germanic root syllable *per se* which results in the different outputs, but the type of derivational suffix added in each case: Old English has (the disarmingly Pythonesque) *-ni*, and Old Norse the *-na* type, and there is nothing characteristically Scandinavian about the latter; the other West Germanic languages all show it too.[36] In principle, then, an unrecorded Old English cognate with this ending type is perfectly possible, and would have given Middle English *lān*, modern *loan* in just the same way as borrowing from Norse would. So how do we choose between these alternative possible accounts? Once again, it is at least partly a matter of perspective. If we look at this word only in the context of other probable loans, it certainly seems like one. The possibility of native origin is usually (at least tacitly) downplayed, with the lack of any record of an Old English *lān* being regarded as significant counter-evidence. But we could put it next to other items of medieval vocabulary which would give a different impression. Figure 3, for instance, shows the two variants of the Germanic root for a word meaning 'voice', respectively **rezð-* and **razð-*. One English descendant of these, even though it surfaces only belatedly as a rare South-Eastern dialect form *(ge)reard* in Middle English, must have come down the right-hand branch (< PGmc **razð-*), and must be native (in this case it is phonologically impossible to get it from Norse)—it is just as much a native word, in fact, as the alternative from the left-hand branch (< PGmc **rezð-*), which happens to be recorded in Old English (as OE *(ge)reord*).[37] Words of this latter type, where there is secure evidence for Old English descent of a form first attested in Middle

[36] The Gmc nouns (declined fem. in OE, and neut. elsewhere) are derived on the root of the strong verb represented by Go *leihwan*, OE *lēon*, OS, OHG *lîhan*, OFris *liā*, OIcel (pres. ind. 1 sg.) *lé*, and ultimately traceable to a Proto-Indo-European root meaning 'to leave'. See *OED* s.v. *loan* (n.1), Pokorny (1959: I.669), Rix *et al.* (2001: 406–8), Torp (1909: 367), Seebold (1970: 327–8, s.v. *leihw-a-*), Bammesberger (1990: 72, 147, s.vv. **laihw-na-*, **laihw-ni-*), Orel (2003: 232, s.v. **laixwnaz*), Kroonen (2013: 323, s.v. **laihna-*), Lehmann (1986: 230, s.v. *leihwan*), Holthausen (1934: s.v. *lǣn*), de Vries (1977: s.v. *lán*), Ásgeir Blöndal Magnússon (1989: s.v. *lán*), Björkman (1900–2: 30 n.), Pons-Sanz (2013: 489). I have followed the standard authorities in listing OFris *lēn* under the *-na* suffix, even though in principle it could equally well descend from an original *-ni* form (Patrick Stiles, pers. comm.).

[37] On the etymologies of these forms see *OED* s.v. *reird* (n.), Pokorny (1959: I.852), Torp (1909: 340), Orel (2003: 299–300, s.v. **razðō*), Kroonen (2013: 407, s.v. **razdō-*), Lehmann (1986: 283, s.v. *razda*), Holthausen (1934: s.v. *reord* (1)), de Vries (1977: s.v. *rǫdd*), Ásgeir Blöndal Magnússon (1989: s.v. *rödd*). The Old Norse word has undergone assimilation of /zð/ > /ðð/ (> /dd/), on which change see e.g. Noreen (1970: §224.2), Brøndum-Nielsen (1968: §254.1). The ME <ea> forms occur in: (1) the London, British Library, Cotton Vespasian A. xxii version (*c.*1200, probably from Rochester) of Ælfric's *De Initio Creaturae* (Morris (1868: 225/35); on the manuscript and its language see Richards (1978), Laing (1993: 82–3) and Dance (2012b: 169–70) and references there cited); and (2) in the *Ayenbite of Inwyt* (Morris (1965: 24/6, 60/34, 210/32, 265/10); on the language see Gradon (1979: 14–107)).

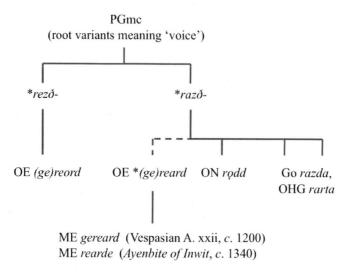

Figure 3.   The etymology of OE *(ge)reord* and ME *reard*.

English, are relatively rare, it is true;[38] but they are also virtually never mentioned when we discuss the case for borrowings from Norse, and this is partly at least, I suspect, because the motivation for finding Vikings in our vocab, the echoes of big cultural collisions from the medieval past, is so powerful, and perennially more exciting than the alternative.[39]

I'm not about to be so controversial as to suggest that we expunge words like *loan* from our received lists of Norse borrowings. But arguments like this are an important indicator that those lists can never be definitive. Over the last few years, I have investigated several hundred proposed Norse loans in Middle English, and the wide range of types of evidence we call on when we identify them as such. About 45 per cent of the stems in my data from *Sir Gawain and the Green Knight* turn out to be of the same broad type as *loan*; that is when a word first attested in late Old or Middle English continues a Germanic root already present in Old English, and when the case for Norse input turns on some more or less remarkable novelty in form or sense or usage

---

[38] For general discussion of words not attested in Old English but (perhaps) able to be reconstructed see Hoad (1985). A classic example is PDE *trust*, which it is now usually agreed cannot be explained as a loan from ON (cp. OIcel *traustr* 'trusty', *treysta* 'to make trusty, trust') but must be referred to a zero-grade derivation on the same PGmc root, which happens not to be recorded in OE; see e.g. *OED* s.v. *trust* adj., d'Ardenne (1961: glossary s.v. *trusten*), Hoad (1985: 139–40). As Patrick Stiles points out to me (pers. comm.), another good analogue is PDE *Wednesday*, which is attested in OE only in the variant with non-mutated stem vowel (OE *wōdnes-*); the alternative in OE *wēdnes-* must have existed (cp. OFris *wednesdei*, MDu *wenesdach*), but is not recorded until early ME (see e.g. *OED* s.v. *Wednesday* n. and adv.).

[39] For some further remarks on the allure of 'the Scandinavian element' see Dance (2013: 51–2). On the comparable phenomenon of 'Nornomania' see Melchers (2012); and for the activities more generally of those he dubs 'contact romantics' see Lass (1997: esp. 201–9).

which is taken to be nearer to Norse, but which could in practice have come about in the native language.[40] Of the 28 examples of very commonly cited Norse loans in Figure 1 above, eleven are moreover of this type. Some of these, notably *both*, *die* and *wrong*, have often been rejected as originally Norse altogether.[41] All in all, this 'grey zone' adds up significantly, resulting in a sizeable discrepancy between the most generous possible lists of Norse borrowings in English on the one hand and the thriftiest on the other. This is a particularly telling instance of how paying attention to the small details, the fine grain of the image as it were, makes an enormous difference to the big picture. It is very important that, wherever possible, we do not present sets of words labelled merely by 'origin' and leave it at that, but that we concern ourselves with the evidence for lexical genealogy and what it means, in other words that we take a properly, analytically etymological approach to our loans.

Such an approach brings other advantages. It is obvious enough to say that a word's history does not stop with identifying its origin; but more than that, it is often the case (especially with a possible borrowing from Norse, though as we shall see not only there) that appreciating its etymological background, the family of words to which it belongs at the level of the Germanic root, can play a fruitful part in understanding its early use in English. *Loan* is again an important example, since it was perhaps its recognisable relationship with the network of words formed on the same root which not only facilitated its integration into English vocabulary in the first place, but which also enabled its take-up and spread by subsequent generations of English

---

[40] A full etymological analysis of the words derived from Old Norse in *Sir Gawain* will appear in a future publication. For the categories of evidence I have employed in this work, see the discussions in Dance (2011) and (2013); *loan* belongs to my 'type C'.

[41] Besides *loan*, these words are: *bank* (cp. ODan *banke*, a formation on the same PGmc root **bank-* as OE *benc* 'bench' (with different suffix) and *hōbanca* 'couch'; see *OED* s.v. *bank* n.1, Björkman (1900–2: 230)); *bond* (cp. OIcel *band*, formed on the same PGmc root **band-* as OE *bend* 'bond' but with a different suffix; see *OED* s.v. *band* n.1, Björkman (1900–2: 229)); *boon* (cp. OIcel *bón*, formed on the same PGmc root **bōn-* as OE *bēn* 'prayer, petition' but with a different suffix; see *OED* s.v. *boon* n.1, Björkman (1900–2: 205, 282)); *both* (cp. OIcel *báðir*, originally a compound of an adj. meaning 'both' and a demonstrative pronoun, which could have arisen independently in English as a combination of OE *bā* + *þā*, and which is sometimes explained in just this way; see *OED* s.v. *both* (adj. and adv.), Björkman (1900–2: 108), Pons-Sanz (2013: 89–90)); *die* (cp. OIcel *deyja*, a verbal formation on the same PGmc root **dau-* as the adj. OE *dēad* 'dead' and the noun OE *dēaþ* 'death'; see *OED* s.v. *die* v.1, Björkman (1900–2: 66, 285), Dance (2000)); *flit* (cp. OIcel *flytja*, a verbal formation on the same PGmc root **flut-* as OE words like *flota* 'boat, sailor'; *OED* s.v. *flit* v., Björkman (1900–2: 210)); *same* (cp. OIcel *samr*, a formation on the same PGmc root **sam-* as OE words like *same* (adv.) 'in the same way'; see *OED* s.v. *same* adj. (pron., adv.), Björkman (1900–2: 218–19)); *seem* (cp. OIcel *sœma*, cognate with OE *(ge)sēman* which had a different sense ('to smooth over, settle, reconcile'); see *OED* s.v. *seem* v.2, Björkman (1900–2: 219)); *sly* (cp. OIcel *slœgr*, an adj. formation on the pret. stem of the verb PGmc **slaxan-* as found in OE *slēan* 'to strike'; see *OED* s.v. *sly* adj., adv. and n., Björkman (1900–2: 219)); *wrong* (cp. OIcel *(v)rangr*, a formation on the same PGmc root **wrang-* as OE *wrang* 'rough, uneven'; see *OED* s.v. *wrong* adj. and adv., Björkman (1900–2: 225, 285), Pons-Sanz (2013: 466–7)).

speakers. Before the later 12th century the main lexical item expressing the concept 'loan' in English texts is the word we encountered above, OE *lǣn*.[42] But, from that point on, our new form *lān* (PDE *loan*) rapidly took over this territory,[43] and was arguably regarded as filling the same space in this etymological word family as *lǣn* had previously occupied. See, for example, its usage in the early 13th-century *Sawles Warde*, where it is the noun corresponding to the related verb *leanen* ('se riche lane . . . þet he haueð ileanet him', 'so rich a loan which he had lent him').[44] It is hard to be sure quite why *lān* caught on in this way at the expense of *lǣn*. But it is worth noticing that, by this period, the form *lǣn* (probably pronounced /lɛːn/) had become somewhat ambiguous in what it could denote—as well as 'a loan', it could now also mean 'a reward' or 'a gift', representing the regular descendant not just of OE *lǣn* but also of the unrelated noun OE *lēan*.[45] Now, you don't need to be a financial mastermind to

---

[42] For OE *lēn* see *BT* s.v. (with additions in *BTS* s.v.), and for other expressions in the same sense area see *TOE* 15.04.01, *HTOED* 02.07.12.04|01 n.

[43] It is first recorded in Bodley 343, in the Ælfric homily called by Irvine (1993) 'The Servant's Failure to Forgive', which is found only in this manuscript. The two instances of *lan(e)* appear in close succession at lines 10–14: 'Ða næfde þe ðeჳen nane mihte to þam þæt he ðam laforde his lane forჳylde; ac þe laford het þa lædon ðone þæჳen mid wife 7 mid alle his cildrum 7 syllæn wið feo, þæt hure his lan wurde him forჳolden' ('Then the thegn had no ability to repay to the lord his loan; but the lord ordered then the thegn with his wife and all his children to be led away and sold for money, so that indeed his loan might be repaid to him.'). For the word's widespread distribution from the early 13th century see *MED* s.v. *lōn(e* n.1, *OED* s.v. *loan* n.1.

[44] Bennett & Smithers (1968: 254, ll. 227–9), based on Oxford, Bodleian Library, Bodley 34. The South-West Midland language of this text is very close dialectally to that found in Bodley 343; see notably Kitson (1992: esp. 33–4).

[45] For OE *lēan* see *BT* s.v. (with additions in *BTS* s.v.), and on its etymology *OED*, s.v. *lean* n.1, Pokorny (1959: I.655), Torp (1909: 371), Orel (2003: 239, s.v. **launan*), Bammesberger (1990: 73, s.v. **lau-na-ⁿ*), Kroonen (2013: 329, s.v. **launa-*), Lehmann (1986: 228–9, s.v. *laun*), Holthausen (1934: s.v. *lēan* (1)). On the monophthongisation of OE /æːa/ and its merger with the reflex of late OE /æː/, usually dated to *c*.1000, see e.g. Schlemilch (1914: 35–6), Campbell (1959: §329.2), Luick (1964: §§355, 356.2 and Anm. 1), Jordan (rev. Crook) (1974: §81), Hogg (1992: §§5.210, 212, 214), Fulk, Bjork & Niles (2008: cxxxiv §7.1), though for an alternative account see Bliss (1949–50). An early instance of the scribal confusion of OE *lēn* and *lēan* has been argued to lie behind *Beowulf* l. 1809b ('sægde him þæs leanes þanc'), a famous crux which has sometimes been resolved by substituting a form of *lǣn* to give the (more plausible) sense 'for that loan'. See Fulk, Bjork & Niles (2008: cxxxiv §7.1, 217–18 (note on ll. 1807–12) and apparatus to l. 1809b) and references there cited; Crépin (1991: 765) goes further and suggests that there is a deliberate play on words by the poet. There is a similar, and less well known, instance of MS <leanes> perhaps for *lǣnes* at *Genesis B* 258a; see Vickrey (1968), but also Doane (1991: 259). In any event, a word spelt <lǣn> could evidently be understood in senses traditionally associated with OE *lēan* by the early 11th century; notice in particular the use of <lǣn> to gloss Lat *commodum* 'profit, reward' and *lucrum* 'gain, riches' at *HlGl* 1061 (Oliphant 1966: 84, gloss 1181), i.e. the 'Harley Glossary' in London, British Library, Harley 3376, dated *s*. x/xi by Ker (1990: 312–13) and localised to Worcester by Cooke (1997: 445–6). The confusion (or merger?) of *lǣn* and *lēan* was presumably facilitated by their semantic contiguity, the basic idea of giving being common to the senses 'loan' and 'gift, reward'; in this connection notice also Rosier (1962: 6 n. 47) (and on lexical merger see Durkin (2009: 79–83)).

work out that not being able clearly to specify whether something was a loan or a gift might have given rise to one or two arguments ('When am I getting my cow back?' 'Oh, but you said it was a /lɛːn/.')[46] The availability of the new variant *lān* (/laːn/) could have helped to resolve this problem, since if one uses it for the sense 'loan', and prefers the form /lɛːn/ to mean 'reward' or 'gift' (and *MED* records this form-type in no other sense), then any potential for confusion is neatly resolved.[47] If *lān* is originally a borrowing from Old Norse, then paying attention to its etymological context in this way gives us an important insight into how it might have caught on in English, how it might have been perceived as a useful, less ambiguous formation on the same root as *lǣn*. And this is hardly surprising: an important corollary of the close genetic similarity of Norse and English is of course the ease with which lexical material from the one could be slotted into the other, and rapidly treated as if it had always been there.[48] But then the same arguments about the early spread of *lān* are true even if we take it as an entirely native variant which was only now coming to prominence. What at one level of etymological discourse is a problem in the identification of origins (is this form

---

[46] For a good example of such ambiguity, notice the Bodley 343 form <læna> at Irvine (1993: 200, text VII.95–7) 'Ne þearf us na tweoȝean þæt he us næle eft þare læna muneȝiæn þæs þe he us her on worlde to forlæt' ('We need not doubt that he will not remind us of those *læna* which he allowed us here in the world'), which can plausibly be interpreted either as 'loans' (as it is by Irvine (1993: 222, glossary s.v. *læn*)) or 'rewards' (as it is by *MED* s.v. *lēn* n., second quotation).

[47] *MED* s.v. *lēn* n. The adoption of ON *lán* as a means to alleviate the confusion of OE *lǣn* and *lēan* is suggested in passing by Crépin (1991: 765). It may be possible to think of this chain of events as an instance of 'homonymic clash', followed by a therapeutic reaction to it; for careful remarks on this phenomenon see more generally Durkin (2009: 88–93), with references, and for the controversy it can generate notice the debate in Samuels (1987) vs. Lass (1987). In any event, the reality in 12th- and early 13th-century usage was evidently somewhat more complex than a clean division between /lɛːn/ 'reward' vs. /laːn/ (/lɔːn/) 'loan'. Notice in particular the instances of *lān* forms being used to mean 'reward, payment' (*MED* s.v. *lōn(e* n.1. sense 1(c)), viz. a1225(?c1175) *PMor.*(Lamb 487) 64 and c1225(?c1200) *St.Kath.(1)* (Einenkel) 805, both in the phrase 'swinkes lan' (the first of which is in fact misleadingly cited by *OED* s.v. *lean* (n.1) (third quotation) as if < OE *lēan*). This is another interesting indication that *lān* was understood as belonging to the same 'family' of words as OE *lēan*, since it is here being slotted into a formulaic collocation formerly occupied by *lēan* or *edlēan*; such a phrase occurs several times in late Old English writers including Ælfric (e.g. *Catholic Homilies* II.31 l. 99 'ures geswinces edlean'; Godden 1979: 271), and for a similar idiom using early ME *læn* compare *The Orrmulum* Dedication l. 333 ('forr hiss swinnc to læn'; Holt 1878).

[48] For some of the consequences of this similarity during the period of contact see Townend (2002: esp. 43–68). It is worth noticing in this connection that borrowings from Old Norse, far from disrupting the 'associative' (or 'consociated') character of the Old English lexical system, as one normally assumes loanwords to do, would in many cases conceivably have reinforced and added to the networks of words formed recognisably on the same roots. This is true of all the words listed above, n. 41, which (it will be recalled, and for the very same reasons) are also amongst those most liable to have their identification as borrowings debated. For some discussion of 'consociated' and 'dissociated' lexis and the effects of borrowing see Durkin (2014: 6), with references; and for a good overview of the characteristics of early English word formation and its development see Kastovsky (2006).

from Old Norse or not?), at another is an opportunity to understand the dynamics of change in the systems of related words in early English, something which seems to me at least as interesting and worthwhile an exercise. In other words, from the point of view of tracing *this* aspect of its early history, at least, it does not necessarily matter whether *loan* is a loan or not.

A CASE STUDY: 'RICH' AND 'POOR'

Bald lists of Modern English words like that in Table 1 are, of course, simplifying in both these respects: they elide etymological complexities, and they tell us nothing about the contexts within the medieval English lexicon upon which so much of our evidence for the early usage and transmission of words depends. If we try to draw conclusions about the history of these words without any of these details, then the results are likely to be superficial, sometimes transparently so. It might momentarily be tempting, for instance, to find in many of the words in our Table (notably *bar, clerk, council, court, custom, duke, ermine, feast, feeble, honour, justice, lecher, mercy, poor, rent, robber, scorn, serve, treasure, war*) evidence for Norman rulers lording it over and oppressing the Anglo-Saxon masses, imposing feebleness, violence, imprisonment and poverty, and introducing them to the horrors of servitude and administration; but such selective readings of the loan-record can in practice be used to serve any socio-cultural stereotype we like, and are best avoided. There are some cognate arguments which, on the face of it, seem more sophisticated, but which proceed from similarly one-dimensional takes on a word's language of origin and modern meanings, and as such are equally insubstantial. The most famous example is the claim popularised by Walter Scott in *Ivanhoe*, namely that animal and meat word-pairs in Modern English with originally French vs. native constituents, like *beef/cow, pork/pig* and *mutton/ sheep*, derive directly from the fact that it was the Norman lords who feasted on the cooked product in their hall, while the (doubtless thoroughly Pythonesque) Anglo-Saxon peasants tended the beast in the field.[49] This theory seems eminently plausible, precisely because it rings so true, at least to popular stereotypes. But when we examine the actual usage of the corresponding items in Middle English it turns out to be a massive simplification; as Kornexl and Lenker have recently shown, a clear specialisa-tion of meat vs. animal terms did not develop in English until much later, with the French-derived words being used to refer to living animals until well into the early Modern period.[50]

---

[49] Scott (1998: 21), cited by Kornexl & Lenker (2011: 179–80). According to Jespersen (1982: 82–3), this observation goes back at least as far as John Wallis's *Grammatica linguae Anglicanae* (1653).
[50] Kornexl & Lenker (2011); see also Durkin (2014: 423).

The fact is that loanwords do not inevitably or quite so obviously bear the stamp of their originary situation on them, and in order to get beyond the impressionistic and try to understand how such words were adopted and used by medieval speakers and writers of English we need to look in as much detail as possible at their occurrences in the extant texts. In interpreting their contexts within these documents, we have to reckon not only with date and geography, but with the effects of other, complex variables like the transmission of manuscript texts through successive strata of scribal copying.[51] When it comes to vocabulary, we also have to deal with that array of factors in word choice which come together loosely under the heading 'semantic'. We rightly now think of language as a 'population of variants moving through time' (in Roger Lass's famous formulation),[52] and this is as true of the contents of semantic fields as it is of systems like phonology and morphology; there will normally be a variety of possible ways of expressing roughly the same idea, with their occurrence motivated by more or less fine nuances not just of denotative meaning but also of connotation, style and idiom.[53] Historically, when we attempt to track the emergence of a new word, we need ideally to consider what this semantic context was like beforehand, how our new word fits in, and how the range of choices and therefore meanings within this system might have changed. Research in this area has been transformed by the completion in 2009, after forty-four years, of the peerless *Historical Thesaurus of the Oxford English Dictionary*—one of the most impressive research projects ever undertaken in the humanities, and one which has helped nurture and develop the whole field of study to which this lecture belongs.[54]

In order to exemplify all these factors, let us look at some changing words and meanings in just one particular corner of English vocabulary in our period. The entry of foreign material into a recipient language is so often conceptualised, as we have seen, in pseudo-economic terms, as cultural capital which can be 'loaned' or 'borrowed';[55] and it therefore seemed appropriate here to explore some expressions

[51] For key discussions of these variables in the context of medieval English dialectology see Benskin & Laing (1981), Laing (2004), Laing & Lass (2006) and the *LAEME* website (especially the 'Introduction' accessible at http://www.lel.ed.ac.uk/ihd/laeme1/laeme1_frames.html).

[52] See e.g. Lass (1997: 377).

[53] For a case-study of some early ME loans in these respects see Dance (2003a: 200–84). For helpful introductions to lexical systems and semantic change see e.g. Smith (1996: 112–40), Durkin (2009: 222–65).

[54] The contents of the full printed *HTOED* are searchable online at http://historicalthesaurus.arts.gla.ac.uk, and are also accessible via the online *OED* (in a slightly revised format, giving dates of first attestation according to *OED3* and omitting words attested only in Old English; it is this latter version on which I base Tables 2 and 3). For accounts of its history and principles see *HTOED* I.xiii–xx, and references there cited.

[55] For introductions to this and related terminology see e.g. Durkin (2009: 132–40), Durkin (2014: 3, 8–11), and see further Fischer (2001).

Table 2. English expressions for 'rich or wealthy' since *c*.1150 (from *HTOED* 02.07.05 adj.); dates of first attestation in brackets.

rich (eOE)	strong (1622)
eadi (OE)	fortuned (1632)
richful (*c*.1300)	affluent (1652)
wealthful (13..)	rhinocerical (1688)
plenteous (*c*.1350)	rough (1721)
wealthy (*c*.1380)	rowthy (1792)
big (?*a*.1400)	strong-handed (1818)
wlouȝ (*a*.1400)	wealth-encumbered (1844)
well (*c*.1405)	nabobish (1857)
golded (*c*.1450)	rhinoceral (1860)
substantious (1490)	ingoted (1864)
opulent (?1518)	tinny (1871)
substantive (1543)	pocket-filled (1886)
fat (1611)	oofy (1896)
juicy (1621)	

Table 3. English expressions for 'poor' since *c*.1150 (from *HTOED* 02.07.06 | 01 adj.); dates of first attestation in brackets.

arm (*c*.1000)	indigent (*c*.1400)	egene (1631)
haveless (*c*.1000)	mean (*c*.1400)	starveling (1638)
waedle (*c*.1000)	naughty (*c*.1400)	necessitated (1646)
naked (OE)	succourless (1412–20)	inopious (1656)
needful (OE)	unwealthy (*c*.1412)	fortuneless (*a*.1666)
helpless (*c*.1175)	behove (1413)	down at heel (1732)
wantsum (?*c*.1200)	misterous (*a*.1425)	parsimonious (1782)
bare (*c*.1220)	miserable (*c*.1485)	lacking (1805)
poor (*a*.1225)	beggarly (1545)	unopulent (1816)
misease (?*c*.1225)	starved (1559)	bushed (1819)
unwealy (*a*.1300)	threadbare (1577)	obolary (1823)
needy (*c*.1325)	penurious (1590)	ill-to-do (1853)
feeble (*c*.1330)	wealthless (1605)	needsome (1870)
poorful (1372)	necessitous (1611)	unrich (1875)
mischievous (*c*.1390)	inopulent (1613)	rocky (1921)
miseased (*c*.1390)	titheless (*a*.1618)	

describing the distribution of wealth, and to look at words meaning 'rich' and 'poor'. Using the *Historical Thesaurus*, we can see at a stroke all the words and phrases which have lexicalised the broad concept of 'rich or wealthy' from about 1150; see Table 2 (dates of first attestation follow *OED*).[56] These make for a very colourful bunch, especially in the 16th and 17th centuries, which gives us expressive terms like *fat, juicy* and *rhinocerical*; more recent highlights include *oofy* (from 1896). But if anything the *HTOED* entry for 'poor' (Table 3) is more varied still, including the likes of *naughty, necessitous, inopious, bushed* and *rocky*—demonstrating perhaps that the only thing

[56] Note that in Tables 2 and 3 I cite the *Thesaurus* entry as accessed via the online *OED* (at http://www.oed.com/view/th/class/144948 and http://www.oed.com/view/th/class/145099 respectively).

Table 4. Principal words denoting 'rich' and 'poor' in Old English (not including developments from the 10th century onwards).

'rich'	'poor'
ēadig	earm
gesǣlig	hēan
spēdig	þearfende (þearfa 'a poor person')
welig (weliga 'a rich person')	wǣdla

people have always been obsessed with more than money is *not* having it. Turning to the *Thesaurus of Old English*, a major off-shoot of the main *Thesaurus* project published in 1995,[57] we can explore in greater detail the most common and productive word families for our two broad concepts in Old English; these are set out in Table 4. Their use and their focal meanings naturally varied according to date, dialect and author, but they can all properly be grouped together as specifically denoting wealth and poverty in at least some texts. Leaving aside developments from the later 10th century onwards (dealt with below), the key Old English adjectives which could mean 'wealthy' were *ēadig*, *gesǣlig*, *spēdig* and *welig*.[58] The idea of poverty was expressed primarily

---

[57] *TOE*, searchable online at http://oldenglishthesaurus.arts.gla.ac.uk. On its principles see *TOE* I.xv–xxxv.

[58] See the words listed under *TOE* 15.01.05, especially the sub-category 'rich' and its various sub-sub-categories ('rich in (worldly) goods', 'very rich, opulent', 'rich in . . .'). Some (perforce impressionistic) remarks on these four adjectives and their attested uses: (1) The basic sense of OE *ēadig*, derived on the root of PGmc **auðaz/*auðan* 'wealth', appears to have been 'fortunate, blessed'. In homiletic and devotional literature it is most frequently encountered with religious connotations, viz. in *DOE*'s senses 2 ('blessed by God, favoured with divine blessing') or 3 ('worthy of reverence or adoration, blessed, revered'); but it was clearly also used to specify material prosperity (*DOE*'s sense 1.b 'referring to good fortune in material possessions'), and it is often found as the formulaic antonym of *earm*, especially but not only in legal texts (including in six out of seven of the citations at *DOE* sense 1.b.i.a 'adjective used as substantive: the rich, the prosperous'; for some remarks on this collocation see Weisweiler (1923: 318–20)). See esp. *OED* s.v. *eadi* adj., *DOE* s.v. *ēadig*, Bammesberger (1990: 54, s.v. **aud-a-z*), Orel (2003: 28, s.v. **auðaȝaz ~ *auðiȝaz*), Kroonen (2013: 40, s.v. **auda-*), Holthausen (1934: s.v. *ēadig*). (2) OE *gesǣlig*, formed on the PGmc adj. stem **sēli-* 'kind, happy', could likewise be used to describe the effects of good fortune in a variety of guises, often spiritual but sometimes specifically material; see esp. *BTS* sense IIa. 'having a fortune, wealthy', and notice also the compound *cornsǣlig*. See esp. *OED* s.v. *seely* adj., *BT* and *BTS* s.vv. *gesǣlig*, Heidermanns (1993: 476–7), Orel (2003: 327, s.v. **sēliz*), Holthausen (1934: s.v. *sǣlig*). (3) OE *spēdig* derives from the noun PGmc **spōði-* 'success, speed', but its literal meaning 'successful' is found alongside numerous instances where it denotes success in material things, i.e. wealth (see *BT*'s sense II 'having means, wealthy, opulent, rich in material wealth'), and it is very frequently found compounded in this sense (e.g. OE *goldspēdig*, *woruldspēdig*). See esp. *BT* and *BTS* s.vv. *spēdig*, Bammesberger (1990: 146, s.v. **spō-di-*), Kroonen (2013: 469, s.v. **spōdi-*), Holthausen (1934: s.v. *spēd*). (4) OE *welig* is formed ultimately on the same root as the adv. *wel* and the verb *willan*. Like the related noun OE *wela* ('prosperity, happiness, riches') it is very frequently used to refer to material riches, but could also denote welfare and well-being more generally. See esp. *OED* s.v. *wealy* adj.1, *BT* and *BTS* s.vv. *welig*, Orel (2003: 453, s.v. **wel(j)anan*), Kroonen (2013: 578, s.v. **weljan-* 1), Holthausen (1934: s.v. *welig* (2)). The remaining uncompounded adj. forms listed by *TOE* under these categories are *gifig*, *maga* and *weleþig*, but each of these is rare and/or only obliquely to be associated with this sense area; see respectively *DOE* s.v. *gyfig*, *gifig*, *BTS* s.v. *maga* ('able'), *BTSC* s.v. *weleþig*.

with *earm* or *hēan*, or a derivative of *þearf*, or with *wǣdla*.[59] All of these words seem to have been reasonably well established ways of describing wealth and its absence, and are sometimes found in variation with one another. For instance, here is an example of Ælfric using a couple of different synonyms for 'rich' and 'poor', for stylistic variety in the same passage:[60]

> Se welega is geworht for ðan þearfan *and* se þearfa for ðam welegan. Þam spedigum gedafenaþ *þæt* he spende *and* dæle; þam wædlan gedafenað *þæt* he gebidde for ðam dælere.

But by early Middle English things have changed considerably, at least to judge by this passage from an early 13th-century life of Saint Katherine, where the rich/poor binary is expressed by the ancestors of precisely our words, *riche* and *poure*:[61]

> sende heaste ant bode . . . þet poure ba ant riche comen þer biuoren him to þe temple i þe tun [of] his heaðene godes, euchan wið his lac forte wurðgin ham wið . . . þe riche reoðeren ant schep—ant bule, hwase mahte—brohte[n] to lake, þe poure cwike briddes

---

[59] See *TOE* 15.01.06, notably the sub-categories 'a poor person' and 'poor, needy, indigent' and their several sub-sub-categories. On these forms notice: (1) OE *earm* (< PGmc **arma-* 'wretched, miserable', of obscure ulterior etymology) is a very common adj. describing misery and wretchedness, often specifically that of material poverty, see esp. *BT* and *BTS* sense (2) 'poor, destitute'. See esp. *OED* s.v. *arm* adj., *BT* and *BTS* s.vv. *earm* adj., Heidermanns (1993: 104–5), Orel (2003: 24, s.v. **armaz* II), Kroonen (2013: 35, s.v. **arma-* 2), Weisweiler (1923: 304–25), Holthausen (1934: s.v. *earm* (2)). (2) OE *hēan* (< PGmc **hauna-* 'shameful') could refer to the condition of being humble, low and/or ignoble in a wide range of circumstances, but often implies or specifies a lack of wealth; see esp. *BTS* sense I.1 ('of low degree, of humble condition, low, poor, as opposed to *rīce, welig, wlanc*'). See esp. *OED* s.v. *hean, hene* adj., *BT, BTS* and *BTSC* s.vv. *hēan*, Heidermanns (1993: 286–7), Orel (2003: 166, s.v. **xaunaz*), Kroonen (2013: 216, s.v. **hauna-*), Holthausen (1934: s.v. *hēan* (1)). (3) OE *þearfa, þearfende* are formed on the (pres. 3 sg. ind. stem of the) preterite-present verb PGmc **þurfan-* 'to need', hence literally 'a needy person', but are usually attested with reference to material poverty. See esp. *OED* s.v. *tharf, thar* v., *BT, BTS* and *BTSC* s.vv. *þearfa, þearfan*, Seebold (1970: 509–10), Orel (2003: 417, s.v. **þarfa*), Kroonen (2013: 552, s.v. **þurfan-*), Holthausen (1934: s.vv. *þearfa, þearfian*). (4) OE *wǣdla* (< PGmc **wēþla-*) is the adj. derived on OE *wǣdl* 'poverty, want', and generally refers to one lacking material wealth, sometimes specifically a beggar (translating Lat *mendicus*). See esp. *OED* s.v. *waedle* adj. and n.2, *BT* s.v. *wǣdla*, Pokorny (1959: I.84), Holthausen (1934: s.v. *wǣdla, wǣðla*). The other synonyms in these categories in *TOE* are mainly compounds, either expressing a lack of possessions (e.g. *næftig, unāga, wanhafa, wanhafol*) or qualifying one of the words for 'wealthy' given above (e.g. *medspēdig, wanspēdig, unmaga*); see the respective entries in *BT, BTS, BTSC*.

[60] Ælfric, *Catholic Homilies* I.18, ll. 205–7, ed. Clemoes (1997: 324), based on London, British Library, Royal 7 C.xii (I have modernised the punctuation and capitalisation and expanded the abbreviations). 'The wealthy person is made for the needy, and the needy for the wealthy. It is fitting for the successful person that he spend and distribute [his goods]; for the impoverished one it is fitting that he pray for the distributor.'

[61] *Seinte Katerine* ll. 17–22, ed. d'Ardenne & Dobson (1981: 4), critical text based on Oxford, Bodleian Library, Bodley 34. 'He sent an order and command that both poor and rich should come before him at the temple of his heathen gods in the town, each one with his offering to honour them with . . . the rich brought cattle and sheep—and bulls, if they could—as offerings, the poor brought live birds.'

The easy assumption at this point is to put this change down to contact with medieval French: *poure* is indisputably a French loan, and *riche* has sometimes been assumed to be one too. Again, could this be an example of the oppressed English masses having words for economic status imposed on them by the people who held the purse-strings, their Norman overlords? To claim a straight rupture between the pre- and post-Conquest vocabularies of wealth is once more, however, to make too much of Old and Middle English as distinct language states, to look backwards from one and forwards from the other. Things get far more complicated, and far more interesting, when we see the fuller picture, and look at the bit in between.

This of course involves us noticing the Old English adjective *rīce*, the history of which is delightfully knotty. As illustrated by the family tree in Figure 4, Old English *rīce* and its siblings elsewhere in the early Germanic languages come from a Proto-Germanic adjective whose stem we can reconstruct as **rīkja-*. But the vowel /iː/ indicates that this stem did not descend straightforwardly via the Germanic line from the Proto-Indo-European word for ruler; instead we have a borrowing here into Germanic from the Celtic family, which must have happened when the two groups were in contact at a very early period in continental Europe.[62] I have given the sense of Old English *rīce* both as 'powerful' and 'wealthy', because (as Malcolm Godden has shown), while 'powerful' was the original sense of the adjective, it had come to be used to denote a particular facet of power, economic wealth, already by the 10th century; it is Ælfric's favourite word for 'wealthy', in fact.[63] The reasons for this semantic shift are potentially complex, but they can very plausibly be linked to socio-cultural developments well before the Norman Conquest. Robin Fleming in particular has written compellingly of the growth of a commercialised, cash economy in later Anglo-Saxon England, and of the extravagent displays of wealth by elite families, including in dress and fine dining—and, as both Fleming and Godden suggest, it seems entirely fitting that an adjective meaning 'powerful' came in this very period increasingly to denote economic riches.[64] As summarised in Figure 4, there were parallel developments in most of the

---

[62] For etymological discussion see *OED* s.v. *rich* adj, n., and adv., Pokorny (1959: I.856), Torp (1909: 342), Lehmann (1986: 283), Heidermanns (1993: 450–1), Orel (2003: 305, s.v. **rīkjaz*), Kroonen (2013: 412–13, s.v. **rīk-*), Ross & Thomson (1976), Green (1998: 150–1), Holthausen (1934: s.v. *rīce* (2)), Durkin (2014: 69–71), Jensen (1976), Ris (1971), Kniezsa (1992: 507–10, 513–15), *DEAF* s.v. *riche* adj., Diensberg (2006: 46).

[63] Godden (1990), with some reference to the earlier discussion in Mincoff (1933: 149–53). The earliest instances of *rīce* clearly denoting material wealth are in the Vercelli and Blickling homilies, argues Godden (1990: 48–50).

[64] Fleming (2001), Godden (1990: esp. 41–2, 53–4). For a different interpretation of the underlying economic phenomena see Sawyer (2013: 106–8), who prefers to explain the semantic shift as symptomatic of the fact that, by the later 10th century, wealth was no longer simply 'an attribute of power' but was now the province also of merchants, traders and others who could be wealthy without also necessarily being powerful.

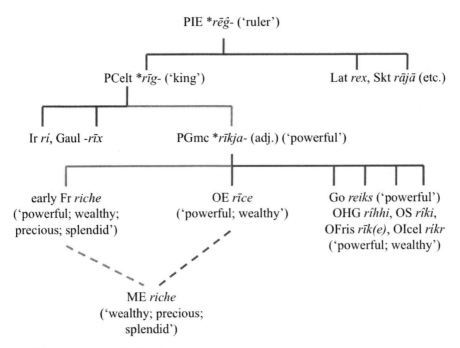

Figure 4.   The etymology of ME *riche*.

Germanic cognates of *rīce*, and also in the early French word *riche*—which, just to complicate the pedigree of these words still further, is itself a borrowing from Germanic.[65] Now, all this of course makes it difficult for us to label the immediate etymological source of early Middle English *riche*, since we have formally and semantically near-identical words in both Old English and French. Some etymologists, notably Skeat, have derived the Middle English word purely from Old English.[66] But we probably need to allow for at least some influence from the sense range of medieval French *riche* in explaining the meanings 'precious, splendid' in Middle English; and

[65] OHG *rîhhi* is recorded meaning 'wealthy' (translating Lat *dives*) from the late 9th century, and OS *rîki* translates *dives* once in *The Heliand*; see Ris (1971: 37–53). (Ris (1971: 53–8) argues that the new meaning developed as a semantic loan from Lat *dives*, though as far as I can see his evidence for this is purely circumstantial, i.e. that the sense 'wealthy' is first attested in literature translated from Latin.) For the senses of early Fr *riche* see *AND* s.v. *riche*, *DEAF* s.v. *riche* adj., *AFW* s.v. *riche* adj., *DMF* s.v. *riche*, Venckeleer (1975: 413–51). Sawyer (2013: 107–8) regards the semantic developments of the English and German words as directly connected, both being products of the economic growth shared by England and Germany in this period (including important trading links between the two; Sawyer (2013: 98–101, 104–5)). Note that the sense 'wealthy' is attested relatively late for OIcel *rîkr* ('about the end of the 13th century', according to Cleasby-Vigfusson s.v.), and in this respect Old Norse as a whole probably shows influence from the use of the cognate word in Low German (so e.g. Falk & Torp (1960: s.v. *Rig*)).

[66] Skeat (1887: 61–2) ('To these we must add *rice*, rich, not borrowed from French, though existing as *riche* in that language . . .'). For some discussion of etymological authorities' differing attitudes in this respect see further Kniezsa (1992: 508, 510).

there are closely related derivatives like Middle English *richesse* which are much more obviously French in form.[67] All in all, we can certainly identify *change* as going on in the usage of early English *rīce* from late Old English to early Middle English; but the Norman Conquest certainly is not the pre-eminent engine of that change that we might have anticipated, and how much in the end we label this word 'native' and how much 'foreign' is another nice problem in etymological hermeneutics. If we do think of Middle English *riche* as effectively a 'blend', a combination of English and French inputs, then this only adds to the complex sequence of to-and-fro between major European language families which characterises this word's history over more than a millennium. Moveable wealth indeed.

If we examine our other words for 'rich' and 'poor' in the period from the early 12th to the early 13th centuries, we find a similarly complex mixture of continuity and change. To recap on our starting point, Table 5 once again shows the key Old English words in these fields, updated now to include *rīce* in the first column. To the words for 'poor' we can moreover add *wrecce*, which began life in Old English meaning 'exiled', but which increasingly in late Old English came to signify 'wretched, unfortunate' and by the 12th century was very clearly being used to mean 'poor' in the sense 'financially impoverished'.[68] In Table 6 are some of the major (wholly or predominantly) 'new' texts of the 12th and early 13th centuries: the interpolations and continuations to the *Peterborough Chronicle* made mainly in the 1120s and 1150s;[69] the *Orrmulum*,

---

[67] For the sense 'precious, splendid' see *MED* s.v. *rīche* adj., senses (2) and (3), *OED* s.v. *rich* adj., n, and adv., sense (5), and compare *AND* s.v. *riche* sense (a) (sub-senses inc. 'costly; splendid, magnificent; precious'), Venckeleer (1975: 413–51). For *richesse* see *MED* s.v. *riches(se* n., *OED* s.v. *richesse* n., and compare *AND* s.v. *richesce*, *DEAF* s.v. *richece* f., *AFW* s.v. *richece* s. f., *DMF* s.v. *richesse* subst. fém., Venckeleer (1975: 437–42).

[68] The OE adj. *wrecce, wrǽcce* is a derivative of the noun *wrecca, wrǽcca* 'exile, adventurer, wretch', formed on the pret. 1/3 sg. ind. stem of the PGmc verb **wrekan-* (original meaning probably 'to pursue'). For etymological discussion see *OED* s.v. *wretch* n. and adj., Pokorny (1959: I.1181), Torp (1909: 415–16), Lehmann (1986: 410, s.v. **wrikan*), Seebold (1970: 568–70), Orel (2003: 471–2, s.v. *wrekanan*), Kroonen (2013: 594, s.v. **wrakjan-*), Holthausen (1934: s.v. *wrecca*). For attested senses of the noun and adj. in OE and ME see further *BT*, *BTS*, *BTSC* s.vv. *wrec(c)*, *wrecca* and *MED* s.vv. *wrecche* adj., *wrecche* n., and for a discussion of the semantic developments in the context of the broader lexical field see Rumball (2008: 7–22). The earliest witness to the adj. unambiguously denoting 'impoverished' (i.e. *MED*'s sense 1(c)) is plausibly the *Life of St Nicholas* in Cambridge, Corpus Christi College 303, Treharne (1997) (*DOE*'s *LS 29 (Nicholas)*) esp. ll. 88 and 109, where it refers to the poor man enriched by the saint. The manuscript is dated *s.* xii[1] or *s.* xii[med], but this text is likely to have been composed in the late 11th century (see Ker (1990: 99–105, no. 57), Laing (1993: 23), Treharne (1997: 19–21, 72–8), Treharne (2010a), Rumball (2008: 21 n. 91), Pons-Sanz (2013: 386)).

[69] For references see above, n. 13. I have searched for words meaning 'rich' and 'poor' in this text using the *Dictionary of Old English Corpus* (*OEC*, at http://tapor.library.utoronto.ca/doecorpus/), and cite references by annal and line number from Irvine (2004). *Rice* is frequent (I count 15 examples in the interpolations and continuations), and often refers unambiguously to material wealth, e.g. s.a. 1137 ll. 40–1, 'Wrecce men sturuen of hungær; sume ieden on ælmes þe waren sum wile rice men', in contrast

Table 5. Principal words denoting 'rich' and 'poor' in Old English (including developments from the 10th century onwards).

'rich'	'poor'
ēadig	earm
rīce	hēan
gesǣlig	þearfende (þearfa 'a poor person')
spēdig	wǣdla
welig (weliga 'a rich person')	wrecce

Table 6. Words denoting 'rich' and 'poor' in major English texts from the 12th and early 13th centuries (unmarked choices in bold face).

	'rich'	'poor'
Peterborough Chronicle (12th-century additions)	**rice**	**wrecc-** (haueleste, ærm)
The Orrmulum	**riche** (sel, sellþe)	**wrecch-**, usell, wædle (wanntsumm)
The Lambeth Homilies	**riche** (eadi; iselhðe)	**wrec(c)h-** (erm, henðe, haueles(te), þarua; pouerte)
The Trinity Homilies	**riche** (richeise)	**wrech-** (haue(n)les, poure)
The AB Language	**riche** (weolie, weoleful)	**poure** (pouerte, poureliche) (wrech-)
Laʒamon's Brut (Caligula MS)	**riche** (weoli, eadi, weorld-seli)	**wrecch-**, hæn (wædle, pouere)

written in Lincolnshire between about 1160 and 1180;[70] the *Lambeth* and *Trinity Homilies*, copied *c.*1200 in the South-West and South-East Midlands respectively;[71]

---

with *wrecce*. I count 6 occurrences of *wrecc-* as a simplex, plus one of the derivative *wreccehed*, the majority of which seem to refer to worldly poverty and its attendant misery (as in the example cited above). There is also one instance of *haueleste* 'poverty' s.a. 675 l. 25. OE *earm* is represented in these annals only once as a simplex, and it is not clear that poverty is what is mainly being denoted by the adj. ('þet ærme folc' referred to s.a. 1124 l. 47 have indeed been deprived of their property, but this is not the only hardship they have suffered, and their pitiableness is more likely to be what is at issue; cp. the adv. *earmlice* s.a. 1127 l. 51 and s.a. 1128 l. 26, which has no evident connection with material poverty and which is best translated 'miserably' or 'grievously').

[70] For references see above, n. 13. My data for *The Orrmulum* is derived from searches of the electronic version of the text in the *Corpus of Middle English Prose and Verse* (*CMEPV*, at http://quod.lib.umich. edu/c/cme/), with citations by line from Holt (1878). *Riche* appears 14 times, often unambiguously referring to earthly wealth, as e.g. 12084 'riche off ahhte'; the nouns *se(o)llþe* (and negative *unse(o)llþe*) are numerous, but alongside *sel* (twice) usually indicate a non-specific 'happiness' and only occasionally might imply material riches, e.g. 14304 'All middellærdess sellþe & sel'. *Wrecch-* (I count 17 instances of the simplex, plus one each of *wrecceliʒ* and *wrecchelike*) does not often seem to denote material poverty *per se*, but notice e.g. 5638, 'All wrecche & wædle & usell mann', where *wrecch-* is found in sequence with the otherwise rarer adjectives *usell* (7 occurrences as a simplex, and once in the nominal derivative *uselldomm*) and the less ambiguous *wædle* (4 occurrences); *wanntsumm* is found once only (14824). (Despite the gloss 'happiness, prosperity' at *OED* s.v. *eadi* adj., Orrm's *ædiʒleʒʒc* does not seem in context to refer to material prosperity; *MED* s.v. *ēdīleǧ(e* n. translates more persuasively as 'One of the virtues blessed in the Beatitudes, a blessing'.)

[71] The *Lambeth Homilies* are found in London, Lambeth Palace Library 487, edited by Morris (1868:

and the texts in the AB Language and the earlier version of Laȝamon's *Brut*, all South-West Midland compositions probably datable to the first half of the 13th century.[72] In each case I have highlighted (in bold face) what seem to be the unmarked

2–159) and in part also by O'Brien (1985); on the manuscript and its language see esp. O'Brien (1985: 12–113), Laing (1993: 111), Laing (2008: 2–3, 125–30), Swan (2010), plus Dance (2011: 82–5) and references there cited. I have searched these texts via *CMEPV*, and cite them by homily number, page and line from Morris (1868). *Riche* occurs 14 times, including 5 times in Homily X, a revised version of a composite Ælfric homily (3 of these 5 occurrences continue Ælfric's *rica* but the remaining 2 replace OE *welega*; cp. the earlier version in Cambridge, Corpus Christi College 178, printed in Morris (1868: Appendix II) and in parallel with the Lambeth text in O'Brien (1985: 203–50), and see also Dance (2011: 84)); *eadi* only once refers to material prosperity, in the doublet 'ne ermne ne eadine' at X. 115/19, retained from the Ælfrician version ('ne earmne ne eadigne'); formations on the *sel-* root generally also have a spiritual connotation, with the exception of *iselhðe* at X. 109/30 'þe ȝitsere þe þurh his iselhðe leoseð' (cp. Corpus 178 *gesælþa*). *Wrec(c)h-* is very common (I count 42 instances of the simplex, plus 3 of *wrechede*), usually referring to non-specific wretchedness, but several instances unambiguously indicate worldly poverty, e.g. III. 39/31 'Nis nan mon swa riche. ne swa wrecche'; in Homily X, comparison with the earlier version in Corpus 178 reveals that the Lambeth redactor has consistently replaced OE *þearfa* (10×) and *wædla* (once) with *wrec(c) h-* (the only exception comes in a pair of synonyms at X. 115/7–8, where OE 'ic eom wædla & þearfa' is updated to 'Ic em þarua and wrecche', thereby giving the only instance of *þarua* in the manuscript); *e(a)rm* occurs 4 times as a simplex (plus 4 *e(a)rming*, 1 *ermðe*, 1 *ermlic*), mainly once more denoting unspecified misery, but material poverty is clearly implied at X. 115/19 in the pair 'ne ermne ne eadine' (noticed above); *haueles* 'poor' appears at X. 111/7 (cp. Corpus 178 *hafenleasan*) and in the phrase 'hafelesen monne' (translating Lat *pauperibus*) at XIII. 135/26, and *haueleste* 'poverty' (alongside *henðe*, probably generic misfortune, loss) at X. 115/3–4 'þe haueleste þe of henðe cumeð' (cp. Corpus 178 'seo hafenleast þe of hynðum becymð'); *pouerte* also appears once only, at XIV. 143/36. The *Trinity Homilies* are in Cambridge, Trinity College B.14.52, edited by Morris (1873: 2–219); see notably Laing (1993: 37–8), Laing & McIntosh (1995), Laing (2008: 31–34), Treharne (2010b). Again, my data is based on a search of *CMEPV*, with references by homily, page and line from Morris (1873). *Riche* occurs 8 times in these texts, including in the sense 'expensive, splendid' which likely shows French influence (e.g. the reference to 'riche weden' at VI. 33/21, 29); there is also the derivative *richeis(s)e*, clearly a French loan, 7 times. *Wrec(c)h-* is found 28 times as a simplex (plus one occurrence each of *wrecchede* and *wrecheliche*), as ever only sometimes specifying material poverty, e.g. at VI. 37/7–8 'doð gladliche . . . elmesse wreche men'; *hauelese* appears at II. 9/11 (translating Lat *non habenti*), and *hauenlese* at XXVI. 157/10 ('hauenlese men' translating *pauperibus*, as in the equivalent passage in the version of this homily in Lambeth (XIII. 135/26, noted above)); *poure* is attested once at VIII. 47/18 (as the opposite of *riche*). (*Arme* (< OE *earm*) occurs only once (at XXV. 149/6, 'tis arme lif'), and only in a generic reference to misery/wretchedness, hence its omission from the table.)

[72] Texts extant in the so-called 'AB Language' are *Ancrene Wisse* in Cambridge, Corpus Christi College 402 (or 'A'), edited by Tolkien (1962) and Millett (2005–6), and the 'Katherine Group' (*Sancte Katerine, Seinte Margarete, Seinte Iuliene, Hali Meiðhad* and *Sawles Warde*) in Oxford, Bodleian Library, Bodley 34 (or 'B'), edited respectively by d'Ardenne & Dobson (1981), Mack (1934), d'Ardenne (1961), Millett (1982) and Bennett & Smithers (1968: 246–61), and as a whole by d'Ardenne (1977). On the texts and their language see further esp. Tolkien (1929), Zettersten (1965), Laing (1993: 24, 124–5), Millett (1996: esp. 17–21 by G.B. Jack), Dance (2003a: 39–43, 49–50; 2003b), Laing (2008: 6–9, 143–6) and references there cited. I have obtained data on 'rich' and 'poor' words by searching the printed concordances in Potts, Stevenson & Wogan-Browne (1993) and Stevenson & Wogan-Browne (2000), and cite instances by manuscript (A or B), folio and line. In the two manuscripts I count 23 instances of *riche*, and two each of the derivatives *richesce* and *richedom*; *weolie* and *weoleful* are much less frequent, found once and 4 times

word choices meaning 'rich' and 'poor', followed by their near-synonyms and some key derivatives in approximately descending order of frequency (very occasional expressions are in brackets).[73] Needless to say, there is a great deal of complexity skulking in the shadows of this list, including when it comes to the broader semantic ranges of the words involved; many of them are polysemous, and ambiguous at least some of the time (it is sometimes hard to tell in a given instance of *wrecc-* or *earm-* whether the focus is on poverty in particular or pitiableness more broadly, for

---

respectively, and always either in alliterative phrases (e.g. A 107b/9 'nam ich weolie wisest') or in close conjunction with the noun *weole* 'riches' (thus B 63v/19). (*Seli* and *ēdī* mean only 'blessed' in spiritual or non-specific usage.) There are 31 occurrences of *poure* (plus 7 *pouerte*, one *poureliche*), and this is clearly the favoured way to denote material poverty in these texts. Compare the 23 cases of *wrecch-* (and 2 of *wrecchedom*, one *wrecchehead*), which is less strongly associated with this sense area in AB; it refers to those in a condition of misery which is often associated with poverty and destitution but which does not necessarily seem to imply it, as becomes evident in the phrase 'wrecche poure peoddere' (A 16a/25–6, contrasted with 'riche mercer'), where *wrecche* was apparently not felt sufficient on its own to indicate that the peddler was lacking in material prosperity. (Formations on *earm* are relatively frequent, and are favoured especially in *Hali Meiðhad*, but again denote generic wretchedness only.) For fuller information on the senses of these words, see the glossaries to the editions cited above. The earlier version of Laȝamon's *Brut* is that in London, British Library, Cotton Caligula A. ix (part I), as edited by Brook & Leslie (1963–78); on its language and for further references see esp. Laing (1993: 69–70), Dance (2003a: 56–60), Laing (2008: 60–5). I have searched for words meaning 'rich' and 'poor' in this text via *CMEPV*, and cite instances by line from Brook & Leslie (1963–78). *Riche* and its derivatives are extremely commonplace, running to many hundreds of occurrences, and this was clearly Laȝamon's favourite word-family with which to refer to material wealth. By contrast I have found forms of *weoli* (<weoleȝen, weoli>) only twice (215, 6939), both alliterating and only the first denoting material wealth (in the antonymous pair 'þa weoleȝen & þa weaðlen'); just four occurrences of *eadi* (*ēdī*, *ædi*), only one of which might refer to material splendour ('an eorð-hus. eadi & feier', 1181, glossed 'of a building: costly, splendid' by *MED* s.v. *ēdī* sense 1.(a); the other cases of *eadi* in the poem all denote blessedness or happiness more generally); and just the one instance of *weorld-iseli* (5509, with the /s/ of *-iseli* probably alliterating on the /s/ of *to-somne* earlier in the line) (other cases of *seli* in the poem mean only 'happy, blessed'). Much the most frequent indicator of poverty is *wrec(c)h-*; I count 32 instances, plus two of *wræccheliche*, a large proportion of which seem to me to specify the absence of material wealth (a number are in collocation with *riche*; see below, n. 97). *Hæn* (< OE *hēan*) is another common way of expressing the same idea, running to 14 occurrences as an adj., the majority of which again refer unambiguously to worldly poverty (and again, several appear as direct antonyms for *riche*, as e.g. 'riche men & hæne', 4899; I count 6 examples of this pairing in the poem). Forms of *wædle* appear only 3 times (two of them alliterating), and *pouere* just once ('riche men and pouere', 11336). (*Ærm* (< OE *earm*) and its frequent derivatives *ærmþe* 8×, *ærmlich(e)* 5×, *ærming* 1× are generally used in this text to foreground the emotional consequences of loss (including military defeat) and hardship (clearly in e.g. 'ærm on his mode. seorhful on heorte', 3295–6), and material poverty does not seem a necessary concomitant.)

[73] In all cases I incorporate adjectives and any substantival equivalents (e.g. *riche* 'wealthy' and *riche* 'wealthy person') under the same head. For some remarks on the data for each text, see above, nn. 69–72, and on the usage of the words concerned in Middle English at large consult *MED* s.vv. *arm* adj., *ēdī* adj., *hāvenlēs* adj. (2), *hāve-lēste* n., *hēn* adj., *henthe* n., *iselthe* n., *povertē* n., *povre* adj., *rīche* adj., *riches(se* n., *sēl(e* n.1, *sēlth(e* n., *tharf* adj. (b), *ūsel* adj., *wantsum* adj., *wēdle* adj., *wēleful* adj., *wēlī* adj., *wrecche* adj., *wrecche* n.

example).[74] But we can draw some preliminary conclusions. It is evident, for one thing, that *riche* is very well established in all these texts as the core word for 'wealthy'. There is nevertheless a certain amount of variation across texts and traditions amongst its near-synonyms and derivatives; the AB texts and the *Brut* are alone in retaining a form of OE *welig*, for example. For 'lacking in wealth', there is a still greater range. There is some continuity from earlier Old English usage, in different ways in the different texts (we meet *wædle* only in *The Orrmulum* and Laʒamon's *Brut*, for instance).[75] There is *wrech-*, an old word with a developed sense which is now the principal choice to mean 'poor' in most of these works. And there are also some brand new items, especially *poure*, which *OED* first records clearly in English as a simplex from the *Trinity Homilies*,[76] but which has already become the dominant adjective in this field by the AB texts; plus in *The Orrmulum* notice the striking *usell* and *wanntsumm*, both clearly containing material derived from Old Norse.[77]

But these famous works are only a part of the English literature produced in this period. Another important category, which until recently was somewhat neglected, consists of versions of pre-Conquest writings copied between the end of the 11th and the turn of the 13th centuries. More than 25 manuscripts survive from this time whose contents are mainly what are sometimes called 'updated' Old English texts; the most significant (though by no means the only type of text represented) are homilies, variously copied, recopied, excerpted, recontextualised, rewritten.[78] In the last couple

---

[74] Notice for instance these two passages from *The Peterborough Chronicle*, where the conditions described respectively by *wrecce* and *earm* certainly *include* the notion of material destitution (note the contrast with *rice* in the first quotation, and the deprivation of property in the second), but where a broader (hypernymous) sense of wretchedness and misery is also highly relevant: 'Wrecce men sturuen of hungær; sume ieden on ælmes þe waren sum wile rice men' ('*wrecce* people died from hunger; some relied upon alms who were once rich people'; s.a. 1137 40–1); 'man læt þet ærme folc mid ealle unrihte: ærost man hem beræfoð her eahte and siþðon man hem ofslæð' ('that *ærme* people are treated entirely unjustly: first they are deprived of their property and afterwards they are killed'; s.a. 1124 47–8).

[75] As will be seen from n. 71 above, much of the variety apparent in this field in *The Lambeth Homilies* depends upon retentions of the varied vocabulary of the Old English original of Homily X.

[76] See *OED* s.v. *poor* adj. and n.1, sense A.1.a., first quotation. As *OED* remarks in its etymological discussion, there are attestations of (what is probably) this word as a byname or surname as early as *c*.1100–30, but in each case these appear with a French article (*le Poer*, *le Poure*) and so 'it is unclear whether these are to be interpreted as reflecting the Middle English or the Anglo-Norman word'.

[77] *Usell* descends from the Old Norse compound represented by OIcel *úsæll* 'wretched', and for the first element of *wanntsumm* compare OIcel *van-t* (nom. or acc. sg. neut.) 'lacking, wanting'. See esp. *MED* s.vv. *ūsel* adj., *wantsum* adj., *OED* s.vv. *usell* adj., *wantsum* adj., Björkman (1900–2: 224–5).

[78] See for instance Conti (2007a: 367 and n. 13), who refers to 'twenty-seven surviving manuscripts containing predominantly Old English material that were written about 1100 or later', drawing on the list in Ker (1990: xviii–xix). For useful and still more extensive lists of manuscripts containing Old English from this period see also Thomson (2006: 10–18), Treharne (2012: 124–6) and the project catalogue of *EMSS* (at http://www.le.ac.uk/english/em1060to1220/catalogue/mss.htm).

of decades, early medieval scholarship (led by the groundbreaking work of Elaine Treharne and Mary Swan) has embraced this material in a serious and imaginative way, putting it in its proper contexts in the multilingual textual environments of the long 12th century and comprehensively dismantling the old assumption that, in the face of the cultural explosion engineered by French and Latin writers in this early medieval 'renaissance', the English decided (in time-honoured fashion) simply to keep calm and carry on copying Ælfric.[79] There is space here to look in detail at only one of these manuscripts, which I have chosen owing to the especially interesting contribution I think it makes to our understanding of lexical history in this period. It is Oxford, Bodleian Library, Bodley 343, which was produced in the second half of the 12th century, near Worcester or Hereford. It contains more than 80 English texts, most by Ælfric.[80] Despite some trail-blazing work especially by Susan Irvine, Peter Kitson and Aidan Conti, most of these texts have been relatively little examined linguistically.[81] This is at least partly attributable to the fact that the great majority have never been printed in their Bodley 343 versions, only in their original pre-Conquest forms.[82] That these texts did begin life in an earlier period is an important reason why their incarnations in this manuscript have sometimes been regarded with disappointment by language historians—not because they are lacking in interest, but simply because they are not unambiguously 'contemporary' documents.[83] As such, as well as all the usual dialectological variables that we have to deal with when we examine a medieval manuscript, we have in cases like this also to reckon with the reactions of

[79] For the key scholarship see above, n. 11.

[80] On the manuscript, and for further references, see notably Ker (1990: 368–75, no. 310), Irvine (1993: xviii–liv), Clemoes (1997: 1–5), Irvine (2000a: 55–60), Conti (2007a: 370–2), Wilcox (2008: booklet 71–101), Conti & Da Rold (2010), Conti (2012). In what follows I refer to the contents according to the article numbers given by Ker (this is the system most commonly cited in previous scholarship; for a revised article numbering, keyed to Ker's, see Conti & Da Rold (2010)).

[81] Irvine (1993: lv–lxxvii; her localisation 'near Worcester' is given at pp. li–ii), Kitson (1992: esp. 28–9, 34–7, 76–80 on dialect; he focuses on art. 77, whose language he localises to eastern Herefordshire or South-West Worcestershire), Kitson (1997: 223–9), Irvine (2000b), Conti (2012: esp. 267–70). See also Laing (1993: 125–6), Napier's (1894: xlvii–lx) discussion of the dialect features of art. 12, and on changes to vocabulary see further Fischer (1996: 32–3), Treharne (2012: 134–5), Dance (2012b: 158–66, 174–82).

[82] The best known exceptions are the homilies edited by Irvine (1993) (arts. 9, 10, 54, 61, 78, 79, 80), Napier (1894) (art. 12, the so-called 'History of the Holy Rood Tree') and Belfour (1909) (as well as those ed. by Irvine, these are arts. 7, 8, 28, 29, 77, 82, 83), most of which survive only in this manuscript; and for an important recent edition of the composite Wulfstan homily at art. 70 see moreover Conti (2007b). For a guide to all available editions of and collations of variant readings from the texts in the manuscript, consult the *EMSS* entry by Conti & Da Rold (2010) alongside Ker (1990: 368–75). For an important collection of (major) variant readings, especially helpful in giving an impression of the sorts of lexical changes made in the Bodley 343 versions of Ælfric texts, see Appendix C in Clemoes (1997: 543–55).

[83] As Kitson (1992: 28) observes, the relative lack of attention paid to the language of Bodley 343 may stem at least partly from Napier's (1894: lvii) somewhat dismissive (and misleading) characterisation of it as not much different from late West Saxon.

scribes to an earlier variety of English (the so-called late West Saxon 'standard') which had longstanding prestige as a written medium.[84] But provided that we allow for these factors, the versions of earlier texts found in this manuscript can and do offer us some important insights into language usage in the 12th century, including some brand new evidence for its vocabulary.

Altogether, in the whole of the English contents of Bodley 343, I count about 215 instances of words denoting 'rich' and 'poor'.[85] Allowing for differences in spelling, most of the texts in the manuscript use precisely the same words for these concepts as do the pre-Conquest original versions to which almost all can be compared.[86] This seems at least a little disapppointing, although it is worth adding that these same Bodley texts often do show changes elsewhere in their vocabulary, and so the retention of 'rich'/'poor' expressions could indicate that these remained acceptable words to 12th-century revisers, at least as part of their passive competence.[87] But there are exceptions to this rule. In two Bodley texts in particular, there is significant alteration of the words for 'rich' and 'poor'; and, since these texts are versions of two Ælfric First Series homilies which take wealth and poverty as central themes, these changes begin to look like deliberate, meaningful acts of revision on the part of whichever redactor introduced them. Let us focus on one of these texts, the Bodley 343 version (article 40 in the manuscript) of an Ælfric homily for Rogationtide, a very important occasion for public preaching and for almsgiving.[88] In Table 7, the relevant readings of an early copy of Ælfric's original are on the left.[89] Ælfric's favoured word for 'wealthy' in this text is *rīce* (which he uses sixteen times), with *welig* and *spēdig* also putting in appearances; for 'poor', he prefers *þearfa* (fifteen times), next to several uses

---

[84] On this 'standard Old English' (sometimes referred to as the 'late West Saxon *Schriftsprache*') see *inter alia* Wrenn (1933), Gneuss (1972), Hogg (1992: §§1.4. 1.10), Gretsch (2001: 41–4, 69–83), Gretsch (2003), Gretsch (2006), Kornexl (2012).

[85] For what I have counted and how see Appendix I.

[86] Differences can be found only in articles 13, 26, 28, 40, 49 and 62, and those in arts. 26 and 28 do not represent substitutions of one word meaning 'rich' or 'poor' for another; see Appendix I. For the changes to arts. 40 and 49 see further the discussion below.

[87] For discussion of lexical changes in Bodley 343, see esp. Kitson (1992: 29 n. 8, with special attention to art. 77), Conti (2012: esp. 267–70), Dance (2012b: 158–66, 174–82). As Conti demonstrates, these revisions are most apparent in the texts copied by the second scribe (art. 6 onwards), and I have suggested elsewhere (Dance 2012b: 161) that 'the likelihood is therefore that a copyist of this part of the Bodley 343 collection essentially as it now stands was the person responsible for these lexical changes—perhaps scribe 2 himself'.

[88] I print a complete text of the Bodley 343 version of this homily below, Appendix II. It is homily XVIII in the first series of Ælfric's *Catholic Homilies*, as edited by Clemoes (1997: 317–24) from London, British Library, Royal 7 C. xii with variants from other witnesses, and commentary in Godden (2000: 145–53). On Rogationtide, for which Ker (1990: 526) counts some forty extant Old English homilies, see Bazire & Cross (1989: xv–xxv).

[89] This is London, British Library, Royal 7 C. xii, probably copied at Cerne Abbas in 'the first half of 990' (Clemoes 1997: 1; Ker 1990: 324–9, no. 257).

Table 7. Words denoting 'rich' and 'poor' in the Bodley 343 copy of Ælfric's 'In Letania Maiore'.

Ælfric	Bodley 343 (revisions highlighted)
rīce 16×	rice 16×
welig 2×	**rice** 2×
spēdig 1×	spediʒ 1×
þearfa 15×	**wrecc-** 9×
	poure 3×
	þearfa 2×
	[omitted 1×]
earm 6×	earm 3×
	wrecc- 2×
	poure 1×
wǣdla 1×	wǣdla 1× (with 1× added in expansion)

of *earm* and one of *wǣdla*. The Bodley version reduces the variety of words for 'wealthy', changing Ælfric's *welig* twice to *rice*, but retaining *spediʒ*. Arguably, this is in keeping with the broader historical trends in this field which we have already noticed in the 12th century, with *riche* gradually becoming still more dominant (see above, Table 6). The same is true for words meaning 'poor': *þearfa* and *earm* both give way to *wrecc-*, eleven times altogether; and, most interestingly of all, these two Ælfric words are both also replaced by what we can now recognise as the earliest known attestations anywhere in English of the French loanword *poure*. Finding *poure* in Bodley 343 is a small but important antedating of the dictionaries (which first record the adjective from *The Trinity Homilies*, from a different part of the country),[90] and an example of the new evidence for lexical history which is still open to discovery if we look outside the 'big name' texts of this period.

At one level, then, such substitutions are an important confirmation of the place of Bodley 343 in the history of English words. If we interpret them as examples of what is often called 'lexical updating', evidence for certain words coming to be felt old-fashioned, and being sporadically replaced in revision, then they present us reassuringly with what we would expect to see in South-West Midland usage a little before better-known texts like *The Lambeth Homilies* and the AB group. And these historical trends are undeniably interesting. But from that point of view things are still disappointingly inconsistent. If this redactor simply didn't like *earm* or *þearfa*, why didn't he replace them every time? and why sometimes change them to *wrecc-*, and sometimes to *poure*? The answer, of course, is that an awareness of lexical fashions, of which items no longer seem 'current', is only one of the things that motivates a writer when he or she chooses words, especially in a rhetorically sensitive text like a homily; and to really understand what might be motivating the choices in this case we have to read the text.

[90] See above, n. 76.

There is space here to examine only a small extract, from the very end of the piece. Here is Ælfric's version, showing the climax of his argument about the role of poverty in securing eternal life (the words denoting rich and poor are highlighted in bold):[91]

> Se **rica** *and* se **þearfa** sind him betwynan nydbehefe. Se **welega** is geworht for ðan **þearfan** *and* se **þearfa** for ðam **welegan**. Þam **spedigum** gedafenaþ þæt he spende *and* dæle; þam **wædlan** gedafenað þæt he gebidde for ðam dælere. Se **earma** is se weig þe læt us to godes rice. Mare sylð se **þearfa** þam **rican** þonne he æt him nime: se **rica** him sylð þone hlaf þe bið to meoxe awend, *and* se **þearfa** sylð þam **rican** þæt ece lif. Na he swa þeah ac crist, se ðe þus cwæð: 'þæt ðæt ge doð anum **þearfan** on minum naman, þæt ge doð me sylfum'.

Ælfric opts for an elegant variety of ways of referring to the rich and the poor in this passage (part of which was cited earlier). He begins with a straight binary of *rīca* and *þearfa* (literally 'the rich and the needy'), before switching to *welega* versus *þearfa* for their chiastic conjunction in the second sentence ('se welega is geworht for ðan þearfan and se þearfa for ðam welegan'). He then expands on the contrast by introducing *spēdig* and *wǣdla* (usually much less common in his writings), describing what it is fitting for first the rich (literally the 'successful person') and then the poor (the *wǣdla*) to do. Then he inserts a new word, *earma* ('Se earma is se weig þe læt us to godes rice'), before finally returning to the terms he began with, *rīca* and *þearfa*, which he pairs consistently as he explains the relative values of their roles in the present and eternal lives.

Now compare the version in Bodley 343:[92]

> Se **rica** *ant* þe **poure** beoð heom betweonan nydbehefe. Se **rice** is iwroht for þa*m* **poure,** *ant* ðe **poure** for þa*m* **rice**. Þam **spediȝe** dafenað þ*et* he spene *ant* dæle þa*m* **wædlan,** *ant* þam **wædlan** dafenað þ*et* heo bidden for þa*m* delere. Se **wrecce** is þe wæȝ þe led up to Godes rice. Mare sylð þe **wrecce** þa*m* **rice** þon*n*e he æt hi*m* nime: se **rice** hi*m* sylð þone

[91] Clemoes (1997: 324, ll. 205–12); I have modernised punctuation and capitalisation and expanded the abbreviations. 'The rich person and the needy person are necessary to each other. The wealthy person is made for the needy, and the needy for the wealthy. It is fitting for the successful person that he spend and distribute [his goods]; for the impoverished one it is fitting that he pray for the distributor. The poor person is the way which leads us to God's kingdom. The needy person gives more to the rich one than he takes from him: the rich person gives him the bread which will turn into manure, and the needy person gives to the rich eternal life. However it is not he but Christ [who does this], who says thus: "What you do for one needy person in my name, you do for me myself".'

[92] f. 80v, ll. 10–15, excerpted from the full text of the homily printed below as Appendix II (ll. 193–200 there), with modernised punctuation and capitalisation. 'The rich person and the poor person are necessary to each other. The rich person is made for the poor, and the poor for the rich. It is fitting for the successful person that he spend and distribute [his goods] to the impoverished one, and for the impoverished one it is fitting that he pray for the distributor. The wretched person is the way which leads up to God's kingdom. The wretched person gives more to the rich one than he takes from him: the rich person gives him the bread which will turn into manure, and the wretched person gives to the rich eternal life. However it is not he [who does this], but the one who says thus: "What you do for one wretched person in my name, you do for me myself".'

hlaf ðe bið to meoxe awend, *ant* þe **wrecce** sylð þa*m* **rice** þet ece lif. Na he swa þeah, ac þe ðe þus cwe*ð*: 'þ*et* ðet ӡe doð ane **wrecce** on mine nome, þ*et* ӡe doð me sylfu*m*'.

Alongside a host of other changes reflecting differences in phonology, morphology and other aspects of its language,[93] the Bodley text substantially recasts Ælfric's rich and poor vocabulary, maintaining some of the variety and interest Ælfric gave it, but regularising and reinforcing the parallels and adding some effects of its own. So in the first two sentences Ælfric's contrast of *rīca* or *weliga* versus *þearfa* is tightened to a single binary, *rice* versus *poure*. In the third, the Bodley version retains Ælfric's variation to *spediӡa* and *wædla*, but it expands the wording to add an extra *wædla* (a word for 'poor' it never otherwise introduces, but is evidently happy to co-opt), conceivably in order to enforce a syntactic parallel between what the rich and poor do by giving the actions of both some recipients ('spene and dæle þam wædlan … bidden for þam delere', 'distribute to the poor person … pray for the distributor'). The second part of the passage changes tack, and brings in a new word *wrecce* as antonym to *rice*, which it employs again slightly more regularly than Ælfric does his pair—and in doing so introduces some sound-play as a bonus, not only highlighting the parallelism of *rice* and its binary *wrecce* ('the rich and the wretch'), but also perhaps punningly exploiting the apparent irony that it is the *wrecca* who is the way to God's *rice*, his kingdom.

The euphonious pairing of 'the rich and the wretch' makes for a very effective rhetorical doublet, and if we look a little further afield it seems in fact to have been a popular contemporary collocation, used a number of times especially in homiletic discourse in that short period of English in which *wretch*- flourished as a common antonym for *rich*.[94] It is hard to resist the temptation to see this doublet being played

[93] Amongst other changes in this passage, notice for example the following (with references following the lineation of Appendix II). Orthography: the use of <ӡ> to represent palatal /j/ (e.g. *spediӡe*, 193), and <g> for velar /g/ (e.g. *godes*, 195). Phonology: Ælfric *ðæt* > Bodley *ðet* (198), Ælfric *naman* > Bodley *nome* (198), both probably representing West Midland dialect forms (second fronting of /æ/, rounding of /ɑ/ before a nasal; see e.g. Jordan (rev. Crook) (1974: §§32, 30)); Ælfric prefix *ge-* > Bodley *i-* (e.g. *geworht* > *iwroht*, 193; a commonplace early ME development). Morphology: Ælfric *se* > Bodley *þe* as the nom. sg. masc. definite article (throughout, though not consistently); Ælfric dat. sg. wk. *-an* and dat. sg. masc. str. adj. *-um* both > Bodley *-e* (e.g. 'anum þearfan on minum naman' next to 'ane wrecce on mine nome', 198). Lexical variants: notice in particular the Bodley form *spene* 'spend' (194), which appears to have developed from OE *spendan* (cp. Ælfric's *spende*) by reinterpretation of the *-d-* in pret. *spende* (etc.) as the dental preterite suffix and creation of a new present stem *spen-*; notice that this Bodley occurrence is earlier than any of those cited by *MED* s.v. *spēnen* v. and *OED* s.v. *spene* v., neither of which gives examples before the *Lambeth* or *Trinity Homilies*. Rephrasing: the Bodley version takes 'þam wædlan' as pl., and hence alters Ælfric's sg. 'he gebidde' to pl. 'heo bidden' in the following clause (194); Bodley alters Ælfric's 'læt us' ('leads us') to 'led up' ('leads up', 195).

[94] A search of *OEC* brings up very few possible attempts by earlier English writers to exploit the two words as a contrasting pair; the nearest I have found is one in the Old English *Boethius*, viz. 'ealle þa ofermodan rican bion swiðe unmihtige and swiðe earme wreccan' (Godden & Irvine 2009: 340, B.36 ll. 62–3). For that matter there are also very few instances where forms of *rich* and *wretch* collocate later in

for similar effect in article 49 in Bodley 343, the other main homily in which 'rich' and 'poor' words are changed. For example:

> Bodley 343: 'ne nemde þe hælend þone ricæ ac þone wrecchæ'
> (Ælfric: 'ne nemde se hælend þone welegan ac þone wædlan')[95]

> Bodley 343: 'þæ wrecce nære fullice iwrecen on þam rican'
> (Ælfric: 'se þearfa nære fullice gewrecen on þam rican')[96]

In the first instance here it is Ælfric's *welega* and *wǣdla* which are reworked to give *ricæ* versus *wreccæ* (exchanging alliteration for part-rhyme); and in the second the change of *þearfa* to *wrecce* extends the sound-play still more pulpit-thumpingly ('þæ *wrecce* nære fullice *iwrecen* on þam *rican*'). The *wretch-/rich* pair is found several times in the *Lambeth* and *Trinity Homilies* and in Laȝamon's *Brut*, can be seen in *The Orrmulum*, and is perhaps operative too as a figure of sound in the Worcester Fragments *Soul's Address to the Body*.[97] Ultimately, of course, 'the rich and the wretch' lost out to the alternative binary, 'the rich and the poor', *riche* and *poure*, which are attested as antonyms in 12th-century Anglo-French texts and arguably came into English directly from French as a phrasal pair like this, on the coat-tails of *riche* (which, as we have seen, led a double life in both languages).[98] But there is no indication that, even though

---

Middle English, the most plausible which arise from a search of *CMEPV* perhaps being: 'Þi lauerd made þe riche: & þou art bicomen a pouer wreche' (Horstmann 1999: 135, ll. 3–4); 'Riche man ich was elles-ware : þei ich beo nouþe a wrechche here' (Horstmann 1887: 330, l. 263); 'wrecchid curatis ben nedid to festen hem richely' (Matthew 1880: 249, ll. 4–5).

[95] Bodley 343, f. 97v l. 7. The Ælfric text is homily XXIII in the first series of *Catholic Homilies* ('Dominica secunda post Pentecosten'), cited from the Royal 7 C. xii text edited by Clemoes (1997: 47). Bodley 343: 'the saviour did not name the rich person but the wretched one'; Ælfric: 'the saviour did not name the wealthy person but the impoverished one'.

[96] Bodley 343, f. 98r l. 9; Clemoes (1997: 368, ll. 100–1). Bodley 343: 'the wretched person would not have been fully avenged on the rich one'; Ælfric: 'the needy person would not have been fully avenged on the rich one'.

[97] I count 3 instances in the *Lambeth Homilies* (e.g. 'Nis nan mon swa riche. ne swa wrecche þet he ne mei sum þing iforðian', Morris 1868: homily III, 39 ll. 31–2); 4 in the *Trinity Homilies* (e.g. 'Swo heneð. and astruȝeð þe riche men þe wrecches', Morris 1873: homily XXXIII, 211 ll. 4–5); and 8 in the *Brut* (e.g. 'Al his cun he wurðede; richen & wrecchen. | þa richen he lette beon stille. Þa wreccen hefden heore wille.', Brook & Leslie 1963–78: ll. 1308–9). There is only one example in *The Orrmulum* ('& off þatt he warrþ wrecche mann | Forr uss to makenn riche', Holt 1878: ll. 3884–5), and one in the *Soul's Address* ('Sone cumeþ þet riche wif þe forhoweþ þene earueþsiþ, | for ufel is þeo wrecche lufe', Moffat 1987: 64, A.41–2).

[98] For some discussion of the use of *riche* and *poure* as a doublet in medieval French see Vanckeleer (1975: 443–6). A 'textbase proximity search' of the *Anglo-Norman On-Line Hub* corpus (accessible via the *AND* website at http://www.anglo-norman.net/s-prox-start.shtml?session=SAB11958T1392910186) produces 12th-century oppositions of *riche* and *poure* including *Les proverbes de Salemon* of Sanson de Nantuil and *Le roman de philosophie* of Simund de Freine. For a lexical field analysis of words for 'rich' and 'poor' based on 15th-century French texts see further Rassart-Eeckhout (1999).

it took off slightly later, 'rich and poor' is a chronologically much newer arrival in English; both phrases were evidently available to the reviser of Bodley 343 article 40, and arguably it was simply a desire for variety, that is a stylistic effect in the course of his refurbished homiletic rhetoric, to which we owe our first occurrence of this idiom, and thus our first attestation of the word *poure*, in the history of English.

I hope that this whistle-stop tour of words meaning 'rich' and 'poor' has been illuminating. At the broader level of word history, I think it highlights the range and types of complications there can be in mapping lexical and semantic change in this period. Change is not all about foreign input, which is sometimes hard to quantify (as we saw with the etymology of *rich*), and when borrowings do appear we have to bear in mind that they are entering systems of words which are already complex and dynamic. On the smaller scale, the contexts of these words in individual works and manuscripts reveal the roles played in the formation of our evidence by textual transmission, literary traditions and the preferences of different writers. And even potentially unpromising books like Bodley 343 are valuable, both for the witness to change that they provide in a period whose record is so patchy, and on their own terms, for their independent and distinctly contemporary stylistic vitality, a literary cultural 'oofiness' which we ignore to our detriment.

CLOSING REMARKS

Throughout this article, I have been arguing for the value of the little stories, that the evidence for vocabulary in the 12th century, and all the fine grain of detail which makes it up, is important in its own right—and not just because it points the way to something more momentous outside of itself. This is true whichever direction we look in, and for that matter whichever metaphors we use to conceive of it. So, the language of this period repays our interest not only by dint of being in 'transition', a suburban milepost on the road to downtown Middle English; and far from simply noticing novelty, studying it is about reading the very various and often complex relationships between old and new. By the same token, knowing where borrowed words came from does have a powerful resonance, since in important ways it connects us to famous cultural encounters of distant ages; but to think of these words *only* as 'loans' is to privilege a debt to the past, to put too much weight on their origins, and their differentness. To my mind, one of the great pleasures of studying medieval words is that it does not have to stop with either where they came from or where they ended up, but can extend to how they were adopted, used and spread, how they found and made their meanings as part of living systems of language; how these elements, whatever their ultimate alterity, whatever their glorious diversity, came and lived together. By using the research resources now to hand, and taking an approach to evidence from the 12th century which is *philological* in all the best senses of that word, we join big stories and little details, language and literature, Old English and Middle English. And we give the language users of this most surprising of ages the chance properly to have their say. Thank you for listening.

Acknowledgements

I would like to record my sincere thanks to the British Academy for the invitation to give this Sir Israel Gollancz Memorial Lecture, which was originally delivered in London on 26 November 2013; and to the Universities of Glasgow and Sheffield for the opportunity to repeat it there (respectively on 6 and 26 March 2014). I am immensely grateful to all those who have commented on versions of the lecture, oral or written, and who have otherwise helped improve it, especially Helen Cooper, Philip Durkin, Mark Faulkner, Miranda Griffin, Sara Harris, Christian Kay, Rosalind Love, Katie Lowe, Rory Naismith, Sara Pons Sanz, Jeremy Smith, Patrick Stiles, Chris Voth, Sheila Watts, Laura Wright, and above all Sarah Meer.

APPENDIX I

Words for 'rich' and 'poor' in Bodley 343

All articles in the manuscript were searched for occurrences of words meaning 'rich' and 'poor' and their derivatives.[99] Instances are listed by article, with spellings normalised to a representative Bodley 343 spelling in each case in order to facilitate comparison. All readings may be assumed to correspond (allowing for changes in spelling) to those of earlier manuscript witnesses to the same text, unless revisions are given in the 'Changes' column.[100]

---

[99] I have included in the main table only those words appearing in Table 5 above and synonymous derivatives on the same stems, plus *poure*. Relevant compounds and derivatives are noticed in footnotes. Note that forms of *eadiʒ* are very numerous in the manuscript, but (with the single possible exception in art. 80) they refer only to spiritual blessedness, and have not been recorded here. Similarly, I have counted only those cases of *earm* which might (or which clearly do) imply material poverty in context. The text of articles 12, 16, 28, 29, 65, 79 and 80 is included in *OEC*; these texts have been searched electronically and, where earlier manuscript witnesses to the same texts are available for comparison, I have indicated in footnotes my sources for the readings in (one or more of) those earlier witnesses. For the other articles, I searched the corresponding Old English copies via *OEC* and compared their readings with the microfiche facsimile of Bodley 343 available in Wilcox (2008); I checked these against the *apparatus criticus* of the standard editions and in the case of art. 68 against the text of the Bodley version printed in Fehr (1966).

[100] Article numbers follow Ker (1990: 368–75, no. 310) (and see also above, n. 80). The figures cited for the results of revisions in the 'Changes' column are included in the total for each stem under 'Readings'; e.g. *ric-* 6× in art. 13 includes the instance of *ric-* revised from *welig*.

Art.	*OEC* short title	Readings	Changes
1	ÆCHom II, 29	*ric-* 1×, *weliʒ* 1×; *þearf-* 1×[101]	
3	ÆCHom I, 17	*ric-* 1×	
11	ÆCHom II, 35	*þearf-* 4×	
12	LS 5 (InventCrossNap)	*weliʒ* 1×	[unique text]
13	ÆCHom I, 19	*ric-* 6×; *þearf-* 1×, *earm* 2×, *hean* 1×	*ric-* 1× < *welig*
14	ÆCHom I, 29	*þearf-* 2×	
15	ÆCHom I, 31	*ric-* 1×	
16	LS 18.1 (NatMaryAss 10N)	*þearf-* 2×[102]	
17	ÆCHom II, 37	*þearf-* 1×	
18	ÆLS (Martin)	*weliʒ-* 1×; *þearf-* 6×, *earm* 1×	
19	ÆCHom II, 33	*þearf-* 1×	
20	ÆCHom II, 34	*þearf-* 2×, *earm* 1×	
21	ÆCHom I, 8	*ric-* 8×; *þearf-* 1×[103]	
22	ÆLS (Peter's Chair)	*þearf-* 1×, *earm* 1×, *wædl-* 1×[104]	
23	ÆCHom I, 13	*ric-* 7×	
26	ÆCHom II, 6	*ric-* 1×, *weliʒ* 2×; *þearf-* 2×, *wædl-* 2×[105]	(1× *welig* omitted)[106]
28	HomS 11.1 (Belf 5)	*wædl-* 2×	*wædligend* 1× < *dwoliend*[107]
29	HomS 15 (Belf 6)	*þearf-* 1×[108]	
30	ÆCHom I, 38	*ric-* 5×, *weliʒ* 1×; *þearf-* 2×, *earm* 3×	
31	ÆLS (Edmund)	*ric-* 1×; *earm* 1×, *wædl-* 1×	
35	ÆCHom II, 3	*ric-* 1×	
36	ÆCHom I, 9	*ric-* 1×; *þearf-* 1×, *earm* 1×[109]	
40	ÆCHom I, 18	*ric-* 18×, *spediʒ* 1×; *þearf-* 2×, *earm* 3×, *wædl-* 2×, *wrecc-* 11×, *poure* 4×	*ric-* 2× < *welig*; *wrecc-* 9× < *þearf-*, 2× < *earm*; *poure* 3× < *þearf-*, 1× < *earm*; *þearf-* 1× omitted; *wædl-* once added in expansion[110]
41	ÆCHom I, 21	*ric-* 1×	
42	ÆCHom I, 22	*wædl-* 1×	
45	ÆCHom I, 26	*ric-* 1×; *þearf-* 1×[111]	
46	ÆCHom I, 27	*ric-* 1×	

[101] And *hafenleas* 'poor' 1×.

[102] Compared with the earlier version (from Oxford, Bodleian Library, Hatton 114) printed in parallel with the Bodley 343 text in Assmann (1889: 117–37).

[103] And *wanspediʒ* 'poor' 1×, *hafenleast* 'poverty' 1×.

[104] And *wanhafel* 'needy' 1×.

[105] And *hafenleast* 'poverty' 1×.

[106] By omission of a phrase corresponding to 'and welig on geearnungum' (Godden 1979: 58, l. 170).

[107] Compared with the e–arlier version in Vercelli, Biblioteca Capitolare CXVII printed by Scragg (1992: 73–83, with variants from other copies).

[108] Compared with the earlier version in Oxford, Bodleian Library, Bodley 340, in the microfiche facsimile edited by Wilcox (2008).

[109] And *wanspediʒ* 'poor' 1×.

[110] See further Table 7 and the discussion above.

[111] And *hafenleast* 'poverty' 1×.

49	ÆCHom I, 23	*ric*- 15×, *weliȝ* 5×; *þearf*- 8×, *earm* 2×, *wædl*- 4×, *wrecc*- 6×[112]	*ric*- 2× < *welig*; *wrecc*- 3× < *þearf*-, 3× < *wædl*-[113]
53	ÆCHom I, 35	*þearf*- 1×	
54	ÆHomM 2 (Irv 3)	*ric*- 1×, *weliȝ* 1×;[114] *þearf*- 1×, *earm* 1×, *wædl*- 1×[115]	[unique text]
57	ÆCHom I, 36	*ric*- 2×; *þearf*- 9×, *earm* 1×, *wædl*- 1×[116]	
62	ÆCHom II, 43	*ric*- 3×; *wrecc*- 1×, *earm* 1×	*wrecc*- 1× < *þearf*-
64	HomU 37 (Nap 46)	*þearf*- 1×	
65	ÆLet 4 (SigeweardB)	*weliȝ* 1×[117]	
68	ÆLet 3 (Wulfstan 2)	*ric*- 1×; *þearf*- 1×	
71	WHom 20.1	*earm* 1×	
73	ÆCHom II, 45	*þearf*- 1×	
74	ÆCHom I, 34	*þearf*- 2×	
79	HomU 2 (Irv 6)	*ric*- 2×; *hean* 2×	[unique text]
80	HomU 3 (Irv 7)	*ric*- 5×, *eadiȝ* 1×;[118] *earm* 2×	[partly unique text][119]

APPENDIX II

An edition of Bodley 343 article 40, 'In Letania maiore'
(f. 78v l. 15—f. 80v l. 16)

Editorial principles

This is a version of Ælfric *Catholic Homilies* I.XVIII. For a text based on London, British Library, Royal 7 C. xii with major variants given in the *apparatus* see Clemoes (1997: 317–24), and the Notes in Godden (2000: 145–53).

---

[112] And *hafenleast* 'poverty' 2×. Retained *weliȝ* is once glossed '.l. diues'; notice also the retained pret. *welgode*. Retained *wædl*- is once glossed '.l. pauper'; notice also the retained *wædlung*. Retained *þearf*- is once glossed 'pauper' and once 'wrecces'.

[113] Including *wreccedlice* < *wædligende* 1×.

[114] Both in the phrase 'þe wælȝa rice' at Irvine (1993: 70, III.255). In her notes Irvine (1993: 76) suggests that Ælfric has used both words here in order to avoid any possible ambiguity as to the sense of *rice*, and perhaps also to alliterate *wælȝa* on *walde* three words later. But it is also tempting to explain this unique construction as the product of more recent revision, perhaps as the result of a scribe copying an interlinear gloss *rice* into a text which originally read simply 'se welega' (a much more typical Ælfrician noun phrase).

[115] *Wædl*- occurs in the pres. ptcp. form *wædliende* 'begging'.

[116] And *hafenleast* 'poverty' 5×.

[117] Compared with the earlier version (from Oxford, Bodleian Library, Laud Misc. 509) printed in parallel with the Bodley 343 text in Crawford (1969: 18–51).

[118] *Eadiȝ* carries at least an implication of material comfort, in contrast with *earm* at Irvine (1993: 202, VII.151).

[119] A composite homily, whose second part (from Irvine (1993: 200, VII.94) onwards) occurs in other, earlier witnesses; for readings see Scragg (1992: 208–13) and his apparatus. The readings which continue those present in earlier copies are *ric*- 3×, *eadiȝ* 1×, *earm* 1×.

I have edited the text from digital photographs of the manuscript (for which I am grateful to the Bodleian Library). To facilitate comparison with Clemoes' text I have followed his paragraph divisions wherever possible. I have regularised the word division, and supplied modern capitalisation and punctuation. I have expanded all abbreviations (in italics). I have in each case expanded to the form most commonly used by the scribe when he writes out the given word in full in this text: hence the Tironian nota (<7>) is expanded to <*ant*> (always so written in full); the barred thorn is expanded to <þ*et*> (the same word is written out <ðet> four times, though also <ðæt> and <þæt> once each); <cw> + suspension mark has been expanded to <cw*eð*> (always so written in full, and the <e> vowel is the only one appropriate to both the frequent pret. forms and to the pres. at ll. 47, 49 etc., both of which are spelt using the same abbreviation); <þa> + suspension mark is expanded to <þa*m*>, except in the phrase <for þa*n* ðe> (since the scribe always makes this distinction when writing out the forms in full); and <þon> plus suspension mark is expanded to <þon*e*>, whether standing for the reflex of the OE adv. *þonne* or the OE acc. sg. masc. demonstr. *þone* (the scribe always writes both words out in full as <þone>, and only once uses a different form for the adv., viz. l. 52 <þōne> which I have expanded as <þo*nn*e>). Scribal revisions and other additions are recorded in the Notes. Editorial emendations are marked with square brackets. I have replaced 'wynn' (<ƿ>) with <w>, but in all other respects I have retained the original spellings, including the scribe's (mildly inconsistent) use of <ȝ > and <g>. (Notice that the scribe has no separate upper case form of <ȝ>, and always uses <G> when an upper case <ȝ> might have appeared, as in ll. 59, 104 etc.).

IN LETANIA MAIORE

Ðas daȝas beoð ihatene Letanie, þ*et* beoð Beddaȝas. On þisse daȝu*m* we sceolon biddan ure orðlicræ wæstmæ nihtsumnesse, *ant* us syndfulnesse *ant* sibbe, *ant*—þ*et* ȝit mare is—ure sunnæ forȝifenessæ. We rædeð on bocu*m* þ*et* þeos hældsumnessæ wurde arered on ðone timan þe ilamp on   5
ane buriȝ þe Uigen is ihaten micel orðsturung; *ant* feollon hus *ant* cirican, *ant* como*n* wilde boren *ant* wulfæs *ant* abiton þæs folces micelne dæl; *ant* ðæs kynges botle wearð mid heofenlice fyre forbernd. Þa bead þe bisceop Mamertus ðreoðra daȝen fæsten, *ant* þeo drecednesse swac; *ant* þe wuna ðæs þæs festenes ðurhwunað ȝehwær on leaffulre laðunge.   10
   Heo naman þa bysene [ð]æs fæstenes æt þa*m* Niniueniscan folce. Þ*et* folc wæs swið fyrenful. Þa walde God heom fordon, ac heo gladedon hine mid heora bereowsunge. God spæc to ane witeȝæ, þe wæs Ionas

ihaten: 'Far to ðære buriȝ Niniuen, *ant* bode ðer þa word þe ic ðe secge.' Þa
wearð þe witega afyrht *ant* wolde fleon Godes sihðe, ac he ne mihte. Ferde 15
ða to sæ *ant* astah to scipe. Þa ða þa scipmen comon ut on sæ, þa sende
God heom to micelne wind *ant* hreownesse, swa ðet heo wæron orwene
heoræ lifes. Heo ða wurpon heora waru ofer bord, *ant* þe witega læȝ slep.
Heo wurpan ða tan betwyx heom, *ant* beden þet God sceolde swutelian
heom hwanon þet unlimp heom become. Ða com þæs witegen ta up. Heo 20
axodon þa hine hwæt he wære, oððe hu he faron wolde. He cweð þet he
were Godes ðeow þe ðe sceop sæ *ant* land, *ant* þet he fleon wolde of
Godes sihðe. Heo cwædon, 'Hu do we embe ðe?' He andswærede,
'Wurpað me ofer bord; þone swicað þeos drecednesse.' Heo ða swa dydon,
ant þeo hreohnes wearð astillod; *ant* heo offrodon Gode heora lac *ant* tugon 25
forð.

God þa ȝearcode ænne hwæl, *ant* he forswealh þone witegan *ant*
aber hine to ðam lande þe he to sceolde, *ant* hine þær ut aspaw. Þa com eft
Godes engel *ant* his word to þam witege *ant* cweð, 'Aris nu *ant* ga to ðære
micelan buriȝ Niniuen, *ant* bodæ swa swa ic þe sæde ær.' He ferde þa *ant* 30
bodade þet heom wæs Godes gramæ onsiȝende | ȝif heo to Gode bugon
noldon. Ða aras þe kyng of his kynesetle, *ant* awearp his deorwurðe reaf ant
dyde hæran to his lice *ant* axan uppan his hæfod, *ant* bed þet ælc man swa
don sceolde. And æȝðer ȝe ða men ȝe ða sukenden cild *ant* eac þa
nytenu ne onbrucedon nanes þinges binnen ðreom daȝum. Ða þurh þa 35
ȝecyrrednesse þet heo yfeles swicon, *ant* þurð þet strange fæsten, heom
milsode God, *ant* nolde heom fordon swa swa he ær þa twa burhwaræ
Sodomam *ant* Gomorram for heora leahtræ mid heofenlican fyre
forbernde.

We sceolon eac on þisse daȝum began ure bedu *ant* fyliȝan ure 40
halydome, ut *ant* æc in, *ant* þone almihtiȝa God mid ȝeornfulnesse heriȝan.
We willað nu þis godspel eow reccen, þe her nu ired wæs, eowre leafan to
trymmingge: Dixit Iesus disci*pu*lis suis, quis u*estru*m habebit amicum *et* ibit
ad illum media nocte *et* dicet illi (et reliqua).

IN LETANIA MAIORE 45

Þe hælend cweð to his leorningcnihtas: 'Hwylc eower is þe hafað sumne
freond, *ant* gæð to him on midre nihte *ant* cweð, "Ðu freond, læn me ðri
hlafas, forþan ðe me sohte sum cumæ *ant* ic nabbe nan þing ȝearlices him
to beodenne." Ðone andswyrað þe hiredes aldor of his bedde *ant* cweð,

"Ne drecce þu me nu on þisse time. Min duræ is beloken, *ant* mine cildræn   50
beoð on heora reste. Ic ne mæȝ nu arisen *ant* þe ðæs tiðan." Ðone ȝif ðe
oþer þurhwunæð mid reame *ant* cnuȝunge, he ariseð þonne for his onrope,
ant na for freondscipe, ant tiðaþ him ðet þe he bid.' Þa sæde eft þe hælend:
'Biddæð *ant* eow bið iseald; secað *ant* ȝe ifindæð; cnukiað *ant* eow bið
iopenæd. Ælc mon þe bit he underfeð; ant þe ðe secæð he ifind; ant þe ðe   55
cnucað him bið iopenod. Hwilc eower bit his fæder hlafes, hu sæist þu,
sylð he him stan for hlafe? Oððe ȝif he bit fisces, sylð he him næddran?
Oððe ȝif he bit æȝes, sylð he him þone wyrm ðe is ihatæn ðrowend? Gif
[ȝ]e cunnon, þa ðe yfelæ beoð, sellon þa godnessæ eowræ bearnum, hu
micele swiðer wile eower heofenlica fæder ȝifan godne gast him   60
biddende?'

Ðe halȝa Augustinus trahtnode þis godspel, *ant* cweð þet ðeo niht
tacnode ða nytennesse þissere weorlde. Þeos weorld is ifylled mid
nytenesse. Nu sceal for ði ȝehwa arisan of ðere nytennesse *ant* gan to his
freond, þet is ðet he sceal buȝon to Criste mid alre geornfulnesse, *ant*   65
biddan þæræ ðrora hlafa, þet is leafan þære halȝan ðrimnesse. Ðe
almihtiga fæder is God, *ant* his sunæ is almihtiȝa God, *ant* þe halȝa gast is
almihtiȝa God: na ðry Godes, ac heo alle an ælmihtiȝa God untodæledlic.
Þone þu becymst to þisse ðrym hlafa, þet is to andȝite þære halȝan
ðrymnesse, þone hæfst þu on þam leafan lif *ant* fodæn þinre sawle, *ant*   70
miht eac oðerne cuman mid þam fedan, þet is ðæt þu miht tæcan þone
leafan oðre freond þe ðe ðæs bit. He cweð 'cuma', for þan ðe we alle beoð
cuman on ðisse life; *ant* ure eard nis na her, ac we beoð her swilce
wæȝferinde men. An cymð, oðer ferð: þe bið acenned, þe oðer forð ferð
ant rymð him setl. Nu sceal ȝehwa for ði wilnian þæs leafan þære halȝa   75
ðrymnesse, for ðan þe ðe leafan hine bringað to ðam ece life.

We willað eft embe þone ȝeleafan swiðor specan, for þan ðe þisses
godspelles traht hafð godne tyȝe. Ðe hiredes aldor ðe wæs on his reste
ibroht mid his cildræn is Crist, | ðe sit on heofenum mid his apostolos *ant*
mid martyros *ant* mid alle þe halȝum þe he on ðisse life fætte. We sceolon   80
eac clypion to Criste *ant* biddan þara þroræ hlafa. Þeah he us þerrihte ne
tyðiȝe, ne sceole we for ði þæra bene swicæn; he ælcð *ant* wile
þæahwæðere forȝifan. Þi he elcað þet we sceolon beon oflyste ant
deorwurðlice halden Godes ȝife. Swa hwæt swa mon æðelice beȝiet, þet ne
bið na swa deorwurðe swa þet ðe bið ærforðlice beȝiten. Ðe hælend sæde,   85
ȝif he þurðwunað cnuciȝende, þone ariseð þe hiredes aldor for þes oðres
onrope, *ant* him tyðað þæs ðe he bit; na for his freondscipe, ac for his
unstilnesse. Ði he cweð 'na for freondraddene' for þan ðe nan man nere

wurðe ne ðæs leafan, ne þæs ecen lifes, ȝif Godes mildheortnesse nære þe
mare ofer mancynne. Nu scele we cnucian *ant* hryman to Criste, for ða[n] 90
þe he wile us tyðian swa swa he sylf *cweð:* 'biddað *ant* eow bið iȝifen;
secað *ant* ȝe ifindæð; cnuciað *ant* eow bið iopenod.' Ælc þæra þe ȝeornlice
bit *ant* ðære benæ ne swicað, þam tyðað God þæs ecan lifes.

He sæde þa oðer bispel: hwuilc fæder wyle syllan his cilde stan ȝif
hit hlafæs bit? oððe neddran ȝif hit fisces bit? oððe þone wyrm ðrowend 95
ȝif hit æȝes bit? God is ure fæder þurð his mildheordnesse, *ant* þe fisc
tacnað þe ileafan, *ant* ðet æȝ ðone halȝan hiht, ðe hlaf ða soðæn lufe. Þæs
ðreo þing ȝifð God his icorenum, for þan ðe nan man ne mæȝ habbæn
Godes rice buton ȝif he habbe þas ðro þing. He sceal rihtlice lefan, *ant*
habban hiht to Gode, *ant* soðe lufe to Gode *ant* to manne, ȝif he wile to 100
Godes rice becuman. Ðe fisc tacnað beleafan, for þan ðe his icunde is swa
hine swiðor þa yða wealcað, swa he strengræ bið *ant* swiðor batað. Swa
eac ðe leafulle man, swa he swiðor bið iswent for his ileafan, swa ðe ileafa
strengra bið þer ðer he ælteowe bið. Gif he abryð on þære ehtnesse, he ne
bið þone ileafa ac bið hiwung. Þæt æȝ tacnað hiht, for ði ðe þa fuȝelas ne 105
tymað swa swa oðer nytene; ac ærest hit bið æiȝ, *ant* þeo moder syððan
mid hihte bryt þet æȝ to bridde. Swa eac ure hiht ne becom na ȝyt to ðam
ðe he hopað, ac is swilce he beo æiȝ; ðone he hafæð þet him behaten is,
he bið fuȝel. Hlaf betacnað þa soðan lufe, þeo is alræ mægne mæst swa
swa þe hlaf bið alra meta fyrmest. Micel mæȝen is ȝelæfe, *ant* micel is 110
soða hiht, þeahwæðere soðe lufe heom ofercumð, for þan ðe heo bið a on
ecnesse *ant* ða oðre twa endiað. We ilefað nu on Gode, *ant* we hopiað to
him. Eft þone we becumað on his rice swa he us behet, þone bið þa ileafa
iendod, for þan ðe wæ beoð habbende þæs ðe we ær hopodan. Ac þeo lufe
ne ateorað nefre; nu is heo for ði heora selost. 115

Ðeo neddræ is iset on ðam godspelle onȝean ðam fisce. On
neddræn hiwe beswac þe deoful Adam, *ant* efre he winð nu onȝean ure
ileafan; ac ðeo iscyldinesse ys æt ure fæder ilang. Ðe wyrm ðrowend þe is
iset onȝean þet æiȝ is attren, *ant* sleahð mid ðam tæȝle to dæðe. Þa ðing ðe
we iseoð on þisse life, þa beoð ateoriȝendlice; þa ðe we ne seoð, *ant* us 120
beoð behatene, heo beoð ece. Strece þærto þinne hiht, *ant* abid a þet þu
heom habbe; ne loca þu under bæc. Ondred ðe þone ðrowend, þe iattræð
mid ðam tæȝle. Ðe mon locað under bæc þe ortruwað on Godes
mildheortnesse; þone bið his hiht iættrod mid þæs ðrowendes tæȝle. Ac we
scelon æȝðer on earforðnesse *ant* on ilimpe *ant* on unlimpe cwæðon swa 125
þe witeȝa *cweð:* 'Ic heriȝe mine drihne on ælcne time.' Getimiȝa us tela on
licomon, ȝetimiȝa us untælæ, simble we sceolon þæs Gode þancian *ant* his

namæn blescian; þone bið ure | hiht ihalden wið ðes wurmes slege.

Stan is iset onȝean þam hlafe for þan ðe heardmodnesse is
wiðerade soðre lufe. Heardheort bið mon þe nyle þurh lufe oðre fremiæn   130
þær ðer he mæȝ. Þet godspel cweð: 'ȝif ȝe cunnon, þa ðe yfele beoð, syllan
þa godnesse owre cildren, hu mycele swiðor wule eower heofenlicæ fæder
ȝifen godne gast him biddende?' Hwæt beoð þa god þe men syllað heoræ
cildren? Hwilwendlicæ godnessæ, swilce swa ðet godspel repede hlaf *ant*
fisc *ant* æiȝ. Gode beoð þas ðing be heora mæðe, for þan þe ðe eorðlice   135
licame behofað þæs foden. Nu ȝe ȝlæwe men nellað syllan eowre cildren
neddran for fisce; nele eac ure heofenlica fæder us syllan þæs deofles
leflæste ȝif we hine biddað *þet* he us sylle soðne ȝeleafan. Ant þu selle nylt
þine cilde þrowend for æiȝ; nele eac God us syllan orwenness for hihte.
Ant ðu nylt þine cilde syllen stan for hlafe; nele eac God us syllan   140
heardhortnesse for soðre lufe. Ac þe goda heofenlica feder ȝifð us ileafan
ant hiht ant þa soða lufe, *ant* deð *þet* we habbað godne gast, *þet* is gode
willan.

Us is to smæȝene *þet* word þe he cweð: 'ȝe ðe beoð yfele'. Yfele
we beoð, ac we habbað godne fæder. We habbað ure namæ 'ȝe þe beoð   145
yfele'. Ac hwa is ure fæder? Ðe almihtiȝa God. Ant hwilceræ mannæ
fæder is he? Swutelice hit is ised, yfelræ mannæ. Ant hwylc is ðe fæder?
Be þam ðe is icwæðen, 'nis nan mon god buton God ane'. Þe ðe effre is
god, he bringað us yfele to gode mannu*m*, ȝif we buȝað fra*m* yfele *ant*
doð god. God wæs ðe mon isceapen Adam, ac þurh his aȝene cyre *ant*   150
deofles tihtinge he wearð yfel, *ant* al is ofspru*ng*. Ðe þe synful bið he bið
yfel, *ant* nan man nis on life buton su*m*mere synnæ. Ac ure goda fæder us
clensað *ant* hæleð, swa swa ðe witega cweð: 'Drihten hel me, *ant* ic beo
ihæled. Gehald þu me, *ant* ic beo ihalden.'

Ðe ðe god beon wile, clypiȝe to ða*m* ðe effre is god, *þet* he hine   155
godne wurce. Ðe man hæf[ð] gold; *þet* is god be is mæðe. He hæfð land
ant welan; ða beoð gode. Ac ne bið þe man na god þurh þas þing, buton he
mid þa*m* god wurce. Swa swa ðe witeȝa cweð: 'He spende his þing *ant*
delde wrecces, *ant* his rihtwisnesse wunað ha on weorlde.' He wanode his
feoh *ant* ehte his rihtwisnesse. He wanode *þet* he forleten sceal, *ant* *þet* bið   160
ieht *þet* *þet* he habbæn sceal on ecnesse. Ðu herest þone man þe beȝit gold
mid leade, *ant* nylt heriȝan þon*e* þe beȝit rihtwisnesse *ant* heofena rice mid
brosniȝendlice feo. Ðe rica *ant* þe wrecca beoð wæȝferinde on þissere
weorlde. Nu berð þe ricæ swære burðene his ȝestreona, *ant* þe þearfæ gæð
emtiȝ. Ðe rica berð mare þon*e* he hofiȝe to his formettu*m*, þe oðer berð   165
emtiȝe pusan. For ði sceal þe ricæ dælen his burðene wið þa*m* wrecce;

þon*e* wanoð he þa byrðene his synnæ *ant* þam wræcce helpað. Ealle we
beoð Godes wrecces; uton we for ði cnawan þa ðe us bid[d]að, þ*et* God
icnawæ us þon*e* we hine bid[d]að ure neodæ. Hwæt beoð þa ðe us
bid[d]að? Earme men *ant* tyddre *ant* dædlice. Æt hwa*m* biddað heo? Æt   170
earme mannu*m ant* tyddre *ant* dædlicu*m*. Buton þam æhtu*m*, ilice beoð þeo
ðe þær biddað *ant* ða þe heo æt biddað. Hu miht ðu for sceame æniȝes
þinges æt Gode biddan, ȝif ðu forwyrnst þine ilice þæs ðe þu ful æðelice
him tyðiȝe miht? Ac ðe ricæ besihð on his pellene gyrlu*m ant* cweð: 'Nis
ðe loddere mid his teattucen min ilica.' Ac þe apostol Paulus hine nebbað   175
mid þissu*m* worde: 'Ne brohte we nan þing to þisse middanearde, ne we
nan þing heonen mid us lædon ne magon.'

Ant ȝif rice wif *ant* poure accenneð togædere, gangon | heo awæȝ,
nast ðu hwæðer bið þære rican wifes cild, hwæðer þæs ærmen. Eft ȝif mon
openað deadra mannæ buriȝene, nast þu hwæðer beoð ðæs rice monnes   180
ban, hwæðer þæs wreccen. Ac þeo ȝitsung is alra yfelræ þingæ wyrtrymæ,
ant ða þe fyliað þære ȝitsunga heo dwæliað fra*m* Godes ȝeleafan, *ant* heo
befallað on mislice costnunge *ant* deriȝendlicu*m* lustu*m* þe heom besencað
on forwyrde. Oðer is ȝif hwa rice beo þ*et* his aldran hi*m* eahta becwædon;
oðer is ȝif hwa þurð ȝitsunge rice wurðe. Þisses mannes ȝitsung is iwreht   185
wið Gode; na þæs oðeres eaht, ȝif his heorte ne bið ontend mid þære
ȝitsunge. Swylce manne bead þe apostol Paulus: 'Beodað þa ricæn þ*et* heo
ne modeȝian, ne heo ne hopiȝan on heora unwisful welu*m*. Ac beon heo
rice on gode weorce, *ant* sylla*n* Godes ðearfu*m* mid cystiȝe mode, *ant* God
hit heom ȝylt mid hundfealdu*m* swa hwæt swa he deð þa*m* wrecce for his   190
lufon.'

Se rica *ant* þe poure beoð heom betweonan nydbehefe. Se rice is
iwroht for þa*m* poure, *ant* ðe poure for þa*m* rice. Þa*m* spediȝe dafenað þ*et*
he spene *ant* dæle þa*m* wædlan, *ant* þa*m* wædlan dafenað þ*et* heo bidden for
þa*m* delere. Se wrecce is þe wæȝ þe led up to Godes rice. Mare sylð þe   195
wrecce þa*m* rice þon*e* he æt hi*m* nime: se rice hi*m* sylð þone hlaf ðe bið to
meoxe awend, *ant* þe wrecce sylð þa*m* rice þ*et* ece lif. Na he swa þeah, ac
þe ðe þus cweð: 'þ*et* ðet ȝe doð ane wrecce on mine nome, þ*et* ȝe doð me
sylfu*m*', þe ðe leofað *ant* rixað mid fæder *ant* mid halȝe gaste, a buton
ende. Amen.   200

Notes

1   IN LETANIA MAIORE] *in red, written in the space left at the end of the final line of the previous
article in the MS*

2   Ðas] *a large initial <Ð> ornamented with red, two lines high, with the decorated tail of the cross-bar
trailing into the left margin*

11   ðæs] *MS* dæs
14   far] *MS* fare *with <e> erased*
18   heoræ lifes] *in between these words there is a small tear in the parchment, formerly stitched, sur-rounded by a decorative doodle*
19   tan] *glossed <.l. lot> probably by the same hand*
28   þe he to] *MS* þe to, *with <he> inserted above probably by the same hand*
31   ʒif] *f. 79r begins*
43–4 Dixit Iesus ... et reliqua] *the <D> of <Dixit>, <Q> of <QVIS> and <E> of <Et> are ornamented in red ink*
45   IN LETANIA MAIORE] *ornamented in red, with the rest of the line blank, as if a new text begins here*
46   Þe] *a very large initial <Þ> ornamented with red, with the decorated ascender (seven lines tall) in the left margin*
59   ʒe] *MS* we *(all other witnesses read* ge*)*
69   hlafa] *a letter has been erased before the beginning of this word, probably another <h>*
79   ðe] *f. 79v begins*
86   hiredes] *the second <e> is written attached to the ascender of the <d>*
90   for ðan] *the suspension mark over the <a> has been omitted*
93   lifes] *the <s> is written above the end of the word, just to the right of the <e>*
96   is] *a letter has been erased before the beginning of this word, probably an <h>*
101 fisc tacnað] *a later hand, in light brown ink, has inserted an <e> in the space between these two words*
128 hiht] *f. 80r begins*
130 wiðerade] *what looks like a thorn has been added above <er> in a later hand*
156 hæfð] *MS* hæf *(final word of line)*
160 feoh] *a letter has been erased at the end of this word, probably a <t>*
165 he hofiʒe] *the prefix <be> has been added (probably by a different hand) above the small space between these two words, in red with a mark of insertion*
168 bid[d]að] *MS* bidðað
169 bid[d]að] *MS* bidðað
170 bid[d]að] *MS* bidðað
175 nebbað] *the second <b> is difficult to read, and seems to have been partially erased*
178 ʒif] *the initial letter of this word is capitalised in the MS (as <G>)*; heo] *f. 80v begins*
188 ne hopiʒan] *MS* ne opiʒan, *with <h> added above the line (in what may be the same hand) with a mark of insertion*

REFERENCES

AFW = *Altfranzösisches Wörterbuch*, ed. A. Tobler, E. Lommatzsch & H.H. Christmann (Wiesbaden, Franz Steiner, 1925–2002).

AND = *Anglo-Norman Dictionary*, ed. W. Rothwell & L.W. Stone, T.B.W. Reid (London, Modern Humanities Research Assocation, 1992); 2nd edn, ed. S. Gregory, W. Rothwell & D. Trotter (London, Maney, 2005–); http://www.anglo-norman.net/.

d'Ardenne, S.R.T.O. (ed.) (1961), *Þe Liflade ant te Passiun of Seinte Iuliene*, repr. with corrections (EETS o.s. 248; Oxford, Oxford University Press).

d'Ardenne, S.R.T.O. (ed.) (1977), *The Katherine Group: Edited from MS. Bodley 34* (Bibliothèque de la Faculté de Philosophie et Lettres de l'Université de Liège 215; Paris, Société d'Édition 'Les Belles Lettres').

d'Ardenne, S.R.T.O. & Dobson, E.J. (eds) (1981), *Seinte Katerine, Re-Edited from MS Bodley 34 and the other Manuscripts* (EETS s.s. 7; Oxford, Oxford University Press).

Ásgeir Blöndal Magnússon (1989), *Íslensk Orðsifjabók* (Reykjavík, Orðabók Háskólans).

Ashe, L. (2007), *Fiction and History in England, 1066–1200* (Cambridge Studies in Medieval Literature; Cambridge, Cambridge University Press).

Assmann, B. (ed.) (1889), *Angelsächsische Homilien und Heiligenleben* (Bibliothek der angelsächsischen Prosa 3; Kassel, Georg H. Wigand).

Bammesberger, A. (1990), *Die Morphologie des urgermanischen Nomens* (Untersuchungen zur vergleichenden Grammatik der germanischen Sprachen 2; Heidelberg, Winter).

Bartlett, R. (2000), *England Under the Norman and Angevin Kings, 1075–1225* (New Oxford History of England; Oxford, Clarendon Press).

Bazire, J. & Cross, J.E. (eds) (1989), *Eleven Old English Rogationtide Homilies*, 2nd edn (King's College London Medieval Studies; London, King's College London).

Beekes, R. (2010), *Etymological Dictionary of Greek*, 2 vols (Leiden Indo-European Etymological Dictionary series 10; Leiden, Brill).

Belfour, A.O. (ed.) (1909), *Twelfth-Century Homilies in MS. Bodley 343* (EETS o.s. 137; London, New York, Toronto, Oxford University Press).

Bennett, J.A.W. & Smithers, G.V. (eds) (1968), *Early Middle English Verse and Prose*, with a glossary by N. Davis, 2nd edn (Oxford, Clarendon Press).

Benskin, M. & Laing, M. (1981), 'Translations and *Mischsprachen* in Middle English Manuscripts', in M. Benskin & M.L. Samuels (eds), *So Meny People, Longages and Tonges: Philological Essays in Scots and Mediaeval English Presented to Angus McIntosh* (Edinburgh, Middle English Dialect Project), 55–106.

Benson, R.L. & Constable, G. (eds) (1982), *Renaissance and Renewal in the Twelfth Century* (Cambridge, MA, Harvard University Press).

Bergs, A. & Brinton, L.J. (eds) (2012), *English Historical Linguistics: An International Handbook*, 2 vols (Handbooks of Linguistics and Communication Science 34.1, 34.2; Berlin and New York, De Gruyter).

Bergs, A. & Skaffari, J. (eds) (2007), *The Language of the Peterborough Chronicle* (Studies in English Medieval Language and Literature 20; Frankfurt am Main, Peter Lang).

Björkman, E. (1900–2), *Scandinavian Loan-Words in Middle English*, 2 vols (Studien zur englischen Philologie 7, 11; Halle, Max Niemeyer).

Bliss, A.J. (1949–50), 'The OE Long Diphthongs *ēo* and *ēa*', *English and Germanic Studies*, 3: 82–7.

Boffey, J. & Edwards, A.S.G. (2005), *A New Index of Middle English Verse* (London, British Library).

Brate, E. (1885), *Nordische Lehnwörter im Orrmulum* (Beiträge zur Geschichte der deutschen Sprache und Literatur 10; Halle, Max Niemeyer).

Brøndum-Nielsen, J. (1968), *Gammeldansk grammatik i sproghistorisk fremstilling*, Vol. 2: *Konsonantisme*, 3rd edn (Copenhagen, Schultz).

Brook, G.L. & Leslie, R.F. (eds) (1963–78), *Laȝamon: Brut*, 2 vols (EETS o.s. 250 and 277; Oxford, Oxford University Press).

Brooke, C. (1969), *The Twelfth Century Renaissance* (London, Thames and Hudson).

BT = *An Anglo-Saxon Dictionary, based on the manuscript collections of the late Joseph Bosworth*, ed. and enlarged by T.N. Toller (London, Oxford University Press, 1898).

BTS = *An Anglo-Saxon Dictionary, based on the manuscript collections of the late Joseph Bosworth, Supplement*, ed. T.N. Toller (Oxford, Clarendon Press, 1921).

BTSC = *An Anglo-Saxon Dictionary, based on the manuscript collections of Joseph Bosworth, Enlarged Addenda and Corrigenda to the Supplement*, ed. A. Campbell (Oxford, Clarendon Press, 1972).

Burchfield, R.W. (1956), 'The Language and Orthography of the Ormulum MS', *Transactions of the Philological Society*, 1956: 56–87. http://dx.doi.org/10.1111/j.1467-968X.1956.tb00564.x

Campbell, A. (1959), *Old English Grammar* (Oxford, Oxford University Press).

Cannon, C. (2005), 'Between the Old and the Middle of English', *New Medieval Literatures*, 7: 203–21.

Cartlidge, N. (ed.) (2001), *The Owl and the Nightingale: Text and Translation* (Exeter Medieval English Texts and Studies; Exeter: University of Exeter Press).

Clanchy, M.T. (2013), *From Memory to Written Record: England 1066–1307*, 3rd edn (Malden, MA, Oxford, Chichester, Wiley-Blackwell).

Clark, C. (1952–3), 'Studies in the Vocabulary of the Peterborough Chronicle, 1070–1154', *English and Germanic Studies*, 5: 67–89.

Clark, C. (ed.) (1970), *The Peterborough Chronicle, 1070–1154*, 2nd edn (Oxford, Clarendon Press).

Cleasby-Vigfusson = *An Icelandic-English Dictionary*, instigated by R. Cleasby, subsequently revised, enlarged and completed by Gudbrand Vigfusson, 2nd edn with a supplement by Sir William A. Craigie, containing many additional words and references (Oxford, Clarendon Press, 1957).

Clemoes, P. (ed.) (1997), *Ælfric's Catholic Homilies, The First Series: Text* (EETS s.s. 17; Oxford, Oxford University Press).

CMEPV = *Corpus of Middle English Prose and Verse*, ed. F. McSparran *et al.* (Ann Arbor, University of Michigan, 2006); http://quod.lib.umich.edu/c/cme/.

CONE = *A Corpus of Narrative Etymologies from Proto-Old English to Early Middle English and accompanying Corpus of Changes*, compiled by R. Lass, M. Laing, R. Alcorn & K. Williamson (Edinburgh, University of Edinburgh, 2013–); http://www.lel.ed.ac.uk/ihd/CoNE/CoNE.html.

Conti, A. (2007a), 'The Circulation of the Old English Homily in the Twelfth Century: New Evidence from Oxford, Bodleian Library, MS Bodley 343', in A. J Kleist (ed.), *The Old English Homily: Precedent, Practice, and Appropriation* (Turnhout, Brepols), 365–402.

Conti, A. (2007b), 'Revising Wulfstan's Antichrist in the Twelfth Century: A Study in Medieval Textual Re-appropriation', *Literature Compass*, 4/3: 638–63. http://dx.doi.org/10.1111/j.1741-4113.2007.00439.x

Conti, A. (2012), 'Individual Practice, Common Endeavour: Making a Manuscript and Community in the Second Half of the Twelfth Century', in Treharne, Da Rold & Swan (2012), 253–72.

Conti, A. & Da Rold, O. (2010), 'Oxford, Bodleian Library, Bodley 343', in *EMSS*; http://www.le.ac.uk/english/em1060to1220/mss/EM.Ox.Bodl.343.htm.

Cooke, J. (1997), 'Worcester Books and Scholars, and the Making of the Harley Glossary (British Library MS. Harley 3376)', *Anglia*, 115: 441–68. http://dx.doi.org/10.1515/angl.1997.115.4.441

Crane, S. (1999), 'Anglo-Norman Cultures in England, 1066–1460', in Wallace (1999), 35–60.

Crawford, S.J. (ed) (1969), *The Old English Version of the Heptateuch, Ælfric's Treatise on the Old and New Testament and his Preface to Genesis*, with the text of two additional manuscripts transcribed by N.R. Ker, repr. with the text of two additional manuscripts (EETS o.s. 160; London, New York, Toronto, Oxford University Press).

Crépin, A. (ed.) (1991), *Beowulf: Édition diplomatique et texte critique, traduction française, commentaires et vocabulaire*, vol. 2 (Göppinger Arbeiten zur Germanistik 329; Göppingen, Kümmerle Verlag).

Curzan, A. (2012), 'Interdisciplinarity and Historiography: Periodization in the History of the English Language', in Bergs & Brinton (2012), 1233–56.

Dance, R. (2000), 'Is the Verb *Die* Derived from Old Norse? A Review of the Evidence', *English Studies*, 81: 368–83. http://dx.doi.org/10.1076/0013-838X(200007)81:4;1-F;FT368

Dance, R. (2003a), *Words Derived from Old Norse in Early Middle English: Studies in the Vocabulary of the South-West Midland Texts* (Medieval and Renaissance Texts and Studies 246; Tempe, AZ, Arizona Center for Medieval and Renaissance Studies).

Dance, R. (2003b), 'The AB Language: the Recluse, the Gossip and the Language Historian', in Y. Wada (ed.), *A Companion to Ancrene Wisse* (Cambridge, Brewer), 57–82.

Dance, R. (2011), '"Tomarȝan hit is awane": Words Derived from Old Norse in Four Lambeth Homilies', in J. Fisiak & M. Bator (eds), *Foreign Influences on Medieval English* (Frankfurt am Main, Peter Lang), 77–127.

Dance, R. (2012a), 'English in Contact: Norse', in Bergs & Brinton (2012), 1724–37.

Dance, R. (2012b), '*Ealde æ, niwæ laʒe*: Two Words for "Law" in the Twelfth Century' (with an appendix by R. Dance & A. Conti), in Treharne, Da Rold & Swan (2012), 149–82.

Dance, R. (2013), '"Tor for to telle": Words Derived from Old Norse in *Sir Gawain and the Green Knight*', in Jefferson & Putter (2013), 41–58.

Da Rold, O. (2006), 'English Manuscripts 1060 to 1220 and the Making of a Re-source', *Literature Compass*, 3/4: 750–66. http://dx.doi.org/10.1111/j.1741-4113.2006.00344.x

Da Rold, O. (2010), 'Oxford, Bodleian Library, Laud Misc. 636', in *EMSS*; http://www.le.ac.uk/english/em1060to1220/mss/EM.Ox.Laud.636.htm.

Da Rold, O. & Swan, M. (2011), 'Linguistic Contiguities: English Manuscripts 1060–1220', in Tyler (2011), 255–70.

DEAF = *Dictionnaire étymologique de l'ancien français*, ed. K. Baldinger, F. Möhren & T. Städtler (Tübingen, Max Niemeyer, 1971–); http://www.deaf-page.de/index.php.

Diensberg, B. (2006), 'Survival of Old English Lexical Units of either Native or Latin Origin or Re-Borrowing from Anglo-French in Middle English', in A.J. Johnston, F. von Mengden & S. Thim (eds), *Language and Text: Current Perspectives on English and Germanic Historical Linguistics and Philology* (Anglistische Forschungen 359; Heidelberg, Winter), 41–56.

DMF = *Dictionnaire de moyen français*, version 2010 (Analyse et traitement informatique de la langue française, CNRS and Nancy Université); http://www.atilf.fr/dmf.

DMIEV = *The DIMEV: An Open-Access, Digital Edition of the Index of Middle English Verse, Based on the Index of Middle English Verse (1943) and its Supplement (1965)*, ed. L.R. Mooney, D.W. Mosser & E. Solopova, with D. Thorpe & D. Hill Radcliffe (1995–); http://www.dimev.net.

Doane, A.N. (ed.) (1991), *The Saxon Genesis: An Edition of the West Saxon Genesis B and the Old Saxon Vatican Genesis* (Madison, University of Wisconsin Press).

DOE = *Dictionary of Old English: A–G*, ed A. Cameron, A.C. Amos, A. diPaolo Healey *et al.*, CD-ROM (Toronto, Pontifical Institute of Mediaeval Studies for the Dictionary of Old English Project, 2008).

Durkin, P. (2009), *The Oxford Guide to Etymology* (Oxford and New York, Oxford University Press).

Durkin, P. (2014), *Borrowed Words: A History of Loanwords in English* (Oxford, Oxford University Press). http://dx.doi.org/10.1093/acprof:oso/9780199574995.001.0001

EEL = *Early English Laws*, ed. J. Winters, B. O'Brien *et al.* (London, Institute of Historical Research and King's College London, 2009–); http://www.earlyenglishlaws.ac.uk.

EMSS = *The Production and Use of English Manuscripts 1060 to 1220*, ed. O. Da Rold, T. Kato, M. Swan & E. Treharne (Leicester, University of Leicester, 2010); http://www.le.ac.uk/ee/em1060to1220.index/html.

Falk, H.S. & Torp, A. (1960), *Norwegisch-dänisches etymologisches Wörterbuch, mit Literaturnachweisen strittiger Etymologien sowie deutschem und altnordischem Wörterverzeichnis*, 2nd edn, 2 vols (Oslo and Bergen, Universitetsforlaget; Heidelberg, Carl Winter's Universitätsbuchhandlung).

Faulkner, M. (2008), 'The Uses of Anglo-Saxon Manuscripts *c*.1066–1200' (unpublished D.Phil. dissertation, University of Oxford).

Faulkner, M. (2010), 'Oxford, Bodleian Library, Junius 1', in *EMSS*; http://www.le.ac.uk/english/em1060to1220/mss/EM.Ox.Juni.1.htm.

Faulkner, M. (2012a), 'Archaism, Belatedness and Modernisation: "Old" English in the Twelfth Century', *Review of English Studies*, n.s. 63: 179–203.

Faulkner, M. (2012b), 'Rewriting English Literary History 1042–1215', *Literature Compass*, 9/4: 275–91. http://dx.doi.org/10.1111/j.1741-4113.2011.00867.x

Faulkner, M. (forthcoming), *Ignota lingua: English Literatures in the Long Twelfth Century*.

Fehr, B. (ed.) (1966), *Die Hirtenbriefe Ælfrics, in altenglischer und lateinischer Fassung*, repr. with a supplement to the Introduction by P. Clemoes (Bibliothek der angelsächsischen Prosa 9; Darmstadt, Wissenschaftliche Buchgesellschaft).

Fernández, F., Fuster, M. & Calvo, J.J. (eds) (1994), *English Historical Linguistics 1992: Papers from the 7th International Conference on English Historical Linguistics, Valencia, 22–26 September 1992* (Amsterdam and Philadelphia, John Benjamins).

FEW = Französisches etymologisches Wörterbuch: eine Darstellung des galloromanischen Sprachschatzes, ed W. von Wartburg *et al.*, 25 vols. (Bonn, Schröder, 1922–78).

Filppula, M. & Klemola, J. (eds) (2009), *English Language and Linguistics*, 13.2 (Special Issue on *Re-evaluating the Celtic Hypothesis*).

Fischer, A. (1996), 'The Vocabulary of Very Late Old English', in M.J. Toswell & E.M. Tyler (eds), *Studies in English Language and Literature: 'Doubt Wisely', Papers in Honour of E.G. Stanley* (London, Routledge), 29–41.

Fischer, A. (1997), 'The Hatton MS of the West Saxon Gospels: the Preservation and Transmission of Old English', in P.E. Szarmach & J.T. Rosenthal (eds), *The Preservation and Transmission of Anglo-Saxon Culture: Selected Papers from the 1991 Meeting of the International Society of Anglo-Saxonists* (Studies in Medieval Culture 40; Kalamazoo, MI, Medieval Institute Publications), 353–67.

Fischer, A. (2001), 'Lexical Borrowing and the History of English: a Typology of Typologies', in D. Kastovsky & A. Mettinger (eds), *Language Contact in the History of English* (Studies in English Medieval Language and Literature 1; Frankfurt am Main, Peter Lang), 97–115.

Fisiak, J. (1994), 'Linguistic Reality of Middle English', in Fernández, Fuster & Calvo (1994), 47–61.

Fleming, R. (2001), 'The New Wealth, the New Rich and the New Political Style in Late Anglo-Saxon England', in J. Gillingham (ed.), *Anglo-Norman Studies XXIII: Proceedings of the Battle Conference 2000* (Woodbridge, Boydell & Brewer), 1–22.

Förster, M. (1900), 'Frühmittelenglische Sprichwörter', *Englische Studien*, 31: 1–20.

Franzen, C. (1991), *The Tremulous Hand of Worcester: A Study of Old English in the Thirteenth Century* (Oxford, Clarendon Press). http://dx.doi.org/10.1093/acprof:oso/9780198117421.001.0001

Friend, A.C. (1954), 'The Proverbs of Serlo of Wilton', *Mediaeval Studies*, 16: 179–218.

Fulk, R.D., Bjork, R.E. & Niles, J.D. (eds) (2008), *Klaeber's Beowulf and the Fight at Finnsburg*, with a foreword by H. Damico, 4th edn (Toronto, Buffalo, London, University of Toronto Press).

Georgianna, L. (2003), 'Periodization and Politics: The Case of the Missing Twelfth-Century in English Literary History', *Modern Language Quarterly*, 64.2: 153–68. http://dx.doi.org/10.1215/ 00267929-64-2-153

Gibson, M., Heslop, T.A. & Pfaff, R.W. (eds) (1992), *The Eadwine Psalter: Text, Image, and Material Culture in Twelfth-Century Canterbury* (Publications of the Modern Humanities Research Association XIV; London, Modern Humanities Research Association; University Park, PA, Pennsylvania State University Press).

Gneuss, H. (1972), 'The Origin of Standard Old English and Æthelwold's School at Winchester', *Anglo-Saxon England*, 1: 63–83. http://dx.doi.org/10.1017/S0263675100000089

Gobbitt, T. (2013), '(Old) English, Anglo-Saxon Legal Texts in the Later 11th to Mid-12th Centuries', *Literature Compass*, 10/8: 618–30. http://dx.doi.org/10.1111/lic3.12086

Godden, M. (ed.) (1979), *Ælfric's Catholic Homilies, The Second Series: Text* (EETS s.s. 5; London, New York, Toronto, Oxford University Press).

Godden, M. (1990), 'Money, Power and Morality in Late Anglo-Saxon England', *Anglo-Saxon England*, 19: 41–65. http://dx.doi.org/10.1017/S0263675100001599

Godden, M. (ed.) (2000), *Ælfric's Catholic Homilies: Introduction, Commentary and Glossary* (EETS s.s. 18; Oxford, Oxford University Press).

Godden, M. & Irvine, S. (eds) (2009), *The Old English Boethius: An Edition of the Old English Versions of Boethius's De Consolatione Philosophiae*, 2 vols. (Oxford, Oxford University Press).

Gradon, P. (1979), *Dan Michel's Ayenbite of Inwyt, vol. II: Introduction, Notes and Glossary* (EETS o.s. 278; Oxford, Oxford University Press).

Green, D. (1998), *Language and History in the Early Germanic World* (Cambridge, Cambridge University Press).

Gretsch, M. (2001), 'Winchester Vocabulary and Standard Old English: the Vernacular in Late Anglo-Saxon England', *Bulletin of the John Rylands University Library of Manchester*, 83: 41–87. http://dx.doi.org/10.7227/BJRL.83.1.3

Gretsch, M. (2003), 'In Search of Standard Old English', in L. Kornexl & U. Lenker (eds), *Bookmarks from the Past: Studies in Early English Language and Literature in Honour of Helmut Gneuss* (Munich, Fink), 33–67.

Gretsch, M. (2006), 'A Key to Ælfric's Standard Old English', in M. Swan (ed.), *Essays for Joyce Hill on her Sixtieth Birthday*, *Leeds Studies in English*, n.s. 37: 162–77.

Harris, S. (2013), 'Twelfth-Century Perceptions of the History of Britain's Vernacular Languages' (unpublished Ph.D. dissertation, University of Cambridge).

Harsley, F.R. (ed.) (1889), *Eadwine's Canterbury Psalter* (EETS o.s. 92; London, Trübner).

Haskins, C.H. (1927), *The Renaissance of the Twelfth Century* (Cambridge, MA, Harvard University Press).

Heidermanns, F. (1993), *Etymologisches Wörterbuch der germanischen Primäradjektive* (Studia Linguistica Germanica 33; Berlin and New York, Walter de Gruyter).

Higham, N. (ed.) (2007), *Britons in Anglo-Saxon England* (Publications of the Manchester Centre for Anglo-Saxon Studies 7; Woodbridge, The Boydell Press).

Hoad, T.F. (1985), 'The Reconstruction of Unattested Old English Lexical Items', in A. Bammesberger (ed.), *Problems of Old English Lexicography: Studies in Memory of Angus Cameron* (Eichstätter Beiträge, Abteilung Sprache und Literatur 15; Regensburg, F. Pustet), 131–50.

Hofmann, D. (1955), *Nordisch-Englische Lehnbeziehungen der Wikingerzeit* (Bibliotheca Arnamagnæana 14; Copenhagen: E. Munksgaard).

Hogg, R.M. (1992), *A Grammar of Old English. Volume One: Phonology* (Oxford, Blackwell).

Holt, R. (ed.) (1878), *The Ormulum*, with the Notes and Glossary of R.L. White, 2 vols (Oxford, Clarendon Press).

Holthausen, F. (1934), *Altenglisches etymologisches Wörterbuch* (Heidelberg, Winter).

Horstmann, C. (ed.) (1887), *The Early South English Legendary; or, Lives of Saints, I: MS Laud 108 in the Bodleian Library* (EETS o.s. 87; London, N. Trübner and co.).

Horstmann, C. (ed.) (1999), *Yorkshire Writers: Richard Rolle and His Followers*, repr. with a new preface by A. Clark Bartlett (Cambridge, D.S. Brewer).

HTOED = The Historical Thesaurus of the Oxford English Dictionary, ed. C. Kay, J. Roberts, M. Samuels & I. Wotherspoon, 2 vols (Oxford, Oxford University Press, 2009); http://historicalthesaurus.arts.gla.ac.uk and (in revised form) http://www.oed.com/thesaurus.

Ingham, R. (ed.) (2010), *The Anglo-Norman Language and its Contexts* (York, York Medieval Press).

Irvine, S. (ed.) (1993), *Old English Homilies from MS Bodley 343* (EETS o.s. 302; Oxford, Oxford University Press).

Irvine, S. (2000a), 'The Compilation and Use of Manuscripts Containing Old English in the Twelfth Century', in Swan & Treharne (2000), 41–61.

Irvine, S. (2000b), 'Linguistic Peculiarities in Late Copies of Ælfric and their Editorial Implications', in J. Roberts & J. Nelson (eds), *Essays on Anglo-Saxon and Related Themes in Memory of Lynne Grundy* (King's College London Medieval Studies 17; London, King's College London, Centre for Late Antique and Medieval Studies), 237–57.

Irvine, S. (ed.) (2004), *The Anglo-Saxon Chronicle, A Collaborative Edition. Volume 7: MS E* (Cambridge, D.S. Brewer).

Jefferson, J.A. & Putter, A. (with the assistance of A. Hopkins) (eds) (2013), *Multilingualism in Medieval Britain (c.1066–1520)* (Medieval Texts and Cultures of Northern Europe 15; Turnhout, Brepols).

Jensen, F. (1976), '*Rich* in the Romance Languages: An Etymological *mise au point*', *Semasia*, 3: 33–7.

Jespersen, O. (1982), *Growth and Structure of the English Language*, 10th edn, with a foreword by R. Quirk (Oxford, Basil Blackwell).

Jordan, R. (1974), *Handbook of Middle English Grammar: Phonology*, trans. and rev. E.J. Crook (Janua Linguarum, Series Practica 218; The Hague and Paris, Mouton).

Kastovsky, D. (2006), 'Typological Changes in Derivational Morphology', in van Kemenade & Los (2006), 151–76.

van Kemenade, A. & Los, B. (eds) (2006), *The Handbook of the History of English* (Blackwell Handbooks in Linguistics; Malden MA, Oxford, Carlton, Blackwell).

Kennedy, R. & Meecham-Jones, S. (eds) (2006), *Writers of the Reign of Henry II: Twelve Essays* (The New Middle Ages; New York and Basingstoke, Palgrave Macmillan).

Ker, N.R. (1990), *Catalogue of Manuscripts Containing Anglo-Saxon*, repr. with supplement (Oxford, Clarendon Press).

Kitson, P. (1992), 'Old English Dialects and the Stages of the Transition to Middle English', *Folia Linguistica Historica*, 11: 27–87.

Kitson, P. (1997), 'When Did Middle English Begin? Later Than You Think!', in J. Fisiak (ed.), *Studies in Middle English Linguistics* (Trends in Linguistics, Studies and Monographs 103; Berlin and New York, Mouton de Gruyter), 221–69.

Kniezsa, V. (1992), '*Rich Lake*: A Case History', in M. Rissanen, O. Ihalainen, T. Nevalainen & I. Taavitsainen (eds), *History of Englishes: New Methods and Interpretations in Historical Linguistics* (Topics in English Linguistics 10; Berlin, Mouton de Gruyter), 506–16.

Kniezsa, V. (1994), 'The Scandinavian Elements in the Vocabulary of the Peterborough Chronicle', in Fernández, Fuster & Calvo (1994), 235–45.

Koopman, W., van der Leek, F., Fischer, O. & Eaton, R. (eds) (1987), *Explanation and Language Change* (Amsterdam Studies in the Theory and History of Linguistic Science, Current Issues in Linguistic Theory 45; Amsterdam & Philadelphia, Benjamins).

Kornexl, L. (2012), 'Old English: Standardization', in Bergs & Brinton (2012), 373–85.

Kornexl, L. & Lenker, U. (2011), 'Culinary and Other Pairs: Lexical Borrowing and Conceptual Differentiation in Early English Food Terminology', in R. Bauer & U. Krischke (eds), *More Than Words: English Lexicography and Lexicology Past and Present, Essays Presented to Hans Sauer on the Occasion of his 65th Birthday—Part I* (Münchener Universitätsschriften 36; Frankfurt am Main etc., Peter Lang), 179–206.

Kries, S. (2003), *Skandinavisch-schottische Sprachbeziehungen im Mittelalter: der altnordische Lehneinfluss* (*NOWELE* suplement 20; Odense, University Press of Southern Denmark).

Kroonen, G. (2013), *Etymological Dictionary of Proto-Germanic* (Leiden Indo-European Etymological Dictionary Series 2; Leiden and Boston, Brill).

Laing, M. (1993), *Catalogue of Sources for a Linguistic Atlas of Early Medieval English* (Cambridge, D.S. Brewer).

Laing, M. (2004), 'Multidimensionality: Time, Space and Stratigraphy in Historical Dialectology', in M. Dossena & R. Lass (eds), *Methods and Data in English Historical Dialectology* (Linguistic Insights 16; Bern etc., Peter Lang), 49–96.

Laing, M. (2008), *A Linguistic Atlas of Early Middle English: Index of Sources*, in *LAEME* at http://www.lel.ed.ac.uk/ihd/laeme1/laeme1_frames.html (accessible under 'Auxiliary Data Sets').

Laing, M. & Lass, R. (2006), 'Early Middle English Dialectology: Problems and Prospects', in van Kemenade & Los (2006), 417–51.

Laing, M. & McIntosh, A. (1995), 'Cambridge, Trinity College, MS. 335: Its Texts and Their Transmission', in R. Beadle & A.J. Piper (eds), *New Science out of Old Books: Studies in Manuscripts and Early Printed Books in Honour of A.I. Doyle* (Aldershot, Scolar Press), 14–52.

Lass, R. (1987), 'On *Sh*tting* the Door in Early Modern English: A Reply to Professor Samuels', in Koopman, van der Leek, Fischer & Eaton (1987), 251–5.

Lass, R. (1997), *Historical Linguistics and Language Change* (Cambridge Studies in Linguistics 81; Cambridge, Cambridge University Press).

Lass, R. (2000), 'Language Periodization and the Concept "Middle"', in I. Taavitsainen, T. Nevalainen, P. Pahta & M. Rissanen (eds), *Placing Middle English in Context* (Topics in English Linguistics 35; Berlin & New York, Mouton de Gruyter), 7–41.

Lehmann, W.P. (1986), *A Gothic Etymological Dictionary (based on the third edition of Vergleichendes Wörterbuch der Gotischen Sprache by Sigmund Feist)*, with bibliography prepared under the direction of H.-J.J. Hewitt (Leiden, Brill).

Lees, C. (ed.) (2013), *The Cambridge History of Early Medieval English Literature* (Cambridge, Cambridge University Press).

Lerer, S. (1999), 'Old English and its Afterlife', in Wallace (1999), 7–34.

Liebermann, F. (ed.) (1903–16), *Die Gesetze der Angelsachsen*, 3 vols (Halle, Max Niemeyer).

LAEME = A Linguistic Atlas of Early Middle English, 1150–1325, ed. M. Laing & R. Lass, version 2.1 (Edinburgh, University of Edinburgh, 2008); http://www.lel.ed.ac.uk/ihd/laeme1/laeme1.html.

LALME = A Linguistic Atlas of Late Mediaeval English, ed. A. McIntosh, M. Benskin & M.L. Samuels, with the assistance of M. Laing & K. Williamson, 4 vols (Aberdeen, Aberdeen University Press, 1986) (online at http://www.lel.ed.ac.uk/ihd/elalme/elalme.html as *An Electronic Version of A Linguistic Atlas of Late Mediaeval English*, ed. M. Benskin, M. Laing, V. Karaiskos & K. Williamson, 2013–).

Liuzza, R.M. (2000), 'Scribal habit: The Evidence of the Old English Gospels', in Swan & Treharne (2000), 143–65.

Lloyd, A.L. & Lühr, R. (eds) (2009), *Etymologisches Wörterbuch des Althochdeutschen*, vol. IV: *gâba—hylare* (Göttingen, Vandenhoeck and Ruprecht).

Luick, K. (1964), *Historische Grammatik der englischen Sprache*, reprint with a glossary by R.F.S. Hamer, 2 vols (Stuttgart, Bernhard Tauchnitz).

Lutz, A. (2002), 'When Did English Begin?', in T. Fanego, B. Méndez-Naya & E. Seoane (eds), *Sounds, Words, Texts and Change: Selected Papers from 11 ICEHL, Santiago de Compostela, 7–11 September 2000* (Amsterdam: John Benjamins), 145–71.

Mack, F.M. (ed.) (1934), *Seinte Marherete, Þe Meiden ant Martyr* (EETS o.s. 193; London, Oxford University Press).

Malone, K. (1930), 'When Did Middle English Begin?', in J.T. Hatfield, W. Leopold & A.J.F. Ziegelschmidt (eds), *Curme Volume of Linguistic Studies* (Language Monographs 7; Baltimore, Waverley Press), 110–17.

Matthew, F.D. ed. (1880), *The English Works of Wyclif Hitherto Unprinted* (EETS o.s. 74; London, Trübner and co.).

Matthews, D. (1999), *The Making of Middle English, 1765–1910* (Minneapolis & London, University of Minnesota Press).

Melchers, G. (2012), '"Nornomania" in the Research on Language in the Northern Isles', in M. Stenroos, M. Mäkinen & I. Særheim (eds), *Language Contact and Development Around the North Sea* (Amsterdam Studies in the Theory and History of Linguistic Science, Current Issues in Linguistic Theory 321; Amsterdam, Benjamins), 213–30.

Menzer, M.J. (2004), 'Multilingual Glosses, Bilingual Text: English, Anglo-Norman, and Latin in Three Manuscripts of Ælfric's Grammar', in J.T. Lionarons (ed.), *Old English Literature in its Manuscript Context* (Morgantown, West Virginia University Press), 95–119.

MED = Middle English Dictionary, ed. H. Kurath, S.M. Kuhn & R.E. Lewis (Ann Arbor, University of Michigan Press, 1956–2001); http://quod.lib.umich.edu/m/med/.

Miller, D.G. (2012), *External Influences on English, from its Beginnings to the Renaissance* (Oxford, Oxford University Press). http://dx.doi.org/10.1093/acprof:oso/9780199654260.001.0001

Millett, B. (ed.) (1982), *Hali Meiðhad* (EETS o.s. 284; London, Oxford University Press).

Millett, B. (1996), *Annotated Bibliographies of Old and Middle English Literature, vol. 2: Ancrene Wisse, The Katherine Group and The Wooing Group*, with the assistance of G.B. Jack & Y. Wada (Cambridge, D.S. Brewer).

Millett, B. (ed.) (2005–6), *Ancrene Wisse: A Corrected Edition of the Text in Cambridge, Corpus Christi College, MS 402, with Variants from Other Manuscripts*, drawing on the uncompleted edition by E.J. Dobson, with a glossary and additional notes by R. Dance, 2 vols (EETS o.s. 325–6; Oxford, Oxford University Press).

Mincoff, M.K. (1933), *Die Bedeutungsentwicklung der ags. Ausdrücke für Kraft und Macht* (Palaestra 188; Leipzig, Mayer & Müller).

Moffat, D. (ed.) (1987), *The Soul's Address to the Body: The Worcester Fragments* (Medieval Texts and Studies 1; East Lansing, MI, Colleagues Press).

Momma, H. (2013), *From Philology to English Studies: Language and Culture in the Nineteenth Century* (Studies in English Language; Cambridge, Cambridge University Press).

Morris, R. (ed.) (1868), *Old English Homilies and Homiletic Treatises (Sawles Warde, and Þe Wohunge of Ure Lauerd: Ureisuns of Ure Louerd and of Ure Lefdi, &c.) of the Twelfth and Thirteenth Centuries, Edited from MSS. in the British Museum, Lambeth, and Bodleian Libraries* (EETS o.s. 29 and 34; London, Trübner and Co.).

Morris, R. (ed.) (1873), *Old English Homilies of the Twelfth Century, Second Series, from the unique MS. B. 14. 52 in the library of Trinity College, Cambridge* (EETS o.s. 53; London, Trübner and Co.).

Morris, R. (ed.) (1965), *Dan Michel's Ayenbite of Inwyt or Remorse of Conscience*, vol. 1: *Text*, rev. P. Gradon (EETS o.s. 23; London, New York, Toronto, Oxford University Press).

Napier, A.S. (ed.) (1894), *History of the Holy Rood-Tree, A Twelfth Century Version of the Cross-Legend* (EETS o.s. 103; London, Kegan Paul, Trench, Trübner and Co.).

Nevanlinna, S. (1997), 'Lexical Variation in the Old English Gospel Manuscripts and a Note on Continuation', in T. Nevalainen & L. Kahlas-Tarkka (eds), *To Explain the Present: Studies in the Changing English Language in Honour of Matti Rissanen* (Mémoires de la société néophilologique à Helsingfors 52; Helsinki, Société néophilologique), 135–48.

Nicolaisen, W.F.H. (1997), 'Periodization in the History of English', *General Linguistics*, 35: 157–76.

Noreen, A. (1970), *Altnordische Grammatik I: altisländische und altnorwegische Grammatik (Laut- und Flexionslehre) unter Berücksichtigung des Urnordischen*, 5th edn (Tübingen, Max Niemeyer). http://dx.doi.org/10.1515/9783111610580

Öberg, J. (ed.) (1965), *Serlon de Wilton: Poèmes Latins* (Acta Universitatis Stockholmiensis, Studia Latina Stockholmiensia 14; Stockholm, Göteborg, Uppsala, Almquist & Wiksell).

O'Brien, B.R. (1999), *God's Peace and King's Peace: The Laws of Edward the Confessor* (Philadelphia, University of Pennsylvania Press).

O'Brien, B.R. (2003), 'The *Instituta Cnuti* and the translation of English Law', in J. Gillingham (ed.), *Anglo-Norman Studies XXV: Proceedings of the Battle Conference 2002* (Woodbridge, The Boydell Press), 177–97.

O'Brien, B.R. (2011), *Reversing Babel: Translation Among the English During an Age of Conquests, c.800 to c.1200* (Newark, University of Delaware Press).

O'Brien, S.M. (1985), 'An Edition of Seven Homilies from Lambeth Palace Library MS. 487' (unpublished D.Phil. dissertation, University of Oxford).

O'Donnell, T. (2011), 'Anglo-Norman Multiculturalism and Continental Standards in Guernes de Pont-Sainte-Maxence's *Vie de Saint Thomas*', in Tyler (2011), 337–56.

O'Donnell, T., Townend, M. & Tyler, E.M., 'European Literature and Eleventh-Century England', in Lees (2013), 607–36.

OEC = *Dictionary of Old English Web Corpus*, ed. A. diPaolo Healey with J. Price Wilkin and Xin Xiang (Toronto, Pontifical Institute of Mediaeval Studies for the Dictionary of Old English Project, 2009); http://tapor.library.utoronto.ca/doecorpus/.

Oliphant, R.T. (ed.) (1966), *The Harley Latin-Old English Glossary* (Janua linguarum, series practica 20; The Hague & Paris, Mouton and co.).

Orel, V. (2003), *A Handbook of Germanic Etymology* (Leiden & Boston, Brill).

OED = *The Oxford English Dictionary* (first published as *A New English Dictionary on Historical Principles*), ed. J.A.H. Murray, H. Bradley, W.A. Craigie & C.T. Onions (Oxford, Clarendon Press, 1928; 2nd edn prepared by J.A. Simpson & E.S.C. Weiner, 1989; 3rd edn. in progress); http://www.oed.com/.

Pantin, W.A. (1930), 'A Medieval Collection of Latin and English Proverbs and Riddles from the Rylands Latin MS. 394', *Bulletin of the John Rylands Library*, 14: 81–114.

Parkes, M.B. (1983), 'On the Presumed Date and Possible Origin of the Manuscript of the "Ormulum": Oxford, Bodleian Library, MS Junius 1', in E.G. Stanley & D. Gray (eds), *Five Hundred Years of Words and Sounds: A Festschrift for Eric Dobson* (Cambridge, D.S. Brewer), 115–27.

Parsons, D.N. (2001), 'How Long Did the Scandinavian Language Survive in England? Again', in J. Graham-Campbell, R. Hall, J. Jesch & D.N. Parsons (eds), *Vikings and the Danelaw: Select Papers from the Proceedings of the Thirteenth Viking Congress, Nottingham and York, 21–30 August 1997* (Oxford, Oxbow), 299–312.

Pelteret, D.A.E. (1978), 'Expanding the Word Hoard: Opportunities for Fresh Discoveries in Early English Vocabulary', *Indiana Social Studies Quarterly*, 31.1: 56–65.

Pokorny, J. (1959), *Indogermanisches etymologisches Wörterbuch*, 2 vols (Tübingen & Basel, Francke).

Pons-Sanz, S.M. (2013), *The Lexical Effects of Anglo-Scandinavian Linguistic Contact on Old English* (Studies in the Early Middle Ages 1; Turnhout, Brepols).

Potts, J., Stevenson, L. & Wogan-Browne, J. (eds) (1993), *Concordance to Ancrene Wisse, MS. Corpus Christi College Cambridge 402* (Cambridge, D.S. Brewer).

Pulsiano, P. (2000), 'The Old English Gloss of the *Eadwine Psalter*', in Swan & Treharne (2000), 166–94.

Rassart-Eeckhout, E. (1999), 'L'expression des concepts "riche" et "pauvre" en moyen français: le matériau lexical d'origine littéraire au service de l'historien', in J.-P. Sosson, C. Thiry, S. Thonon & T. van Hemelryck (eds), *Les Niveaux de vie au Moyen Age: Mesures, perceptions et représentations, Actes du Colloque international de Spa, 21–25 octobre 1998* (Louvain-la-Neuve, Academia-Bruylant), 249–75.

Richards, M. (1978), 'Cotton Vespasian A.XXII: The Vespasian Homilies', *Manuscripta*, 22: 97–103.

Richards, M. (1988), *Texts and their Traditions in the Medieval Library of Rochester Cathedral Priory* (Transactions of the American Philosophical Society 78.3; Philadelphia, American Philosophical Society).

Ris, R. (1971), *Das Adjektiv* reich *im mittelalterlichen Deutsch: Geschichte—semantische Struktur—Stilistik* (Quellen und Forschungen zur Sprach- und Kulturgeschichte der germanischen Völker 40 (164); Berlin & New York, Walter de Gruyter).

Rix, H., Kümmel, M., Zehnder, T., Lipp, R. & Schirmer, B. (2001), *Lexikon der Indogermanischen Verben*, 2nd edn (Wiesbaden, Dr Ludwig Reichert Verlag).

Roberts, J. (2009), 'On the Disappearance of Old English', in J. Roberts, E. Stanley, T. Shippey & M. Carver, *The Kemble Lectures on Anglo-Saxon Studies, 2005–8*, ed. A. Jorgensen, H. Conrad-O'Briain & J. Scattergood (Dublin, School of English, Trinity College), 12–44.

Rosier, J.L. (1962), 'Design for Treachery: The Unferth Intrigue', *Publications of the Modern Language Association of America*, 77: 1–7. http://dx.doi.org/10.2307/460680

Ross, A.S.C. & Thomson, R.L. (1976), 'Gothic *reiks* and Congeners', *Indogermanische Forschungen*, 81: 176–9.

Rumball, J. (2008), 'Anglo-Saxon Exiles and Outlaws: A Philological and Historical Study' (unpublished Ph.D. dissertation, University of Cambridge).

Rynell, A. (1948), *The Rivalry of Scandinavian and Native Synonyms in Middle English, Especially Taken and Nimen (with an excursus on Nema and Taka in Old Scandinavian)* (Lund Studies in English 13; Lund, Gleerup).

Samuels, M.L. (1987), 'The Status of the Functional Approach' and 'A Brief Rejoinder to Professor Lass', in Koopman, van der Leek, Fischer & Eaton (1987), 239–50, 257–8.

Sawyer, P. (2013), *The Wealth of Anglo-Saxon England* (Oxford, Oxford University Press). http://dx.doi.org/10.1093/acprof:oso/9780199253937.001.0001

Schlemilch, W. (1914), *Beiträge zur Sprache und Orthographie spätaltengl. Sprachdenkmäler der Übergangszeit* (Studien zur englischen Philologie 34; Halle, Niemeyer).

Scott, W. (1998), *Ivanhoe*, ed. G. Tulloch (Edinburgh edition of the Waverley novels 8; Edinburgh, Edinburgh University Press).

Scragg, D.G. (ed.) (1992), *The Vercelli Homilies and Related Texts* (EETS o.s. 300; Oxford, Oxford University Press).

Seebold, E. (1970), *Vergleichendes und etymologisches Wörterbuch der germanischen starken Verben* (Janua Linguarum, series practica 85; The Hague & Paris, Mouton).

Short, I. (2007), *Manual of Anglo-Norman* (Anglo-Norman Text Society, Occasional Publication Series 7; London, Anglo-Norman Text Society).

Skaffari, J. (2009), *Studies in Early Middle English Loanwords: Norse and French Influences* (Anglicana Turkuensia 26; Turku, University of Turku).

Skaffari, J. (2012), 'English in Contact: French', in Bergs & Brinton (2012), 1671–86.

Skeat, W.W. (1887), *Principles of English Etymology. First Series: the Native Element* (Oxford, Clarendon Press).

Smith, J. (1996), *An Historical Study of English: Function, Form and Change* (London, Routledge).

Smith, W.G. (1970), *The Oxford Dictionary of English Proverbs*, 3rd edn (Oxford, Clarendon Press).

Southern, R.W. (1960), 'The Place of England in the Twelfth-Century Renaissance', *History*, 45: 201–16. http://dx.doi.org/10.1111/j.1468-229X.1960.tb02299.x

Stanley, E.G. (1985), 'The Treatment of Late, Badly Transmitted and Spurious Old English in a Dictionary of that Language', in A. Bammesberger (ed.), *Problems of Old English Lexicography: Studies in Memory of Angus Cameron* (Regensburg, F. Pustet), 331–67.

Stengel, E. (1899), 'Die beiden Sammlungen altfranzösischer Sprichwörter in der Oxforder Handschrift Rawlinson C 641', *Zeitschrift für französische Sprache und Literatur*, 21: 1–21.

Stevenson, L. & Wogan-Browne, J. (eds) (2000), *Concordances to the Katherine Group, MS. Bodley 34, and The Wooing Group, MSS Nero A XIV and Titus D XVIII*, with the assistance of B. Douglas (Cambridge, D.S. Brewer).

Swan, M. (2010), 'London, Lambeth Palace, 487', in *EMSS*; http://www.le.ac.uk/english/em1060to1220/mss/EM.Lamb.487.htm.

Swan, M. (2012), 'Using the Book: Cambridge, University Library, MS. Ii.1.33', in Treharne, Da Rold & Swan (2012), 289–97.

Swan, M. & Treharne, E. (eds) (2000), *Rewriting Old English in the Twelfth Century* (Cambridge Studies in Anglo-Saxon England 30; Cambridge, Cambridge University Press).

Swan, M. & Roberson, O. (2010), 'Oxford, Bodleian Library, Rawlinson C.641', in *EMSS*; http://www.le.ac.uk/english/em1060to1220/mss/EM.Ox.Rawl.C.641.htm.

Swan, M. & Kato, T. (2010), 'London, British Library, Cotton Titus D. xxiv', in *EMSS*; http://www.le.ac.uk/english/em1060to1220/mss/EM.BL.Titu.D.xxiv.htm.

Sweet, H. (1873–4), 'The History of English Sounds', *Transactions of the Philological Society* (1873–4): 462–623.

Sweet, H. (1892), *A New English Grammar, Logical and Historical. Part 1: Introduction, Phonology and Accidence* (Oxford, Clarendon Press).

Thomson, R.M. (1998), *England and the 12th-Century Renaissance* (Variorum collected studies series; Aldershot, Ashgate).

Thomson, R.M. (2006), *Books and Learning in Twelfth-Century England: The Ending of 'Alter Orbis' (The Lyell Lectures 2000–2001)* (Walkern, Herts., The Red Gull Press).

Tobler, A. (ed.) (1895), *Li proverbe au vilain: Die Sprichwörter des gemeinen Mannes altfranzösische Dichtung* (Leipzig, Verlag von S. Hirzel).

TOE = *A Thesaurus of Old English*, ed. J. Roberts & C. Kay, with L. Grundy, 2 vols (King's College London Medieval Studies 11; London, King's College Centre for Late Antique and Medieval Studies, 1995); revised online edn, ed. F. Edmonds, C. Kay, J. Roberts & I. Wotherspoon (Glasgow, University of Glasgow, 2005–), http://oldenglishthesaurus.arts.gla.ac.uk.

Tolkien, J.R.R. (1929), '*Ancrene Wisse* and *Hali Meiðhaď*', *Essays and Studies*, 14: 104–26.

Tolkien, J.R.R. (ed.) (1962), *Ancrene Wisse, The English Text of the Ancrene Riwle edited from MS. Corpus Christi College, Cambridge 402* (EETS o.s. 249; London, Oxford University Press).

Torp, A. (1909), *Wortschatz der germanischen Spracheinheit, unter Mitwirkung von Hjalmar Falk* (Vergleichendes Wörterbuch der indogermanischen Sprachen 3; Göttingen, Vandenhoeck and Ruprecht).

Townend, M. (2000), 'Viking Age England as a Bilingual Society', in D.M. Hadley & J.D. Richards (eds), *Cultures in Contact: Scandinavian Settlement in England in the Ninth and Tenth Centuries* (Studies in the Early Middle Ages 2; Turnhout, Brepols), 89–105.

Townend, M. (2002), *Language and History in Viking Age England: Linguistic Relations Between Speakers of Old Norse and Old English* (Studies in the Early Middle Ages 6; Turnhout, Brepols).

Traxel, O.M. (2004), *Language Change, Writing and Textual Interference in Post-Conquest Old English Manuscripts: The Evidence of Cambridge, University Library, Ii. 1. 33* (Münchener Universitätsschriften, Texte und Untersuchungen zur englischen Philologie 32; Frankfurt am Main, Peter Lang).

Treharne, E.M. (ed.) (1997), *The Old English Life of St Nicholas with the Old English Life of St Giles* (Leeds Texts and Monographs n.s. 15; Leeds, School of English, University of Leeds).

Treharne, E.M. (2006), 'Reading from the Margins: The Uses of Old English Homiletic Manuscripts in the Post-Conquest Period', in A.N. Doane & K. Wolf (eds), *Beatus Vir: Studies in Early English and Norse Manuscripts in Memory of Phillip Pulsiano* (Tempe, AZ, Arizona Center for Medieval and Renaissance Studies), 329–58.

Treharne, E.M. (2010a), 'Cambridge, Corpus Christi College, 303', in *EMSS*; http://www.le.ac.uk/english/em1060to1220/mss/EM.CCCC.303.htm.

Treharne, E.M. (2010b), 'Cambridge, Trinity College, B. 14. 52', in *EMSS*; http://www.le.ac.uk/english/em1060to1220/mss/EM.CTC.B.14.52.htm.

Treharne, E.M. (2010c), 'Cambridge, Trinity College, R. 17. 1', in *EMSS*; http://www.le.ac.uk/english/em1060to1220/mss/EM.CTC.R.17.1.htm.

Treharne, E.M. (2011), 'The Vernaculars of Medieval England, 1170–1350', in A. Galloway (ed.), *The Cambridge Companion to Medieval English Culture* (Cambridge Companions to Culture; Cambridge, Cambridge University Press), 217–36.

Treharne, E.M. (2012), *Living Through Conquest: The Politics of Early English, 1020–1220* (Oxford Textual Perspectives; Oxford, Oxford University Press).

Treharne, E., Da Rold, O. & Swan, M. (eds) (2012), *New Medieval Literatures*, 13 (Special Issue: *Producing and Using English Manuscripts in the Post-Conquest Period*).

Trotter, D. (ed.) (2000), *Multilingualism in Later Medieval Britain* (Cambridge, D.S. Brewer).

Tyler, E.M. (ed.) (2011), *Conceptualizing Multilingualism in Medieval England, c.800–c.1250* (Studies in the Early Middle Ages 27; Turnhout, Brepols).

de Vaan, M. (2008), *Etymological Dictionary of Latin and the Other Italic Languages* (Leiden Indo-European Etymological Dictionary Series 7; Leiden, Brill).

Venckeleer, T. (1975), *Rollant li proz: contribution à l'histoire de quelques qualifications laudatives en français du Moyen Age* (Lille, Atelier reproduction des thèses, Université Lille III).

Verfaillie-Markey, D. (1989), 'Le Psautier d'Eadwine: Édition critique de la version hébräique et sa tradition interlinaire anglo-normande (MSS Cambridge, Trinity College R. 17. 1, et Paris, B. N. latin 8846)' (unpublished Ph.D. dissertation, University of Ghent).

Vickrey, J.F. (1968), 'An Emendation to *L[æ]nes* in *Genesis B* Line 258', *Archiv für das Studium der neueren Sprachen und Literaturen*, 204: 268–71.

de Vries, J. (1977), *Altnordisches etymologisches Wörterbuch*, 2nd edn (Leiden, Brill).

Walberg, E. (ed.) (1922), *La Vie de saint Thomas le Martyr par Guernes de Pont-Sainte-Maxence. Poème historique du XIIe siècle (1172–1174)* (Skrifter utg. av Kungl. humanistiska vetenskapssamfundet i Lund 5; Lund, C.W.K. Gleerup).

Wallace, D. ed. (1999), *The Cambridge History of Medieval English Literature* (Cambridge, Cambridge University Press). http://dx.doi.org/10.1017/CHOL9780521444200

Weisweiler, J. (1923), 'Beiträge zur Bedeutungsentwicklung germanischer Wörter für sittliche Begriffe', *Indogermanische Forschungen*, 41: 13–77, 304–68.

Whiting, B.J. & Whiting, H.W. (1968), *Proverbs, Sentences and Proverbial Phrases from English Writings Mainly Before 1500* (Cambridge, MA, Belknap). http://dx.doi.org/10.4159/harvard.9780674437364

Wilcox, J. (ed.) (2008), *Homilies by Ælfric and Other Homilies* (Anglo-Saxon Manuscripts in Microfiche Facsimile 17; Tempe, AZ, Arizona Center for Medieval and Renaissance Studies).

Wogan-Browne, J., with Collette, C., Kowaleski, M., Mooney, L., Putter, A. & Trotter, D. (eds) (2009), *Language and Culture in Medieval Britain: The French of England c.1100–c.1500* (York, York Medieval Press).

Wormald, P. (1999), *The Making of English Law: King Alfred to the Twelfth Century, Volume I: Legislation and its Limits* (Oxford & Malden, MA, Blackwell).

Wrenn, C.L. (1933), 'Standard Old English', *Transactions of the Philological Society* (1933): 65–88. http://dx.doi.org/10.1111/j.1467-968X.1933.tb00190.x

Younge, G.R. (2012), 'The *Canterbury Anthology*: An Old English Manuscript in its Anglo-Norman Context' (unpublished Ph.D. dissertation, University of Cambridge).

Zettersten, A. (1965), *Studies in the Dialect and Vocabulary of the Ancrene Riwle* (Lund Studies in English 34; Lund, Håkan Ohlssons Boktryckeri).

Zupitza, J. (ed.) (1966), *Ælfrics Grammatik und Glossar*, repr. with introduction by H. Gneuss (Sammlung englischer Denkmäler 1; Berlin, Zürich, Dublin, Weidmannsche Verlagsbuchhandlung, Max Niehans Verlag).

The author: Richard Dance is Reader in Early English in the Department of Anglo-Saxon, Norse and Celtic and a Fellow of St Catharine's College, Cambridge. He is the author of a number of books and articles about Old and Middle English language and literature, and his special interests include the influence of Old Norse on early English. Recent publications include: the *Glossary* in *Ancrene Wisse: A Corrected Edition of the Text in Cambridge, Corpus Christi College, MS 402, with Variants from Other Manuscripts*, ed. B. Millett, 2 vols. (EETS o.s. 325–6; Oxford, Oxford University Press, 2005–6); 'The Old English Language and the Alliterative Tradition', in C. Saunders (ed.), *A Companion to Medieval Poetry* (Blackwell Companions to Literature and Culture; Oxford, Blackwell, 2010), 34–50; '"Tor for to telle": Words Derived from Old Norse in *Sir Gawain and the Green Knight*', in J. Jefferson & A. Putter (eds), *Multilingualism in Medieval Britain (c.1066–1520)* (Medieval Texts and Cultures of Northern Europe 15; Turnhout, Brepols, 2013), 41–58.

rwd21@cam.ac.uk

This article was first published in 2014 in *Journal of the British Academy* (ISSN 2052–7217).

To cite the article: Richard Dance (2014), 'Getting a word in: Contact, etymology and English vocabulary in the twelfth century', *Journal of the British Academy*, 2: 153–211. DOI 10.5871/ jba/002.153

Journal of the British Academy, **2**, 213–230. DOI 10.5871/jba/002.213
Posted 18 December 2014. © The British Academy 2014

What are prime ministers for?

Lecture in Politics and Government[1]
read 13 October 2014

PETER HENNESSY

Fellow of the Academy

Abstract: The article draws up an assessment of the resources and instruments a new prime minister inherits on his or her first day in 10 Downing Street. It examines the growth in the functions that have fallen to successive prime ministers, as heads of government, over the seven decades since the end of the Second World War. It explains the very special and personal nuclear weapons responsibilities that belong to a prime minister. It touches, too, on the physical and mental strains that often afflict those who carry the office of prime minister. The article examines Jack Straw's proposal that the United Kingdom prime minister and the collective Cabinet system over which he or she presides should be placed on a statutory basis by Parliament.

Keywords: Prime minister, Cabinet, collective governments, nuclear weapons, Parliament.

I owe my title question to a young boy in the late 19th century who may well have not existed beyond what one might call plausible and useful legend about the day Queen Victoria opened Blackfriars Bridge across the River Thames. As the little old lady in black passed in her carriage between her loyal and cheering subjects on either side of said bridge, the lad turned to his papa and enquired 'Dad. What is that lady for?' Unless Dad by chance was an avid reader of 'The Monarchy' chapter in Walter Bagehot's *The English Constitution*,[2] he would have been a bit pushed to provide the precocious child with a pithy answer.

One way of approaching the question is to think a bit about what a prime minister inherits once he has kissed hands with the Queen, delivered his or her well-rehearsed spontaneity on the step of No. 10 and marched down the corridor to the prime ministerial office past the same applauding Principal Private Secretary and Downing

---

[1] An edited version of the Q&A session that followed this lecture is published in *British Academy Review*, issue 25.
[2] Bagehot ([1867], 1963: 82–120).

Street staff who had clapped the predecessor out about an hour earlier as he or she set off for the Palace to resign.

Here is my top 20 of the bounty which falls into the lap of the new prime minister:

1. A £744 billion pot of public expenditure a year (the 2015–16 forecast from the Office of Budget Responsibility).
2. Twenty-two seats around the Cabinet Table for those ministers who will fight it out in front of you as to who will spend how much of the money pot and on what.
3. A direct labour force of about 400,000 people called the civil service.
4. Forty government departments.
5. Three secret agencies and some high class security and intelligence coordination and analytical machinery in the Cabinet Office.
6. Some 160,000 personnel in the Armed Forces.
7. A bomb of thermonuclear proportions and four very sophisticated submarines to carry it.
8. An interesting and usually leak-proof chat with the Queen each week if you are both in town or you pop up to Balmoral to see her in September.
9. A nice place in town plus a decent house in the Buckinghamshire countryside.
10. Round-the-clock protection from some highly trained and agreeable policemen noted for their sharpshooting.
11. A dominant share of parliamentary time.
12. The weekly torment of Prime Minister's Questions when the House of Commons is sitting.
13. Heaps of patronage in Whitehall and quangoland.
14. A press pack watching—or imagining—your every move on a 24-hour basis.
15. A seat—through your New York diplomatic representative—on the United Nations Security Council as one of its five permanent members.
16. A seat on the European Council as one of its 28 members; ditto the NATO Council.
17. Certain special operational functions such as the shooting down (or not) of a civilian nuclear airliner that might be in the process of carrying out a 9/11-style attack on the United Kingdom.
18. A slew of intractable problems at home and abroad, some of them centuries in the making, and a hand of history that falls upon you straightaway which is, for most premiers, both awesome and covered in calluses.
19. Very few direct levers of power.
20. And, finally, perhaps the most daunting responsibility of all, the writing and signing of four 'last resort letters' for placing inside the inner safe of the four Trident submarines containing your wishes—to retaliate; or not to retaliate; if you and much of your country are wiped out by a nuclear bolt-from-the-blue.

My first reaction to any list of this kind is 'why on earth would anybody wish to do the job of Prime Minister of the United Kingdom?'

My second thought is to be intrigued by the absence of any job description for those who become the Queen's First Minister. Neither is there any statute which lays out the parameters for the premiership or for Cabinet government. (I'll come back to that, too, in a moment.) You just have to get on with it.

Most of the prime ministers who have taken office during the past century had sat in Cabinets before and seen other prime ministers in action. Some had not: Ramsay MacDonald in 1924; Tony Blair in 1997; David Cameron in 2010.

Mr Cameron, however, did possess an unusual characteristic in May 2010. He had been schooled as an undergraduate in Oxford by the ace professor Vernon Bogdanor at Brasenose and, as part of the PPE formation, familiarised himself with the great rolling debates about Cabinet government and prime ministerial government—a gratifying thing for those of us who labour our way through The National Archives and slog our way through the lecture halls and seminar rooms. And, in an interview he kindly gave me last year, the prime minister was intriguing on the themes which have turned into a thousand exam questions since John Mackintosh[3] and Dick Crossman[4] revived the old creeping prime ministerialism debate 50 years ago.

'Vernon had trained me', said the prime minister. 'Dare I say I'd even read your book on the Prime Minister.'[5] ('Dare away', I thought—albeit silently. Those of us in universities who live under the curse of the Research Excellence Framework have to find 'impact' where we can.)

I asked the prime minister what else, apart from the Bogdanor training, had helped him form his view of what the job of prime minister involved before he found out for himself after May 2010? Our conversation ran like this:

> CAMERON: The picture of the job I had was formed by watching John Major a bit because I'd helped him with Prime Minister's Questions. So I'd seen inside the black box of No. 10. I'd worked in the Conservative Research Department when Mrs Thatcher was Prime Minister . . . trying to understand how much a chairman and how much a chief executive—that was something I'd thought about quite a bit having worked in business. Having studied the whole debate about how much Cabinet and Cabinet committees . . . informed decision-making structures, I'd thought about that a bit. I think I was determined to try and make it a little bit more formal and structured than it had been under my two immediate predecessors. Not necessarily because I had some sort of deep view that there was ever a perfect kind of Cabinet government, not that, just that I'm a fairly structured person. I like meetings to start on time, finish on time. I like process . . . and making decisions . . .

[3] Mackintosh (1962).
[4] Crossman (1963: 1–57).
[5] Conversation with David Cameron, 10 Downing Street, 3 Oct. 2013; Hennessy (2001).

HENNESSY: So it's for temperamental reasons rather than constitutional propriety?

CAMERON: A bit of both. I think things had gone too far towards the sofa and it needed to come back a bit.

Mr Cameron added that much 'depends on circumstance, it depends on what's happening politically, it depends on the characters'.

I asked him if he had talked to previous prime ministers before he came into office?

CAMERON: I talked to John Major. I did talk a bit to Margaret Thatcher. John Major I talked to quite a bit.

HENNESSY: What did John Major tell you in terms of do's and don'ts?

CAMERON: He gave me quite a lot of don'ts, of things he'd done, as it were. He said that he didn't manage his time as well as he should have. He wished he had made more time to think.

The prime minister's answer made me think that I'd missed an important 21st item in that list with which I began of what a premier inherits—finite time; thinking time especially. Mr Cameron has plainly pondered that a good deal. Later in the interview I put a follow-up question to him on the time/thought theme.

HENNESSY: Walter Bagehot writing on Peel. . . said that a Prime Minister needs a 'mind in reserve' for those things that come out of the blue and really stretch.[6] Do you think you're good at the mind in reserve?'

CAMERON: Oh, that's a very good one. I think there's enough flexibility . . . in the job so that when something does come up, you can extract yourself from some of the things you're doing. So when, for instance, a Libya happens or a hostage crisis happens . . . you can step outside some of the day to day. . . . I try to make sure that my life is not too cluttered. You do need to have time to read, to think, to not get exhausted so then when something does come up that means you are really burning the candle at both ends, you've got the energy and the time to do it.

David Cameron has, in a way, done a Bagehot on himself—a bit of self-placement in the great rolling debate about prime minister and Cabinet. His prior thinking had led him to see the job as an executive chairman of the Cabinet and he reckons that is what he has been.

CAMERON: . . . you're the executive chairman; you're chairing the Cabinet; you're driving progress . . .

HENNESSY: Before the election you said that you wanted to be more collective, in the way you described earlier. But would I be right in thinking that the Coalition made sure you were virtuous?

[6] In fact, Bagehot used the phrase 'mind in reserve' in a later 1875 essay entitled 'The Premiership'. St John-Stevas (ed.) (1974: 67).

CAMERON: I think there's probably some truth in that. I think that I am quite a collegiate person . . . I think it will be true that Coalition adds an extra sort of buckle to prevent too much sofa government.[7]

A prime minister can shape—has to shape—the tone, pitch and style of a government. And it's possible—as David Cameron had plainly done—to think a good deal about it before you reach No. 10. But, after that, there's no road map, war book or cunning plan about what you do and how you do it. You are, to borrow a phrase Winston Churchill liked, the 'spear-point'.[8] Everybody knows it and expects you to be spear carrier-in-chief. But what are you really for?

The question may seem a touch luxurious for those who have held the office of prime minister because you're never short of things people are asking you to do on top of that most terrible of special delivery parcel labelled 'events' that turns up on the doorstep of No. 10 with wearing frequency. And, as Henry Kissinger once described the US system, the prize is 'to rescue an element of choice from the pressure of circumstance'.[9] And the sheer rapidity and variety of decisions you need to make is very sapping on the energy levels and the grey cells. As the neuroscientist, Daniel Levitin, expresses it: 'Each time we shift attention, there is a metabolic cost we pay in glucose. We don't actually do two, or three or 10 things at once, we just switch from one to another to another. Some brain activities are more expensive than others, and switching attention is among the most expensive.'[10] This applies to prime ministers in buckets.

One way I have tried to get a bit of purchase on 'What are prime ministers for?' is to attempt a functional analysis—to look at the mix of three things:

1. The functions that only prime ministers can carry out.
2. The things they have to do when certain events dump themselves on the prime ministerial desk.
3. The new functions the job has acquired over the decades that tend to stay in No. 10 once they have arrived and are rarely shed or passed to somebody else thereafter.

The idea of trying such a functional analysis came to me in the late 1980s and early 1990s after just such an attempt—an internal secret one conducted within Whitehall in 1947—had finally reached The National Archives. It had been prepared

[7] Conversation with David Cameron, 3 Oct. 2013.
[8] House of Commons (1947: cols. 203–4). It was in this same debate on House of Lords reform that Churchill famously remarked that: 'No one pretends that democracy is perfect or all-wise. Indeed, it has been said that democracy is the worst form of Government except all those other forms that have been tried from time to time.'
[9] Kissinger (1979: 54).
[10] Levitin (2014).

by a young Treasury official, William Armstrong, in response to a request from the Institute of Public Administration for help in preparing a paper on the functions of the British prime minister to be presented at an international conference on government chief executives in western democracies.

William Armstrong, who went on later to head the Treasury and the Civil Service, sought the help of the senior and the wise in the Cabinet Office and Buckingham Palace before sending off a brief to the public administrators and placing the result, for the purposes of the Whitehall collective memory, in what was then a new artefact of the constitution called 'The Precedent Book'.[11] There is, incidentally, a fine thesis for someone in 'The Precedent Book'. Its creation in 1947 was not made public nor, until recently, was its demise. The final edition was created in 1992[12] and, as Lord Wallace of Saltaire told me in a written Parliamentary answer last August to my question inquiring whether or not HMG 'intend to restore and update the Cabinet Office Precedent Book', the volume 'has largely been superseded by the Cabinet Manual,[13] the Ministerial Code[14] and the Code of Conduct for Special Advisers,[15] which are public documents'.[16]

Back to the prime minister's functions as placed in the Precedent Book in 1947. The collective wisdom of Whitehall and the Palace came up with 12:

1. Managing the relationship between the Monarch and the government as a whole.
2. Hiring and firing ministers.
3. Chairing the Cabinet and its most important committees.
4. Arranging other 'cabinet business', i.e. the chairmanships of other committees, their memberships and agendas.
5. Overall control of the civil service as First Lord of the Treasury.
6. The allocation of functions between departments, their creation and abolition.
7. Relationships with other heads of government.
8. An especially close involvement in foreign policy and defence matters.
9. Top civil service appointments.
10. Top appointments to many institutions of 'a national character'.
11. Certain scholastic and ecclesiastical appointments.
12. The handling of 'precedent and procedure'.[17]

---

[11] Hennessy (2001: 58).

[12] See the evidence of Sir Jeremy Heywood, Secretary of the Cabinet, to the House of Commons Political and Constitutional Reform Committee on 17 July 2014, Questions 112–14.

[13] Cabinet Office (2011).

[14] Cabinet Office (2010a).

[15] Cabinet Office (2010b).

[16] Lord Wallace of Saltaire answered the question (HL 1518) on 5 Aug. 2014.

[17] The National Archives.

Had I been at William Armstrong's side (I was but a few months old at the time) I would have added to that core dozen. But its contents intrigued me. I made a few enquiries and, as far as I could establish, there had been no such audit before and none since. What's more, no prime minister had seen this job description.

So, a cunning plan of Baldrickian proportions formed in my mind. Why not pretend to be the William Armstrong of the early 1990s, draw up a modern list along 1947 lines, send it to the discreet and the wise on the inside for a bit of tweaking and then 'contrast and compare', as we like to say in exam questions. This I did in the mid-1990s and placed the result in a book I was then preparing on the constitution called *The Hidden Wiring*.[18] I had another crack at it three years ago with my friend and former student, Dr Andrew Blick, and placed it in a study of the writing of contemporary history entitled *Distilling The Frenzy*.[19]

I shan't go into the details here but some interesting things emerged from the exercises to update the 1947 taxonomy of prime ministerial tasks as head of government (not leader of party), which would have lengthened all three lists quite a bit had they been added.

First, the 1995 audit produced 33 functions compared to William Armstrong's 12 in 1947. Even allowing for those that should have been there originally—such as dealing with Opposition on a Privy Counsellor basis, overseeing the preparation of War Books, the distribution of honours, contingency planning for industrial disputes that might jeopardise the essentials of life and a few more—this represented quite an accumulation of functions and, it might be argued, an accretion of prime ministerial power that altered the balance within what we like to think of as a collective Cabinet executive.

The biggest change in terms of the quantum of personal prime ministerial responsibility was the question of authorising the release of nuclear weapons which had fallen to successive premiers since the first United Kingdom atomic bomb was delivered to the RAF in November 1953.[20]

A particular function that one does not associate with the *diminuendo* qualities of Mr Attlee was an increasing preoccupation with the media either in terms of attempting to massage and manipulate it or to fend it off. The Attlee years, too, were almost entirely free of the counter-terrorism work that fell to prime ministers after the Troubles recrudesced in Northern Ireland from the late 1960s.

When Andrew Blick and I set to work on our 2011 audit we wrote down 47 functions, nearly four times William Armstrong's. A swathe of them was specific to the Coalitionist requirements of the job after May 2010 and may disappear after the

[18] Hennessy (1995: 86–92).

[19] All three taxonomies are published. Hennessy (2012: 109–22).

[20] Hennessy (2007: 9).

May 2015 general election. Examples include managing intracoalition relationships within the so-called 'Quad' of prime minister, deputy prime minister, chancellor and chief secretary meetings, plus a more complicated process for some ministerial appointments such as agreeing with Nick Clegg who shall be the law officers.

Other accretions since the mid-1990s are not Coalition-specific such as deciding with the relevant minister whether or not to use the ministerial override on disclosing information as allowed by clause 53 of the Freedom of Information Act 2000. An area where, unusually, a prime minister has shed power is, in effect, choosing the moment to trigger a general election by asking the Monarch for a dissolution of parliament which is now a matter of statute under the Fixed-Term Parliaments Act 2011.

The wider national security responsibilities of the prime minister have also increased and Mr Cameron's most important innovation within the machinery of government—the creation of the National Security Council—reflects this. Indeed, when I asked him in our conversation of autumn 2013 'What surprised you most about the job when you started?', the prime minister said: 'I knew that the national security, terrorism, intelligence services role of the job was very big, but it still surprises you how big it is.'[21]

A very sombre and sobering aspect of a premier's national security responsibilities that most intrigues audiences at literary festivals when one gives talks on the secret state or related themes is the preparation of the 'last resort letters' for the inner safes of the Royal Navy's Trident submarines. These answer the question of retaliate or don't retaliate after a nuclear attack which has wiped out the prime minister and his two or three alternate nuclear deputies drawn from the Cabinet on a personal basis.

In an interview this summer for the BBC Radio 4 'Reflections' series, I asked Sir John Major how he had felt in the early days of his premiership when he had been briefed on this intensely prime ministerial duty? 'It is a shock', he replied:

> The first I realised that I was going to have to write post-Armageddon instructions to our four Trident submarines [they were, in fact, Polaris boats still doing the patrolling in 1990] was when the Cabinet Secretary told me. And it is quite an extraordinary introduction to the premiership.
>
> I remember I went away over the weekend and I thought about it a lot. And it was one of the most difficult things I ever had to do—to write those instructions; the essence of them being that if the UK is wiped out but its Trident submarines are at sea with their weaponry, what should they then do with their weaponry. Eventually I reached a conclusion and I set it out.[22]

[21] Conversation with David Cameron, 3 Oct. 2013.
[22] John Major, 'Reflections', BBC Radio 4, 13 Aug. 2014.

I'd heard that David Cameron had called him in before writing his letters for the submarines:

> I talked to David about that. I'm not going to say what I said. But we discussed the parameters of it and I left him to make his own decision, as he did.[23]

Last year I'd asked the prime minister about his nuclear session with John Major when we talked in his office at No. 10. 'Yes', said the prime minister,

> I asked John Major in and asked for his advice and I talked to him about it. I also talked to the Chiefs of Staff, I talked to CDS [Chief of the Defence Staff] I think. But then, in the end, it is you know, it is you in the office on your own. I sat at that chair and there's a great big shredder that was placed right here and you write . . . you choose which basic letter you want, make any amendments to it you want and then you seal it up and you shred all the rest. And so nobody hopefully will ever see these letters. It goes into the safe of the Trident submarine and then hopefully when you stop being Prime Minister they take it out and burn it and no one will have ever opened it.

As with John Major, I suggested that this 'must be when you realise what being prime minister really is all about because no one else ever does that'. It is, Mr Cameron replied, one of the 'big moments',

> —going to see the Queen, walking through the door of No. 10, chairing your first Cabinet. It's probably, yes, because it's the oddest in a way. You've seen prime ministers drive up to Buckingham Palace. You've seen them walking through the door of No. 10. You can't really believe you are doing it yourself. But that bit in the office, writing out the letters, with the shredder . . . is such an extraordinary thing to have to do, you can't really imagine it until you do it.[24]

If Parliament ever manages to create a system, either through a House of Commons resolution or a war powers statute, to regulate the capacity of a prime minister and Cabinet to take military action, this 'last resort' prime ministerial function will obviously remain prerogative pure, by which I mean that, heaven forbid, if those letters are ever opened and they say retaliate, it will be under the ancient prerogative powers of the Crown that the Trident missiles will fly.

Is it possible—or desirable—for Parliament to acquire a say in the powers and reach of a British prime minister and Cabinet in the carrying out of their normal functions far away from the contingency planning for nuclear war? There's a little noticed section in Jack Straw's memoir, *Last Man Standing*, published in 2012, which takes a look at this very question.

---

[23] Ibid.
[24] Conversation with David Cameron, 3 Oct. 2013.

In the book, Straw is critical of some of the style of decision-taking on the road to the Iraq War of 2003 in which he was closely involved as Tony Blair's Foreign Secretary. 'Tony's reputation', wrote Straw,

> has suffered because he used informal 'sofa government' methods of decision-making rather than ensuring that Cabinet (and its committees) were proper, formal bodies where collective decisions were made. The criticism is justified. Look at Iraq.

Straw went on:

> I was fully involved in the decisions over Iraq, made informally and formally. Because Tony had agreed that any decision to take military action would have to go through the Commons, there had to be a high degree of involvement by Cabinet (and the Parliamentary Labour Party) in the final decision. The end point of this discussion chain was very formal indeed—a resolution of the House of Commons. But it would have been better—for Tony and his reputation, as well as for good government—if he, and I, and the Defence Secretary, had had to discuss progress with, and seek decisions from, a National Security Council, in turn reporting to Cabinet—and on paper, not by way of oral briefing.[25]

Straw reached the conclusion that: 'The days of self-regulation of Cabinet Government should be over.'[26] As a result he's been drafting a Cabinet Government and Executive Powers Bill for that purpose and, to declare an interest, I've been helping him with this. It's still a work-in-progress but here, briefly, are its essential provisions:

- Cabinet to consist of not less than 16 members and no more than 22.
- Cabinet will have two standing committees reporting to it—a National Security Council and a National Economic Council (whose duties and composition are set out in a pair of schedules to the Bill).
- The prime minister to be required to make an annual report to Parliament on the operations and effectiveness of the Bill's clauses that deal with Cabinet Government.
- That a consultation period of at least three months should be completed prior to major changes in the machinery of government with the Commons Public Administration Committee affording them prior scrutiny before the changes are approved by both Houses of Parliament on an affirmative resolution.
- 'That the prime minister shall not authorise the active, and large-scale, deployment of British forces overseas without the approval of the House of Commons' except where 'the operations of the Special Forces or where the circumstances require that no prior public notice of the deployment should be given.'

---

[25] Straw (2012: 544–5).
[26] Ibid. (545).

The schedule dealing with the National Security Council, which, of course, already exists but on a non-statutory basis, specifies that it shall oversee all questions related to national security, foreign policy, defence strategy and policy (including decisions to deploy United Kingdom armed forces abroad on active service) as well as the coordination of intelligence and security.

The schedule touching upon the National Economic Council, which does not exist, tasks it with oversight of all questions relating to economic, fiscal and monetary policy as well as policy for industry, trade, investment plus energy and climate change. It also requires the Chancellor of the Exchequer to bring before the National Economic Council all Budget proposals and spending reviews before they are presented to Parliament and that the meeting of this requirement should be reported on the face of the resulting Budget or Spending Review.

To ensure that the collective work of the NSC and the NEC are at the core of the government's work cycle the schedules lay out that each shall meet at least 11 times a year.[27]

Of course any such Act, were Parliament to pass it, would create a collective framework for the conduct of central government—which is meant in the United Kingdom to be the norm as enshrined in *The Cabinet Manual*, *The Ministerial Code* and the code's predecessor, *Questions of Procedure for Ministers*, which ran as the core constitutional document (though it was secret until John Major declassified it in 1992) from 1945 until 1997.[28] But such a statute would not—could not—ensure that a collective spirit prevailed always and everywhere in the Cabinet Room.

For the style of a particular government would, as David Cameron suggested, continue to be shaped by the circumstances of the day and the temperament of the occupant of No. 10. And prime ministers, after all, set out their own stalls. Some set out to be transformers—Harold Wilson in 1964 to substantially raise the rate of economic growth (which he failed to do[29]) and Margaret Thatcher in 1979 to, as she put it to a Cabinet Office official, 'change the facts'[30] of the United Kingdom's political economy (which to a large extent she did by injecting successive tranches of economic liberalism and curbing trades union power). Ted Heath, though rarely seen as a transformer premier, also qualifies by steering the United Kingdom into membership of the European Economic Community in 1973; and Harold Macmillan did so between 1957 and 1963 by engineering the United Kingdom out of great tracts of its remaining territorial Empire. A side thought—would a prime minister who saw us out of the

---

[27] The draft Cabinet Government and Executive Powers Bill has yet to be published.
[28] Baker (2000).
[29] Kitson (2004: 32).
[30] John Ashworth quoted in Hennessy (2001: 422).

European Union qualify in that sense? I think so. As would perhaps a prime minister who presided over a Scottish separation.

Others because of circumstances or temperament do not set such high bars for themselves. Jim Callaghan was obliged to be a survivor or get-us-through premier during the protracted economic and industrial crises of his three years in No. 10, 1976–9. John Major, in his 'Reflections' interview with me, was eloquent about what he wished he could have done for health and education had he possessed the funds and a further governing spell after 1997 (which he made plain he never expected).

Historical memory can be—usually is—hard on the incumbents of No. 10. By seeking the highest office they set themselves up to be brought down in a variety of ways. It's partly what E.P. Thompson called, in a very different context, 'the enormous condescension of posterity'.[31] Is the premiership a victim of Enoch's Law? Here I mean Enoch Powell who famously wrote in his study of Joe Chamberlain that: 'All political lives, unless they are cut off in midstream at a happy juncture, end in failure, because that is the nature of politics and human affairs.'[32]

For me Quintin's Law fits better than Enoch's. Quintin being Quintin Hogg, Lord Hailsham, who for a few days came close to succeeding Harold Macmillan as prime minister in October 1963. In a 1989 interview with Anthony Clare for BBC Radio 4's 'In the Psychiatrist's Chair', Hailsham was asked did he regret not making it to the premiership? He replied:

> I've known every Prime Minister to a greater or lesser extent since Balfour, including Balfour, and most of them have died unhappy . . . It doesn't *lead* to happiness.[33]

It's as if, in their often lengthy post-premier life, reflecting in tranquillity is not their lot—to have had that position and power and yet to have left substantial things undone that might have been done.

The nature of prime ministerial memory, too, can linger on what might have happened but did not in terms of catastrophe avoided. Harold Macmillan told his grandson, Alexander (now the Earl of Stockton), 'that as an old man he only had nightmares about two things: the trenches in the Great War and what would have happened if the Cuban missile crisis had gone wrong'.[34]

I suspect for David Cameron, the early hours of Friday, 19 September 2014, will come into the category of catastrophe avoided when the results from the Scottish Referendum counts indicated that the United Kingdom would stay together. I've been keeping a diary of the unfolding story which I'll publish next year under the

---

[31] Thompson (1966: 12).
[32] Powell (1977: 151).
[33] 'In the Psychiatrist's Chair', BBC Radio 4, 16 Aug. 1989.
[34] Hennessy (2001: 102–3).

title of *The Lion and the Unicorn Revisited.*

I scribbled down in my entry for Tuesday, 16 September, that I thought 'David Cameron made the speech of his life in Aberdeen yesterday' followed by snatches of what the prime minister had said:

> On Friday we 'could be living in a different country with a different place in the world . . . We are a family. Four nations in a single country. That can be difficult; but it's wonderful. Please, please don't let anyone tell you, you can't be a proud Scot and a proud Brit.'

I've been around the block a bit; fairly hardened when it comes to political rhetoric. But David Cameron meant every word.

On top of his convictions about the United Kingdom, he was facing a personal abyss on Thursday, 18 September. In my diary entry for that day, I sketched how Friday, 19 September, would play out for the prime minister if Scotland had voted yes.

> PM and HM Queen. Surely he will want to go to Balmoral in person rather than phone from Downing Street. So swift flight from Northolt to Aberdeen to Balmoral and back. You can't tell the Sovereign you've lost her kingdom by telephone.
>
> Announcement that both Houses of Parliament will be recalled—probably for Monday.

I'd heard a whisper it could be Saturday and gathered subsequently that it would have been the first Saturday session since the Falklands War debate in April 1982. Back to my diary note:

> Treasury and Bank of England (which does have a contingency plan) will be active from the moment the markets open.
>
> Cabinet meets on Friday afternoon.
>
> We will, as a wise insider friend of mine puts it, be 'in completely uncharted territory'. The *Cabinet Manual* is silent on how to dismember the kingdom.

Had events panned out that way, Friday, 19 September 2014, would have been one of the most dramatic days in the history of the country and the modern premiership, let alone David Cameron's Downing Street tenure.

Last month's answer to the overarching Scottish Question *has* changed the functional configuration of David Cameron's premiership. His Downing Street Declaration at six minutes past seven on the morning of Friday the 19th has seen to that. From worrying about the possible dissolution of the United Kingdom overnight we woke up to find ourselves on a vast constitutional building site without plan or blueprint. The master document was the front page splash of the *Daily Record* for Tuesday, 16 September 2014. Signed by David Cameron, Ed Miliband and Nick Clegg, it was the nearest the Brits can manage to 'We Hold These Truths To Be Self Evident'. It was entitled

THE VOW[35]

Which is more Hollywood than Philadelphia, and it encompassed

- Making the Holyrood Parliament permanent.
- Devolving to it extensive extra powers beyond those already transferred.
- Continuing the Barnett formula put in place by the eponymous Joel as Chief Secretary to the Treasury in 1978 during the Callaghan administration and intended to last two years.

As of first light on Friday, 19 September, the Scottish Question took a brief breather, the English Question, previously a growl, grew to a roar. Mr Cameron intends to tackle the two together—and fast.

His Downing Street Declaration made this plain.[36] He has placed the Leader of the Commons, the admirably historically minded William Hague in charge of the Cabinet committee to act as Clerk of Works of the great constitutional building site. But the overall responsibility for remaking the kingdom is undoubtedly—inescapably— prime ministerial. It is right up there in the list of prime ministerial functions and every political history of the Cameron years will linger upon that fact. It is—and will remain—intellectually stretching and energy-sapping.

Friday, 19 September 2014, and the seven days that followed will linger long as one of the strangest weeks in the history of the premiership. From facing the possibility that the kingdom might rupture until the early hours of that Friday morning to Friday, 26 September, when, with the approval of the House of Commons, David Cameron and his Cabinet took us to war again in Iraq,[37] there can never have been a week quite like it.

As if to add to the spectacle, not to mention the strain on the PM, he inadvertently blew his conversation with the Queen early on the morning of the 19th when it was plain her kingdom was safe for the time being. The Head of State/Head of Government net is one of the very few that does not leak. For observers of this most sensitive and most special membrane it felt rather like GCHQ getting a rare, revealing and wholly unexpected Signals Intelligence breakthrough.

Talking to Michael Bloomberg, the former Mayor of New York, while in the city for the United Nations General Assembly, Mr Cameron's words were picked up by a nearby television crew. This is what he said:

---

[35] 'The Vow', *Daily Record*, 16 Sept. 2014.
[36] Press Release. *Scottish Independence Referendum: Statement by the Prime Minister*, 19 Sept. 2014. See https://www.gov.uk/government/news/Scottish-independence-referendum-statement-b.
[37] Coates, Elliot & Haynes (2014).

The definition of relief is being the Prime Minister of the United Kingdom and ringing the Queen and saying: "It's alright, it's OK". That was something. She purred down the line . . .

But it should never have been that close. It wasn't in the end, but there was a time in the middle of the campaign when it felt . . .

The PM's voice drifted away at this point. He went on:

I've said I want to find these polling companies and I want to sue them for my stomach ulcers because of what they put me through. It was very nervous moment.

The BBC and Channel 4 news applied their best technology to decipher the next bit. The BBC's version was the prime minister concluding by saying 'I've never heard someone tear up like that. It was great.' Channel 4 reckoned Mr Cameron had said 'cheer up' not 'tear up'.[38] The whole thing should be captured in the equivalent of those great Scottish oil paintings—a huge canvas entitled 'The Relief of Balmoral'. The prime minister was mortified. Apologies were offered and, no doubt, graciously received.

As I mentioned earlier, who on earth would want the job of prime minister—especially in the era of directional microphones and 24-hour rolling news—however much they cherish the United Kingdom and its well being?

Yet the British prime ministership remains *the* 'glittering prize', as F.E. Smith put it, nearly 90 years ago, 'to those who have stout hearts and sharp swords' and relish political power.[39] Gaining it is invariably an exhilarator but rarely a joy-bringer in the longer run.

It's not a job one would wish on anybody—and perhaps you have to be a little odd to want to do beyond a certain level of appetite. But I have, I confess, a sneaking regard for those who have walked through that famous door, felt that inheritance and taken that range of tasks on. And, we can't do without a prime minister. We may be—and I hope will be—a collective executive nation; but we need a man or woman to take the flak that assaults those at the point of the spear. The United Kingdom is still one helluva kingdom to lead.

Finally, if pressed to confine the answer to the little boy on Blackfriar's Bridge to a single sentence, I would reply that the prime minister has to be a keeper and explainer of the government's overall strategy. This was certainly Margaret Thatcher's view, as those who worked most closely with her in Downing Street attest.[40] A prime minister, she liked to say, needs stars to steer by. And so, in my view, does a government.

---

[38] Mason (2014); Dominiczak (2014).

[39] Lord Birkenhead, as he was by then, delivering his Rectorial Address to the students of Glasgow University, 7 Nov. 1923, in Jay (ed.) (1996: 343).

[40] Private information.

REFERENCES

Bagehot, Walter ([1867], 1963), *The English Constitution* (London, Fontana edn).

Bagehot, Walter (1974), 'The Premiership', in Norman St John-Stevas (ed.), *The Collected Works of Walter Bagehot, vol. 6* (London, The Economist), 65–8.

Baker, Amy (2000), *Prime Ministers and the Rule Book* (London, Politico's).

Cabinet Office (2010a), *Ministerial Code* (London, Cabinet Office, May).

Cabinet Office (2010b), *Code of Conduct for Special Advisers* (London, Cabinet Office, June).

Cabinet Office (2011), *The Cabinet Manual: A Guide to Laws, Conventions and Rules on the Operation of Government* (London, Cabinet Office, October).

Coates, Sam, Elliot, Francis & Haynes, Deborah (2014), 'RAF poised to strike', *The Times*, 27 September.

Crossman, R.H.S. (1963), 'Introduction', Bagehot, *The English Constitution* (London, Fontana edn), 1–57.

Daily Record (2014), 'The Vow', 16 September.

Dominiczak, Peter (2014), 'Cameron says Queen "purred" at Scotland result', *The Daily Telegraph*, 24 September.

Hennessy, Peter (1995), *The Hidden Wiring: Unearthing the British Constitution* (London, Gollancz).

Hennessy, Peter (2001), *The Prime Minister: The Office and Its Holders since 1945* (London, Penguin).

Hennessy, Peter (2012), *Distilling the Frenzy: Writing the History of One's Own Times* (London, Biteback).

Hennessy, Peter (2007), *Cabinets and the Bomb* (Oxford, Oxford University Press for the British Academy).

House of Commons (1947), *Official Report*, 11 November, cols. 203–4.

Jay, Anthony (ed.) (1966), *The Oxford Dictionary of Political Quotations* (Oxford, Oxford University Press).

Kissinger, Henry (1979), *White House Years* (London, Weidenfeld and Michael Joseph).

Kitson, Michael (2004), 'Failure followed by success or success followed by failure? A re-examination of British economic growth since 1949', in Roderick Floud and Paul Johnson (eds), *The Cambridge Economic History of Modern Britain, Volume III, Structural Change and Growth, 1939–2000* (Cambridge, Cambridge University Press), 27–56.

Levitin, Daniel (2014), 'It's all too much', *New Scientist*, 16 August.

Mackintosh, John (1962), *The British Cabinet* (London, Stevens).

Mason, Rowena (2014), 'Cameron: Scotland result made Queen "purr down the line"', *The Guardian*, 24 September.

National Archives, The (TNA), CAB 21/1638, 'Function of the Prime Minister and His Staff'.

Powell, Enoch (1977), *Joseph Chamberlain* (London, Thames and Hudson).

Straw, Jack (2012), *Last Man Standing: Memoirs of a Political Survivor* (London, Macmillan).

Thompson, E.P. (1966), *The Making of the English Working Class* (New York, Vintage).

Note on the author: Peter Hennessy, FBA, is Attlee Professor of Contemporary British History at Queen Mary, University of London, an independent crossbench peer in the House of Lords where he sits as Lord Hennessy of Nympsfield, and author of *The Prime Minister: The Office and its holders since 1945*.

hennessyp@parliament.uk

This article was first published in 2014 in *Journal of the British Academy* (ISSN 2052–7217).

To cite the article: Peter Hennessy (2014), 'What are prime ministers for? ', *Journal of the British Academy*, 2: 213–229. DOI 10.5871/jba/002.213

Journal of the British Academy, **2**, 231–268. DOI 10.5871/jba/002.231
Posted 18 December 2014. © The British Academy 2014

What if? Models, fact and fiction in economics

Keynes Lecture in Economics
read 16 October 2013

MARY S. MORGAN
Fellow of the Academy

Abstract: Economists build models to understand the economy, but to outsiders these often seem to be imagined or fictional worlds, accounts that seem closer to those of science fiction than to matters of science. Such a judgement underrates the importance of fictional elements and the imagination in the way economists make and use their models. Paying attention to the 'what-if' questions that economists ask when they use their models reveals how they create the keys that enable them to translate between their imaginary model worlds and the real economic world we all live in.

Keywords: economists, economic models, fictional worlds, 'what-if' questions.

I FICTION IN SCIENCE

Economists use models as a way to understand the world. But their ways of working with models often appear quite strange, and even worthy of suspicion to commentators, because those worlds that economists picture in their models seem to be imaginary worlds, not the one we live in. This fictional quality of economists' models makes them interesting for an historian and philosopher of economics. Are economists' models fictions (in which case how do they become so)? Or is it that economic models function as fictions? If they are fictions, are they a form of science fiction, or are economists creating fictions in the service of science? And most important, how do economists reason with these imagined worlds—with their seemingly fictional qualities—to understand the real world?

The idea that we might—in general terms—think of scientific models as fictions has recently become fashionable in the philosophy of science, particularly amongst younger scholars in that field.[1] One direction in this literature takes heart from the

---

[1] Three recent collections show the breadth and depth of this initiative—those edited by Suárez (2009), by Frigg & Hunter (2010) and by Wood (2010); individual works of particular relevance to this essay are Frigg (2010), Toon (2010, 2012), and Suarez (2010).

philosophical discussions of fiction itself, their idea is that we can think of the models of science as props in a game of make believe.[2] So, these philosophers argue, rather than make a model to represent or describe the world we live in, scientists prescribe, or imagine, a world which is pictured in the form of a model—in equations or diagrams or even made into a machine. The idea of models as fictions seems particularly apt for the kinds of model that are popular in economic theorising.

If models are props in a game of make believe, we can use the term 'playing games with the model' as a short-hand description for how economists work with their models—typically by asking 'what-if' questions of their models and telling answering stories about their imagined worlds. By playing these games, economists figure out how each of their imagined worlds works, explore its limitations, and see how far they can stretch its possibilities. As in all games of make-believe, there are rules for playing the game. When economists play games with their models for their own scientific purposes, those rules come from two different sources (see Morgan, 2012: chapter 1). One source of rules comes with the medium or language of the model (whether it is made up of equations or diagrams or is an hydraulic model). The other source of rules is the economics subject knowledge which acts both as a constraint on, and a prompt for questions about, the kinds of things that are imagined to happen within that world in the model. Constraints might be factual ones: for instance, economists will rule out a solution within a mathematic model that requires them to imagine that people live negative lives, that is, imagining people might live a minus number of years not a positive number of years—this is a fiction too far.[3] Prompts might be theoretical hunches about how economic society might work, for example, about the wealth transfers between generations. The rules set by the kind of medium that the model is made in (geometry, algebra, arithmetic, etc.) determine the kinds of manipulations that are allowable but it is the economists' subject knowledge that determines which manipulations are relevant and of interest.

Many of these games seem not to have immediate or obvious relations to any concrete events or characteristics of the economic world, they are often theory-making or theory-exploring games. Playing games with the model according to those rules makes truths, but only about the imagined world in the model not about the real world. So the idea of models as fictions, and game playing in using those fictions, raise puzzling questions about how such games with imagined worlds relate to factual kinds

---

[2] The usual starting point is Kendall Walton (1990), but equally relevant is the distinction he draws in 1993 between fictions that are a means to understand the props (e.g. model airplanes) and those that focus attention on the make-believe that props stimulate (e.g. a hobby horse).

[3] See Hausman's investigation (1994) of the overlapping generations model in economics which reveals some of these fictional aspects.

of economic knowledge, and how such models could be used to gain insight into the real economic world.

The notion of scientific models as fictions held by philosophers of science, and economists' own usage of their imagined world models, prompts a number of questions. The first question to address is what kind of imaginings are going on here? If we treat economic models as fictions, we might wonder: do economists prescribe a world of science fiction, or do they rather offer imaginative accounts of the real world that we live in? The difference may be difficult to draw even if we have some sense that science fiction is different from a scientist's imaginative account. Leila, the 3-year old daughter of a friend, for several weeks saw dragons everywhere: every corner that she went round might contain a dragon; and if a cobweb grabbed her hair 'it's a dragon mummy'. Even though for a 3-year old, dragons might be pretty real, perhaps there is a difference compared to the classic example used in philosophy of fictions which concerns the taking of tree stumps (as props) to be bears, so that children playing a game about bears in the forest, whether they are hunting them or running away from them, will regard tree stumps as bears and behave accordingly.

My instinct is to put the dragons example into the category of science fiction, and using tree stumps in the forest as props for bears as being rather an imaginative account of the world (particularly relevant for children in America, who grow up with bears in their forests). If so, it may seem as if facts only come into the second kind of games, those of bears (factual stumps in the forest) versus those of dragons. But this dependence on factual props may not provide a useful dividing line when one looks at the practices of science. So, the second question to be raised is how do facts and fictions interrelate in the construction and use of models: are they used together, do the facts limit the fictions, or are they embedded inside the fictions or prescribed imaginings?

Third, following on from the second point, I question whether labelling models as 'fictions' is not too narrow and restrictive a way to think about economic models. *Artefacts* maybe a more helpful term for what they are and how they are used. Both terms refer to something human made, but artefact points also towards the tool aspect of modelling. This does not mean that imagination (and its props) is not part of the modelling recipe, indeed, imagination remains a critical ingredient, as one of the roots of the term artefact hints. I will return to this particular idea later, after a discussion of the place of imagination in economic modelling.

II SCIENCE FICTION VS IMAGINATIVE FICTIONS IN ECONOMICS

A good place to begin questions about imagination and economic science is in the restaurant at the end of the universe in Douglas Adams's *Hitchhiker's Guide to the*

Galaxy. Ford, one of the main characters, sees an old friend Hotblack Desiato sitting at a table, minded by some heavies. Ford tries to speak to his friend who does not react, and after several attempts to get a response, he is pushed away by the minders who tell him that Hotblack Desiato is 'spending a year dead for tax purposes' (1986/92: 225).[4] This is a wonderful idea, just the kind of idea that an imaginative economist might have written into their model, one that escapes the factual constraints of life, but only by one, admittedly critical, step! Let me compare this with another example, from Francis Edgeworth, a famous Irish economist of the late 19th century, in a book called *Mathematical Psychics* which in some respects is not so unlike *The Hitchhiker's Guide to the Galaxy*. Edgeworth begins his investigation into the far mysterious areas of economic life with a discussion of the nature of happiness or 'atoms of pleasure' and their properties:

> *Atoms of pleasure* are not easy to distinguish and discern, more continuous than sand, more discrete than liquid . . . We cannot *count* the golden sands of life, we cannot *number* the 'innumerable smile' of the seas of love, but we seem to be capable of observing that there is here a *greater*, there a *less*, multitude of pleasure-units, mass of happiness; and that is enough.   (1881: 8–9)

That is enough at least for Edgeworth to begin his mathematical investigations into how exchange relations are conducted:

> To gather up and fix our thoughts, let us imagine a simple case—Robinson Crusoe contracting with Friday. The *articles* of contract: wages to be given by the white, labour to be given by the black. Let Robinson Crusoe = X. Represent y, the labour given by Friday, by a horizontal line measured *northward* from an assumed point, and measure x, the remuneration given by Crusoe from the same point along an *eastward* line. Then any point between these lines represents a contract.   (1881: 28)

This passage leads into the first drawing of a very famous model in economics that came to be called the Edgeworth Box, a prosaic looking object, but one that takes some explanation, and which was developed over the following 60 years as a wonderfully flexible theorising tool. The point here is not to understand the model, but to recognise the same imagination and structure of argument going on in both of these sites. For Edgeworth, imagining the exchange relations between Crusoe and Friday, and making an image of those imagined relations, is an act of prescribing the world in the model. By the same token, imagination is clearly driving the *Hitchhiker's Guide to the Galaxy* example. And the latter seems almost more real than the Crusoe–

---

[4] The first elements of the *Guide* were radio scripts broadcast in 1978; the first full set of adventures (if that is the right word) were put together by 1986 (according to the introductory notes by Adams to the 1986 volume).

Friday affair, after all, more people 'play dead' by leaving their country for a year for tax purposes, than are wrecked or abandoned on isolated islands.

It is not easy to tell what we should be concentrating on here, and what might be the relevant differences. One might think that anyone called Hotblack Desiato must be a fictional character. But in fact Adams borrowed the name from a real estate agent in London, and during a period of house hunting, years ago, I would regularly meet Mr Hotblack, but never Mr Desiato. There were various stories circulating about his absence; perhaps he had merely gone away for a year for tax purposes, perhaps he never existed. Robinson Crusoe is an even more interesting case if one tries to distinguish fiction and fact. *Robinson Crusoe* is understood as a novel written by Daniel Defoe (1719), but it was written as if it were a news account of something that had happened in his day—so we are already in a fiction/fact ambiguity. If it is a novel, Robinson Crusoe must be imagined, but the character and part of the story were probably based on a Scottish sailor called Alexander Selkirk who was abandoned on an island 700 km off Chile in 1704. He was picked up in 1709 by a passing ship, and his landing back in Britain became a big news item in London before Defoe wrote Robinson Crusoe. So, Adams's character Hotblack Desiato and Defoe's Robinson Crusoe each have an opaque status between facts and fictions.

What matters here for thinking about economics? Is it that the people and their actions are fictional, or that their situations are fictional, or that the interrelations between people or groups and other elements in the economy are fictional, or that the stories told about them are fictional? For most economists, model building usually involves some 'as if' assumptions about behaviour. Just as children may imagine tree stumps as bears, economists imagine people in their models as always rational (according to economists' ideas of rationality). Fictional 'as if' assumptions about the behaviour of 'agents' (individuals, firms, organisations etc.) are typical in the building of economic models and have been the subject of extensive discussion by philosophers of economics ever since Milton Friedman's seminal 1953 discussion of them. But in considering the *use* of models (rather than their *construction*), those 'as if' questions are less important, than the 'what-if' questions used when economists play games with their models, and it is the 'what-if' fictional *usages* of models that are the focus here. For such 'what-if' questions, situation descriptions are often important: for example, the prisoner's dilemma situation prompts lots of what-if accounts (see Morgan, 2012: chapter 9). Other stories may rely more heavily on the time relations of events, or interrelations between groups of economic actors, proposed in the model. Imaginative stories prompted by the what-if questions that economists like to ask about their model worlds are where we see economists playing their games of make-believe.

Once again, *Hitchhiker's Guide* has a neat example—in a what-if story about the planet Magrathea in one of the *Guide's* entries. A long time ago (where all stories start), when many men became rich, they also became dissatisfied with the planets they lived in . . .

> either the climate wasn't quite right in the later part of the afternoon, or the day was half an hour too long, or the sea was exactly the wrong shade of pink.

> And thus were created the conditions for a staggering new form of specialist industry: custom-made luxury planet building. The home of this industry was the planet Magrathea, where [new planets were designed and made] . . . to meet the exacting standards that the Galaxy's richest men naturally came to expect.

> But so successful was this venture that Magrathea itself soon became the richest planet of all time and the rest of the Galaxy was reduced to abject poverty. And so the system broke down, the Empire collapsed, and a long sullen silence settled over a billion hungry worlds, disturbed only by the pen scratchings of scholars as they laboured into the night over smug little treatises on the value of a planned political economy.   (1986/92: 87)

The what-if question—what happens if people get very rich—prompts the answer worked out in a story (with a distinctly moral flavour): some people get very rich, a new luxury industry starts, that industry is so successful that the distribution of income becomes even more unequal, and so forth until the system breaks down.[5]

Exploring economists' what-if questions reveals why, and when, the fictional qualities of economic models matter to the ways that economists use them. There is no one way for economists to play these games. Three examples explored in the rest of the paper must suffice to give a sense of their variety. In the first example, an economist imagined an entirely fictional USA in order to work out something factual about that economy: perhaps the most famous use of a counterfactual experiment relying on models in economic history by Robert Fogel. The second case involves a very standard model in economics, namely the supply and demand model, in which fictional elements are used to define what facts are economically interesting and the possibilities of locating matching facts in the world by economic historical work, by econometrics and in experimental economics. The final example involves a splicing of facts into fiction in the creation and usage in the Newlyn–Phillips machine, a model which imagines the economy as an hydraulic system. In each case, we find combinations of fact and fictions, and what-if questions at work.

---

[5] *The Hitchhiker's Guide* invites historiographical speculations: textual evidence from his final comment suggests that perhaps Douglas Adams recognised these imaginative accounts given by economists, and made fun of them, and perhaps Thomas Pikkety (2013) had read this story.

III   WHAT IF . . . THERE WERE NO RAILROADS?

In the economic history of the first half of the 20th century, railroads were considered to be absolutely indispensable to the US economy, not just to its growth but in determining its development: where people settled, what occupations they followed, how cities and regions grew up, and what kind of economy each region turned out to be. A salient example of this general thesis is offered by an historian Leland Jenks who (in 1944) wrote about the railroad as an invention with three domains of impact. The first domain was as the idea of a new transportation system, with economic effects even before it was built as towns, communities, and industries located in the proposed path of the railroad and agricultural areas were opened up ahead of time. Second, it was effective as a construction enterprise: building the railways created a demand for raw materials, new labourers, and industries, with knock-on effects on wages, migration, and so forth. And, as a result of those demands, there were both consumer multiplier effects on local communities, and, from the effects of financing the railroads, on banking and finance. Only third, did Jenks countenance the effect of the railroad as a producer of new transport services with new characteristics, for instance refrigerated trucks (which allowed agriculture to specialise in different goods for urban centres), and with added speed which affected the costs of many other industries and created new supply chains. In addition, the railway companies formed new large organisations, which, according to Alfred Chandler, were the locus for the development of managerial capitalism. In other words, the railroads' tentacles were felt everywhere in economic life.

   Leland Jenks's article is narrative in form and economic analytical in argument—it swings along in fine style to cover a huge terrain. In effect he made use of his historical imagination to piece together an impressive narrative of the highly complex pattern of the geographical and economic interrelations of American development. But it is clear that each individual cause–effect link in Jenks's account needed to be separately evidenced and this became a very popular area of research for American economic historians in the period. By the mid 1960s, Jenks's style had begun to look increasingly old fashioned in both technological and evidential terms compared to the explosion of cliometric and statistical studies of railroads in that decade. Yet what was more important than this change of technical style was the change in starting point, which brings us to Robert Fogel, who radically questioned the standard view. Fogel (1964) set out to assess the railroad's dispensability (not its indispensability). He began with the counterfactual: What if there had been no railroad in the US in 1890? Asking the question this way around immediately moved his economics into the world of fiction, and for Fogel, this involved an elaborate re-imagining of US economic history.

   Of course there are lots of different ways of setting up a counterfactual to challenge

Jenks's ideas; and equally there are many different ways in which the 19th-century US economy could be re-imagined without the railroads. Fogel attacked just one little strand of Jenks's many different elements by specifying his counterfactual world very narrowly: he considered only how life would be different in transporting, by water and cart from farm to final shipment point, only four agricultural products—corn, wheat, pork and beef. He reasoned that the cost of such imagined transportation compared to the cost of moving these goods by railroads in 1890 would give a starting measure of the effect of the railroads on the American economy. Even just to figure out what those transport costs would have been in his imagined world proved an immense data task because there were 4.5 million farms sending goods to regional shipment points (the intraregional shipments), and then on by interregional shipment to final market points. For the comparison of transport costs for the latter interregional transport, he largely replaced railroads with the alternatives of canals and rivers, which would have been cheaper than railroads, but slower, and with winter closures. The social savings in 1890—the difference between not having and having the railroads—for this interregional part of the transport system, amounted to only a very tiny proportion of the total income of the economy. The more problematic bit of the imaginary world, and so of his calculations, was to figure out the alternative cost of all the transport from the farms to the main regional shipping points by water and road. Including these intraregional costs (along with the interregional costs) for those four main farm commodities still only saved 2.8 per cent of total economic income. That is, if America had no railroads, they would have been 2.8 per cent less well off as an economy in 1890 than they were, which is very small (perhaps only 1 year's growth).

Fogel had made a huge factual effort within his imagined world to prove that the railroads didn't make much difference to the real world, but he thought his figure of 2.8 per cent was still an overestimate because if you took away the railroads in 1890, you must have them taken away over the previous decades, so people wouldn't have settled where they settled and wouldn't be shipping stuff from where they shipped it to the markets—they would probably have settled somewhere else, and perhaps would not even be keeping pigs and cattle but growing crops, or even living in cities.

This prompted Fogel to an even greater imaginative effort. Before the railroads came along in mid century, canals had been built and rivers improved such that 76 per cent of the cultivatable land used in 1890 could still have been reachable without the railroads. He argued that if there hadn't been any railroads then there would have been further development of those existing transport systems. Fogel imagined and designed 5,022 miles of new canals and waterways that he claimed could have been built to fill in many of these spaces, leaving only 7 per cent of good land unreachable. Figure 1 shows the new waterways that he imagined would have been built to fill in

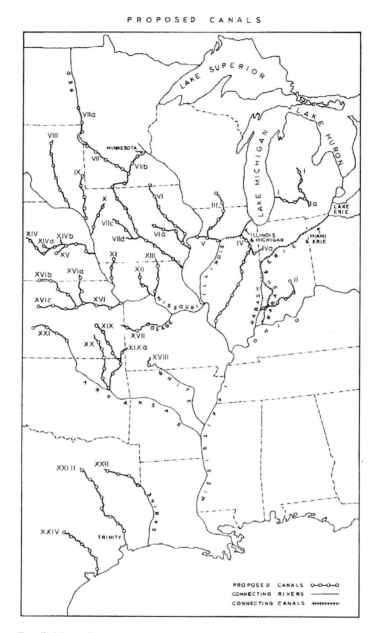

Figure 1. Robert Fogel's Map of Imagined New Waterways.
Source: R.W. Fogel (1964), *Railroads and American Economic Growth*, (Baltimore, Johns Hopkins University Press), p. 93.

PROFILES OF PROPOSED CANALS IN MICHIGAN, INDIANA, ILLINOIS, WISCONSIN, MINNESOTA AND IOWA

HORIZONTAL SCALE IN MILES
VERTICAL SCALE IN FEET

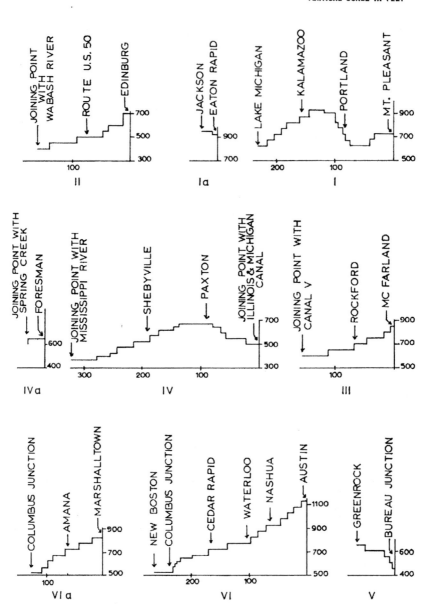

Figure 2. Robert Fogel's Profiles of Imagined Canals.
Source: R.W. Fogel (1964), *Railroads and American Economic Growth*, (Baltimore, Johns Hopkins University Press), p. 101.

much of that space, and Figure 2 shows one set of his canal designs. (There are in fact 5 pages of new canals designed to fill in his map of new waterways.) As can be seen, each canal path, its length and all the locks are planned; some of them are very long (several hundred miles) and some have more rises and falls than those canals that were built in the US economy before the railroads came along. Each canal was costed for construction and usage in order to measure properly the transport costs for his chosen goods in this newly designed counterfactual world. Having these additional waterways in his imagined economy meant that his calculations of the social savings of having railroads versus not having them dropped to only 1.5 per cent of GDP—peanuts. One of the reviews of Fogel's work captured the outcome in a nutshell: 'The iron horse was the paper tiger of the nineteenth century' (Rubin, 1967: 230).

Economists and historians who were sympathetic to Fogel's project and those of other 'new economic historians' (or cliometricians, as they came to be called) found the number rather small, but Fogel's calculations were so grounded in all those facts that it was hard to disagree with his numbers. 'Fogel's techniques are less striking than his use of imagination and a detailed knowledge of, and scrupulous regard for, the facts' (Williamson, 1965: 111). Most of the complaints from his sympathisers were that he hadn't covered enough of the agricultural goods let alone the industrial ones (raw and manufactured). Adding non-agricultural freight brought Fogel's saving calculation up to 4.7 per cent, still only a couple of year's growth; but he still hadn't covered passengers. Others thought that he had chosen the wrong date to make the calculations, and that transport services were not the most important domain for assessing the effects of the railroads on American development. Jenks would probably have agreed with this last point, for transport of agricultural produce was only one strand in his tapestry of effects, and one he thought not very important.

Fogel was criticised by other economic historians for using facts constructed from models rather than ones that were 'found' in the archive, or that could have in principle have been found in the archive but had got 'lost', or even ones which could have been interpolated in between other facts. Indeed, although Fogel's book was extremely heavy with facts, it was not quite clear where the facts stopped and the fictions began. One historian recalled his feeling of drowning in Fogel's facts when reading his book— and then suddenly, out the blue, there were 'new' facts about the cost of transport in the absence of railways—but where did they come from?[6] Still other reviewers were more overtly critical, describing Fogel's work as 'science fiction' (Erickson, 1966: 107), 'quasi-history', based on 'a figment' rather than on 'an hypothesis' (Redlich, 1965: 486, 484), and an 'imaginary journey into what might have been' (Kirkland, 1967: 1494). For this last group of historians, there was a fundamental difference between the facts

---

[6] In personal discussion at University of Pennsylvania seminar.

that could have been there and the ones that never were there, between theoretically underpinned quantitative economic history (such as Albert Fishlow's contemporary studies of the railroad's impact) versus model-builders and counterfactualists, that is, between those who dealt in facts and those who dealt in fictions.

Where indeed were these models? Rereading Fogel now it its pretty hard to see them as they slide in rather quietly and early in his account. He had used a 'linear programming model'—a relatively new form of model-basis for calculating the most efficient use of resources, one that had been developed in solving the logistical problems of the Second World War.[7] The use of this model to calculate the most efficient use of transport available for the 1890 economy with, and without, railroads meant that there were fictions on both sides of the social saving measurement. This is because the linear programming model calculated what would have been the most efficient use (at lowest cost) of the railroads in 1890 (not the actual cost of transporting goods by rail in 1890), and compared this cost with the imagined transport by his replacement waterways, also most efficiently used. In other words, they were both imagined economies, they were both model-based calculations, providing reason for Fogel to argue that his social savings numbers must be overestimates.

So the battles over the status of facts and fictions in this counterfactual were not just old versus new economic history, nor just a narrative with analytical economics (of the kind offered by Jenks) versus lots of data collection and counting. Rather this was also an argument within quantitative economic history between those who were theoretically informed but held steadfast to actual data in their statistical work and the model builders and counterfactualists who did not necessarily want to be held by what actually happened but by what could or should have happened in the most efficiently working economy that could be imagined. Fogel's world was a fictional world and one that depended, in the final moment, upon fictional data.

There are many layers of imagining and fictions going on here. Nevertheless they are all very grounded in facts compared to another counterfactual advanced by R. Preston McAfee (later a coeditor of the prestigious *American Economic Review*), who asked: What would have happened by 2000 if Columbus had not discovered America but fell off the edge of the flat earth? This was clearly a light hearted take-off piece of the counterfactualist project and began with Fogel's work:

> . . . if the railroads did not exist in 1890, they probably do not exist now, for there is no record of them being invented in the last ninety-two years. Non-existent railroads are unsafe to use. (1983: 735)

---

[7] The technique was rather new—developed by Leonid Kantorovich in Russia in 1939 (for war-time resource planning) and by George Dantzig and John von Neumann in the USA (see Klein, 2001: 128–33).

While using non-existent railways may seem less daunting than falling off the edge of a flat earth, McAfee's counterfactual has very few facts indeed to ground it in any account of American economic development. In contrast to Fogel's heavily quantitative and fact-driven work that produced his imaginative account of the economic world, McAfee's counterfactual is a piece of science fiction.

Since Fogel and McAfee both deal with imagined events and do so within imagined worlds, why does it seem reasonable to regard one as science fiction and the other as an imaginative account of the world we live in? Fogel's imagined world is more plausibly our world in the sense argued by Geoffrey Hawthorn's writings about counterfactuals and the conditions he found necessary for creating 'plausible worlds' (as he calls them, 1991). He argues that in order to create a sensible counterfactual you need first to choose a sensible node point—as in Fogel's case 1890, when most of the railroads had been pretty much filled in. Second, you have to keep as much as possible the same rather than changing everything; that means you shouldn't choose a counterfactual that requires you completely to rewind the past and to rewind the future—as McAfee does. Third, counterfactuals, as Hawthorn reminds us, don't start with theories and models but start with some fact-like situation counter to the actual facts, and only bring in models and theories when they are needed to help generate those counterfacts. McAfee breaks these conditions and Fogel follows them, which offers a useful way to validate the distinction between McAfee's science fiction and Fogel's imaginative but plausible reconstruction.

In another comparison, one could say that both Jenks and Fogel give an imaginative description of the world but they use their imagination and facts at different points of analysis. If we recall Jenks's big canvas account, he relies on broad facts, not heaps of little facts (data points), and the ability to imagine all the interconnections between them. Fogel imagines the details of only a small part of Jenks's canvas, but this in turn requires him to imagine the whole transport landscape in a different way, an exercise that relies heavily on factual information. Both Fogel and Jenks keep their imagination firmly grounded in facts, both offer plausible world accounts, but facts and fictions intersect in very different ways in their two accounts.

IV WHAT IF . . . PLAYING GAMES WITH THE LAWS OF SUPPLY AND DEMAND

Philosophers of science, when they think about models, worry about the problem of representation: How do we know when a model offers a good representation of the part of the world that is being modelled? For the scientist, this is the problem of assessing the similarity of their model of the world to the world that we live in and know. The second major problem for the philosopher of science is to wonder about scientists' incipient claims that their models explain things in the world. How do economists use their models to do more than say 'this is a picture of the world' but use it to explain things in the world, and perhaps even change things in the world via economic policy? In the philosophical account of models as fictions, the suggested solutions to the problem of representation, and thence perhaps to explanation, relies on 'keys' (see Frigg, 2010; Bokulich, 2012; and earlier Goffman, 1974) that translate elements of the prescribed fictions on to the facts of the world. We can think of these as map keys. Drawing a map requires one to key in the things in the world onto the map. Typically, elements in the world are represented on the map with conventional symbols: maps in Britain have beer mugs where there are pubs and round red dots where there are stations (which isn't quite so obvious). These conventional symbols act as keys to tell us what we are going to find when we look at the map without knowing the territory, and just as important, where we will find them when we are in the territory (assuming we know how to read the map and its symbols). So keys as a matching device work both ways—from the world to the map, and from the map back to our actions in the world.

Having elements keyed onto a map helps us to learn things about the world from the map—in particularly about the relationships of things to each other in that world. Keying on a map enables the user to make inferences, for example: where the nearest railway station is in relation to a pub. This is what was happing in Fogel's counterfactual, where each set of real world facts and counterfacts from the imagined worlds created from the linear programming models could be compared. Because he could make the comparisons (between transport by rail or by water, alternatively imagined), he could also make the measurements, and inferences could be made from those comparisons. In his imagined counterfactual world, each set of objects and activities can be easily compared with the world actually happening in 1890 because the factual keys are there.

But unlike maps, keys don't necessarily work both ways for models. The first great difficulty with the notion of 'keys' as a solution to the fiction–fact translation for models is that it relies on the scientist first knowing an awful lot about the world to make the model, just as it does for someone to draw a map, that is to make a good geographical representation of the world and key the relevant social and environmental symbols that depict the elements in the right places. As with any scientist, the economist does not necessarily understand enough about how the world works to build their models as accurately as a map. This is indeed the reason they need to use their imagination to build models—to try out their ideas about how the economic world might be, and how it might work with their what-if questions. Because models are not full enough or accurate enough representations of the world, economists' what-if discussions enable inferences to be made within the model about the things that are keyed there, but do not necessarily enable us to infer back to the world that the model represents.

The second problem is that, in many cases of models, it is not obvious that there are factual equivalents to those imagined elements, for model elements are often concept-based not fact-based, so that keys chosen to translate from models to things in the world might be quite misleading. Even if there are not missing or misleading elements, 'props' may not be easy to 'reverse', as required if the model elements are to be translated back for understanding the world or for policy action in the world. Models are not the same things as maps. And key fashioning clearly requires more than just prescribing that a stump is a bear in a game of make believe. Indeed, it may be reasonable to argue that the task of scientific modelling is *both* to create models and to fashion the keys for using them.

Creating the means and processes of translation from fictions to facts can be well illustrated in the ways that economists build and use their supply and demand models. The supply and demand model—how economists imagine market relations—is probably the most recognisable diagram of economics for people who are not economists: an early example from Marcel Lenoir (1913) is given in Figure 3. The

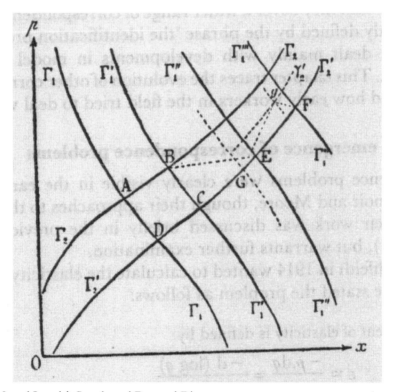

Figure 3. Marcel Lenoir's Supply and Demand Diagram.
Source: M. Lenoir (1913), *Etudes sur la Formation et le Mouvement des Prix*, (Paris, Giard et Brière), p. 58, fig. 44.

vertical axis measures prices and the horizontal one quantities; supply curves (usually) slope upwards to the right and demand ones upwards to the left. Each curve represents how economists imagine or hypothesise what a set of consumers and producers imagine they would buy or sell at the different prices in the market place (and these diagrams also show that these curves shift). So there's a double level of imagination going on here. The demand curve is not such a strange thing to imagine because people know, from their own introspection, how they might respond to prices: if prices are higher or lower, they might buy less or more of the good, which is surely why the diagram is easy to explain. But there are serious problems here. This introspection is for the individual, and these curves model the market. And while casual observations of markets may support these diagrams, the diagrams themselves were not initially based on any direct observations of supply and demand curves because those things are not there to be seen in the market. Rather, these diagrams are constructed objects on paper that economists use to describe market relations and they believe that different kinds of markets might require different shaped curves. Notice also that there is (usually) no scale, these diagrams have this abstract quality because they are conceptual constructs—another element of imagination. These now standard items of economics were first drawn in the mid-19th century (though they were imagined before that) and they are used to ask a whole range of what-if questions using different technologies of investigation.

Fashioning the keys for the demand and supply curve diagrams took place between 1860 or so and 1960. It involved four different kinds of research work to understand what kinds of supply and demand facts might be expected from theory and might be found in data. These activities involved: (1) experimenting with different versions of this abstract conceptual model; (2) defining what interesting economic facts implied by the model might or might not exist in the world; (3) fitting statistical facts from markets to the fictional curves; and (4) using the models in experimental designs for the first classroom experiments done in economics. Starting from a simple, abstract, imagined model, these projects have not only explored what kinds of keys are possible, and fashioned some usable ones, for the model, but also generated lots of different kinds of interesting findings.[8]

(1) Although Marshall (1930 [1890]) was not the first to draw these supply and demand diagrams (see Humphrey, 1992), he did develop both the diagram and its standard usage in model experiments. Figure 4 shows a block of six of his diagrams, where we can see that the supply curve has different shapes—horizontal, upward (the normal case) and wavy. We can also see that in the top three, the demand curve is shifting upwards (perhaps because there is an increase in income for consumers) and

---

[8] Discussion of examples (1) and (4) is drawn from Morgan (2012: chapter 7).

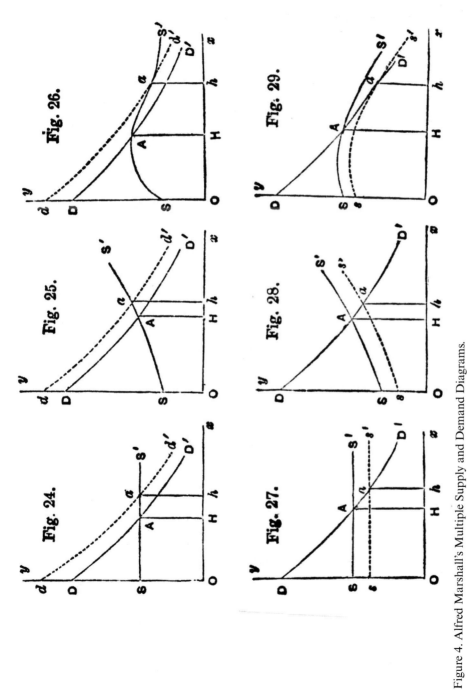

Figure 4. Alfred Marshall's Multiple Supply and Demand Diagrams.

Source: A. Marshall (1890), *Principles of Economics* Book V, Chapter XIII, Figures 24–6, note 1, p. 464; and Figures 27–9, note 1, p. 466. Reproduced with acknowledgement to Marshall Library of Economics.

in the bottom three, supply is shifting downwards perhaps because of a technical change which makes production cheaper at all levels of output). Marshall developed the method of using these little models of supply and demand in 'what-if' experiments: such as what happens if the supply or demand curve rises or falls, or what happens if a tax is put on the price of the good. (For example, in the top left-hand one, where the supply curve is horizontal, he asked what would happen to the price and quantity if the demand curve shifted slightly upwards. Clearly, the quantity along the horizontal axis would increase but the price would not change.) Some of these what-if experiments were simple, others (such as the far right pair) had outcomes which were less obvious, and some quickly took him into quite big questions about ethics and distribution. As already noted: this diagram is an imagined set of relations about how people as a group are imagined to behave, not a map of what was already known and already tied down. Marshall used these what-if experiments as a testing ground for theories about supply and demand, and so each of these little diagrams offers a site of different experiments about what we might expect to see happening if each one offers a good picture of the world. Already it is clear that one diagram is not enough, supply and demand relations of the economic world are quite varied in Marshall's imagination, which means that there must be several keys depending on the circumstances of the industry.

(2) This imaginative quality of the supply and demand diagram was problematic for those such as John Clapham, an economic historian, who argued that these diagrams were only 'mental furniture' for the economist and could not be made applicable to things in the world. He was interested in real industries, real goods, real prices, real quantities, and complained that whereas he would expect to go into a hat factory and find boxes of hats on the shelves, these conceptual devices of Marshall were like so many 'empty boxes' on the 'shelves of his [an economist's] mind' (1922: 305). They were labelled with constant return industries (the horizontal supply curve), increasing return industries (the supply curve falls with more produced) and decreasing return industries (the supply curve rises with more produced). Not only were these boxes mental constructs, but he argued that no keys were possible to take you to anything in the world: thus those boxes are empty. They are empty, Clapham argued, because it is very difficult to get any kind of information that would give you these supply curves as observational or factual things, based on the point that the supply curve refers to an industry not a single producer or firm. He gave four reasons. First, there is no such thing as a standard commodity (in manufacturing rather than in raw materials) and so no well-defined industry: 'a standard hat is not a mathematical concept' (Clapham, 1922: 311). Second, there are no existing statistical keys which would tell which real firms, if they could be collected together into industries, were examples of any of these idealised returns to scale curves. Third, it was impossible—in

practical ways—to separate out increases in efficiency due to increase in scale from those due to technical change, or 'to separate out the effects of organisation from those of invention' (313), so independent ways of measuring returns to scale were not viable. Finally, even if the economists could turn their conceptual boxes into actual boxes (by solving these measurability and classificatory problems), it is not clear what the practical use of such actual boxes could be. Thus these model boxes are empty as a matter of principle, and you can not fill them up, or fashion any keys, to enable these curves to refer to objects in the world.

Taking up the challenge, Arthur Pigou (1922), one of the leading figures following Marshall, agreed that these little model diagrams did indeed exist as boxes on the shelves of the economist's mind—they are the economists' mental furniture: they provide the 'intellectual machinery' (461) that helps them work things out analytically (rather than realistically). As with Marshall, the logical machinery of these various arrangements of things in the world enabled the economist to 'disentangle and analyse the causes by which the values of different things are determined' (460). For Pigou, not only are these boxes, containing different shaped curves and labelled with different returns to scale, in economists' minds, but if you opened any box, you would find even smaller boxes fitting inside which offer further subdivisions. In other words, there are classes of different kinds of things in the industrial world—as Marshall's diagrams show—but there are also sub-kinds or classes within these. Each box can be opened for what-if reasoning using the logical machinery inside it. Boxes do not have different kinds of goods in them as Clapham hoped, they have different kinds of industries with different market behaviours, as conceptualised into models by these imaginative economists. The keys had not yet been fashioned to match realistic markets, but the investigation of the basic model and its proliferation into kinds and sub-kinds revealed that, rather than any uniform or master key, many different keys might well be needed.

(3) In the 1920s and 1930s, economists made a determined effort to find statistical facts to match these supply and demand mathematical and diagrammatic models, that is to make the curves themselves measurable and factual. Although Clapham had pointed to the absence of data for manufactured industry goods, there were quite good data on market prices and quantities for agricultural goods, and for some industrial raw products. These are the markets where such measuring initiatives were made, for this was—above all—a keying project, matching facts and fictions together. But whether such curves were measurable proved not to be a simple question of finding data, but of the specific patterns of stability and variability in the behaviour of the buyers and sellers in the market. As we can see from the earlier Figure 3, the abstract model suggests supply and demand curves are both liable to shift around because of other factors that affect either demand or supply or both. The implication of this was explored by the economist Philip Green Wright (father of the famous

geneticist Sewall Wright) who was one of the first to work on this problem as a statistical problem. His charts (1929), found in Figure 5, point both to the problem and to a new kind of machinery developed to fashion statistical keys. He asked: What if just the demand curve shifts in the market place and nothing else changes? Then those shifts will trace out the data points on the supply curve (see his Chart I) and the statistical matching will measure the supply curve. Vice-versa: What if just the supply curve shifts and nothing else changes? Then the statistical matching will trace out and measure the demand curve (his Chart II). So, under certain behaviour conditions in the world, the supply or demand curve could be recovered from the market statistics and measured, in these two cases—simple statistical keys will work. But what happens if both curves are shifting from some other reason over time—then the outcome will be as in his Chart III. There, the curve traced out by the statistics of supply and demand is neither the supply nor the demand curve, but simply a trace of changes in prices and quantities over time. A simple statistical key will not do for whatever this final statistical curve was, it was not something imagined in the original abstract model.

This problem of figuring out what relations could be keyed to the world became known as 'the identification problem'. The specific problem here—of identifying the supply and demand relations when market curves were each subject to lots of different influences—was the first exemplar of this generic problem. The point is that just having statistical data does not make the keys that unlock the problem of turning those imagined models of markets into factual ones. Creating such keys that would reveal the factual relations in the world involves some imaginative work in solving identification problems, and econometricians (as such statistical economists came to be known) developed some very nifty technical solutions to these very knotty problems, and this continues to be a vibrant research area in econometrics.[9]

Sometimes the identification problem is irrelevant because the market does not even exist in a form that would create any such data. Thus, we find economists in the 1950s trying to measure market quantities to fit into a wider computation of national income, for which an accounting of all the goods produced in a country is needed. If much of the material produced is subsistence, or is exchanged in barter, then it is problematic to measure the production of those goods accurately via any kind of limited market statistics. In such cases, the original imagined supply and demand model does not seem to apply, yet economists developed processes of indirectly deriving measurements of exchange quantities even where those markets did not exist. In other words, 'factual curves' were produced even when the market itself was only an imagined and never a real market. This solution is akin to Fogel's use of the linear

---

[9] Wright was also the first to use what has come to be called 'instrumental variables' as a solution, using a variable that acts as an instrument so that the relationship of real interest can be measured accurately. Discussion of the identification issue with this example (3) is drawn from Morgan (1990: chapter 6).

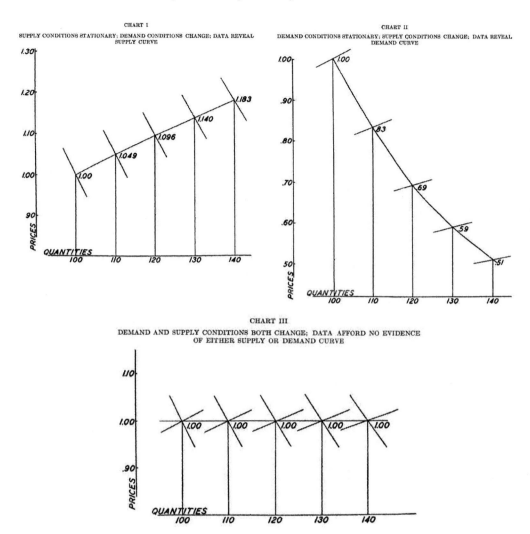

Figure 5. Philip Green Wright's Identification Diagrams.
Source: P.G. Wright (1929), 'Review of Henry Schultz: *Statistical Laws of Demand and Supply*', *Journal of the American Statistical Association*, 24: 207–15. Charts I, II and III, pp. 211–13. Reprinted by permission of the publisher, Taylor & Francis Ltd.

programming model to create facts for his imagined US economy of 1890, with similar responses from the critics, as we see in this reaction from a team asked to create data for the missing market for Nigeria in the 1950s:

> Where goods and services are not marketed it is possible to go as far as asking what they might be worth if they were. To take the further step of inventing functional relationships such as demand and supply curves, or even appearing to invent such relationships, seems to us unwarranted ... Where complex economic transactions do not exist, little purpose is served by making them appear to do so.   (Prest, Stewart & Lardner, 1953)

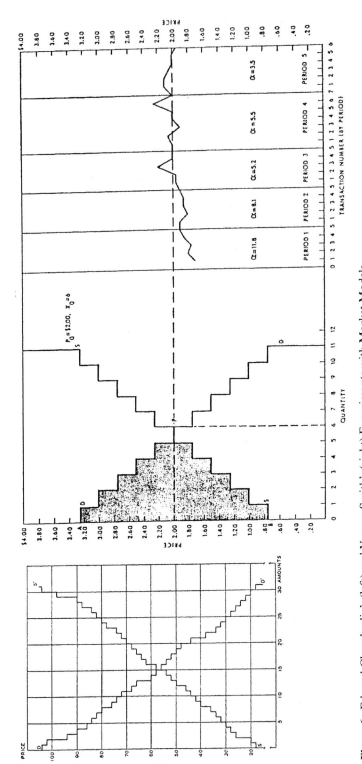

Figure 6. Edward Chamberlin's (left) and Vernon Smith's (right) Experiments with Market Models.
Source: E. Chamberlin (1948), 'An Experimental Imperfect Market', *Journal of Political Economy*, 56: 95–108; Figure 1, p. 97; V. Smith (1962), 'An Experimental Study of Competitive Market Behavior', *Journal of Political Economy*, 70: 111–37, Chart 1, p. 113. Reprinted by permission of the publisher, University of Chicago Press.

(4) Another mode of keying models to factual materials began with the first ever classroom experiments in economics. Edward Chamberlin in 1948 and Vernon Smith in 1962 developed the process of using the imagined supply and demand model to create a model market in the classroom. Chamberlin's stated aim was to 'observe a real model'—notice he did not seek to observe a real market, but to observe the actions of real people in the imagined model market of economics. The tradition he established was to draw out a set of demand and supply schedules with numbers attached and give to each member of the class a card telling them if they were buyers or sellers, and what their 'reservation price' was (the price above or below which they would not trade). There were rules of trading to govern how the model market worked, and in the graphs (Figure 6) we can see recorded examples from both Chamberlin's and Smith's model markets. Factual keys to the objects of the model (the demand and supply prices and quantities of the two curves) had already been created as part of the experimental design and its protocols, while the classroom experiment was undertaken to fashion outcome keys to the intersection points of the curve. Chamberlin's outcomes were not quite as predicted by the model, but Smith soon discovered how the rules of trading in the protocols (such as one period of exchange or more, open-outcry or individual contracting) could be varied to obtain the 'correct' outcomes for the classroom market as predicted by the model. None of these keys—created in the design or outcome of the experiment—were initially related to real world markets. Only later did economists draw on these kinds of results and their findings about trading rules to design real world markets that worked according to their models.

V WHAT IF . . . THE ECONOMY IS AN HYDRAULIC MACHINE

Thinking about models as fictions and the ways in which models involve fictional elements has proved fruitful. It has given insight into the importance of imagination in model making, pointed to the myriad ways in which the fictional and factual intersect in economists' modelling activities, and to the difficulties of translations between factual and fictional elements. But the presence of these factual elements suggests that we might consider another label, and might indeed prefer to consider scientific models as *artefacts* (Knuuttila, 2011). This notion of models as artefacts is not to be understood here as being in opposition to that of models as fictions, but rather to offer a more generous notion. The new label still implies that models embed or require some kind of imagination to make and use. And fictional elements are not ruled out, for the label has the advantage of openness: model inputs are unrestricted, models can contain both factual and fictional things, intuition, analogies, indeed, all sorts of stuff: there is no fixed or single recipe for making a scientific model, and lots of ingredients are possible (see Boumans, 1999). The notion of artefacts accurately refers to the fact that not only are the models that economists use human-made but that they are material objects, even if only pen and paper objects, or written into machine code. That material quality of models is itself an important characteristic, for it this which enables them to function as a technology of enquiry (see Morrison & Morgan, 1999). In Morgan (2012), I argued that this technology of enquiry is manifest in the way models are used as experimentable objects answering what-if questions—both to extend the imaginative reach of the modeller and to offer materials that *might*, with difficulty, be keyed to events in the world. And while understanding models to be artefacts does not solve the classic philosophical problems of representation and inference, it does hold open some of the possibilities that the idea of models of fictions particularly seems to close off, namely about how answering what-if questions with models can be informative about the world.

To show how this artefactual understanding of models is rewarding while at the same time building on the ideas developed while thinking about models as fictions, the final model to be discussed is an hydraulic machine. It was built just after the Second World War to understand the macroeconomic system, and as it is a machine, it is difficult to refer to this model as a fiction, but certainly the notion of artefact fits it perfectly well. J.M. Keynes imagined that the aggregate economy needed to be treated as a system with its own behavioural laws. But Keynes was no modeller, he really wasn't. Rather, his *General Theory* (1936) gave a primarily verbal account of the aggregate economy in a book that many of his contemporaries found opaque. The young economists of his day immediately set out to write down some little mathematical or diagrammatical models in order to understand exactly what Keynes was trying to say, and whether—indeed—he was saying anything new.[10] These arguments continued into the post-war period and provide the context for one of the most unusual models in the history of economics, built in the late 1940s, to model the macroeconomic system as an hydraulic machine.[11]

The machine is constructed from a combination of observations, facts and fictions

[10] For economists, the most famous of these is the ISLM diagram, drawn by Hicks (1937) in an explicit attempt to figure out whether Keynes was saying anything new, and it became the standard model to understand Keynes's economics. Two other models are particularly relevant to the keying discussion. One is J. Tinbergen's (1937) fitting of statistics to a Keynesian model of the Dutch economy in the 1930s in order to see how to get out of the great depression (see Morgan, 1990: chapter 4). The other is P. Samuelson's (1939) simulation model that he used to explore what kind of policies would have what effects in a Keynesian model, and found that almost anything can happen, in other words, providing some very implausible stories (see Morgan, 2012: chapter 6).

[11] The tradition of thinking of money as liquid goes way back in the history of economics and there are designs for, and built, hydraulic machines to be found in the late 19th century, particularly in the work of Irving Fisher (see Morgan, 1997).

all intertwined together. There are keys that translate both the elements built into the model and the outcomes from experiments with the model back to the world. Although the artefact looks like a rather low-budget piece of schoolboy imagination, it functions as a carefully crafted and subtly imaginative account of the economic world.

The machine is normally known as the Phillips Machine, but it is more accurate to call it the Newlyn–Phillips Machine because it was jointly built by Bill Phillips and Walter Newlyn, and I want to write Newlyn back into the history.[12] These two economists can be seen here (Figure 7) with two generations of the machine. The one on the left is the first prototype machine, the Mark 1 machine, with Newlyn leaning over it. Its inauguration was reported by the *Yorkshire Evening Post*, because this machine was commissioned by Leeds University where Newlyn was working, and now stands in the entrance to their Business School building. Phillips on the right is shown with the second generation, Mark 2, machine (which might perhaps be labelled the Phillips–Newlyn machine). It is about 7 ft by 5 ft (slightly bigger than the prototype), and stands in the computation gallery of the London Science Museum (and is possibly its only exhibit from economic science). It has been restored, and a video display shows one of the last times it was used when televised by the BBC for a budget report in the 1990s.

These two inventors, Walter Newlyn and Bill Phillips, both left school with no qualifications. They made their way through the depressed 1930s world, to fight in the Second World War. Newlyn was an expert in communications equipment, was evacuated in the last days from Dunkirk and then served in India. Phillips worked in the air force on aircraft systems. He was taken prisoner of war by the Japanese and there are some wonderful stories about clandestine radio systems, which he managed to keep going, and about the Japanese failing to understand why the lights dimmed every evening (because Phillips had managed to figure out how the soldiers could get themselves hot tea) (see Blyth, 1975; Leeson, 2000). They returned from the war, and as they had both done some evening courses at the University of London before the war, they went to LSE as returning veterans and became friends there.

The traditional story, as I have said, has written Newlyn out and it is very important to bring him back in because of his experience in the 1930s. He started off in the 1930s as a very junior clerk to Darlings, the big Australian grain merchants and he worked his way up to be their chartering clerk on the Baltic exchange. The Baltic exchange then was not just an exchange for grain trading it was also the major exchange for trading freight. If you wanted to carry something around the world in a freighter you would come and make a contract in the Baltic exchange. Newlyn wasn't the trader; he

---

[12] A full version of the short history of the machine that follows draws on Morgan (2012: chapter 5). See also Morgan & Boumans (2004).

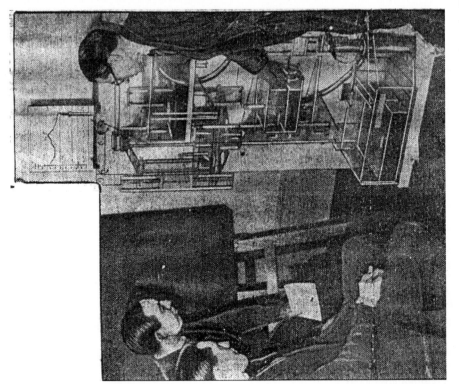

Figure 7. Walter Newlyn with the Prototype Mark I Machine (left) and Bill Phillips with the Mark II Machine (right).
Source: *Yorkshire Evening Post*, Friday, 20 January 1950; and LSE STICERD Archive.

was in some sense more important—he was the person writing the charter contracts, so he really understood how money went round the system because he was right there sending cargos round the world and writing the contracts for the monetary exchanges. Here is an extract from his theory of money, which speaks from his experience of how flows of money don't depend on large stocks:

> Take, for example, the case of a large scale merchanting firm disposing of a bulk cargo of grain purchased abroad. Having received the cheque at 2:45 pm a messenger will have deposited it at the merchant's bank at 2:50. The messenger then proceeds round the corner and at 2:55 deposits a cheque for the same amount drawn on his firm's bank account to one of the London discount houses. Moreover, he probably passes in his walk a messenger of the buying firm who has collected a cheque of similar amount from another discount house and deposited it in the buyer's bank at 2:45 pm.   (Newlyn, 1971: 75)

So all the money had been moved around within 10 minutes.

Bill Phillips had a very different but equally important early experience, for in some sense he grew up inside a hydraulic machine. His childhood was spent on a New Zealand dairy farm in a very rural area, which had no electricity. His parents were both equally important in organising the stream that went through their farm not only for farm use, but to give them electricity, and a flush toilet, inside the house. This is an account from his sister about how they lived at the mercy and control of this hydraulic system:

> Of course, it was wasteful to run a generator when not required. Consequently, Dad built a neat winch into the ceiling in their bedroom and when they decided it was 'lights out' time, the sound of the winch being wound alerted us to the imminent 'blackout' . . . As the winch wound in the cable, the trap-door was raised the water was then diverted to the side of the water-wheel to rejoin the stream . . . the wheel stopped turning, generation stopped and 'LIGHTS-OUT'.   (Carol Ibbotsen-Somervell: 5)[13]

In other words, he understood from his early life, how water flows can make a domestic economy work.

These two individuals who grew up with very different experiences came together, made friends at the LSE, and spent social time together, going on walks, going to the theatre and meeting over the refectory table. They invented the machine together in three important steps. First, Phillips transformed a standard economics diagram of supply and demand into a diagram of domestic plumbing. Second, Newlyn developed the blueprint for this hydraulic machine. Third, they built the prototype of the Newlyn–Phillips machine. All this happened over a short time in 1949, when they spliced their own experiences of hydraulics and of money flows in an economic system into this analogical machine.

---

[13] From a memoir in the STICERD archive, LSE.

In the first step, Phillips wrote an undergraduate essay where he took that standard supply and demand model and queried what was on the horizontal axis: is it quantities of something at a point in time, or is it flow per unit of time? As he pointed out, stocks and flows could not be represented on this same diagram, and the what-if experiments could not be conducted, unless stocks were constant. So he took advantage of a diagram from a recent textbook by Kenneth Boulding (1948), who had drawn a domestic plumbing example—the cistern from a lavatory—to show how one might get stocks and flows working together. Phillips developed Boulding's plumbing diagram to design his own version (both shown, Figure 8). The second half of his paper is an attempt to do the same for a macroeconomic system, but it is very clear from his text that he did not understand the macroeconomics of his time.

Phillips showed this essay to his friend Newlyn in early 1949,[14] who thought this idea of making a hydraulic account of the macroeconomy was just the way to go—in fact he had already, in one of his own undergraduate essays, played around with an idea of a hydraulic process for a monetary system. Newlyn's essay showed he really understood the professional literature on macroeconomics even as an undergraduate, and he took Phillips's ideas of plumbing and his own knowledge of macroeconomics to develop them into a blueprint (Figure 9) for a macroeconomy machine. (The copy is poor as it is on a large sheet and had been cut in half in order to be stored.) The blueprint was taken to Leeds, where Newlyn was already a lecturer, to persuade the head of the department to fund the prototype machine shown in the figure. In the summer of 1949, they constructed the machine together—Newlyn explaining the requirements of the macroeconomic system to Phillips the junior economist, and Phillips the senior engineer being helped by Newlyn the junior one.[15]

A drawing of the machine (Figure 10) made to market the Mark II machine around the world in the early 1950s, shows the machine more clearly than photographs do. The basic design is of a circular flow, the channel up the left-hand side is the income flow going up; when it starts coming down as expenditure, it divides itself. The first thing that comes off on the left is taxes, consumption goes down the centre part, investment comes off on the right-hand side and then exports and imports and the external sector are shown underneath that. There are a number of tanks, which hold different stocks of money. So the whole economy is pictured, all the bits of the Keynesian system in terms of aggregate national income, aggregate expenditure, aggregate consumption, imports and exports, savings, taxes and so forth. Each of these can be keyed back to the categories of the national income accounts, which were

---

[14] Newlyn kept the essay and it is now owned by his son-in-law, the economist Martin Slater.
[15] They published separate articles about the machine, expressing their own interests and knowledge (see Newlyn, 1950; Phillips, 1950).

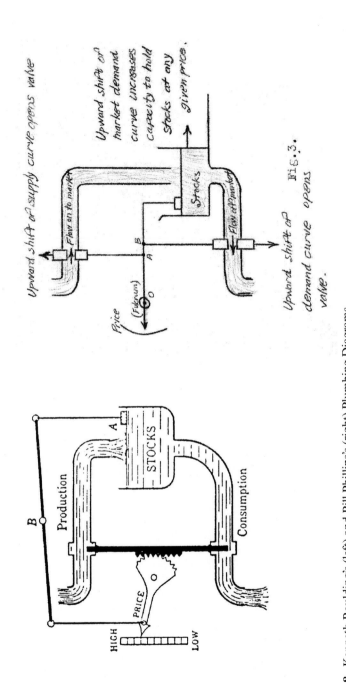

Figure 8. Kenneth Boulding's (left) and Bill Phillips's (right) Plumbing Diagrams.
Source: K. Boulding: *Economic Analysis* (1948), Figure 9, p. 117, reproduced by courtesy of the Bentley Historical Library, University of Michigan;
A.W.H. Phillips's Undergraduate Essay, Figure 3, reproduced by courtesy of Martin Slater.

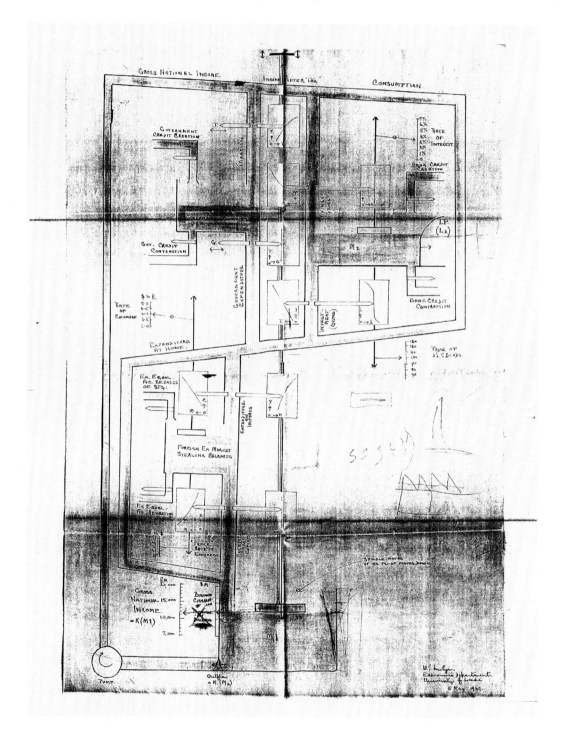

Figure 9. Walter Newlyn's Blueprint for the Machine.
Source: STICERD Phillips Machine Archive, reproduced by courtesy of Lucy Newlyn.

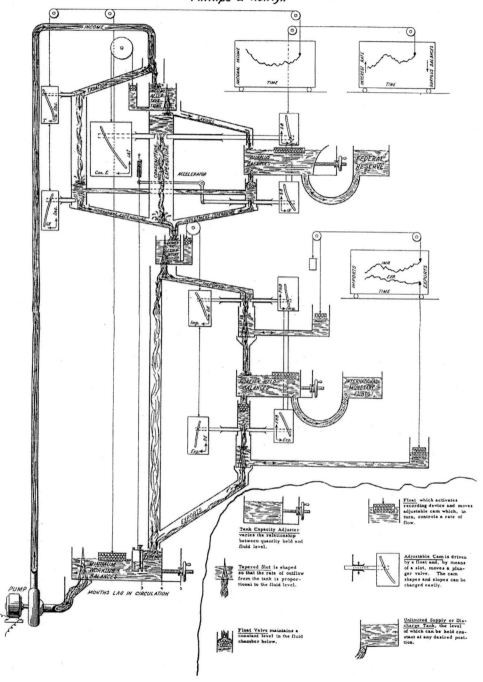

Figure 10. Marketing Drawing of the Hydraulic Machine.
Source: James Meade Archive, LSE.

established in the late 1940s largely using Keynes's aggregate economy concepts as definitions.

Despite its looks, the machine has wonderful resources for game playing which involve both the hydraulic format and the economic content of the machine. For example, the economist can set the levels of money in the tanks; change the 'function slides' that describe the aggregate behavioural relations in the system and thereby control the valves; unhook or hook-up parts of the machine; and even link two machines so that you can have an international economy (e.g. America and Britain linked up). All sorts of policy interventions can be enacted in the world of the model. It also acts as a computer (which is why it is in the Science Museum), for each time an experiment is done, the outcomes are charted in graphs on the top right corner, which show what happens to national income (and the interest rate: the price of borrowing money) over time. When economists played games with the machine, conducting what-if experiments with it, they found they could tell quite a lot of plausible stories about the world of the 1950s from the world of the machine. There were also, of course, some implausible stories from experiments when the red water (which represents the money flows) went all over the floor. The point is that the 'what-if' experiments have their own keying system, because not just the parts, but also all the relationships between parts, are embedded in the machine.

The Newlyn–Phillips (and its successor, the Phillips–Newlyn) machine is a very subtle model and its plausibility depends a lot on that subtlety—not just on the parts and their relationships, for those parts and relations are not passive when the machine is set in motion. Stocks and flows of money, income, expenditure etc., really work together, as indeed they do in real life—which is what Phillips was worried about. The time delays in the system, or the lack of them, was what Newlyn was really concerned about and understood from his chartering days: this was manifest in the time-lag in the machine because it takes time for a flow of 'money' (red water) to work its way round the system in any given experiment, and that time can be calibrated in certain respects. It also has a continuous pattern of circulation to give a real dynamics rather than the set of comparative static points taken as standard for working with models at the time (a mode of model work we saw in Marshall's diagrammatic reasoning). Finally, the interactions in the system worked in a real way as opposed to being imagined as working.

Of course, the Newlyn–Phillips model is in such a different medium that one can still think this is a pretty strange model, a wonderful world of make-believe science fiction as much as a serious piece of economic science. Its quirkiness generated a tradition of cartoons, beginning with one that Rowland Emett did in *Punch* for the government's budget day in 1953 and going on through the years up to the cover of *The Economist* in 2008 during the financial crisis. Emett depicted the machine as a

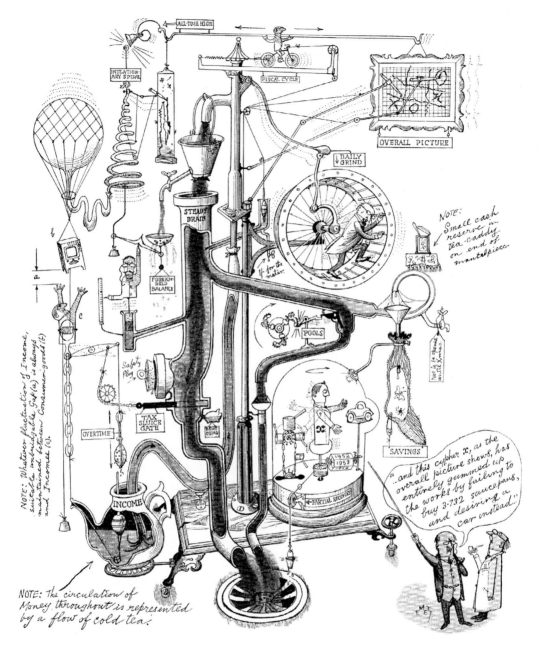

MACHINE DESIGNED TO SHOW THE WORKING OF THE ECONOMIC SYSTEM

Figure 11. Rowland Emett's Cartoon of the Hydraulic Machine.
Source: *Punch*, 15 April 1953, p. 457. © Punch Limited, reproduced by permission.

Heath-Robinson machine run on cold tea (Figure 11). (The small print and details are wonderful.) In the 1970s and 1980s economists got embarrassed by this machine and put it away in cupboards; more recently a number have been restored and it has become an artefact to be proud of, an icon of the modelling age in economics.

VI CONCLUSION

What is the importance and value of what-if questions? These examples have shown a range of different ways in which versions of that question are asked by economists in their work with models. We have also seen that economists' methods of answering such questions provide them not just with a way to understand the worlds they create in their models, but give them a variety of indirect ways of interrogating what kind of world we live in. We have also seen that these interrogations, and so the process of gaining understanding of the real world, depend on a lot of crossings over between facts and fictions, just as games of fictions do. The philosophers' of science notion of models as fictions proved a good starting point, but analysing the practical work of modelling pointed towards the multiple interactions between facts and fictions that offer scientists the chances of learning about the world from their models. These cross-overs may hold clues to why scientists often speak of 'explaining' the world with their models.

Focusing on 'keys' as the critical link that facilitates that back and forth between model world and real world was also helpful. This paper paid attention to the process of keying from the world to the model in both Fogel's case and in the Newlyn–Phillips machine case. These showed the sources for those keys to be in many respects factual: statistical data materials for Fogel and experiential knowledge for Newlyn and Phillips. This offers a contrast to the usual discussion of the building blocks of economic model building in which economists' 'as if' assumptions about behaviour have been justly criticised as unrealistic. Focusing more consistently on the usage of models in all three cases involved examining the keying processes prompted by what-if questions and the ways model stories were related back to the world. It is in the process of answering these questions (as much as in the 'as if' assumptions of model building), that the plausibility of models are questioned, their fictional/factual status assessed, and their contributions to understanding the world brought into focus. And if the plausibility of any particular model rests much more firmly on the kind of claims that come with what-if questions, then it is not whether the exact status of the model is fictional or factual that matters, rather it is the stories that are told with the model in answering those questions. Working backward from these analyses, it appears crucial for economists that models have this flexible status, sometimes as fictions, sometimes as factual, and sometimes as mixtures. This flexibility enables economists to use them for model experiments to explore their theories, and so to think about what would happen if the world was like their models, but also to think about what might be learnt about the real world when facts and statistics can be keyed into their models.

Economic models are human-made, not natural objects like the model organisms of biology (such as the fruit fly), which is the primary reason why the terminology of models as artefacts offers both a broader umbrella, and a more relevant, term. It also fits with the idea that—for the scientists—the primary function of models is to work as a technology of scientific enquiry, a function which is entirely consistent with this artefactual status and is less obviously a function of fictions. Nevertheless, fictional qualities are involved, for imagination is critical in this cognitive use of models, both in creating and using them, just as in science fiction. At this point, I return to my question about the difficulty of drawing distinctions between science fiction and economists' imaginative accounts of the world using scientific models. In the science fiction galaxy of the *Hitchhiker's Guide*, the planet Magrathea had built up an industry of making custom-made planets for rich men in the galaxy. When it had gathered all the wealth to itself, leaving the rest of the galaxy poor, miserable, and unfairly depressed, it had put itself into hibernation, awaiting a return to bursting economic activity and wealth accumulation again, sometime in the future. The ability to forget the economic disasters of the past was a feature of that world of science fiction, just as of our own world. For later explorers, Ford and his friends, the planet and its history existed only as legend, only as fiction. As the entry in the *Guide* tells them: 'In these enlightened days of course, no one believes a word of it. . . . Magrathea is a myth, a fairy story, it's what parents tell their kids about at night if they want them to grow up to become economists' (87–8). Whereas Douglas Adams's science fiction seems to assume that the 'dismal science' (as economics is often labelled) will naturally tell dismal stories, the inference that I draw from the comparisons of this paper is that what economists excel at is telling stories about the imagined worlds in their models, accounts that sometimes capture salient experiences of real life even when fictional elements are involved.

Acknowledgements: The Keynes lecture had one dummy run (to the science studies community at University of Pennsylvania, September 2013), and two further outings (to the economics faculty of University of Buenos Aires; and to a group working on models at the Courtauld Institute of Art). I thank those who kindly questioned and commented at all three events (and at an earlier discussion of 'Fictions and its Use' at the ZiF, University of Bielefeld in July 2013). In particular my thanks go to Sidney Winter, Roman Frigg and Tarja Knuuttila for more extended discussions, and to Janet Carsten (editor of this journal) and an anonymous referee for very helpful comments.

I also thank Marcel Boumans for permission to use materials on the hydraulic machine and to Walter Newlyn's family for supplying information and materials. The lecture drew on research undertaken from the 'How Well Do Facts Travel?' project (funded by the Leverhulme Trust) and from my work on models originally funded by a British Academy Research Readership.

REFERENCES

Adams, Douglas (1986/92), *The Hitchhiker's Guide to the Galaxy* (2nd edn, London, Pan Books).

Blyth, C.A. (1975), 'A.W.H. Phillips, M.B.E.: 1914–1975', *Economic Record*, 51: 303–7. http://dx.doi.org/10.1111/j.1475-4932.1975.tb00255.x

Bokulich, A. (2012), 'Distinguishing Explanatory from Nonexplanatory Fictions', *Philosophy of Science*, 79: 725–37. http://dx.doi.org/10.1086/667991

Boulding, K.J. (1948), *Economic Analysis* (New York, Harper).

Boumans, M.J. (1999), 'Built-In Justification', in Morgan & Morrison, *Models as Mediators*, (Cambridge, Cambridge University Press), 66–96. http://dx.doi.org/10.1017/CBO9780511660108.005

Chamberlin, E.H. (1948), 'An Experimental Imperfect Market', *Journal of Political Economy*, 56: 95–108. http://dx.doi.org/10.1086/256654

Clapham, J.H. (1922), 'Of Empty Economic Boxes', *Economic Journal*, 32: 305–14. http://dx.doi.org/10.2307/2222943

Defoe, D. (2003 [1719]), *Robinson Crusoe* (London: Penguin).

Edgeworth, F.Y. (1881), *Mathematical Psychics* (London, Kegan Paul).

Erickson, C. (1966), 'Review of *Railroads and American Economic Growth* by Robert William Fogel', *Economica*, ns 33: 106–9.

Fishlow, A (1965), *American Railroads and the Transformation of the Ante-Bellum Economy* (Cambridge, MA, Harvard University Press).

Fogel, R.W. (1964), *Railroads and American Economic Growth: Essays in Econometric History* (Baltimore, Johns Hopkins University Press).

Friedman, M. (1953), 'The Methodology of Positive Economics', in *Essays in Positive Economics* (Chicago, University of Chicago Press), 3–46.

Frigg, R. (2010), 'Models and Fiction', *Synthese*, 172: 251–68. http://dx.doi.org/10.1007/s11229-009-9505-0

Frigg, R. & Hunter, M.C. (eds) (2010), *Beyond Mimesis and Convention: Representation in Art and Science* (Dordrecht, Springer).

Goffman, E. (1986 [1974]), *Frame Analysis* (Northeastern University Press).

Hawthorn, G. (1991), *Plausible Worlds* (Cambridge, Cambridge University Press). http://dx.doi.org/10.1017/CBO9780511621222

Hausman, D. (1994), 'Paul Samuelson as Dr. Frankenstein: When idealizations escape and run amuck,' in B. Hamminga & N. de Marchi (eds), *Idealization in Economics.* (Amsterdam, Rodopi), 229–43.

Hicks, J.R. (1937), 'Mr Keynes and the "Classics": A suggested interpretation', *Econometrica*, 5: 147–59. http://dx.doi.org/10.2307/1907242

Humphrey, T.M. (1992), 'Marshallian Cross Diagrams and Their Uses before Alfred Marshall: The origins of supply and demand geometry', *Economic Review*, 78: 3–23.

Jenks, L. (1944), 'Railroads as an Economic Force in American Development', *Journal of Economic History*, 4: 1–20.

Keynes, J.M. (1936), *The General Theory of Employment, Interest and Money* (London, Macmillan).

Kirkland, E.C. (1967), '*Review* of *Railroads and American Economic Growth: Essays in Econometric History* by Robert William Fogel', *American Historical Review*, 72: 1493–5. http://dx.doi.org/10.2307/1847978

Klein, J.L. (2001), 'Reflections from the Age of Measurement', in J.L. Klein & M.S. Morgan (eds), *The Age of Economic Measurement, History of Political Economy, Annual Supplement to Vol 33* (Durham, Duke University Press), 111–36.

Knuuttila, T. (2011), 'Modelling and Representing: An artefactual approach to model-based representation', *Studies in History and Philosophy of Science*, 42: 262–71. http://dx.doi.org/10.1016/j.shpsa.2010.11.034

Leeson, R. (2000), 'A.W.H. Phillips: An extraordinary life', in R. Leeson (ed), *A.W.H. Phillips: Collected Works in Contemporary Perspective* (Cambridge, Cambridge University Press), 3–17. http://dx.doi.org/10.1017/CBO9780511521980.003

Lenoir, M. (1913), *Etudes sur la Formation et le Mouvement des Prix* (Paris, M. Giard et E. Brière).

McAfee, R. Preston (1983), 'American Economic Growth and the Voyage of Columbus', *American Economic Review*, 73: 735–40.

Marshall, A. (1930 [1890]), *Principles of Economics* (8th edn, London, Macmillan).

Morgan, M.S. (1990), *The History of Econometric Ideas* (Cambridge, Cambridge University Press). http://dx.doi.org/10.1017/CBO9780511522109

Morgan, M.S. (1997), 'The Technology of Analogical Models: Irving Fisher's monetary worlds', *Philosophy of Science*, 64: S304–S314. http://dx.doi.org/10.1086/392609

Morgan, M.S. (2012), *The World in the Model: How Economists Work and Think* (Cambridge, Cambridge University Press). http://dx.doi.org/10.1017/CBO9781139026185

Morgan, M.S. & Boumans, M.J. (2004), 'Secrets Hidden by Two-Dimensionality: The economy as an hydraulic machine' in S. De Chadarevian & N. Hopwood (eds), *Models: The Third Dimension of Science* (Stanford, Stanford University Press), 369–401.

Morgan, M.S. & Morrison, M. (eds) (1999), *Models as Mediators: Perspectives on Natural and Social Science* (Cambridge, Cambridge University Press). http://dx.doi.org/10.1017/CBO9780511660108

Morrison, M. & Morgan, M.S. (1999), 'Models as Mediating Instruments' in Morgan & Morrison, *Models as Mediators*, 10–37.

Newlyn, W.T. (1950), 'The Phillips/Newlyn Hydraulic Model', *Yorkshire Bulletin of Economic and Social Research*, 2: 111–27. http://dx.doi.org/10.1111/j.1467-8586.1950.tb00370.x

Newlyn, W.T. (1971), *Theory of Money* (2nd edn, Oxford, Clarendon Press).

Phillips, A.W. (Bill) (1950), 'Mechanical Models in Economic Dynamics', *Economica*, 17: 282–305. http://dx.doi.org/10.2307/2549721

Pigou, A.C. (1922), 'Empty Economic Boxes: A reply', *Economic Journal*, 32: 458–65. http://dx.doi.org/10.2307/2223427

Piketty, T. (2013), *Capital in the Twenty-First Century* (Cambridge, MA, Belknap Press).

Prest, A., Stewart, I.G. [& Lardner, G.] (1953), *The National Income of Nigeria, 1950–51*, Colonial Office: Colonial Research Study, no. 11 (London, HMSO).

Redlich, F. (1965), '"New" and Traditional Approaches to Economic History and Their Interdependence', *Journal of Economic History*, 25: 480–95.

Rubin, J. (1967), '*Review* of *Railroads and American Economic Growth: Essays in Econometric History* by Robert William Fogel', *Technology and Culture*, 8: 228–34. http://dx.doi.org/10.2307/3101979

Samuelson, P.A. (1939), 'Interactions Between the Multiplier Analysis and the Principle of Acceleration', *Review of Economics and Statistics*, 21: 75–8. http://dx.doi.org/10.2307/1927758

Smith, V.L. (1962), 'An Experimental Study of Competitive Market Behaviour' *Journal of Political Economy*, 60: 111–37. http://dx.doi.org/10.1086/258609

Suárez, M. (ed) (2009), *Fictions in Science: Philosophical Essays in Modeling and Idealization* (London, Routledge).

Suárez, M. (2010), 'Fictions, Inference, and Realism', in J. Woods (ed.), *Fictions and Models* (Munich, Philosophia Verlag), 225–45.

Tinbergen, J. (1937), *An Econometric Approach to Business Cycle Problems* (Paris, Hermann & Cie).

Toon, A. (2010), 'The Ontology of Theoretical Modelling: Models as make-believe', *Synthese*, 172: 301–15. http://dx.doi.org/10.1007/s11229-009-9508-x

Toon, A. (2012), *Models as Make-Believe: Imagination, Fiction and Scientific Representation* (Basingstoke, Palgrave-Macmillan).

Walton, K. (1990), *Mimesis as Make-Believe* (Cambridge, MA, Harvard University Press).

Walton, K. (1993), 'Metaphor and Prop Oriented Make-Believe', *European Journal of Philosophy*, 1: 39–56. http://dx.doi.org/10.1111/j.1468-0378.1993.tb00023.x

Williamson, G.G. (1965), 'Review of *Railroads and American Economic Growth: Essays in Economic* [*sic*] *History* by Robert William Fogel', *Economic Development and Cultural Change*, 14: 109–13. http://dx.doi.org/10.1086/450147

Woods, J. (2010), *Fictions and Models: New Essays* (Munich, Philosophia Verlag).

Wright, P.G. (1929), 'Review of *Statistical Laws of Demand and Supply* by Henry Schultz', *Journal of the American Statistical Association*, 24: 207–15. http://dx.doi.org/10.2307/2276697

The author: Mary S. Morgan is Professor of History and Philosophy of Economics at the London School of Economics and University of Amsterdam, and Distinguished Visiting Fellow at University of Pennsylvania. She is a Fellow of the British Academy and also an Overseas Fellow of the Royal Dutch Academy of Arts and Sciences.

M.Morgan@lse.ac.uk

This article was first published in 2014 in *Journal of the British Academy* (ISSN 2052–7217).

To cite the article: Mary S. Morgan (2014), 'What if? Models, fact and fiction in economics ', *Journal of the British Academy*, 2: 231–268. DOI 10.5871/jba/002.231

Journal of the British Academy, **2**, 269–303. DOI 10.5871/jba/002.269
Posted 19 December 2014. © The British Academy 2014

Central banks:
Powerful, political and unaccountable?

Keynes Lecture in Economics[1]
read 18 September 2014

WILLEM H. BUITER
Fellow of the Academy

Abstract: The economic and political importance of central banks has grown markedly in advanced economies since the start of the Great Financial Crisis in 2007. In this article I argue that the preservation of the central bank's legitimacy and independence requires that a clear line be drawn between the central bank's provision of liquidity and the Treasury's solvency support for systemically important financial institutions. Central banks should not be materially involved in regulation and supervision of the financial sector. All activities of the central bank that expose it to material credit risk should be guaranteed by the Treasury. In addition, central banks must increase their accountability by increasing the transparency of their lender-of-last-resort and market-maker-of-last resort activities. Central banks ought not to engage in quasi-fiscal activities. Finally, central banks should stick to their knitting and central bankers should not become participants in public debates and deeply political arguments about matters beyond their mandate and competence, including fiscal policy and structural reform.

Keywords: Quasi-fiscal, independence, legitimacy, accountability, regulation, supervision.
JEL Classification: E02, E42, E52, E58, E61, E62, E63, G18, G28, H63

1. INTRODUCTION

The economic and political importance of central banks has grown markedly in advanced economies since the start of the Great Financial Crisis (GFC) in 2007. An

[1] This is the background paper for the British Academy's Keynes lecture I gave on 18 September 2014. I would like to thank Anne Sibert for extensive and stimulating discussions on the subject matter of the lecture. Ebrahim Rahbari made very useful comments on an earlier version. The views and opinions expressed are mine alone. They cannot be taken to represent the views and opinions of Citigroup, or of any other organisation I am affiliated with.

unwillingness or inability of governments to use countercyclical fiscal policy has made monetary policy the only stabilisation tool in town. However, much of the enhanced significance of central banks is due to their lender-of-last-resort and market-maker-of-last-resort roles, providing liquidity to financially distressed and illiquid financial institutions and sovereigns. Supervisory and regulatory functions—often deeply political—have been heaped on central banks. Central bankers also increasingly throw their weight around in the public discussion and even the design of fiscal policy and structural reforms—areas which are way beyond their mandates and competence. In this lecture I argue that the preservation of the central bank's legitimacy requires that a clear line be drawn between the central bank's provision of liquidity and the Treasury's solvency support for systemically important financial institutions. All activities of the central bank that expose it to material credit risk should be guaranteed by the Treasury. In addition, central banks must become more accountable by increasing the transparency of their lender-of-last-resort and market-maker-of-last-resort activities. Central banks ought not to engage in quasi-fiscal activities. Finally, central banks should stick to their knitting.

Central banks' fiscal and quasi-fiscal roles have grown dramatically during the GFC as their balance sheets have swollen and their seigniorage revenues have increased. The reversal of the pre-GFC tendency to take financial regulatory and supervisory tasks away from central banks has further enhanced the responsibilities and powers of central banks, most dramatically in the United Kingdom, but also in the euro area and the USA. The delegation to central banks of an expanding list of quintessentially political interventions and responsibilities and the expansion of their arsenals of policy instruments with important redistributive impacts has not been matched by an increase in central bank accountability, either formal or substantive. In a representative democracy this matters because without accountability there can be no legitimacy and without legitimacy institutions eventually fail. Even those who believe that the 'output' legitimacy conferred by good performance is more important than 'input' or 'process' legitimacy should worry that the accumulation of heterogeneous responsibilities by central banks has proceeded to the point that it outstrips the capacity of a single institution to discharge them effectively.

It appears that central banks did not actively seek their additional roles and responsibilities; rather they were thrust upon them. However, a growing number of central bank officials are as keen to defend the independence of their institution against all comers, including governments and parliaments, as they are uninhibited in lecturing the political classes and the public at large on fiscal policy and structural reform. Some central bank interventions have even been made conditional on the implementation of specific fiscal policies and structural reforms. Central banks should stick to monetary policy and desist from activities, including participating in public discourse, outside their mandates.

The increased power and, at times, arrogance of unelected and unaccountable technocrats is largely due to established political institutions and processes failing to handle the GFC and its aftermath effectively. Elected officials played a prominent role in creating the political, legislative, regulatory and supervisory failures that allowed the GFC to happen. Once the GFC had erupted, they also failed to formulate an effective response from the legitimate institutions. Few elected politicians have been willing to take responsibility for the creation and accountable oversight of institutions, and for the promulgation and enforcement of laws and rules to prevent/reduce the likelihood and severity of future financial crises or mitigate their effects.

A significant reduction in the scope and scale of central bank responsibilities is necessary to prevent a crisis of legitimacy that could leave the advanced economies even less prepared for the next financial crisis than they were for this one. Ideally, the central bank should stick to monetary policy, defined here as *narrow monetary policy*, that is choosing (a rule for) the policy interest rate, the size of the monetary base or the value of an exchange rate and managing the size and composition of its balance sheet in the absence of lender-of-last-resort- and market-maker-of-last-resort interventions. The only further role of the central bank would be its *legitimate financial stability role* as lender of last resort and market maker of last resort in providing funding and market liquidity to systemically important institutions and markets. It might even make sense, as suggested by Buiter (2008e) and Sibert (2012), to split the narrow monetary policy role from the legitimate financial stability role, by entrusting the narrow monetary policy role to a body (a monetary policy committee (MPC), say) that is independent of and located outside the central bank. One or more senior executives of the central bank—the Governor comes to mind—could make up a minority of the members of the MPC, but its Chair should come from outside the central bank.

The central bank should take the least possible amount of credit risk. Conducting effective lender-of-last-resort or market-maker-of last-resort operations may entail taking on material credit risk through outright purchases of risky securities or by lending to counterparties that are at risk of insolvency against collateral issued by entities that are also at risk of insolvency. But, when this is the case, the central bank should only take on unavoidable credit risk with a full sovereign guarantee, as is the case with the Bank of England's Special Liquidity Scheme (now closed) and Asset Purchase Facility.[2] The Fed's Term Asset-Backed Securities Loan Facility was an example of how a central bank ought not to take on credit risk, as only 10 per cent of the $200 bn facility benefited from a US Treasury guarantee.

---

[2] In the context of the ECB, whose fiscal counterparty in the euro area consists of 18 (from 2015 of 19) national treasuries, any credit risk taken on by the ECB/Eurosystem should be jointly and severally guaranteed by all euro area national sovereigns.

There is no obvious reason why the central bank should manage wholesale payment, clearing and settlement systems. Any institution with a credit line from the central bank, guaranteed by the Treasury, could do this equally effectively. Institutions other than the central bank should supervise and regulate financial institutions and markets, provide deposit insurance and resolve systemically important financial institutions. The central bank should not manage or supervise macro-prudential instruments or arrangements. As with other fiscal matters, the inevitable fiscal roles of any central bank in managing its assets and liabilities and having a monopoly over the issuance of domestic currency legal tender must be subject to careful legislative oversight.

Central bankers should not participate in or attempt to influence fiscal policy or structural reforms, let alone attempt to oust elected politicians. There is a fine line between trying to influence fiscal policy and structural reforms and making sure that those legitimately in charge of these policies and reforms understand how the central bank, in pursuit of its mandate, would react to different fiscal policies or structural reforms. In recent years it is apparent that central banks, perhaps because they believed it was necessary to prevent a financial and economic calamity, have overstepped this line. The unwillingness or inability of other political and economic institutions to assume responsibility and to act effectively in the face of potential or actual financial disaster must be corrected if central banks are to revert to being solely monetary policy makers.

There is a case for elected (or otherwise politically legitimate) officials to specify a monetary policy goal, such as an inflation target, and then allowing central banks independence in using their narrow monetary policy instruments to attain this goal. However, in performing other roles—including their legitimate financial stability role—central banks must be subject to material substantive accountability. It can be problematic, however, to allow the same officials independence in one area while requiring them to be accountable in others. Unfortunately, if central banks continue to act independently in areas where they should not, they may end up losing their independence in the area where it may be desirable for them to have it: making monetary policy, narrowly defined.

2. THE GROWING SCOPE AND SCALE OF CENTRAL BANK ACTIVITIES, POWERS AND RESPONSIBILITIES

The range of activities undertaken by central banks has expanded since the GFC. This section examines the stabilisation policy, lender-of-last-resort and market-maker-of-last-resort activities, supervisory and regulatory powers, fiscal and quasi-fiscal roles, and the increasingly invasive and pervasive interventions in areas of policy making that are well beyond the expertise, comparative advantage and mandate of the central bank.

2.1 Stabilisation policy

In many advanced economies, monetary policy has become the only available macro-economic stabilisation instrument. Fiscal policy is not used for a number of reasons. German official anti-Keynesianism prevents the largest euro area member state (and the one with the largest amount of fiscal space) from employing fiscal policy to stimulate demand. Political gridlock in the United States makes discretionary fiscal stabilisation policy impossible, although it does not so far interfere materially with the operation of the automatic fiscal stabilisers. Fiscal stimulus would probably be most effective in the EA periphery (Ireland, Spain, Portugal, Italy, Greece and Cyprus), where the output gaps are widest, if it could be funded at rates no more than 1.5 to 1.0 per cent above German sovereign yields. Unfortunately, these countries either have only limited market access or would be likely to encounter market resistance if a debt-funded discretionary fiscal stimulus were to wake euro area sovereign debt markets from the stupor they fell into on 26 July 2012, when Mario Draghi uttered the magical words: 'Within our mandate, the ECB is ready to do whatever it takes to preserve the euro. And believe me, it will be enough.' (Draghi (2012))[3]. Moreover, some of these unfortunate countries also face external political constraints imposed by supranational entities such as the European Commission (with the German official position lurking behind them) and the Troika (the European Commission, the European Central Bank (ECB) and the International Monetary Fund (IMF)).

Given a mandate that has been chosen by a process that is seen as legitimate, narrow monetary policy is sufficiently apolitical to be entrusted to expert unelected technocrats. In practice such operational independence includes (limited) goal independence when the objective or objectives of monetary policy are qualitative rather than quantitative/numerical. This is the case for the ECB, the Bank of Japan, and the Fed. The former two central banks are to attain price stability and the Fed is to pursue stable prices, maximum employment and moderate long-term interest rates. Given their qualitative mandates, these three (limited) goal-independent central banks then choose their own numerical targets. In contrast, the goal-dependent Bank of England is to pursue price stability and the Chancellor of the Exchequer assigns it a specific numerical inflation target for a specific price index.

Although some governments provide numerical inflation targets, no government makes any attempt to lay down verifiable quantitative targets for real economic

---

[3] The specific policy, Outright Monetary Transactions, that backs up this statement is developed in ECB (2012a, 2012b).

objectives such as the unemployment rate, the output gap or economic growth. The central banks too tend to avoid measurable, verifiable targets for the unemployment rate or for GDP growth. There was a short-lived attempt at 'forward guidance' through quantitative thresholds/knock-outs or triggers for the unemployment rate by the Fed and the Bank of England. These were abandoned in a hurry, when the real-economy forward guidance thresholds were crossed but the conditions for raising the official policy rate were nevertheless deemed not to be satisfied by the FOMC[4] and the MPC (see Buiter (2013a)). Forward guidance was replaced with 'fuzzy guidance' expressed in terms of unobservable and non-measurable concepts such as 'economic slack'.[5] Thus, when it comes to real objectives, central banks are given de facto quantitative goal independence by default.

During the GFC and the mostly sub-par subsequent recovery, the FOMC has followed a sensible monetary policy (other than its forward misguidance), although it may be slow in raising its target Federal Funds rate, both in regard to its employment and inflation mandates and in regard to its responsibility for financial stability. UK monetary policy too has been adequate (again, give or take some forward misguidance), although there was a rather surprising tolerance towards the persistent and predictable overshooting of its 2 per cent inflation target from December 2009 till November 2013. Prior to the appointment of Governor Haruhiko Kuroda in March 2013 the Bank of Japan's (BoJ) monetary policy was far too restrictive. After a good start on its escape from deflation, the BoJ underestimated the downward effect of the April 2014 sales tax on demand and was behind the curve once more until the material enhancement of the scale and scope of its Quantitative and Qualitative easing on Friday, 31 October 2014. The ECB may have saved the euro in July 2012 when Mario Draghi said 'whatever it takes', but its monetary policies have been persistently too restrictive since the crisis began. This may in part be due to its 'consensus' model of decision making, where policy is changed only if a majority of the Governing Council wants a policy change *and* the dissenting minority is not too unhappy with it—especially if the dissenting minority includes the German members of the Governing Council. Another contributing factor is Article 123 TFEU[6] which, in the interpretation common in Germany and the rest of the Teutonic fringe, means that the ECB/Eurosystem cannot directly purchase euro area sovereign debt and is also constrained

---

[4] The Federal Open Market Committee of the Federal Reserve (FOMC) is responsible for open market operations. The FOMC consists of twelve members—the seven members of the Board of Governors of the Federal Reserve System; the president of the Federal Reserve Bank of New York; and four of the remaining eleven Reserve Bank presidents, who serve one-year terms on a rotating basis.

[5] See Bank of England, Forward Guidance, 7 Aug. 2007,
http://www.bankofengland.co.uk/monetarypolicy/Pages/forwardguidance.aspx

[6] Treaty on the Functioning of the European Union, which is one of two core functional treaties of the European Union. The other is the *Treaty on European Union*.

in its ability (or at least inhibited as regards its willingness) to buy euro area sovereign debt in the secondary markets.

As their official policy rates got stuck near to or at the zero lower bound, the communication strategies of the Fed, the ECB and the Bank of England have been ineffective and confusing. Forward guidance about changes in the size and composition of the balance sheet, about the timing of the first official policy rate increase, about, in the case of the Fed and the Bank of England, the observable thresholds whose crossing would be necessary and perhaps sufficient to trigger the first rate increase, about the speed of subsequent increases or about the central bank's view of the likely level of the neutral policy rate has been incoherent, contradictory and at times inconsistent. In part this is the unavoidable by-product of 'communication by committee' (see Buiter (2013a) and Buiter *et al.* (2014b)).

2.2 Financial stability

2.2a The 'twin delusions'

The 'twin delusions' of modern central banking are, first, that monetary policy is best made by an operationally independent central bank and, second, that the objective of monetary policy is either price stability or price stability along with some real economic activity target such as unemployment. The pursuit of price stability is generally operationalised as targeting a low rate of inflation for some price index for goods and services over the medium term—two or three years, typically. A minority favours targeting a path for the price *level* that grows at a moderate rate, or targeting the growth rate of or a path for nominal GDP. The price index whose stability is sought is generally some broad index of consumer prices, such as the consumer price index (CPI) and harmonised index of consumer prices (HICP) or the personal consumption expenditure deflator. Two per cent annual inflation became the norm for many advanced economy central banks. Some central banks adopted a form of *flexible* inflation targeting, which traded off deviations of inflation from target against deviations of output from potential output or against deviations of the actual from the natural rate of unemployment. The Fed's so-called 'dual mandate' of maximum employment and stable prices is an example of flexible inflation targeting.[7] The ECB and the Bank of England have a lexicographic or hierarchical mandate. Price stability

---

[7] The Fed's monetary policy mandate is really a triple one. Section 2A of the Federal Reserve Act calls for the growth of monetary and credit aggregates to promote 'the goals of maximum employment, stable prices, and moderate long-term interest rates'. Somehow, the third wheel on the bicycle, moderate long-term interest rates gets lost in the official statements of the monetary policy objectives of the Fed. In a way that is a pity, because it is the dimension in which the Fed has been most successful since the onset of the GFC.

comes first and subject to that, or without prejudice to that, these central banks can support growth and full employment.

The 'great moderation', the period from the mid-1980s till the onset of the GFC in mid-2007, was characterised by robust and stable real growth in the global economy and low and stable inflation. For the second time in my life as an economist, I heard central bankers, other economic policy makers and academic economists declare victory over the business cycle: the dawning of an era of economic stability.[8] Lucas (2003) professed that the 'central problem of depression-prevention [has] been solved, for all practical purposes' and Gordon Brown proclaimed 'no return to boom and bust' (Summers (2008)). When the GFC hit there was too much familiarity with Dynamic Stochastic General Equilibrium (DSGE) modelling in central banks (see e.g. Buiter (2009) and MathWorks (2014)) and in the economics profession at large, and too little familiarity with the work and insights of Hyman Minsky (1986, 1992). The pre-GFC quantitative and policy-oriented macroeconomic models produced by the DSGE school incorporated no meaningful role for financial institutions other than the central bank, and no special role for financial instruments other than base money. There was no role for financial intermediation, liquidity, bubbles, default and bankruptcy. Insights from behavioural economics were ignored. Minsky emphasised the inherent instability of financial capitalism, and especially how periods of financial calm and stability germinated the seeds of future financial instability and crises. Unfortunately these valuable qualitative insights were not operationalised in a quantitative way that could have guided monetary policy makers.

In the world of advanced economy central banking, the 'great moderation' hubris manifested itself as the 'twin delusions' of central banking. The analytical foundations for operational independence of the central bank are effectively non-existent. The most common justification for independence is that it overcomes a commitment problem (or time-inconsistency problem) that results in an inflation bias when monetary policy is run by the Treasury. Kydland & Prescott (1977) and Barro & Gordon (1983) assume that the natural unemployment rate is higher than the socially optimal unemployment rate, that the flexible inflation targeting monetary policy maker wants to maximise society's welfare and that the monetary authority cannot credibly commit itself to a monetary policy rule that will govern its future policy actions. They demonstrate that the result is an inflation bias: equilibrium inflation

---

[8] In Council of Economic Advisers (2000), Section 3 of Chapter 2 has the heading: 'The End of the Business Cycle?'. The academic economists that made up this Clinton Council of Economic Advisers (Martin N. Baily, Robert Z. Lawrence and Kathryn L. Shaw) did not quite declare the US business cycle dead ('Of course, it is premature to declare the business cycle dead' (Council of Economic Advisers (2000) page 79)). The reader is, however, left with the firm impression that if the business cycle is not dead, it is at least seriously incapacitated. See also Burns (1960) and Romer (1999).

under the time-consistent (that is, no commitment) monetary policy rule will be higher than the optimal inflation rate but the unemployment rate will be at the natural rate. Their logic is impeccable.

Unfortunately, this commitment problem has nothing to do with central bank independence. Unless we *assume* that making the central bank independent will somehow allow it to credibly commit itself to a monetary policy rule, an independent central bank will produce the same inflation bias as a non-independent monetary authority. This was pointed out by McCallum (1995, 1997). Only if, as suggested by Rogoff (1985), we take away the root cause of the inflation bias by appointing central bankers who do not care about unemployment and are solely interested in producing the socially optimal inflation rate will the inflation bias be eliminated and the optimal inflation rate be achieved (see also Besley (2005)). But operationally independent central banks with an objective function that penalises both deviations of inflation from its optimum value and deviations of unemployment from its optimum value will produce an inflation bias if the optimum unemployment rate is below the natural rate. Independence and an inability to commit are fully compatible. What is the invisible commitment technology that somehow prevents an independent central bank from reneging on its commitments? Operational independence of a central bank means that no other person, committee or institution can force it either to do things it does not wish to do or not to do things it wishes to do and that would be feasible but for the outside interference. It does not mean that the independent entity is capable of commitment. The belief that an operationally independent central bank overcomes the commitment problem and thus eliminates the inflation bias inherent in time-consistent monetary policy is based on proof by repeated assertion, a popular mode of proof in the social sciences but not quite on a par with proof by induction or deduction. That said, I have considerable sympathy for the view expressed by Blinder (1999), that one problem that never reared its head during his time on the Federal Reserve Board was the problem of credible commitment. Of course this could have been due to the FOMC at the time operating according to the time-consistent (but sub-optimal) strategy but not being aware of it . . .

Operational independence of the central bank can also make sense if the design and conduct of monetary policy, narrowly defined, can be viewed as a technical business that can be performed only by highly trained technical experts, rather like performing a root canal job on an abscessed tooth. If conducted properly and professionally, it does not involve overtly political matters of redistribution and reassignment of property rights. Those without the right training as well as the right sense of civic duty, especially elected politicians, can be blinded by myopia, motivated by political ambition and distracted by emotions, and as a result might pursue monetary policies that are likely to be excessively expansionary and therefore inflationary. In the end everyone loses. Better therefore to take monetary policy out of the hands of the ambition-driven and emotion-ridden politicians and entrust it to the disinterested trustees of economic stability and guardians of financial virtue—the appointed leaders of the operationally independent central bank.

Later in this article I address the issue of the political economy of central bank independence in some depth. What I want to emphasise here is that maintaining financial stability all but disappeared as a central bank responsibility in some key countries during the 'great moderation' years. In the United Kingdom this was formalised when Gordon Brown stripped the Bank of England of all its regulatory and supervisory responsibilities and powers in 1997. When I joined the first MPC as an external member in June 1997, financial stability was the last thing on my mind. When I left, three years later, the only fleeting consideration of financial stability matters had come during the Russian financial crisis of August 1998 and its aftermath when we briefly monitored corporate credit risk spreads to track possible spillovers/ contagion from the Russian turmoil into the Sterling markets. For me, monetary policy involved one instrument, the Bank Rate, one primary objective, price stability (operationalised as a specific inflation target) and, subject to that, the promotion of growth and employment. Simple really.

The ECB was created in 1999 with just one tiny, throwaway reference to financial stability in the European Treaties and Protocols. It was to be an operationally independent central bank focused on price stability. It had no regulatory or supervisory powers and no micro-prudential or macro-prudential instruments. Article 25.2 of the Protocol (No. 4) on the Statute of the European System of Central Banks (ESCB) and the ECB permitted the Council to assign the ECB 'tasks concerning policies relating to the prudential supervision of credit institutions and other financial institutions with the exception of insurance undertakings'.[9] The Fed never lost its regulatory or supervisory role, which it shared with a bewildering array of other institutions. Just at the federal level there are the Federal Deposit Insurance Corporation (FDIC), the Office of the Comptroller of the Currency (OCC), the Office of Thrift Supervision (OTS) and the National Credit Union Administration (NCUA), the Securities and

---

[9] In the Protocol (No. 4) On the Statute of the European System of Central Banks and of the European Central Bank (part of the Consolidated version of the Treaty on the Functioning of the European Union), Chapter V, Prudential Supervision, Article 25, Prudential Supervison, reads:

25.1. The ECB may offer advice to and be consulted by the Council, the Commission and the competent authorities of the Member States on the scope and implementation of Union legislation relating to the prudential supervision of credit institutions and to the stability of the financial system.

25.2. In accordance with any regulation of the Council under Article 127(6) of the Treaty on the Functioning of the European Union, the ECB may perform specific tasks concerning policies relating to the prudential supervision of credit institutions and other financial institutions with the exception of insurance undertakings.

Exchange Commission (SEC), the Commodity Futures Trading Commission (CFTC), the Federal Housing Finance Agency, among others and, since 2010, also the Financial Stability Oversight Council (FSOC).[10] The Fed had (and has), however, no macro-prudential instruments at its disposal other than margin requirements for stocks, something that has been set at the same level for these past 40 years. It is sometimes argued that the Fed's army of bank inspectors can be given countercyclical macro-prudential instructions, but evidence on the use and effectiveness of this instrument is hard to come by, and I am extremely sceptical. In addition, the Fed and the Bank of England— and to a lesser extent the ECB—were blinded by the light of the Efficient Markets Hypothesis. Under Greenspan and under Bernanke until mid-2007, self-regulation was often assumed and indeed asserted to be the best form of regulation. Few understood that self-regulation is to regulation as self-importance is to importance and self-righteousness to righteousness. Only the Bank of Japan had financial stability as an objective on a par with (or even ahead of) price stability.[11]

2.2b Bagehot's revenge

Central banks and treasuries (or ministries of finance) are the two ultimate guarantors of financial stability and, with the benefit of hindsight, it is incomprehensible that the financial stability role of the central bank was so comprehensively forgotten. Although guaranteeing financial stability was not their oldest role, which was funding the war efforts of the sovereign, it was emphasised by Bagehot (1873). Although he was not the first to use the phrase 'lender of last resort' in its modern sense,[12] he did provide the first characterisation of the job of the lender of last resort during a financial panic: lend freely, at a penalty rate of interest against good collateral.[13] Bagehot's lender of last resort was hamstrung somewhat by the gold standard, which required convertibility on demand of legal tender fiat money into gold. A modern central bank in a fiat money economy in which the vast majority of public and private contracts are denominated in domestic currency and can be settled in domestic currency, has a unique ability to provide open-ended domestic currency funding liquidity to banks and other systemically important counterparties. In an economy where much financial intermediation bypasses banks and instead takes place through arms-length transactions in financial markets, the provision of funding liquidity by the central bank is

---

[10] The FSOC is a mainly consultative body, chaired by the Secretary of the Treasury that brings together federal and state regulators of financial and credit institutions and an insurance expert appointed by the president.

[11] The Bank of Japan Act mentions financial stability as a purpose of the Bank of Japan in Article 1(2). Price stability appears as a purpose in Article 2. Bank of Japan (1997).

[12] It was probably Sir Frances Baring (1797).

[13] Presumably this means 'against collateral that would be good during normal times, or if held to maturity'.

not enough to forestall or mitigate financial crises. The central bank must act as market maker of last resort as well, providing domestic currency market liquidity for markets trading systemically important financial instruments.

The financial stability role of the central bank should at least be on a par with its macroeconomic role of providing price stability and possibly promoting some aspect(s) of real economic performance. I have some sympathy for the argument that, if one takes a long enough view, macroeconomic stability requires financial stability, because the inevitable consequences of financial instability are economic crisis, likely resulting in unemployment, excess capacity, volatile inflation and the risk of deflation. With most central banks not looking further ahead than two or three years in their analyses of macroeconomic prospects, they have tended to lose sight of financial cycles, which usually have longer durations than the typical business cycle (see Borio (2012)). Emphasising the financial cycle in its own right therefore makes practical sense. I would go further than that and argue that if there is a conflict between supporting the dual mandate over a two to three year horizon and acting to halt incipient financial froth and excess, financial stability should be given priority. Whether the pursuit of financial stability requires just the use of macro-prudential tools or in addition calls for leaning against the wind in asset market and credit markets, raising the official policy rate to dampen incipient financial excess when the dual mandate at a two to three year horizon does not call for such rate increases, is an exercise I leave to the reader. Stein (2012, 2013, 2014) provides an eloquent argument in support of the use of the policy rate increases in pursuit of financial stability even when this is not called for by the dual mandate. Clearly, if there are no sufficiently effective counter-cyclical macro-prudential instruments (or, as in the US, no meaningful countercyclical macro-prudential instruments at all), the use of the policy rate in support of financial stability cannot be avoided.

There should be a clear distinction between the liquidity-providing role of the central bank and the solvency support that should only be provided by the Treasury. Therefore, it is essential that any credit risk that the central bank takes on when it acts as market maker of last resort or lender of last resort be covered by a full sovereign guarantee. Ideally, the non-sovereign-guaranteed assets of the central bank should only be Treasury debt and loans secured against Treasury debt. Such a 'treasuries only' approach to the assets of the central bank that are not sovereign guaranteed, establishes a clear division of responsibilities between the Treasury and the central bank: the central bank provides funding liquidity and market liquidity; the Treasury fills solvency gaps. With a sovereign guarantee, the central bank is able to purchase the necessary assets outright and lend against whatever collateral may be offered by systemically important but at-risk counterparties. Because few treasuries write blank cheques, there would likely have to be an agreement between the Treasury and the central bank on the kind of risky securities the central bank could purchase outright, on the counterparties it can deal with, on the collateral it can accept and on the maximum scale of its risky operations. Positive or negative lists that would evolve over time could fulfil that role.

After years of lending to borderline insolvent banks that frequently offered as collateral debt issued by borderline insolvent euro area periphery sovereigns, the ECB has stated that in its purchases of asset-backed securities (ABS) it will only buy the higher-risk 'mezzanine' tranches if they are covered by a sovereign guarantee. In principle it is right to make such a demand. Indeed, I would argue that the guarantee should be a joint and several one by all euro area sovereigns. However, if some or all of the euro area sovereigns are unwilling to provide such guarantees or if the guarantee is not worth much because of the precarious fiscal position of the sovereign providing the guarantee, the ECB is faced with an unpleasant dilemma. Either it goes ahead and purchases the risky ABS without a sovereign guarantee (or with a sovereign guarantee that is not worth much), thus engaging in fundamentally inappropriate quasi-fiscal activities, or it does not purchase the high risk ABS and thus increases the risk that the Eurozone will fall in a deflationary trap or even into secular stagnation (see Summers (2014) and Buiter *et al.* (2014a)). It is clear that the design of the Eurosystem and the division of duties, responsibilities and powers between the ECB and the national fiscal authorities are deeply flawed. Why these issues have not been addressed and resolved since the GFC erupted in the summer of 2007 is a mystery and an indictment of the political institutions and political leadership in the Eurozone.

2.2c Central banks and liquidity

Financial assets are liquid if they can be bought and sold quickly, the transaction costs and the bid-ask spread are small and the price is not significantly below that justified by the fundamentals. Liquidity depends upon the subjective beliefs of market participants; any store of value will be liquid if there is trust, confidence and optimism. If enough people believe an asset is liquid then it will be—even bitcoin. Conversely, when there is mistrust, lack of confidence, fear and pessimism, any store of value can become illiquid.

Commercial banks are characterised by a mismatch between liabilities and assets as regards maturity or duration and liquidity. The same is true for governments, whose main asset, the ability to tax, is illiquid. In the absence of central bank intervention, bank runs—both the old-style depositor type and the new-style wholesale creditor type—and sovereign debt runs are always possible, even when banks and sovereigns are fundamentally solvent. As the unique provider of potentially unlimited domestic currency funding and market liquidity, the central bank must stand ready to act as lender of last resort and market maker of last resort for banks and sovereigns.

Unfortunately, central banks are unable to stop a bank run or a run on the sovereign if the debts of the bank or the sovereign are denominated in foreign currency. Iceland provides a spectacular example of this for the case of banks (see Buiter & Sibert (2008)). And even a central bank's base money liabilities can become illiquid if faith in the domestic currency is lost. In open economies, direct currency substitution between a rapidly depreciating domestic currency and a foreign currency is a not uncommon phenomenon in emerging markets and developing countries where the authorities have lost control of the public finances and force the central bank into aggressive deficit and debt monetisation. Hyperinflations are another means of making base money illiquid.

2.2d Central banks and solvency

Modern central banks are highly profitable businesses that can command vast resources, even if they are constrained by (low) inflation targets. This makes them an obvious source of cheap funding for weak banks (or other financial firms) that need to fill a solvency gap. The Treasury too will tend to prefer what is effectively an off-budget and off-balance-sheet quasi-fiscal financing mode through the central bank to an on-budget and on-balance-sheet open fiscal intervention.

In principle, the division of labour between the central bank, the shareholders and unsecured creditors of a bank and the Treasury is clear. The central bank provides funding liquidity and market liquidity to help banks that are solvent but illiquid. Shareholders and unsecured creditors take haircuts when a bank is insolvent. The Treasury steps in if and only if the bank is systemically important and the imposition of the maximum possible haircuts on shareholders and unsecured creditors is not enough to restore it to solvency. At that point either the Treasury comes up with the capital necessary to restore the bank to solvency or secured creditors and special, protected categories of unsecured creditors such as deposit holders, possibly even insured ones, take a haircut.

In practice, the tax payer is frequently subordinated to both senior and junior unsecured creditors—indeed at times even to bank shareholders. Central banks have provided large back-door injections of capital into capital-deficient banks by using a variety of clever mechanisms to underprice their loans. Paying over the odds for assets banks are trying to get rid of is another common way in which central banks effect a quasi-fiscal subsidy. This is partly because of the practical problem of distinguishing institutions that are illiquid but fundamentally solvent from institutions that are both illiquid and fundamentally insolvent. Often, however, it has been a reflection of a widespread belief that some large banks are too important, too systemically connected or too politically connected to fail. This is slowly changing. Mechanisms to permit an orderly resolution of systemically important financial institutions (SIFIs) are being cobbled together in the US, where there was considerable experience resolving smaller and less complex banks through the FDIC, and in the EU, through the reinterpretation of state aid rules by the European Commission, the Bank Recovery and Resolution Directive and the Single Resolution Mechanism with its Single Resolution Fund and Single Resolution Board. If these efforts are successful we will be closer to a world in which any financial support for banks from the tax payers is provided through legitimate, open and transparent procedures, with control and responsibility residing with accountable, elected officials.

2.3 Enhanced financial stability, supervisory and regulatory responsibilities of central banks

One point virtually all disinterested observers will agree on is that, when it comes to the GFC, no central bank saw it coming until well after it had started. Our leading central bankers did not have a clue: they did not anticipate it and as a result they did not act pre-emptively to prevent or mitigate it. This cognitive vacuum was shared by virtually all observers and analysts outside the central banks as well, including those who have been widely credited with seeing the GFC coming. In every case I know of, the allegedly successful prophet of a full-blown financial crisis was a professional doomsayer who had been predicting a major crisis every year for years on end—sometimes for well over a decade. Even then they failed to gauge not just the timing but also the magnitude and scope of the crisis that was about to engulf the North Atlantic region, and they did not provide any coherent argument supporting their predictions of doom. Diagnosing a boom or even a bubble in the US housing market or predicting looming problems in the securitisation of subprime mortgages is deserving of credit but it does not make the diagnostician the canary in the GFC coalmine.[14]

During the crisis years of late 2007 through 2009 the performance of central banks as lenders of last resort and market makers of last resort was mixed (see e.g. Buiter (2008c)). However, on average it was better, fortunately, than their crisis-preventing and crisis-anticipating performance.

Since the crisis started, every leading central bank has seen its regulatory and supervisory responsibilities enhanced. The Fed has been given supervisory powers over non-bank SIFIs and is a prominent member of the Financial Stability Oversight Committee. The ECB dominates the European Systemic Risk Board and has just assumed the leadership of the Eurozone's Single Supervisory Mechanism, which supervises the 120-odd largest banks in the Eurozone. This is despite the failure of

---

[14] For a contrary opinion—that there were many who predicted the GFC with a reasonable degree of accuracy—see Bezemer (2009a,b) and Katz (2014).

both banks to anticipate the crisis and, in the case of the Fed, despite its failure to use the regulatory and supervisory powers that it already possessed to prevent or mitigate the crisis.

The most impressive enhancement of the central bank responsibilities and powers has occurred in the United Kingdom. Having concluded that the tripartite arrangement between the Treasury, the Bank of England and the Financial Services Authority (FSA) of 1997 (amended in March 2006), did not function properly, the UK Treasury transferred most of the responsibilities of the FSA to the Bank of England.[15] In addition, quite a few macro-prudential instruments that in other countries are often controlled by the Treasury, including the maximum loan-to-value ratio or loan-to-income ratios for residential mortgages, are now under the control of the Bank of England or about to be transferred to it. The central bank now includes and dominates the macro-prudential regulator (the Financial Policy Committee) and the micro-prudential regulator/supervisor (the Prudential Regulation Authority (PRA) and the Prudential Regulation Authority Board). It plays a central role in bank resolution, a process for which the role of the custodian of the fiscal deep pockets—the Treasury—is specified with far too little precision. In addition, through the PRA, it is also responsible for the oversight of and rules relating to the Financial Services Compensation Scheme, the UK deposit insurance scheme. This institutional responsibility overload is a clear example of the 'central planning fallacy'—the common belief that, when a decentralised regime is not working properly, the solution is to centralise authority. It is also worrying that the new 'bi-partite' Bank of England and Treasury arrangement to address financial stability in the UK fails to recognise the central role of the Treasury not just in bank resolution but also in maintaining financial stability generally. This role is essential whenever systemically important institutions are threatened with insolvency and this problem cannot, for whatever reason(s), be addressed adequately through the bail-in of equity owners and unsecured creditors. Only the deep fiscal pockets of the Treasury are, providing recourse to them is transparent, legitimate sources of funding for a bail-out by the tax payer.

2.4 The fiscal and quasi-fiscal roles of the central bank

No matter how independent a central bank is and despite formal ownership structures which are often bizarre, the Treasury is the beneficial owner of its country's central banks and it is entitled to receive its stream of profits, less reserves or provisions. In the United Kingdom the Treasury has owned the stock of the Bank of England (tech-

---

[15] This excludes 'conduct' or consumer protection responsibilities which have been assigned to the Financial Conduct Authority.

nically a joint stock company) since 1946. The ECB is owned directly by the central banks of the member states of the euro area and these national central banks are in turn owned beneficially by their national treasuries.[16]

The present discounted value of the future 'seigniorage' profits of central banks in the advanced economies (the product of their monopoly of the issuance of domestic-currency legal tender) is large. For the Eurosystem, my team has calculated it to be well over €2 trillion (see Buiter (2013b) and Buiter & Rahbari (2013). In addition to distributing its profits to the Treasury, central banks can provide a wide range of hidden subsidies or impose hidden taxes on the financial counterparties they deal with. The terms on which the central bank lends to eligible counterparties, including the interest rate charged, the maturity of the loans, the collateral that is accepted, the haircuts on the market value or fair value of the collateral and the margin requirements over the life of the loan, can involve implicit subsidies, as can the terms on which the central bank purchases securities outright from banks and other counterparties. The two three-year Longer-term Refinancing Operations (LTROs) of the ECB in December 2011 and February 2012 provide an example of this.

Unfortunately, no central bank publishes estimates of the flow of implicit subsidies it provides to private and public counterparties, let alone of their present discounted value. The subsidies are buried in the yields on assets and liabilities that are paid or charged, for which a subsidy-free benchmark is often not available. Indeed, central banks do not publish and refuse to reveal the actual yields on many of their assets and liabilities and refuse to say who the counterparties were in their financial transactions, even after commercial sensitivity is no longer an issue, because sufficient time has passed since the transactions took place. Many appear to view accountability and

---

[16] The Federal Reserve System is indeed a federal institution consisting of a central, governmental agency, the Board of Governors and 12 regional Federal Reserve Banks. The 12 regional Federal Reserve Banks—the operating arms of the Federal Reserve system, are owned by their member banks. Reserve Bank stock may not be sold, traded, or pledged as security for a loan and dividends are fixed at 6 per cent per year, which makes this 'stock' look rather like a fixed rate perpetuity. The Board of Governors and the Federal Reserve System as a whole aren't 'owned' by anyone. The Federal Reserve System describes itself as an independent entity within government (see Federal Reserve System (2005)). Since the US Treasury gets the profits of the Federal Reserve System, it would minimise confusion if the private 'ownership' of the Federal Reserve Banks were abolished and the entire system (Board and Regional Reserve Banks) were explicitly owned by the US Treasury. The Banca D'Italia is owned by banks, insurance companies and social security institutions (see Banca D'Italia (2013)). Although these shareholders are not supposed to influence the policies of the Banca D'Italia, this pseudo-private ownership structure is by no means innocuous. By revaluing its equity from a notional amount of euro 156,000 to euro 7.5 bn, the Banca D'Italia made a large quasi-fiscal capital transfer to its shareholders in 2014—boosting their capital from 2015 on. The Bank of Japan is capitalised at 100 million yen and about 45 per cent of the stock is held privately (see Bank of Japan (2014)). The stock trades in the over the counter market—quite possibly the most astonishing ownership structure I have come across.

transparency, even *ex post*, as the enemy of effectiveness and even of financial stability.[17]

These payments of implicit subsidies or imposition of implicit taxes represent the quasi-fiscal role of the central bank. It can reduce or increase the profits the central bank remits to its beneficial owner, the Treasury, or it can redistribute income and wealth between different counterparties.

2.5 Central banks not 'sticking to their knitting'[18]

The notion that central banks should focus exclusively on their mandates and not be active participants in wider public policy debates, let alone be active players in the negotiations and bargaining processes that produce the political compromises that will help shape the economic, social and political evolution of our societies is, I believe, sound. Alan Blinder described this need for modesty and restraint for central bankers as sticking to their knitting.

Central banks sticking to their knitting—the design and conduct of monetary policy in the pursuit of macroeconomic stability and financial stability—has always been the exception rather than the rule. Especially in Continental Europe, central bank annual reports in the post-Second World War era often devoted more space to the discussion of fiscal policy and structural policies than to monetary policy. In the UK, different Governors of the Bank of England engaged in budgetary pontification to varying degrees. Under Eddie George the sound of silence was the norm, but his predecessors and his successors were much more vocal. Speaking out beyond their remit afflicted both central banks without any material degree of independence (operational or target), like the Bank of England pre-1997 and the Banque de France pre-1999, and central banks with a higher degree of operational and some target independence, like the Fed and the pre-1999 Bundesbank.

Although always inappropriate, central banks straying into policy debates on matters outside their mandates and competence is less of a concern when there is little central bank independence and the central bank functions mainly as the liquid arm of the Treasury. It becomes a matter of grave concern when central banks have a material

---

[17] The ECB and the BoE still refuse to provide any information on counterparties and the terms of transactions with individual counterparties. The Fed tried to prevent disclosure of the names of its counterparties to whom it provided emergency loans, and the terms of these emergency loans, made between 2007 and 2010. Fear of counterparty stigmatisation is a frequently given excuse. The Fed was finally (in March 2011) forced to provide the information under the Freedom of Information Act, following a lawsuit by Bloomberg.

[18] I originally attributed this phrase to Alan Blinder, only to discover, first, an earlier use of a central bank should stick to its knitting by David Laidler (2004) and then a reference from 1920 (Trust and Estates, Volume 31, page 120).

degree of operational independence (and sometimes of target independence also). Many advanced economy central banks achieved a measure of operational independence for the first time during the last decade of the 20th century, starting with the Reserve Bank of New Zealand in 1989.[19,20]

Former Fed Chairman Bernanke routinely lectured Congress and the White House on fiscal sustainability and appropriate fiscal stimulus measures. He played a prominent, high profile public role in gathering support for a fiscal stimulus package to counteract the US slowdown/recession from late 2007 through to 2009. On Thursday, 17 January 2008, for instance, in testimony to the House Budget Committee, he backed calls for a fiscal package to stimulate the economy, but stressed such a plan should be 'explicitly temporary.' . . . 'Any program should be explicitly temporary, both to avoid unwanted stimulus beyond the near-term horizon and, importantly, to preclude an increase in the federal government's structural budget deficit'. He went on to say that the nation faced daunting long-run budget challenges associated with an aging population, rising health-care costs, and other factors, and that a fiscal program that increased the structural budget deficit would only make confronting those challenges more difficult. 'Fiscal action could be helpful in principle, as fiscal and monetary stimulus together may provide broader support for the economy than monetary policy actions alone'.

Chairman Bernanke may be right or wrong about the usefulness of this kind of fiscal policy package at the time (for what it is worth, I believe he was largely right), but it is an indictment of the American political system that we have the head of the central bank telling members of Congress how they ought to conduct fiscal policy. Fiscal policy is not part of the Fed's mandate. Nor is it part of the core competencies of the Chairman of the Federal Reserve Board to make fiscal policy recommendations for the US federal government. It is true that Bernanke acting ultra vires was likely the lesser of two evils: usurping the constitutional roles of the Congress and the Executive versus permitting a re-run of the Great Depression. The point is that political institutional reforms are required in the US (and elsewhere) to prevent a recurrence of this 'rule by technocrats' which creates a scary precedent.

This is not the first time the Chairman of the Fed has strayed into controversial policy issues that are none of his and the Fed's business. Bernanke has lectured, as Chairman of the Fed, on free trade, on aspects of globalisation that are not relevant to the conduct of monetary policy, and on equality, equality of opportunity, educational achievement and teenage pregnancy (see Bernanke (2007a,b,c)).

The President of the ECB, Mario Draghi, like his predecessor Jean-Claude Trichet,

---

[19] The Bundesbank had a high degree of operational independence ever since its inception in 1957.
[20] The RBNZ was also the first to introduce inflation targeting, in 1989 and 1990, as the primary objective of the central bank and the operational expression of the pursuit of price stability. See Buiter (2006).

is actively trying to influence and shape EA policies in the areas of fiscal stimulus and structural reform, using a range of possible monetary policy interventions (mostly unconventional) as sticks or carrots to get national governments and the European Commission to do what he considers to be 'the right things'. Draghi's recent address at the Jackson Hole Conference organised by the Federal Reserve Bank of Kansas demonstrates how broad the range of economic issues is on which the President of the ECB feels comfortable to lecture, some might say badger, the political leadership of the EA (Draghi (2014)). Regardless of the economic merits of Draghinomics, there is something worrying, from a constitutional/legal/political/legitimacy perspective, if unelected central bank technocrats become key movers and shakers in the design and implementation of reforms and policies in areas well beyond their mandate and competence.[21]

An earlier, even more striking example of a central bank(er) acting ultra vires was when Italian Prime Minister Silvio Berlusconi resigned on 12 November 2011. It was widely reported in the media that the ECB supported his replacement with Mario Monti.[22] Some reports go further and allege that the President of the ECB played an active, albeit indirect, part in Berlusconi's resignation, by restricting the ECB's buying of Italian sovereign debt during the days leading up to the announcement of his resignation.[23] This certainly has a ring of plausibility, as on 29 September 2011 the then President of the ECB, Jean-Claude Trichet and the ECB President-in-waiting, Mario Draghi both signed a letter to Berlusconi that contained a detailed list of fiscal and structural reforms the Italian government ought to implement as soon as possible. The words 'or else' were not part of this missive, but were clearly implied.[24]

I don't wish to assign all or even most of the blame for this usurpation of parliamentary and executive power to the individual central bankers involved. The

[21] The Term Draghinomics (by analogy with the three arrows of Abenomics) due to Nouriel Roubini (2014).

[22] See e.g. the *New York Times* of 12 Nov. 2011, which reported: 'Mr. Monti met on Saturday with Mr. Berlusconi and earlier in the day with Mario Draghi, the recently installed president of the European Central Bank, reinforcing the notion that financial and European institutions supported Mr. Monti's appointment' (*New York Times, Europe*, 'Berlusconi Steps Down, and Italy Pulses with Change', http://www.nytimes.com/2011/11/13/world/europe/silvio-berlusconi-resign-italy-austerity-measures.html?_r=0; also the *Wall Street Journal*, 13 Nov. 2011, 'Berlusconi Bows Out; Austerity lies ahead', http://online.wsj.com/news/articles/SB10001424052970204358004577033703085619754 and NPR, 13 July 2012, 'The European Central Bank's Guide to Influence', http://www.npr.org/blogs/money/2012/07/13/156705409/the-european-central-banks-guide-to-influence.

[23] See *Financial Times*, 7 Nov. 2011, 'Berlusconi fights to the end as debt costs soar', http://www.ft.com/intl/cms/s/0/62b7533c-095b-11e1-a2bb-00144feabdc0.html#axzz3DPMNHbHf

[24] The text of the letter (in English), which was leaked to the Italian press, can be found here: http://www.corriere.it/economia/11_settembre_29/trichet_draghi_inglese_304a5f1e-ea59-11e0-ae06-4da866778017.shtml

blame for this intolerable situation lies mainly with the defective institutional design of the monetary union in the euro area and the unwillingness and/or inability of the euro area political class to correct the manifold deficiencies of the EMU and the European Treaties. Banking union is proceeding only slowly and incompletely; there is no sovereign debt restructuring mechanism; there is no European Monetary Fund with mutualised sources of funding from the member state sovereigns capable of providing conditional liquidity to sovereigns on a scale sufficient to avoid the risk of fundamentally unnecessary sovereign debt restructuring, or to mitigate the trauma associated with unavoidable sovereign debt restructuring; there are no adequate mutualised 'fiscal pots' to back up the Single Resolution Mechanism for systemically important banks or the Single Deposit Guarantee Scheme which may one day materialise. The ECB was and is therefore stuck with the uncomfortable choice between letting the euro area collapse and taking on responsibilities and acting in ways that are well beyond its mandate. It is time to correct this situation.

2.6 Legitimacy and accountability of central bank power

In liberal democracies, where political office is achieved through free and fair elections, the fighting of wars is nevertheless delegated to unelected technocrats—the military. The elected, legitimate politicians decide whether or not to fight wars. They do not typically fight wars themselves, but leave the conduct of wars to the specialists. Likewise, the task of intelligence gathering for national security purposes is delegated to unelected technocrats in the public sector and increasingly sub-contracted to private entities. I still hope that elected, legitimate politicians will continue (or perhaps at last begin) to make the decisions on what kind of information is to be sought and retained, which individuals or which kind of people and organisations are to be monitored or have their communications intercepted, and what constitutes acceptable and unacceptable practices and procedures.

I have long described the notion of an independent central bank—even just an operationally independent central bank—as a mythos (Buiter (2004, 2005, 2008d)). Both the traditional definition of mythos, myth or mythology—a traditional or recurrent narrative theme or plot structure (in literature), or a set of beliefs and assumptions about something (in philosophy or science)—and the modern meanings of myth as a folk tale, legend, fable, and fairy tale, or a widely held but false belief or idea, are appropriately associated with the notion of an (operationally) independent central bank.

Since the early 1990s central banks in most advanced economies have been viewed as operationally independent, and have often viewed themselves as operationally independent, in part because, through some cosmic coincidence, what central banks would choose to do if they really were operationally independent coincided with what the consensus among the political classes and in the polity at large wanted them to do: pursue low inflation, act symmetrically in a countercyclical manner, tightening monetary policy in the upswing and loosening during downturns; do not use interest rates aggressively to tackle credit and asset market booms; at most lean against the wind a little in the credit markets and financial markets, if this can be done without prejudice to the price stability mandate or the dual mandate.

I am convinced that, should it come to a direct conflict between the monetary policy priorities of the central bank and those of the Treasury, there is likely to be no such thing as central bank operational independence. The only conceivable exception would be the ECB, although it is doubtful whether the Eurozone could survive a 'monetary dominance' outcome in a game of chicken between the fiscal and monetary authorities. Except in highly unusual circumstances, there is, in the final analysis, likely to be fiscal dominance when a single national central bank faces a single national Treasury. The game of chicken between an operationally independent central bank and the Treasury can only have one outcome: the central bank swerves or gives way.

The reasons why the ECB today and (possibly) the pre-1999 Bundesbank are exceptions to the rule that fiscal dominance is the norm and monetary dominance the exception, make it clear that the ECB is likely to be the only exception in the foreseeable future. The ECB as monetary authority faces not one but eighteen national fiscal authorities. There is no supranational or federal euro area fiscal authority or Treasury. The 18 (19 when Lithuania joins on 1 January 2015) national treasuries of the euro area are internally divided and, despite the existence of the Eurogroup of EA finance ministers, seldom act in a coordinated, purposeful manner. Even the most powerful of the individual EA finance ministers, German finance minister Wolfgang Schäuble, is therefore much less powerful when dealing with the ECB than his pre-1999 predecessors were in dealing with the German Bundesbank. The relatively high degree of de facto operational independence enjoyed by the Bundesbank from when it was established in 1957 till the start of the common currency in 1999 was due to the unique historical circumstances preceding its birth. The Weimar Republic hyperinflation between 1921 and 1924, the Great Depression, the rise of Nazism, the defeat in the Second World War and the dismemberment of Germany that followed it created a unique and virtually impossible to replicate intensity of popular political support for keeping everyday politics out of the running of the central bank.

The divine coincidence between what operationally independent central banks want to do and what their political masters would like them to do was in part a result of (1) the high inflation episodes experienced by many advanced economies that accompanied the 1973 and 1979 oil price shocks and the collapse of the Bretton Woods system between 1971 and 1973 and (2) the 'great moderation'. In addition, the operational independence of the greatly enhanced central banks since the onset of the GFC also reflects the dysfunctional politics and unfit-for-purpose political and economic institutions of the euro area, the US and, perhaps to a lesser extent the UK (although the near-exit of Scotland from the UK suggests otherwise). It is an interesting question, and one I am not sure I know the answer to, whether it makes sense to reduce the scope of central bank power and influence before these wider political and institutional dysfunctionalities have been corrected.

The reason for the prevalence of fiscal dominance outside the special cases of the ECB and the old Bundesbank is obvious. The only form of legitimacy a central bank can aspire to is 'output legitimacy': how well it performs its assigned tasks, or how successful it is in its pursuit of its mandate. Central banks and those who serve in them have little or no 'input legitimacy'. Input legitimacy refers to procedural legitimacy—the design of the institution (notably the manner in which the decision makers are selected), the manner in which decisions are made and communicated, and the sources of whatever authority the institution commands. In the words of Sharman (2008: 6–7), 'Both forms of legitimacy express public assessment of the worth of an institution, but input legitimacy is a matter of the design of the institution while output legitimacy must be earned by the institution's performance.'

Central banks tend to be short on input legitimacy. The origins of the Bank of England are found in the war financing needs of King William III (an expatriate Dutchman who successfully invaded England in 1688 and took the crown in 1689 (which he shared with his wife, Mary II)). The Fed is a Johnny-come-lately among advanced economy national central banks, established in 1913 through an Act of Congress (The Federal Reserve Act). The ECB derives its even more recent right of existence from the Treaty on European Union and the Treaty on the Functioning of the European Union—documents whose length and opacity render them abject failures as sources of input legitimacy among the wider population in the EU or the EA.

Central bankers are appointed officials. They therefore lack the unique input legitimacy of being elected to the public offices they occupy. Although many central bankers have outstanding character and intellect, the selection processes involved are only partly based on merit and qualifications. Often partisan political infighting results in both type I and type II errors in the selection of central bankers.

Output legitimacy of central banks is fragile. Inevitably there will be periods with bad outcomes for the economic variables the central bank is targeting. Sometimes this bad performance may be due to bad performance by the central bank, sometimes it will be due to circumstances beyond the control of the central bank (bad luck). Most of the time even a well-informed and disinterested observer won't be able to assign bad outcomes confidently to bad performance or bad luck. To avoid the risk of central bank independence being swept away on a groundswell of popular and political discontent, even where operational independence makes sense, it is important to enhance the input legitimacy of central banks.

This requires, in my view, the return to a view of the central bank as, first, the monetary authority, narrowly defined, in charge of conventional and unconventional monetary policy and, second, as lender of last resort and market maker of last resort for sovereigns and systemically important financial institutions. All balance sheet activities of the central bank should either involve sovereign debt or be guaranteed by the sovereign (jointly and severally by all EA sovereigns in the case of the ECB). There is even a case for taking the MPC (the body setting the policy rate and choosing the size and composition of the balance sheet of the central bank under orderly market conditions) out of the central bank completely. The central bank would implement the rate and balance sheet decisions of the MPC and would alone decide on lender-of-last-resort and market-maker-of-last-resort operations (see Buiter (2008e) and Sibert (2012)).

Beyond that the central bank should have no regulatory or supervisory functions (macro-prudential, micro-prudential or conduct related). It should not play a significant role in bank resolution and none in deposit insurance. It should be part of something like FSOC, the supreme financial stability council, headed by the Treasury, that brings together the central bank and all financial supervisors and regulators. Unlike the real-world FSOC in the US, this FSOC+ should be able to take decisions that are binding on all institutions that participate in it.

The reason for getting the monetary authority out of the supervision, regulation and resolution business is that these are inherently political tasks, in which property rights are reassigned and reallocated routinely and redistributive decisions are taken all the time. No unelected technocrats should be in charge of such decisions without the kind of close parliamentary scrutiny, oversight and interference that would make an operationally independent monetary policy impossible. Clearly, if the Governor of the central bank is both in charge of setting interest rates and of the regulation and supervision of the key banks, it is not possible to fire him/her for incompetence in the performance of his/her supervisory and regulatory responsibilities while retaining him/her as the head of the monetary policy making committee.

Even if the central bank were to become the limited monetary authority I favour (with or without the lender-of-last-resort and market-maker-of-last-resort responsibilities), its operational independence, even in these restricted domains, would be at risk unless it were highly accountable.

2.7a Formal and substantive accountability
Formal accountability is the aspect of responsibility involving giving, *ex post*, a statistical or judicial explanation for events, actions and outcomes. Such formal

accountability requires that those to whom account is given (the Principal) can properly monitor the actions of the Agent (Trustee or Custodian). The Principal must have enough information to be able to make an informed judgement as to how well the party held to account has performed. Clear objectives for the Agent and the most complete possible information about the actions of the Agent are necessary for formal accountability to be possible.

Formal accountability requires openness and transparency, at least *ex post*. I will focus in what follows on the formal accountability of the least formally accountable central bank in the visible universe, the ECB. It is clear from its own website, that the ECB has a minimalist interpretation of accountability as the least demanding kind of formal accountability only. Until recently, it identified accountability with the (written and oral) reporting obligations of the ECB to the European Parliament, the European Commission and the European Council. Published staff forecasts, press conferences with prepared statements and Q&A, speeches, interviews and other forms of communication by members of the Executive Board and by the Governors of the national central banks with the wider public supplemented these treaty-based communication requirements. In the view of the ECB, public knowledge of the objectives of the ECB and the ability to observe some of the actions taken by the ECB would suffice, together with the communication channels just outlined, to make the ECB fully accountable. Of course, the central bank policy actions that are publicly observable (interest rate decisions, some of the decisions concerning the size and composition of the balance sheet) represent but a subset of the total set of central bank policy actions. We don't know the identity of the counterparties of the ECB in their financial transactions or the terms on which these transactions are conducted—not even with an appropriate time lag that would respect legitimate commercial sensitivities about pending or recent transactions.

Recently, the ECB has decided to start publishing (as of 2015) minutes of its Governing Council policy meetings, following the Fed and the Bank of England and most other advanced economy central banks. These would be unattributed minutes, not transcripts, and they would not contain individual voting records. As the ECB seldom if ever has had a formal vote on monetary policy decisions, not having the individual voting record of a vote that does not take place may not seem to be much of an issue. I believe this logic to be wrong (see e.g. Buiter (1999) and Issing (1999)). First, formal votes ought to be taken on every material policy decision and, second, individual voting records of all Governing Council members should be published as an integral part of formal accountability. Without this, substantive accountability cannot be achieved.

The standard ECB-stalwart's objection to publishing the individual votes of Governing Council members is that it would leave the national central bank Governors (and possibly the members of the Executive Board as well) open to improper pressures from their national constituencies to vote not in the euro-area interest, as they are supposed to do according to the treaties, but in the national interest (if and when the two are thought to be in conflict). I believe this argument gets it exactly backwards. Voting in the national rather than the European interest is a lot easier if one cannot be held to account for such mandate-violating actions because these votes are not in the public domain. Any formal political or judicial sanctions against such mandate violations become impossible if there are no formal votes or if the individual votes remain a secret.

Substantive accountability means that, following such reporting, explanation and justification as can be achieved through formal accountability, judgement (or other pleasant or unpleasant consequences) may follow for the responsible parties. There is substantive accountability if the reporting, explanation and justification is 'payoff-relevant' for the party doing the reporting, that is, if there can be punishments, sanctions or rewards for those deemed responsible for actions or outcomes.

Logically, truly operationally independent central banks can have no substantive accountability at all. Central bank operational independence requires the following:

- Political independence (don't take or seek instructions).
- Technical independence (does the central bank have the tools to do the job?).
- Financial independence and security from external raids on its financial resources, to the extent that these are necessary to fulfil its mandate.
- Security of tenure and of terms of employment.
- An independent body (a court, say) to settle disputes.

Independence has to mean that those in charge of monetary policy cannot be fired except for incapacity or serious misconduct, and that financial remuneration and working conditions likewise cannot be used to reward or punish them. It ought to mean also that monetary policy makers cannot be sued in civil courts or be dragged into criminal courts for actions taken in their capacity as monetary policy makers.[25] Operationally independent central banks are therefore not substantively accountable.

I have come round to the view that the very high degree of operational independence sought and thus far achieved by the ECB is not necessary for the design and implementation of effective monetary policy. Substantive accountability of a central bank can be enhanced by making it possible for members of the central bank's

[25] In the advanced industrial countries we have not (yet) witnessed recourse to the law by those disgruntled with the conduct of monetary policy—in emerging markets many such instances can be found. The legal immunities and liabilities of central bankers in the performance of their monetary policy making tasks are, however, an uncharted area.

monetary policy making committee (the Governing Council in the case of the ECB) to be fired for reasons other than incapacity or serious misconduct. The parliament that the ECB is formally accountable to (the European Parliament) should be able to fire/dismiss any member of the ECB's Board if a qualified majority (say two thirds plus 1) of those entitled to vote are in favour of this. I would favour extending to the European Parliament the right also to dismiss the National Central Bank (NCB) governors, using the same qualified majority rule. Leaving this to national parliaments would reinforce the unfortunate legal fiction that the Eurozone has 19 (next year 20) central banks—the ECB and 18 (next year 19) NCBs—rather than one central bank (the ECB) and 18 (next year 19) branches. Fundamental policy disagreement between (a qualified majority of) the European Parliament and any member of the ECB's Governing Council would be a valid ground for dismissal.

The absence of substantive accountability for central banks and individual central bankers means that it is difficult to provide them with the proper incentives to do the best possible job. Although many central bankers may be motivated in their approach to the job by a sense of public service, by duty and by unflinching commitment to the central bank's mandate, one would like to see these higher motives reinforced by such primitive and crass but frequently more reliable motives as the desire for power, prestige, wealth, comfort and leisure.

This problem of motivating central bankers is especially acute when the monetary policy decision is a group decision; it gets more severe the larger the monetary policy making committee. This is because when monetary policy is made by a committee, two further factors can adversely influence the quality of the decision making. The first is the problem of free riding and shirking by individual members whose incremental contribution to the joint product (the interest rate decision, say) cannot be identified clearly (see Blinder (1999, 2007a, 2007b), Sibert (2003, 2006), Mihov & Sibert (2006)). The second concerns some well-known problems and pathologies associated with small-group decision making, of which 'groupthink' is a well-known example (see Sibert (2006); for a more optimistic perspective on group decision making see Blinder (1999), and Blinder & Morgan (2005)).

How can one incentivise monetary policy makers in operationally independent central banks to pull their finger out? Linking pay to performance would be one obvious mechanism. For a 'lexicographic' inflation targeting central bank this would be rather straightforward. Members of the Governing Council of the ECB would currently be having a rather spartan year, with inflation undershooting the 'below but close to two per cent' target consistently and persistently. It is true that the inflation outcome (and the behaviour of all other nominal and real economic variables of interest) is driven by many forces other than monetary policy. Most of these other drivers are not under the control of the monetary authority. Some cannot even be observed or measured. Payment by result rewards good luck as well as good policies and punishes bad luck as well as bad policies. That, however, is the case with most real-world incentive pay systems that base pay on the behaviour of verifiable performance indicators that are only partially under the control of the payee. Elsewhere I have made proposals to provide financial incentives for better forward guidance about the timing and speed of future increases in the policy rate and about its long-run neutral level, by making monetary policy makers' pay a function of the behaviour of financial options that would pay off handsomely if actual future policy rates pan out in line with the forward guidance but would inflict losses if the forward guidance turns out to have been a poor guide to the future behaviour of rates (see Buiter (2013a)).

Proposals for linking central bankers' pay to performance have not been wildly successful. Without this, the only consequences of poor individual performance (if it can be identified), are damage to reputation (shame and embarrassment), poorer prospects for honours and impaired career prospects following one's term of office with the monetary authority.

Employment prospects in the public sector or the prospect of honours would not be morally appropriate, legitimate or even legal incentives to induce central bankers to put their shoulder to the wheel, but this does not mean they play no role. Post-central bank employment prospects in the private sector would, however, subject to the appropriate safeguards and purdah/garden leave/cooling-off-periods, be a useful way of incentivising central bankers.

If we grant the assumption that the outside world's perception of one's competence is a major determinant of one's future employment prospects, it is essential that the most complete information about each monetary policy maker's contribution to the monetary policy decision is publicly available. This is not an issue when monetary policy is made by one person, as is the case in New Zealand. It *is* an issue when monetary policy is made by a committee, as it is now in the majority of central banks. Revealing the individual votes of all members of a MPC as soon as practicable following a monetary policy decision, is an effective way of structuring incentives and represents a tiny step towards substantive accountability.

The sight and sound of the ECB describing itself as the most accountable central bank in the world, when the truth is zero substantive accountability and a minimal and inadequate set of formal reporting duties (even if non-attributed minutes will now be released), is not a pretty one. I also do not think it is politically sustainable. Either the ECB will become more open, or its independence will be taken from it.

How would the operational independence of central banks be destroyed? In Japan most likely, with the central bank maintaining the appearance of operational independence while shedding its substance. This process appears to be underway already. Overt political confrontation between the Ministry of Finance (or the prime minister) and the Bank of Japan is not the way things are done. The emergence of an 'occupy the BoJ' movement is also unlikely.

In the US the Fed has always lived, to a greater or lesser extent, in fear of what Congress could do to it. The US Senate not confirming presidential nominees for the Federal Reserve Board or delaying their confirmation are small pin-pricks. Legislative initiatives to 'Audit the Fed', although perfectly legitimate and indeed desirable in my view, are other ways for the US Congress to harass the Fed. Some members of Congress have gone further than that. In 2007, Congressman Ron Paul sponsored a Federal Reserve Board Abolition Act (H.R. 2755 (110th)). The bill died, but undeterred, Ron Paul wrote a book in 2009 with the self-explanatory title 'End the Fed'.[26] The book spent time on the New York best seller list. It may be viewed as the work of a crank, but if there are enough cranks, surprising and disturbing things can happen. More importantly, the Fed is a 'creature of Congress', created by an ordinary federal law, the Federal Reserve Act, without any Constitutional protection. The threat of Congressional legislation undermining the operational effectiveness of the Fed, despite the safety valve of a presidential veto, is a real one. The 'Kill the Fed' movement is a sideshow at the moment, but could go mainstream under the right (or rather, wrong) set of circumstances.

In the UK, the Chancellor can change the inflation target of the Bank of England without even a Parliamentary vote. The Treasury also has 'reserve powers' that permit the Chancellor to take over the power to set interest rates from the Bank of England's MPC, again without the need for a prior vote in the Commons, although the House of Commons has to endorse this decision within 28 days.

In the euro area, the ECB may appear safer from political interference than the Fed, the BoE or the BoJ, because of the extreme difficulty of amending the European treaties that define the tasks, competencies, rights and obligations of the ECB and the European System of Central Banks (the Eurosystem, for all intents and purposes). This is correct in a legal, or perhaps legalistic sense. The protection provided by a treaty, a constitution or any other piece of paper, no matter how many significant signatures it contains, is limited. As Stalin is supposed to have said to French Prime Minister Pierre Laval in 1935: 'How many divisions does the Pope have?'[27] There have been demonstrations in Greece and Spain against Germany and its leadership. Not, thus far, I believe, against the ECB and its leadership. But this could change.

Individual euro area member states can, even when they are committed to remain members of the euro area, exercise pressure on the ECB to change its policies. They

---

[26] See Paul (2009).

[27] This was in response to Stalin being asked by Laval whether he could influence Russian Catholics to help Laval win favour with the Pope, to counter the increasing threat of Nazism. See Wikipedia, Joseph Stalin, Quotes, http://en.wikiquote.org/wiki/Joseph_Stalin.

can do this at the level of the Eurogroup or at the street level. Those desperate enough can exercise pressure by using the threat of exit from the Eurozone. The credibility of such a threat depends on complex local and Eurozone-wide political dynamics that are hard to predict. Eurozone exit by a disgruntled member state must be more than a tail risk, however: if Scotland can get within an inch of exiting a 307 years-old political (and monetary) union with England, Northern Ireland and Wales, it is not inconceivable that any Eurozone member state could exit from a 15-year old monetary union. I believe that Mario Draghi was speaking the truth when he said that the ECB would, within its mandate, do 'whatever it takes' to keep the euro area together. Even if 'whatever it takes' includes surrendering the substance of operational independence. The formal trappings of operational independence can of course be retained to keep the legal eagles satisfied.

3. CONCLUSION

Central banks in most of the advanced economies have become too powerful, mainly as a result of systemic political failures in Western Europe and North America. In particular, they have accrued a host of deeply political responsibilities and powers. They have neither the legitimacy nor the capability or skills to discharge all these responsibilities effectively. I propose a return to narrow central banking. In its purest version, narrowly defined monetary policy could be decided outside the central bank. Even if the MPC remains part of the central bank, the central bank is just the monetary authority, narrowly defined, and the lender of last resort and market maker of last resort for sovereigns and systemically important financial institutions. It should have no regulatory or supervisory functions. Its unavoidable fiscal role should be transparent. Its quasi-fiscal actions should be minimised through a sovereign guarantee for all financial transactions/operations carrying credit risk, and a transparent accounting for each transaction with every counterparty.

As central banks exit many of their current responsibilities and activities, other institutions, better qualified and more legitimate, must take their place. A vacuum is not an attractive alternative to an overreaching central bank. In practice, this means the following:

- National treasuries (in the euro area, 18 (19 as of 2015)) provide sovereign guarantees for the credit risk central banks take on as a result of their lender-of-last-resort and market-maker-of-last resort operations.
- Macro-prudential regulation, micro-prudential regulation, conduct regulation, recovery, resolution and recapitalisation of SIFIs and deposit insurance are

assigned to institutions other than the central bank. Anything that puts public money at risk (notably recovery, resolution and recapitalisation of SIFIs) has to involve the Treasury as an actor with veto power.

• A body similar to the former Tripartite Arrangement of the UK, or to the FSOC in the US today, must be created to coordinate the financial stability policies of the central bank, the Treasury and the other regulatory and supervisory bodies. The fact that the UK's Tripartite Arrangement failed and that FSOC thus far appears to be little more than a talk-shop or paper tiger does not mean we should stop trying to create a variant that works. There is no alternative that has any chance of being both reasonably effective (output legitimate) and input legitimate.

Even a minimalist central bank will have considerable power to influence the path of inflation, output and employment and to redistribute resources through its fiscal and remaining quasi-fiscal instruments. Substantive accountability is incompatible with operational independence. For the minimalist central bank there is not much to choose between operational independence and granting parliament the power to dismiss members of the central bank's policy making committee for reasons other than incapacity and malfeasance, provided a qualified majority of those eligible to vote supports the dismissal. Any lack of substantive accountability should be compensated for with maximum formal accountability, including full procedural transparency, mandatory voting on all policy decisions with the individual voting records in the public domain.

Operational independence will be taken away from the ECB, the Bank of England and the Fed if they continue to perform their current broad range of regulatory, supervisory and (quasi-)fiscal tasks. Even the operational independence of the minimalist central bank I favour is likely to be tested severely in the years to come. It is likely that the short interlude of highly operationally independent central banks will not last in most countries much beyond the end of the current decade.

REFERENCES

Bagehot, Walter (1873), *Lombard Street: A Description of the Money Market* (London, Henri S. King), third edn.

Banca D'Italia (2013), 'Updating the Valuation of Bank of Italy's Equity Capital', http://www.bancaditalia.it/media/notizie/aggiornam_quote_capitale_BdI/en_quote_capitale.pdf

Bank of England (2006), Memorandum of Understanding Between HM Treasury, The Bank of England and the Financial Services Authority. http://www.bankofengland.co.uk/about/Documents/legislation/mou.pdf

Bank of England (2014), *Annual Report 2014*. http://www.bankofengland.co.uk/publications/Documents/annualreport/2014/boereport.pdf

Bank of Japan (1997), Bank of Japan Act, Law number: Act 89 of 1997, Amendment: Act No. 102 of
     2007. http://www.japaneselawtranslation.go.jp/law/detail_main?id=92&vm=2
Bank of Japan (2014), Outline of the Bank, http://www.boj.or.jp/en/about/outline/index.htm/
Baring, Francis (1797), *Observations on the Establishment of the Bank of England* (London, The
     Minerva-Press, for Sewell, Cornhill & Debrett).
Barro, R.J. & Gordon, D.B. (1983), 'A positive theory of monetary policy in a natural-rate model',
     Journal of Political Economy, 91, 4: 589–610. http://dx.doi.org/10.1086/261167
Bernanke, B.S. (2007a), 'The Level and Distribution of Economic Well-Being'. Remarks before the
     Greater Omaha Chamber of Commerce, Omaha, Neb., 6 Feb. 2007.
     http://federalreserve.gov/BoardDocs/Speeches/2007/20070206/default.htm.
Bernanke, B.S. (2007b), 'Recognizing Leadership', address given at the Princeton Prize in Race Relations
     Awards Program, Washington, D.C., 22 May,
     http://www.federalreserve.gov/newsevents/speech/bernanke20070522a.htm.
Bernanke, B.S (2007c), 'Education and Economic Competitiveness', speech given at the US Chamber
     Education and Workforce Summit, Washington, D.C., 24 September,
     http://www.federalreserve.gov/newsevents/speech/bernanke20070924a.htm.
Besley, Timothy (2005), 'Political Selection', *Journal of Economic Perspectives*, 19(3): 43–60.
     http://dx.doi.org/10.1257/089533005774357761
Bezemer, Dirk J (2009a), '"No One Saw This Coming": Understanding financial crisis through —
     accounting models'. Unpublished.
     http://som.eldoc.ub.rug.nl/FILES/reports/2009/09002/09002_Bezemer.pdf 21q
Bezemer, Dirk (2009b), 'No one saw this coming—or did they?', *Vox EU*, 30 September 2009.
     http://www.voxeu.org/article/no-one-saw-coming-or-did-they.
Blinder, Alan S. (1999), *Central Banking in Theory and Practice* (Cambridge, MA, MIT Press).
Blinder, Alan (2007a), 'Monetary policy by committee: Why and how?', *European Journal of Political
     Economy*, 23(1): 106–23. http://dx.doi.org/10.1016/j.ejpoleco.2006.01.003
Blinder, A.S. (2007b), 'Monetary Policy Today: Sixteen questions and about twelve answers', in
     S. Fernández de Lis & F. Restoy (eds), *Central Banks in the 21st Century: An International
     Conference*, Sponsored by the Banco de España, Banco de España, Madrid, 31–72 (conference
     volume).
Blinder, Alan (2012), 'Central Bank Independence and Credibility During and After a Crisis', Jackson
     Hole Symposium, 1 September 2012.
     https://www.kansascityfed.org/publicat/sympos/2012/ab.pdf
Blinder, Alan S. & Morgan, John (2005), 'Are Two Heads Better than One? Monetary policy by
     committee', *Journal of Money, Credit, and Banking*, October: 789–812.
Borio, Claudio (2012), 'The financial cycle and macroeconomics: What have we learnt?', BIS Working
     Papers No 395, December, http://www.bis.org/publ/work395.pdf.
Buiter, Willem H. (1999), 'Alice in Euroland', *Journal of Common Market Studies*, 37(2): 181–209.
     http://dx.doi.org/10.1111/1468-5965.00159
Buiter, Willem H. (2004), 'Two naked emperors? Concerns about the Stability and Growth Pact and
     second thoughts about central bank independence', *Fiscal Studies*, 25(3): 249–77 (presented as the
     Institute for Fiscal Studies 2003 Annual Lecture).
Buiter, Willem H. (2005), 'New developments in monetary economics: Two ghosts, two eccentricities, a
     fallacy, a mirage and a mythos', *Economic Journal*, 115(502): C1–C31 (presented as the Royal
     Economic Society 2004 Hahn Lecture).
Buiter, Willem H. (2006), 'Stabilisation policy in New Zealand: Counting your blessings, one by one', in
     Bob Buckle & Aaron Drew (eds), *Testing Stabilisation Policy Limits in a Small Open Economy
     Proceedings from a Macroeconomic Policy Forum* (Reserve Bank of New Zealand and The
     Treasury), 37–74.

Buiter, Willem H. (2007), 'Seigniorage', *Economics*, the Open-Access, Open-Assessment E-Journal, 2007–10.

Buiter, Willem H. (2008a), 'Central bankers should stick to their knitting', Willem Buiter's Maverecon Blog, *Financial Times*, 28 January, http://blogs.ft.com/maverecon/2008/01/central-bankershtml/#axzz3ChPNKVLm

Buiter, Willem H. (2008b), 'Can central banks go broke?', *CEPR Policy Insight No. 24*, May.

Buiter, Willem H. (2008c), 'Central banks and financial crises', paper presented at the Federal Reserve Bank of Kansas City' s symposium on Maintaining Stability in a Changing Financial System, Jackson Hole, Wyoming, 21–3 Aug.

Buiter, Willem H. (2008d), 'Monetary economics and the political economy of central banking: Inflation targeting and central bank independence revisited', in Jorge Carrera (ed.), *Monetary Policy Under Uncertainty; Proceedings of the 2007 Money and Banking Seminar* (Buenos Aires, Banco Central de la Republica Argentina), 218–43.

Buiter, Willem H. (2008e), 'Clipping central bankers' wings', *Central Banking*, 43(2): 28–32.

Buiter, Willem H. (2009), 'The unfortunate uselessness of most "state of the art" academic monetary economics', *Vox EU*, 6 March. http://www.voxeu.org/article/macroeconomics-crisis-irrelevance.

Buiter, Willem H. (2013a), 'Forward Guidance: More than old wine in new bottles and cheap talk?', *Citi Research, Economics, Global Economics View*, 25 September.

Buiter, Willem H. (2013b), 'The Role of Central Banks in Financial Stability: How has it changed?', in *The Role of Central Banks in Financial Stability*, World Scientific Studies in International Economics: Volume 30, ed. Douglas D. Evanoff, Cornelia Holthausen, George G. Kaufman & Manfred Kremer.

Buiter, Willem H. (2014), 'The Simple Analytics of Helicopter Money: Why it works—always', *Economics*, The Open-Access, Open-Assessment E-Journal, 8(2014–28): 1–51. http://dx.doi.org/10.5018/economics-ejournal.ja.2014-28

Buiter, Willem H. & Rahbari, Ebrahim (2013), 'The ECB as Lender of Last Resort for Sovereigns in the Euro Area', *Journal of Common Market Studies*, Special Issue: The JCMS Annual Review of the European Union in 2011, September 2012, 50, S2: 6–35

Buiter, Willem H. & Sibert, Anne C. (2008), 'The Icelandic banking crisis and what to do about it: The lender of last resort theory of optimal currency areas', *CEPR Policy Insight No. 26*, Oct.

Buiter, Willem H., Rahbari, Ebrahim & Seydl, Joe (2014a), 'Secular Stagnation: Only if we really ask for it', Citi Research, Economics, Global, Global Economics View, 13 January.

Buiter, Willem H., Lee, William, Anderson, Michael & Seydl, Joe (2014b), 'Fed Creates Maginot Line to Defend Against Financial Stability', Willem H. Buiter, William Lee, Michael Anderson and Joe Seydl, Citi Research, Economics, North America, U.S. Economics Market and Policy Comments, 25 July.

Burns, Arthur F. (1960), 'Progress Towards Economic Stability', *American Economic Review*, 50: 1–19.

Council of Economic Advisers (2000), *Economic Report of the President*, http://www.gpo.gov/fdsys/pkg/ERP-2000/content-detail.html.

Draghi, Mario (2012), Verbatim of the remarks made by Mario Draghi—Speech by Mario Draghi, President of the European Central Bank at the Global Investment Conference in London 26 July, http://www.ecb.europa.eu/press/key/date/2012/html/sp120726.en.html.

Draghi, Mario (2014), 'Unemployment in the euro area', Speech by Mario Draghi, President of the ECB, Annual central bank symposium in Jackson Hole, 22 August 2014, http://www.ecb.europa.eu/press/key/date/2014/html/sp140822.en.html.

ECB (2012a) Introductory statement to the press conference (with Q&A) Mario Draghi, President of the ECB, Vítor Constâncio, Vice-President of the ECB, Frankfurt am Main, 2 August 2012, http://www.ecb.europa.eu/press/pressconf/2012/html/is120802.en.html.

ECB (2012b), Press Release, 6 September 2012—Technical features of Outright Monetary Transactions http://www.ecb.europa.eu/press/pr/date/2012/html/pr120906_1.en.html.

EU (2008), CONSOLIDATED VERSION OF THE TREATY ON THE FUNCTIONING OF THE EUROPEAN UNION, http://euwiki.org/TFEU#Article_123.

Federal Reserve System (2005), The Federal Reserve System, Purposes and Functions, ninth edn, June.

Issing, Otmar (1999), 'The Eurosystem is Transparent and Accountable, or Willem in Wonderland', *Journal of Common Market Studies*, 37(3): 503–19. http://dx.doi.org/10.1111/1468-5965.00175

Katz, Gary (2014), 'Who Predicted the Global Financial Crisis?', Investor Home, http://investorhome.com/predicted.htm.

Kydland, F.E. & Prescott, E.C. (1977), 'Rules rather than discretion: the inconsistency of optimal plans', *Journal of Political Economy*, 85(3): 473–91. http://dx.doi.org/10.1086/260580

Laidler, David (2004), 'Sticking to its Knitting: Why the Bank of Canada should focus on inflation control, not financial stability', C.C. How Institute Commentary, No 196, February, http://www.cdhowe.org/pdf/commentary_196.pdf.

Lucas, Robert E. (2003), 'Macroeconomic Priorities', *American Economic Review*, 93(1): 1–14.

MathWorks (2014), DSGE, http://www.mathworks.com/discovery/dsge.html.

McCallum, Bennett T. (1995), 'Two Fallacies Concerning Central Bank Independence', *American Economic Review*, Papers and Proceedings, 85: 207–11.

McCallum, Bennett T. (1997), 'Crucial Issues Concerning Central Bank Independence', *Journal of Monetary Economics*, 39: 99–112. http://dx.doi.org/10.1016/S0304-3932(97)00007-X

Mihov, Ilian & Sibert, Anne C. (2006), 'Credibility and Flexibility with Monetary Policy Committees', *Journal of Money, Credit and Banking*, 38: 23–46. http://dx.doi.org/10.1353/mcb.2006.0021

Minsky, Hyman P. (1986), *Stabilizing An Unstable Economy*, Yale University Press.

Minsky, Hyman P. (1992), 'The Financial Instability Hypothesis', The Jerome Levy Economics Institute of Bard College, Working Paper No. 74, May.

Paul, Ron (2009), *End the Fed* (New York, NY, Grand Central Publishing).

Rogoff, Kenneth (1985), 'The Optimal Degree of Commitment to an Intermediate Target', *Quarterly Journal of Economics*, 100: 1169–90. http://dx.doi.org/10.2307/1885679

Romer, Christina (1999), 'Changes in Business Cycles: Evidence and Explanations', *Journal of Economic Perspectives*, 13(2): 23–44. http://dx.doi.org/10.1257/jep.13.2.23

Roubini, Nouriel (2014), 'Draghinomics—Abenomics European-style', *The Guardian*, 1 September, http://www.theguardian.com/business/2014/sep/01/draghinomics-abenomics-european-style.

Sharman, Campbell (2008), 'Political Legitimacy for an Appointed Senate', *IRPP Choices*, 14(11): 2–24.

Sibert, Anne C. (2003), 'Monetary Policy Committees: Individual and Collective Reputations', *Review of Economic Studies*, 70: 649–66. http://dx.doi.org/10.1111/1467-937X.00260

Sibert, Anne C. (2006), 'Central Banking by Committee', *International Finance*, Wiley Blackwell, vol. 9(2): 145–68, 08.

Sibert, Anne C. (2012), 'Monetary Policy, the Provision of Financial Stability and Banking Supervision', European Parliament, Directorate General for Internal Policies Policy Department A: Economic and Scientific Policy, http://www.europarl.europa.eu/document/activities/cont/201212/20121210ATT57792/20121210ATT57792EN.pdf.

Stein, Jeremy C. (2012), 'Monetary Policy as Financial-Stability Regulation', *Quarterly Journal of Economics*, 127: 57–95. http://dx.doi.org/10.1093/qje/qjr054

Stein, Jeremy C. (2013), 'Overheating in Credit Markets: Origins, measurement, and policy responses', Federal Reserve Bank of St Louis, 7 February, http://www.federalreserve.gov/newsevents/speech/stein20130207a.htm.